"THE BLOOD OF OUR SONS"

"The Blood of Our Sons"

Men, Women, and the
Renegotiation of British Citizenship
During the Great War

Nicoletta F. Gullace

First published 2002 by
PALGRAVE MACMILLAN™
175 Fifth Avenue, New York, N.Y. 10010 and
Houndmills, Basingstoke, Hampshire, England RG21 6XS.
Companies and representatives throughout the world.

PALGRAVE MACMILLAN IS THE GLOBAL ACADEMIC IMPRINT OF THE PALGRAVE MACMILLAN division of St. Martin's Press, LLC and of Palgrave Macmillan Ltd. Macmillan® is a registered trademark in the United States, United Kingdom and other countries. Palgrave is a registered trademark in the European Union and other countries.

ISBN 0–312–29446–8 hardback

Library of Congress Cataloging-in-Publication Data
Gullace, Nicoletta.
The blood of our sons : men, women, and the renegotiation of British citizenship during
the Great War / by Nicoletta Gullace.
   p.   cm.
ISBN 0–312–29446–8
   1. Citizenship—Great Britain.   2. Great Britain—Politics and government—1910–1936.   3. Suffrage—Great Britain—History—20th century.   4. World War, 1914–1918—Great Britain. I. Title.

JN906.G85 2002
940.3′1′0941—dc21

                                                    2002016917

A catalogue record for this book is available from the British Library.

Design by Letra Libre, Inc.

First edition: August 2002
10 9 8 7 6 5 4 3 2 1

Printed in the United States of America

TO LIGE, WITH ALL MY LOVE

CONTENTS

PART III
THE CULTURAL CONSTRUCTION OF THE LAW

INTRODUCTION

In March 1916, at the height of the Great War, militant suffragette Annie Kenney had a revealing conversation with a "pro-German" spirit at an exclusive London seance. The ghost was an American physician named Dr. Coulter, who had lived a previous life as Voltaire, and was presented to Kenney through one Mrs. Herbine, a medium rumored to be the rage among Britain's Liberal leadership. Although Miss Kenney suspected Mrs. Herbine of "earthly trickery," it was clear to her that, authentic or not, Herbine and Coulter were working for the enemy. "The Herbine-Coulter influence is used in the cause of pro-German pacifism," reported Kenney's newspaper accusatorily. "It is directed towards undermining the confidence of Britain in her Allies and . . . silencing . . . criticism of weak and inadequate Government methods of waging war against Germany."[1]

Although Dr. Coulter and Mrs. Herbine seemed somewhat baffled by Miss Kenney's pointed questions regarding the war, their statements clearly revealed to Kenney and her colleagues that the Germans were "exploiting spiritualist influences in furtherance of their attempt to conquer Europe." The part of Dr. Coulter's advice that Kenney found so alarming was his injunction to stop criticizing Britain's Liberal government, which she and many Conservative critics believed to be entirely too relaxed in waging total war. Instead, the ghost recommended that Kenney resume her prewar career of agitating for women's suffrage. "Your work and your mission are to rouse the public in your special sphere, which is women's votes and the wonderful work that women are doing in this war," insisted the apparition. "You have been too critical. You must stop all this and do as I tell you . . . I see peace. Therefore you must be preparing the ground so that after the war is over they will be ready to give you your vote as you will have proved that women are worthy of it."[2]

It was odd advice to give a militant suffragette. In the years before the war, Kenny's organization, the Women's Social and Political Union, waged a violent campaign against the British authorities that involved bombing churches, slashing paintings, burning houses, and smashing the windows of London's most fashionable shops. The campaign caused thousands of pounds worth of damage and earned militant suffragettes the scorn and animosity of press, public, and legislators alike. To the consternation of both constitutionalist suffragists (who feared the bad publicity) and the Liberal government (which was charged with restoring order), the militants had transgressed all boundaries of propriety, legality, and good sense.[3] Now, however, Dr. Coulter begged Kenney to agitate for women's votes instead of resuming her shrill, nationalistic call for sterner military measures. Long feared by a hesitant British establishment, the enfranchisement of women had become a moderate and reasonable reform.[4]

What facilitated this embrace of women's suffrage—by earthly as well as celestial commentators? In the following pages, I will suggest that the cultural environment created by the war reconfigured the way Britons understood the rights and obligations of citizenship.[5] Rather than examining suffrage as a purely political event, this study reconstructs the cultural landscape of wartime Britain in order to map the way propaganda, advertising, and popular entertainment absorbed images of the war to promote new ideas about gender and civic participation. During the war, the political claims of men no longer seemed so absolute, nor the arguments of feminists so unreasonable. In accounting for these changes, I have written a book that is as much about perceptions as it is about reality, as much about culture as it is about politics, and as much about men as it is about women.

My story begins with the terrifying news of the German invasion of Belgium on August 4, 1914. With this event, rumors of violent atrocities against women and children began to saturate the press, providing British authorities with a horrifying, popular, and easily understood rationale for waging war against Germany. Not only had the Germans violated treaty law in their invasion of a small, neutral land, but German soldiers allegedly raped and mutilated women, cut the hands off children, and bayoneted babies in their bid to pacify the unwilling victims of their brutal occupation.[6] As I will argue, atrocity propaganda not only shaped popular imagination of the enemy, but changed the lived experience of men and women on the home front. As the press, the government, and a host of amateur publicists justified the war in terms of the safety of the family and the sanctity of the woman's body, the imperative for military intervention became increasingly difficult to dispute.

No one was more deeply affected by these images than young unenlisted men and the women who loved them. While Britons hailed the common soldier as the savior of innocent women and children, the civilian male was jeered on the streets, mocked in the press, and handed white feathers by cheeky flappers policing manhood in the West End of London.

In a nation where military service was still voluntary and where the army desperately needed more recruits, atrocity propaganda provided an unanswerable rhetoric to hurl against those reluctant to serve. The mothers and sweethearts of young men were also mercilessly exhorted to send them to war, implicating women in the most fearsome decision of a young man's life—the decision to face death on the Western Front. Ideas about military obligation promoted in theaters, on hoardings, and in the press thus found their way onto the streets and into the home, exposing the emotional and political repercussion of what I call "propaganda in action."

Tracing the language of citizenship through streets and alleyways, as well as into the halls of Westminister, my study reveals the way military obligation and service to the state gained an ever more authoritative place in measures of civic worth. Such assumptions would have a particular impact on the lives of the young. Drawing on letters, diaries, and journals, my study foregrounds the experiences of men who were harassed into enlisting and those who were branded as "cowards" for failing to serve. Equally, it is about the women who were so successfully beguiled into sending men to war. Female patriotism, particularly in its most sacrificial guise, gave women a powerful language with which to lay claim to the war. It was a language, however, that worked in more ways than one. Not only were mothers expected to offer uncomplainingly the blood of their sons, but critics of female recruiting began to lay responsibility for male deaths at the feet of women, who had allegedly been responsible for cajoling men into service.

If women's relationship to the production of armies was complicated and ambiguous, their bravery nevertheless informed political discourse as the conflict dragged on. As I will argue, the war gave women the opportunity to renegotiate conceptions of citizenship in two distinct but complimentary ways. At a historic moment when citizenship was defined in terms of service to the nation, women displayed their own patriotism in ways that ranged from making munitions to offering sons. They also undermined the idea that citizenship was ineluctably tied to the male body. In addition to the suffragettes' scathing attacks on the inadequate war measures taken by a government elected by men, women of many persuasions brandished their patriotism in highly revealing ways. Through recruiting activities such as handing out white feathers to reputed "cowards" and offering petticoats to male "shirkers," female war enthusiasts drew attention to the fact that manhood alone was an inadequate marker of civic responsibility.

Such attitudes would become deeply embedded in wartime suffrage debates. Comparing the sacrifices of women to the sacrifices of soldiers and participating in the almost universal deprecation of men who failed to enlist, a host of commentators began to cast patriotism, rather than manhood, as the fundamental qualification for citizenship. Significantly, the same bill that granted the parliamentary vote to women over thirty disenfranchised conscientious objectors and gave the vote to underage boys who had served at the front. And while women drew attention to their loyalty, their Britishness, and their exemplary service to their country, patriotic organizations—including feminist ones—launched a concerted attack on overly generous franchise laws that allowed naturalized aliens and male pacifists to vote while excluding loyal women of British birth. Despite this extensive public discussion over the nature of both male and female citizenship, historians have generally examined the granting of women's suffrage during World War I in isolation from other questions of citizenship that arose simultaneously. This tendency is so pronounced that most studies of women's suffrage end with the outbreak of war in 1914, even though the Representation of the People Bill, which granted the parliamentary vote to women over thirty, was not signed until 1918, following three and a half years of brutal warfare.[7]

There are a number of reasons for this surprising gulf. Postwar scholars—including feminists who lived through the war—assumed that women received the vote as a "reward" for patriotic service, a point so apparently obvious that it deserved little elaboration.[8] More recently, feminist historians have chosen to emphasize the achievements of the prewar suffrage movement rather than looking at the vote as a gift from the generous hand of male legislators willing to recognize women's war work. Sandra Stanley Holton's influential claim that the vote was practically won by 1914, along with the fact that only women over thirty received the vote, also seemed to discredit the idea that the war service of younger women had been a significant factor in achieving the victory. The widely held belief that women's suffrage agitation "ended" with the Great War gave a further narrative rationale to the use of 1914 as a terminal date, distinguished not only by the commencement of hostilities but by a declared "truce" between suffragists and the government.[9]

This study takes issue with each of these assumptions. Women's suffrage was forged in the crucible of war, where both male and female citizenship were increasingly defined and evaluated by the ability to wage war. Feminists were quick to grasp this fact. Indeed, despite professions to the contrary, wartime suffragists never abandoned their campaign for the vote. Although both the militant Women's Social and Political Union

(WSPU) and the constitutionalist National Union of Women's Suffrage Societies (NU) proclaimed a suspension of suffrage activity until the end of the conflict, neither organization lost the opportunity to harness feminism's newfound nationalism to the cause of women's suffrage. While both the WSPU and the NU alienated pacifist members, even some left-leaning suffrage societies found it hard to resist relating women's patriotic service to their claim for the vote.[10] As the *Anti- Suffrage Review* noted with irritation at the time, "They sew and knit comforts for the soldiers but with such a perpetual running accompaniment of suffragist self-laudation that they might as well embroider the sacred name of Mrs. Pankhurst or Mrs. Fawcett on every sock and every muffler. . . ."[11]

The Great War marked a tremendous ideological break for suffragists, as the two principal organizations and a multitude of their followers abandoned feminist pacifism for a hardy love of country. Yet despite this nationalistic shift, feminist organizations retained a remarkable coherence. Not only did feminists continue to publish a host of weekly and monthly newspapers, maintain connections with provincial branches, and raise money, hold meetings, and fill public halls with those eager to hear their message, but they used their extraordinary notoriety to draw attention to the patriotic service of the women of Britain. In the period before the war, feminists succeeded in putting the issue of female citizenship onto the national agenda. Whether it was the militants with their vandalous campaign of arson, sabotage, and window-breaking, or the constitutionalists with their daunting ability to flex women's financial muscle and lobbying ability in the political arena, the relentless work of prewar feminists assured that no wartime franchise bill could be introduced without reckoning with the issue of women's votes. In this way, arguments framed by feminists before the war were not "dropped," but refashioned and explicitly tied to the question of national defense as feminism's patriotic move to the right insured its growing appeal to new audiences.

Few women's historians have chosen to address the pro-war activities of suffragists.[12] Indeed, the rabid nationalism of Christabel and Emmeline Pankhurst (who, during the war, turned the once radical WSPU into the proto-fascist Women's Party), is almost as embarrassing to contemporary feminists as it was to their pacifist kinswoman, Sylvia. As a result, feminist scholarship devoted to the war years has tended to focus on a small but important group of feminist pacifists, while the Pankhursts have been relegated to the lunatic fringe of the women's movement in most scholarly accounts.[13] The WSPU was in fact highly influential in reshaping public attitudes toward women's suffrage during the Great War. Drawing upon grassroots displays of female patriotism, the WSPU exploited its own celebrity and penchant for spectacle to give both female loyalty and male cowardice a higher profile than they would otherwise have had. Filling meeting halls, staging parades, and offering interviews for circulation in the press, the Pankhursts fashioned an image of nationalist feminism perfectly attuned to popular tastes. Their continual juxtaposition of female patriotism with male failure—what I term "comparative patriotism"—was echoed and amplified throughout public culture during the war years. Whether in a parliamentary debate over conscientious objection or on the alluring lips of a flapper castigating a boy out of uniform, the denigration of the unenlisted man, the pacifist, and the conscientious objector was central to disrupting a notion of citizenship based on manhood alone. Such sentiments constituted one of the cultural variables that gave resonance to arguments grounding citizenship in personal sacrifice and service to the state—an idea with revolutionary implications for both women who wished to vote and men who were expected to fight.

WSPU militants were in no way solely responsible for these changes. The constitutionalist NU, led by the highly respected Millicent Garrett Fawcett, ruthlessly purged its pacifist wing and devoted itself to promoting women's war work, using the spectacle of female patriotism to legitimize renewed agitation for the vote. Refuting anti-suffrage arguments that denied women's claim to the vote on the grounds that women did not exert "physical force" in defense of the state, patriotic suffragists used the war to graphically demonstrate women's military utility and civic worth. By providing women with unprecedented opportunities to serve the military state, the Great War gave patriotic suffragists of all persuasions a more auspicious environment in which to justify claims that had a long and important history within the feminist movement.

Rather than undercut the suffrage movement, as so many scholars have assumed, the Great War provided a context in which long-standing feminist claims seemed increasingly persuasive to the press, to legislators, and to the general public. Women's war work, the sacrifices of mothers and wives, and the patriotic performance of well-known suffragists all validated feminists' long-standing arguments about national and imperial value of female citizenship. Susan Kingsley Kent, Lisa Tickner, and Cheryl Jorgensen-Earp have shown the way prewar rhetoric, tactics, and concerns were carried over and refashioned by suffragists during the war, while Sandra Holton has demonstrated the remarkable alacrity with which constitutionalists renewed political alliances at crucial moments in 1916 to press their case with Britain's Liberal leadership.[14] In many ways, the suffrage performance remained the same; only the set had changed, the theater improved, and the audience received the spectacle with standing applause rather than rotten fruit. Indeed, the power of ridicule had shifted from "Antis"—who had used it so ruthlessly before the war—to suffragists, and feminists seemed to be having the last laugh as the case against female en-franchisement deteriorated in an environment where women so visibly as-sisted in the waging of war and where pacifist men chose not to serve.

—◦∞◦—

Women's legislative victory was not just the work of suffragists, however, but was also deeply embedded in the idiosyncracies of Britain's wartime political culture. The Representation of the People Bill of 1918 was the broadest reform act in British history, adding more than twice as many voters to the electorate as any other franchise reform. As Neal McCrillis notes, the bill increased the enfranchised portion of the adult population from 28 percent to 78 percent, giving the vote to 5 million men and nearly 9 million women who had been ineligible to vote before. Tory MP Sir J. A. R. Marriot aptly commented in 1927 that "compared to the 1918 act, previous reform acts 'almost sink into insignificance.'"[15] Yet the 1918 act has received surprisingly little scholarly attention. Legislative historians have generally assumed that the 1884 reform bill, which enfranchised agricultural workers, actually achieved nearly universal manhood suf-frage, despite the fact that it included registration requirements that left 40 percent of the adult male population unable to vote.[16] Historians of women's suffrage, as already noted, tend to end their studies in 1914, rel-egating the reform bill of 1918 to a mere footnote, significant only in that it was the piece of legislation that recorded the suffrage victory. Yet the 1918 act was one of the most significant domestic results of the war—a legislative milestone drawn up not to enfranchise women but to enfran-chise soldiers, many of whom had lost their votes when they were mobi-lized for foreign service.

The tale of how this caste of untouchables—the common soldier—came to be seen as the repository of national virtue is, strangely enough, part of the story of votes for women. Unlike any other European power, Britain entered the Great War with a volunteer army. As the quintessen-tial symbol of Britain's domestic freedom, the volunteer army was a cor-nerstone of Liberal commitment to consensual governance. Even at the outset of war, Prime Minister Herbert Asquith's Liberal administration was determined to preserve this institution and refused to implement conscription. Instead, the government launched a propaganda campaign imploring men to join up voluntarily—a project reinforced by the press and the patriotic efforts of private citizens, often acting entirely on their own. The voluntary recruiting campaign permeated national life for the first two years of the war. Not only did recruiting propaganda celebrate the common soldier as a national savior, but it castigated those men who chose not to volunteer, claiming that their reluctance to serve was a national disgrace. The ubiquitous denigration of unenlisted men insured that when conscription was proposed in 1915, few Britons would scruple about violating the liberty of "slackers," especially since mandatory service would benefit the "brave lads" already at the front. Indeed, as the army required ever more men, voluntarism fell into disfavor, even among Liberals who began to worry that voluntary methods would not raise sufficient recruits to insure a total military victory. A severe manpower shortage forced Asquith to accept conscription in 1916, and the following December he was ousted by David Lloyd George, a radical patriot who favored the stern military measures endorsed by the *Times*, the Tories, and much of the popular press.

Despite this resounding defeat, the voluntary recruiting campaign had a defining impact on parliamentary reform. Recruiting propaganda, newspaper articles, and the everyday remarks of people on the street made literal the hitherto theoretical predication of citizenship on military service. Drawing upon a propaganda campaign that depicted conquered women and children as the victims of German atrocities, recruiters lionized common soldiers while turning unenlisted civilians into national pariahs. Not only did such images help to justify conscription, but in 1916 they fueled an unprecedented call for reforms that would give soldiers more political power.

While most professional soldiers had never qualified to vote, patriotic Britons became deeply troubled when electoral residency requirements resulted in the disenfranchisement of men who left home to join the army. Had legislators been content to simply re-enfranchise those who were struck from the registers, women might not have seen the inside of the polling booths in 1918. But few politicians were content to end the project of reform there. Conservatives called for the enfranchisement of all soldiers, including underage boys, while Liberals argued that male munitions workers, who also forfeited votes when they moved to distant armament centers, performed essential war work and ought to be re-enfranchised too. Finally, a broad array of commentators began to cry for the disenfranchisement of conscientious objectors, whose ability to vote was an insult to the logic that grounded citizenship in military service.

These concessions profoundly shaped the case of women. Not only did many feminists refuse to sit by while the franchise was awarded to new classes of men, but the extension of the logic justifying enfranchisement on the basis of military service immeasurably bolstered the women's case. As feminists relentlessly pointed out, nearly one million women were working in munitions production, and their claim to the vote was indistinguishable

from that of the male munitions workers whom Asquith proposed to enfranchise. Furthermore, military nurses, female ambulance drivers, and,
most poignantly, the mothers of soldiers all risked their lives for the state,
either indirectly through childbirth or directly in France, Eastern Europe,
and other arenas where female medical staff performed perilous and essential war work. Most importantly, the move to disenfranchise conscientious objectors decisively undercut the sexual basis of the parliamentary
vote, since men who refused to serve were to be deprived of ballots for
which they would have otherwise qualified, allowing feminists to demonstrate that service, rather than sex, entitled Britons to vote.

In examining these issues, this book brings the study of female enfranchisement back into the context in which it took place. Once war service,
rather than male gender, became the basis of British citizenship, feminists
had won a crucial victory. While suffragists had long questioned masculinity as a qualification for the parliamentary vote, it was only in the
context of total war that the seemingly unanswerable correlation between
manhood, military service, and citizenship began to break down. Serving
as army nurses, munitions workers, and the mothers of those who fought,
women could proclaim that they, like soldiers, risked their lives for the
state. Indeed, instead of vindicating the "physical force" argument, war
ironically revealed its two fundamental flaws: first, that not all men able
to bear arms were willing to do so and, second, that women's contribution
to making war was far from negligible.

This is the story of how these two glaringly obvious facts captured the
public mind, and the human and legislative consequences of their imaginative power. The Representation of the People Bill and the extension of
the parliamentary franchise to women over thirty was part of a larger cultural process fostered by war and expedited not only by patriotic female
service but by the concerted denunciation of those men who refused to
"do their bit." Introduced as a measure to insure the enfranchisement of
soldiers, the Representation of the People Bill applied the litmus test of
loyalty to other social groups as well. Indeed, during the war, sacrifice, service, and British blood began to take precedence over sex, property, and
legal majority, while patriotism replaced manhood as the fundamental
qualification for the parliamentary vote. This shift, of course, was never
absolute. The new franchise laws not only included millions of civilians
who, because of age, infirmity, or sex, were unable to serve, but in order
to avert a female electoral majority, legislators excluded countless patriotic young women who ought logically to have qualified to vote. Despite
its practical inconsistencies, however, the rationale of service was essential
to breaking the barrier of sex. As part of the nation in arms, patriotic men
and women could share citizenship status while pacifists, "shirkers," and

conscientious objectors had their rights challenged in the press, in Parliament, and in the courts. Although many of these more extreme measures were corrected following the war, this public discourse created the context—momentary though it might have been—in which women were enfranchised, suggesting that pro-war women, rather than their progressive sisters, were responsible for British feminists' most significant victory.

In order to undertake this project, I have drawn on the methodological insights of the new cultural history.[17] It is my contention that systems of representation bear directly on historical change by establishing habits of thought crucial to rationalizing particular actions. In this way, culture and social practice are inextricably linked. Drawing on a large and unusually diverse array of sources, including legislative debates, advertisements, novels and poems, cartoons, paintings, political speeches, propaganda pamphlets, government documents, newspapers, songs, theatrical productions, letters, and non-verbal gestures such as handing out white feathers, my work investigates the creation of a cultural episteme in which notions of duty, loyalty, and Britishness gained an authoritativeness that undercut the hegemony of sex in defining the rights of citizenship. Such sources are important because they reveal a cultural environment where, in music halls and municipal halls alike, Britons clamored for men to enlist and where wives, mothers, and women on the street were implicated in articulating expectations about male behavior that saturated legislative debates. In contrast to studies that examine the relationship of gender to war as purely a cultural phenomenon, this book traces the way the cultural construction of gender actually shaped the law.[18] Since the war's epistemic shift coincided with discussion of an electoral Reform Bill, this extraordinary cultural moment was indelibly imprinted on the most important piece of legislation passed in Britain during World War I. This book thus offers a cultural explanation for a political event that has generally been studied in isolation from the wider context in which it occurred—the enfranchisement of British women in 1918.

I would like to take this opportunity to thank those who contributed to the completion of this project. Foremost are Tom Laqueur and Reggie Zelnik, whose generous mixture of criticism and encouragement were crucial to the development of this work in its earliest stages. They read with patience often painfully long drafts of my early chapters, offering caution, praise, and guidance at the moments when I most needed it. Tom Laqueur's exuberance, in particular, showed me that it was possible to write serious history with a sense of play. I also wish to thank Susan Kent, whose generous sharing of her work helped me to define the parameters of my own project. She, along with Angela Woollacott and Jay Winter, have not only inspired me with their careful and provocative scholarship but offered insightful readings of my work as well as abundant encouragement and support.

Many colleagues contributed to the intellectual development of this project, either through opportune comments at professional meetings or by reading of parts of my work. I would like to thank especially Regina Sweeney, Sue Grayzel, John Gillis, Susan Pedersen, Fred Leventhal, and Maura O'Connor for timely comments and suggestions. Maura O'Connor, particularly, has been more than a friend and reader, but over the years has become almost a fairy godmother. Not only did she secure me cheap housing in fashionable Highbury and Inslington (the first of two nice apartments that she passed on to me), but she was instrumental in securing a publisher for my book. Through her intervention during a very busy quarter, I was happily matched up with Deborah Gershenowitz, whose enthusiasm and insightful comments have helped me shape this work in its final stages.

In addition to those people who contributed to the conception of this book are the institutions that made its execution possible. The substantive research was completed in Britain under the auspices of the Fulbright-Hays Commission and the Mabelle McLeod Lewis Memorial Fund. Additional research and write-up support was provided by the Institute on Global Conflict and Cooperation at the University of California. A John M. Olin Postdoctoral Fellowship at Yale University allowed me to commence turning my doctoral dissertation into a book. While in England my work was greatly facilitated by the help of the librarians and archivists at the Imperial War Museum, the Museum of London, and the House of Lords Record Office, as well as by the staff of the Modern Manuscripts room at the Bodleian Library and David Doughan of the Fawcett Library. I am very grateful to those who patiently located obscure materials for me and offered their own expertise in helping me to decipher them. I am also indebted to the Public Record Office and the British Library for sending me additional materials through the post.

The institution to which I am most indebted, however, is the University of New Hampshire, where I have received abundant support and encouragement for the completion of this work. Not only did my colleagues in the History Department Faculty Seminar offer me useful and timely intellectual advice, but my former chair Jeff Diefendorf and my current chair Bill Harris have worked in every way possible to give me the resources necessary to complete this book. I am also deeply indebted to Dean Marilyn Hoskin, who generously provided me with summer research money; Provost David Hiley, who through the Hortense Cavis Shepherd Professorship allowed me a discretionary research budget; and Burt Feintuch, the director of the University of New Hampshire Center for the Humanities, who permitted me to remain at the Center well past my tenure as a Gustafson Junior Fellow. He and Jennifer Beard have made the Center for the Humanities an extraordinarily welcoming intellectual environment, and without their support I could not have finished this book. My colleagues Lucy Salyer and Sara Wolper have offered countless bits of useful advice on long walks and over (sometimes) healthy lunches. They, along with my other colleagues in the History Department, have created at UNH a sense of community and intellectual excitement that few people have the good fortune to experience outside of graduate school. Finally, I would like to thank the History Department Undergraduate Committee for awarding me funds to hire my superb research assistant, Genevive Tremblay, whose only fault is that she moved to Oregon.

Those to whom I owe the greatest debt are the friends and family members who helped sustain me for the duration of this often taxing project. First, I would like to thank my parents, Carmelo and Hilary Gullace. Although a number of institutions supported my work in its most promising phases, only my parents were willing to support it when its outcome looked decidedly less secure. Their generosity, both emotional and financial, was essential to my success and has shored me up many times since. The often lonely moments of living in a foreign city were made more than bearable by Mary Brunton and David Brown, my London roommates. Frequent trips to the country to visit my Granny, Florence Tallerman, and my aunt and uncle, John and Ruth Keeble, were among the happiest times I have spent abroad. I also wish to thank Ron Yanosky, Sabrina Klein, and Sylvia Schafer, whose friendship in graduate school has carried over into sustaining phone conversations and who have been sympathetic about the vicissitudes of this project ever since. My friends Kari Horowicz and Jim Mott and my brothers John and Joe Gullace have also helped in countless ways, with advice, good sense, and, above all, friendship and much love. Finally, I owe a tremendous debt of gratitude to my husband's parents, Glen and Mildred Gould. My baby daughter, Emma Hilary, was born ten days late, allowing me to finish my last chapter and earning her own acknowledgment. Her grandparents slept on a lumpy futon in our living room for six weeks, providing care for

Emma Hilary, solace for her brother Charlie, and meals for the whole family. Their presence allowed me to prepare the manuscript for the publisher while my husband finished up the semester. Without them, I could not have brought this project to its final stages.

Above all, I am grateful to a man who, in marrying me, agreed to recognize editorial support as a conjugal right. Eliga Gould has been my most persistent editor, my most constructive critic, and my dearest friend. He has read every word of this project, often many times over, making intellectual and stylistic comments that were essential to developing my work. As one of the few fathers I know who is comfortable ministering to every need of his baby daughter and his precocious four-year-old son, he generously took over primary responsibility for childcare while I finished this book. The image of him with my introduction in one hand and our daughter in the other will be my most enduring memory of the final stages of this project. Without his patience, his love, and his infectious enthusiasm, this project could never have come to a successful end.

Part I

Propaganda and the Public Mind

CHAPTER ONE

———— ～✥✥～ ————

THE RAPE OF BELGIUM AND
WARTIME IMAGINATION

On December 28, 1914, Kate Hume, a seventeen-year-old girl from Dumfries, was tried before the Edinburgh High Court for publishing two forged letters in her local newspaper. The first letter, allegedly from her sister Grace, was written in the form of a deathbed farewell. The second, from Grace's fictional colleague Nurse Mullard, gave details of how Nurse Hume's breasts had been cut off by German soldiers who left her to bleed to death on the floor of the Belgian hospital at Vilvorde where she purportedly served as a field nurse. Although leniency in Kate's sentencing was recommended when the jury discovered that her brother had died aboard the *Titanic*, the offence was considered serious enough to warrant Kate's immediate imprisonment and her trial before one of the highest courts in Scotland.[1]

Nine months after the publication of Kate's letter, the British government's *Report on Alleged German Outrages in Belgium* was released to the English-speaking world, causing an international sensation. In the report, Lord James Bryce, former ambassador to the United States, and his distinguished colleagues claimed that after conducting a thorough investigation they had indisputable evidence that German soldiers had cut off women's breasts, bayonetted babies, chopped the hands off little children, and generally raped, pillaged, and maimed the citizens of that peaceful and neutral country.[2] Kate Hume was convicted, put on probation, and charged with fabricating an "abominable and revolting story" that intentionally "shocked and horrified" the public.[3] In the opinion of Sir Thomas Clouston, one of the psychiatrists who examined Kate, "The prisoner at the time was in a state of adolescent hysteria, and such conditions might have made her quite abnormal in fancy and action. The letters were stupid, inconsistent, illogical and absurd, and such as might have been written by a person in the condition he had described."[4] Lord Bryce, on the other hand, was applauded for having verified and made public the atrocious behavior of the German army. Sir Otto Trevelyan summed up the thoughts of many correspondents when he wrote to Bryce, "I can hardly say what a friendly relief and pleasure I feel in the accomplishment of your immense, most arduous, and all important task. What a public service by you, and your rare set of colleagues. I earnestly hope that no pains will be spared by the government in making it widely known at home and abroad."[5]

What distinguished the Bryce Report from Kate Hume's letter to the *Dumfries Standard* was not the lurid details of the atrocities described nor, according to many scholars, the truth of the tales—both of which were based on equally exaggerated evidence.[6] It was not even the possibility that Kate Hume was, as the psychiatrist described her, "in a state of adolescent hysteria": indeed, much of Bryce's evidence was founded on the alleged testimony of witnesses as young and distraught as Kate herself. The distinction lay in the official sanction of the Bryce Report, which allowed it to claim the increasingly valuable commodity of publicly accepted truth and thus to appropriate a series of powerful gendered images into the arsenal of official propaganda.

This would prove to be a potent marketing tool indeed. Using images of violence against women, children, and the family created a set of seemingly irrefutable moral imperatives with which to silence the pacifist opposition, cajole unwilling recruits, and demand even the most horrendous sacrifices from a population incessantly beseeched to give up its sons. This chapter will examine the authentication and distribution of atrocity stories and discuss the symbolic value of wartime imagery that was at once sentimental and sexual, patriotic and pornographic, effective and subversive.

German Atrocities and the Marketing of War

With the German invasion of Belgium on August 4, 1914, the British gained access to an almost limitless supply of material alleging brutality of the most sadistic sort. Comparing the German army to "one vast gang of Jack-the-Rippers," the popular writer William Le Queux was only one among hundreds of patriotic publicists who described in lurid detail such random horrors as a governess hanged "stark naked and mutilated," the bayonetting of a small baby at Corbeek Loo, and the "screams of dying women" raped and "horribly mutilated" by German soldiers accused variously of cutting off the feet, hands, or breasts of their innocent and hapless victims.[7]

From the start the British regarded such images as a potentially powerful way of interesting the domestic and international public in the war. "It is remarkable to note how instant is the response in the United States to every fresh German atrocity," the British propaganda administrator Sir Gilbert Parker noted with satisfaction in 1916. "It might have been expected . . . [that] German atrocities would have by this time become somewhat stale. But this is not the case. There seems to be no more certain appeal to the American public than through the medium of such atrocities."[8] In addressing such issues as the invasion of Belgium, the sinking of the passenger liner *Lusitania*, or the shooting of nurse Edith Cavell, the British created a highly sexualized image of German monstrosity and used it to market an evocative, sentimental, and deeply gendered version of the conflict to an international and domestic public.

There are a number of reasons why the British government found itself compelled to authorize such a disturbing campaign. First, the invasion of Belgium was unquestionably a brutal affair. Thousands of civilians evacuated their villages, and Britain was flooded with refugees rendered homeless by invading armies that behaved with ferocity against any civilian resistance.[9] Yet, as Susan Kingsley Kent has shown, the invasion of Belgium, with its very real suffering, was nevertheless represented in a highly stylized way that dwelt on perverse sexual acts, lurid mutilations, and graphic accounts of child abuse of often dubious veracity.[10] From the three-hundred-page *Appendix* to the Bryce Report, "Crimes against Children and Women" were extracted and reprinted with special frequency, often organized into separate and highly prominent sections in popular atrocity books.[11] Because a reference to the Bryce Report ensured the credibility of any tale, highly improbable accounts came to be accepted as sworn truth. Thus in one frequently reprinted deposition, "a married woman" reported seeing "eight German soldiers [coming] round a corner. . . . They were singing and . . . dancing about." A two-year-old child wandered into the street getting in the way of the soldiers. "The [soldier] . . . on the left stepped aside and drove his bayonet with both hands into the child's stomach, lifting the child into the air . . . and carrying it away on his bayonet, he and his comrades still singing."[12]

Accounts like these served a number of purposes. On the most basic level, they sold newspapers, captivated public attention, and provided the British with an irrefutable imperative with which to justify their intervention in the war. Having suffered a humiliating propaganda defeat during the Boer War, with Emily Hobhouse's shocking revelations regarding the treatment of Boer women and children in British concentration camps, the British authorities were prepared to take the moral offensive during World War I. In doing so they returned, at least subconsciously, to an older trope dating back to the Sepoy Rebellion of 1857, when the British press represented imperial insurrection in terrifying sexual terms and when abused women and children became the evocative symbols of a lawlessness and treacherous enemy.

The official endorsement of such stories, however, had as much to do with the fact that these images had already taken on a life of their own in the popular press. For British publicists and their sympathizers, the central issue of the war—the "cause"—both in the sense of the trigger and the moral impetus, was German violation of Belgian neutrality at midnight on August 4, 1914. As the former president of Harvard, Charles W. Eliot, wrote to James Bryce in December 1914, "From my point of view, that violation of Belgian neutrality by Germany was a very fortunate happening for the cause of freedom and democracy; because it consolidated British opinion in favor of immediate war. . . . It certainly was a most extraordinary display on the part of Germany of rashness, insolence, and lack of intelligence."[13] Unlike Serbia, Belgium was not party to any of the conflicts being disputed in the summer of 1914. British propagandists were thus eager to move as quickly as possible from an explanation of the war that focused on the murder of an Austrian archduke and his wife by Serbian nationalists to the morally unambiguous question of the invasion of neutral Belgium.[14] Bryce wrote to his friend A. V. Dicey in August 1914 that "There must be something fatally wrong with our so-called civilization when for this Servian cause so frightful a calamity has descended on all Europe."[15] Yet later he was able to remind the same correspondent that "The one thing we have to comfort us in this war is that we are all absolutely convinced of the justice of the cause, and of our duty, once Belgium had been invaded, to take up the sword."[16]

The invasion of Belgium consolidated parliamentary and press support of the war and, in the eyes of most Britons, invalidated the isolationist case.[17] British officials hoped that this diplomatic trump card would have similar effect in securing the opinion of the rest of the world, and the story of Belgium was dispersed around the globe. As advocates of foreign intervention used the invasion of Belgium to justify the British cause, however, the case against Germany went through subtle but significant change. What began as an outcry among intellectuals over the violation of European treaty law ended as a condemnation of brutal acts of atrocity committed against Belgian women and children. Accordingly, British foreign policy was publicly invested with a series of gendered meanings.[18] This transformation, however, did not happen overnight.

Before the invasion of Belgium was endowed with significance for the family or depicted in terms of a woman's body, British liberals regarded this breach of a formal treaty as a threat to the fundamental system of human relations ordered through the law. In the eyes of the Oxford faculty of Modern History, Britain was at war because "we are a people in whose blood the cause of law is the vital element." Regarding Belgium as the testing ground for the principle of legality itself, these academics argued that "The war in which England is now engaged with Germany is fundamentally a war between two different principles. . . . The one regards international covenants to which it has pledged its own word as 'scraps of paper' . . . the other regards the maintenance of such covenants as a grave inevitable obligation."[19] In a famous interview with the British ambassador in Berlin, the German chancellor, lamenting war with England, coined the phrase that would become the focus of such fears. Referring to the Treaty of London, which guaranteed Belgian neutrality in 1831 and 1839, Chancellor Theobald von Bethmann Hollweg told Sir Edward Goschen: "We are at war today . . . just for a word—'neutrality'—a word which in war-time has so often been disregarded—just for a scrap of paper."[20]

In Britain, the "scrap of paper" became one of the most infamous phrases of the war, appearing in sources ranging from popular music-hall songs to propaganda pamphlets aimed at the rural poor.[21] Arthur Hassall published a book on the subject entitled *Just for a Scrap of Paper* to "explain why England stands for the sanctity of European treaty law," the Parliamentary Recruiting Committee issued a series of posters depicting it, and both the Liberal prime minister and Conservative party leader agreed that "it is for that Scrap of Paper and all that it means that we . . . have already watered with the blood of our sons the fair fields of France."[22] The German chancellor's statement figured prominently in British self-justification, and the "scrap of paper" with Goschen's reply was one of the centerpieces of the British White Book, an official collection of documents illustrating the events that lead up to the outbreak of the war.[23]

To educated Britons, the German chancellor's readiness to draw attention to the fact that treaties are "scraps of paper" threatened to subvert the very philosophical basis of legal agreement.[24] For these observers, the authority of the law rested upon the idea that the contract, as a physical testament of the act of signing or swearing, could freeze a moment of opinion or volition, making it eternally valid.[25] Because international treaties attempted to apply this precept of civil law to the international sphere, Bethmann Hollweg's repudiation of the Treaty of London carried social, political, and financial reverberations well beyond the diplomatic realm.[26] Indeed, Arthur Conan Doyle classified the violation of Belgium as "perjury," while Chancellor of the Exchequer David Lloyd George denounced Germany as a "great nation behaving like a fraudulent bankrupt."[27] "Have you any £5 notes about you?," Lloyd George ironically inquired to the laughter of a packed audience gathered at London's Queen's Hall. "If you have burn them; they are only scraps of paper. . . . What are they made of? Rags. . . . What are they worth? The whole credit of the British Empire. (Loud Applause). . . . This doctrine of the scrap of paper . . . goes under the root of all public law. It is the straight road to barbarism. . . . It is as if you were to remove the Magnetic Pole because it was in the way of a German cruiser."[28]

To British observers, Germany's refusal to accept the symbolic significance of the "scrap of paper" not only rendered diplomatic commitments as worthless as the parchment they were printed on, but also posed an intellectual threat to the entire contractual basis of international and civil law.[29] In this context the "scrap of paper" was crucially important. Money was a scrap of paper, debt was a scrap of paper, marriage was a scrap of paper, treaties were scraps of paper, and international law was a scrap of paper. In the words of the patriotic commentator G. W. Prothero, "If international morality is regarded as of no account, a heavy blow is dealt at commercial and private morality as well. The Reign of Law, the greatest mark of civilization, is maintained in all its parts."[30] Not only did the Germans seem to attack all these contracts in a violation that broke a treaty obligation and included rape, requisitioning of property, and the symbolic destruction of law and order in the shooting of mayors and public officials, but they divested the "scrap of paper" of all meaning in a rhetorical act that threatened the sanctity of the written word. The German rejection of symbolism, language, and representation in favor of a stunning literalness hit liberals with a force comparable to the one experienced throughout Europe when the French revolutionaries divested their king of his mystical body and claimed that he was just a man. The "scrap of paper," like the execution of Louis XVI, was a literalist moment that forced a counterattack in the deployment of an image whose literal and symbolic meaning could not be so easily separated.

Although the German disregard of European treaty law was shocking to an educated elite, many middle-class observers expressed anxiety that the campaign to rally the British public was not having as much effect as it should on the classes that would become the backbone of the war effort. In August 1914, during the height of "war fever," Scottish miners organized anti-war demonstrations, the Independent Labour Party avowed pacifism, and numerous observers expressed anxiety about the sluggishness of recruiting among the working classes. According to the British

Empire Union, Labour politician Ramsay MacDonald responded to the "scrap of paper" by exclaiming, "Never did we arm our people and ask them to give up their lives for a less good cause than this."[31] And Coulson Kernahan, an experienced recruiting officer from Sussex, believed that explaining the origins of the war in legalistic terms could have only a limited influence on popular enlistment.[32]

In a much admired letter to the *Times*, G. W. Prothero argued that "even if the demands of honour and the maintenance of treaties make a widely understood appeal, the fact that our vital interests as a nation are involved is not fully apprehended."[33] Prothero, like many patriotic commentators, recommended a more systematic educational campaign in working-class constituencies that would focus on Germany's unscrupulous aristocracy, her aggressive military caste, and the ruling German principle of "Might makes Right." Prothero's suggestion, with its emphasis on such standard working-class enemies as the aristocracy and military, is an example of the idea that the so-called truth could be tailored to specific audiences. The central premise of propaganda throughout the war was that truth, properly presented at the right time, would inspire the individual to act rightly—or in a way desired by the educator.[34] In this way the control of information was crucial as a means of maintaining the ranks of right-thinking citizens who would support the cause. Gradually the official range of truth began to expand as commentators like Prothero noted that to broaden the appeal of the war, it would be necessary to explain that "the reasons which . . . compel us to take up the glove [are] for the sake of ourselves and, still more for our posterity."[35]

Although the educative campaign explaining the complex origins of the war continued to play a role in propaganda, the terms of that education began to expand as the government was forced to recognize that its own hold over the symbols of civilization—humanity, liberty, culture, and democracy—would remain tenuous unless these symbols came to represent more than the political institutions of an elite government and the ever-shrinking liberties guaranteed by the liberal state. As Coulson Kernahan put it, the public must be convinced that "this is a war which is *their* business . . . and that if they, the public, did not make it their business, they not only might not have any business to which to attend, but might live to see their own homes burning, their own women and children treated even more brutally and inhumanly than the enemy had treated the women and children of France and Belgium."[36]

While the call of King and Country and the "scrap of paper" remained staples of government propaganda throughout 1914, the official depiction of the ideals over which the war was being fought began to give way to a far more violent and gendered portrayal of Belgian occupation. Thanks to reports coming from Belgium, atrocity stories were gaining currency in the British press, occasioning intermittent embarrassment (as in the Kate Hume case) and offering an almost irresistible means by which to interest even the humblest reader in the war. The first official reports from Belgium appeared in the *Times* on August 26. As the Germans accurately noted, however, the *Belgian Reports* were far more restrained than the sensationalistic accounts produced by the British press. By 1915, the British government was receiving complaints from Belgium that its official documents were no longer being reproduced in British papers. Indeed, the accounts of rape and bizarre mutilations favored by English tabloids and "qualities" alike siphoned public interest from the endless inventory of stolen property and requisitioned goods, which, by the thirteenth official inquiry, had become the staple of the *Belgian Reports*.[37]

While the public officials who received the Belgian complaints seemed somewhat embarrassed, they did nothing to rein in the flamboyant nature of British atrocity reportage. Instead, the government launched a propaganda campaign that appropriated lurid representations of the war and enlisted newspapermen and advertisers to market them to a broad democratic public.[38] The official appropriation of popular imagery and the tailoring of propaganda to mass audiences is most clearly evident in the central metaphor of the war—the rape of Belgium. Here, in the event that inspired both the pen of Kate Hume and the appointment of Lord Bryce, the initial justification of the war in terms of democracy and treaty violation began to meld with a version of the conflict that stressed the safety of women and children and the sanctity of the home. Not only did the government propaganda bureau at Wellington House employ an array of novelists, poets, and fiction writers to create such propaganda, but it shrewdly endorsed popular and sensational ideas about the war, allowing a range of unofficial propagandists (borrowing on government credibility) to do its work for it.

The wedding of the "scrap of paper" to German atrocities is evident in both popular prints and the rhetoric of the penny press. Louis Raemaeker's cartoon of "Germany's Pledged Word" depicts the violation of international conventions as a prostrate female Belgium lying on the altar of *Deutschland über Alles*.[39] A similar idea is evident in the poetic caption to "In the Trail of the Hun" where "Broken pledges" and "treaties torn" are illustrated with a picture of women being used as human shields.[40] In the press and in popular imagination, the invasion of Belgium was transformed into the rape of Belgium, an image that informed the entire iconography of the war.[41]

In this context, Kate Hume's perverse fabrication is perhaps more understandable. According to the *Times*, Kate "had read a great deal about

German cruelties to women, and she had got it into her head that her sister had been killed at the front." "I do not know why I wrote it," Kate testified, "but I fancied what I said would be the way Grace would have written of herself in her last minutes. . . . I cannot say what made me do it, except the cruelties which the Germans were committing. I was seeing and imagining the things I wrote."[42]

In fact there was no difference between what Kate imagined and what could be read in the newspapers except that it came to the attention of the authorities that what Kate had said was false. While the government had begun by explaining the war in terms of the liberal values it held most dear, the newspapers began to represent it in a way that melded concern with the safety of home and family with genres of pornography and hagiography often denied a Protestant and respectable audience. The rape of Belgium thus came to be depicted not just as a rape but as a particularly lurid and brutal rape involving mutilation, repetition, and the public exposure of the violated female body to the eyes of parents, husbands, soldiers, and readers.[43] "A woman, 22 years old . . . was successively violated by five soldiers," declared the international lawyer Coleman Phillipson describing a bloody orgy at Corbeek Loo. A sixteen-year-old girl, "forced to drink," was "violated successively" on the lawn. "She continued to resist and they pierced her breasts with their bayonets. . . ." Even nuns were allegedly raped "in such horrible circumstances that it is difficult to believe the assailants to have been human at all."[44] And according to J. H. Morgan, the British attorney investigating German violations of international law in occupied France, "cases of sodomy and of the rape of little children did undoubtedly occur on a very large scale. . . . There is very strong reason to suspect that young girls were carried off to the trenches by licentious German soldiery, and there abused by hordes of savage and licentious men. . . ." Describing one blood-curdling rape after another, Morgan coolly declared that "One of our officers . . . heard a woman's shrieks in the night coming from behind the German trenches . . . when we advanced in the morning . . . a girl was found lying naked on the ground 'pegged out' in the form of a crucifix."[45]

Despite their sensational impact, however, atrocity stories put the British government in a difficult and embarrassing position since their veracity was frequently questioned both at home and abroad. To R. L. Orchelle, the American translator of Dr. Ernst Müller-Meiningen's defense of German international law, it was "The vexed and murky question of Belgian neutrality, that cunning cry and device that won our sentimental American sympathies above all other pleas or principles."[46] If a German apologist like Orchelle and a British spokesman like Bryce could agree on one thing, it was that the question of Belgian neutrality lay at the heart of the public understanding of the war. Because atrocities were widely exploited by the *Times,* a newspaper often considered an official organ by readers abroad, the government had a powerful investment in the credibility of these tales. To squash them would have been to exonerate Germany, to suggest British newspapers were printing falsehoods, and to let slip away a mode of representing the war that was proving far more popular than any government lecture on treaty violation. As the *Times* put it, "these outrages, if they are really happening, are part, and a powerful part of our case. It is true, therefore, that we should not have merely haphazard and informal reports of them in the newspapers, but that evidence should be carefully taken and sifted, and that all evidence which appears should be published to the world."[47] It was out of a need to stabilize this powerful and controversial imagery—an imagery able to arrest domestic and international attention—that the British government lent its considerable moral authority to the question of credibility.

Rape and the Creation of a Belief System

According to Kate's judge, the real danger of her letters was that they were "a gruesome document, so cleverly composed that anybody reading them would not doubt their authenticity."[48] The concern of the judge, however, seems to have been precisely the opposite of that of the government. In investigating questionable atrocity stories, the Press Bureau, charged with censoring British news, was much more concerned about whether a story could ultimately be proved false than whether it might be believed. As Press Bureau official E. T. Cook wrote to a renegade clergyman accused of spreading false atrocity stories from his pulpit, "The dissemination of unauthenticated charges which break down under enquiry is, apart from other considerations, undesirable in the national interest, as tending to weaken the force of much weighty material which exists on the subject of misconduct by the enemy."[49]

The Bryce Report, like the trial of Kate Hume and the reprimand of the clergyman, demonstrates the government's frantic attempt to gain control of public discourse and to adjust itself to the representational necessities of a democratic war.[50] It was out of a need to bring atrocity images under government authority that the attorney general and the director of Public Prosecutions set up the Bryce Commission in December 1914. Using the form of an official inquiry, the Bryce committee endorsed popular and unlikely atrocity stories and gave them government sanctity. Appended to its thirty pages of text were three hundred pages of evidence. The report was in fact designed to be excerpted and the choicest tales of

Hun barbarism were often nuggets found among bland accounts of burned buildings and stolen property. The result was that the Bryce Report, in the main rather dull, became a source-book for numerous popular publications and semiofficial spinoffs. Establishing an official idiom of violence, in which innocent women and children became the symbols of the British cause, the report helped fuel rampant atrocity reports and inspired the gendered representation of such acts as the sinking of the *Lusitania* and the execution of nurse Edith Cavell.[51]

Much and perhaps most propaganda was popularly generated and dispersed, yet its widespread credibility was established only through the painstaking efforts of official organizations. As accounts of atrocities began to appear with increasing frequency in the British press, the newspapers and the government were flooded with demands for their confirmation. In September 1914, a letter allegedly written by the son of a London vicar serving in France caused considerable consternation after it was published in the *Times*. The letter gave an account of three naked girls who had taken refuge in the British trenches after one had had her breasts cut off by German soldiers: "We have got three girls in the trenches with us, who came to us for protection. One had no clothes on, having been outraged by the Germans. I have given her my shirt. . . . Another poor girl has just come in having had both her breasts cut off. Luckily, I caught the Uhlan officer in the act and with a rifle at 300 yards killed him. And now she is with us, but poor girl, I'm afraid she will die. She is very pretty and only about 19, and only has her shirt on. . . ."[52]

The illicit material of pornography, once relegated to the streets of Soho, instead became a staple in the pages of the *Times*. Melding the discourse of pornography with the language of battle, this tale of rape and mutilation both eroticized the war and, in the name of news, legitimated a discourse that on all accounts was "unspeakable." To many commentators, this letter and others like it made a sufficient case for the instigation of an official inquiry into the accuracy of atrocity stories. "Such statements as these cannot possibly be allowed to rest on anonymous authority," wrote Lord Selborne to the *Times*. "If they are untrue, I am sure that you sir, would most deeply regret having given them publicity in any form. . . . But if they are true then God and man will judge. . . . Would it not be possible for trained lawyers or Judges belonging to a neutral nation . . . to conduct a sworn inquiry?"[53] Although the editor of the *Times* assured readers that he had "received in confidence the name and regiment of the officer in question," Asquith had considerably more difficulty answering similar questions in the House of Commons.[54] Since the Press Bureau did not censor the stories, the government was implicated in the question of their credibility and came under

increasing pressure from at home and abroad to make an official pro-
nouncement on their veracity.[55]

One difficulty that the government faced was that the origin of stories
like that of the vicar's son printed in the *Times* was not entirely clear.
Whether culled off the streets or reported by correspondents seeking information from Belgium and France, the only traceable stories seemed to
be those that were proven false.[56] It is even possible that stories such as
these did, as the editor of the *Times* claimed, come from the front itself.
Captain Martin Hardie, serving on the censor's staff in the Third Army in
France, commented that the soldiers, "consider it their duty—or some of
them do—to send home thrilling tales. One writes that a zeppelin has
been over their camp, dropping bombs and killing two men. (This is pure
fiction.) Another gay youth writes to a girl, . . . enclosing a set of postcards
'given to me by a French girl called Rosie (!) who is sweet on me because
me and my pal killed 5 Huns and rescued her from their clutches.'"[57]

Both the proliferation of these stories and the questioning of their veracity compelled the government to act, especially since both the German
and the American press disputed the authenticity of allied sources. The
Kate Hume atrocity hoax was repeatedly denounced by German apologists while an incredulous German-American press was so successful in
fostering skepticism over atrocity stories that on the eve of World War II,
the journalist Allan Jay commented that "in the Midwest you have the
feeling that men are waiting with shotguns to shoot down the first propagandist who mentions Belgian babies."[58] The way the government handled this crisis was to prosecute the tellers of demonstrably false atrocity
stories and to endorse officially those reports that could not be closely examined. The result of this strategy was to create out of a rampant popular discourse an official mode of representing the war that borrowed on
the prestige of the Crown to create a believable narrative from disparate
stories of rape, mutilation, and sadism.

The trial and conviction of Kate Hume turned an embarrassing incident
into a testament to the determination of the authorities to uncover the facts
regarding the outrages of war. Yet, as the director of Public Prosecutions
pointed out, prosecution always *highlighted* embarrassing falsehoods, making it useful only in cases that had already received a certain amount of notoriety.[59] Official corroboration was thus far preferable to the suppression
of false news. It was in the search for such corroboration that the attorney
general and the director of Public Prosecutions appealed to James Bryce in
late 1914 to head the Committee on Alleged German Outrages.

Had the commission been in earnest about verifying atrocities, its task
would have been considerable. Given the inaccessibility of the occupied
territories, contemporaries were baffled by how to prove accusations for

which little physical evidence existed. Throughout the war unsuccessful efforts to locate victims of atrocities testified to the difficulty of discovering the maimed even among the thousands of Belgian refugees housed in England. The attempts by one correspondent of Lord Bryce to find a pregnant women who carried the child of a German soldier yielded nothing, just as the reward Lord Northcliffe offered for a child with its hands cut off went unclaimed. The validation of private crimes against women's bodies was becoming a bureaucratic nightmare.[60]

The appointment of the Bryce Commission was an attempt to overcome these evidentiary limitations in a way that is deeply revealing about the gendered construction of truth during the war. As German apologists pointed out, it was very difficult in Britain to prove a case of rape and the penalties were relatively minor. Like the letter from the vicar's son, which was printable primarily because it was allegedly written by an officer at the front, the testimony of rape, to be credible, would have to be presented through the oracle of respected men. Lord Bryce was chosen to head the committee because of his prewar philo-Germanism, his legal expertise, and his tremendous reputation in the United States, where he had served as the British Ambassador in Washington. As Attorney General Sir John Simon noted, "The value of the investigations entirely depends upon the known impartiality and authority of those who compose the committee, and the Government very much hope that you may be disposed to accept this invitation."[61]

Simon placed his emphasis on the credibility of the committee rather than the reliability of the witnesses. Indeed, the Bryce committee was allowed to interview neither witnesses nor those who took evidence. Its job was simply to endorse typed depositions presented to it by the committee secretaries, Brodrick and Mears. According to Simon, this truncated procedure had been established to save time. A team of barristers had already taken depositions from Belgian refugees residing in Britain, and the work of the Bryce Committee was to be made as simple as possible by taking up the work where the barristers left off. Yet on reviewing the voluminous correspondence surrounding the issue of proof, one is left with the uncomfortable feeling that the government was looking for endorsement rather than verification of these disturbing accounts.[62] As *Edinburgh Review* editor Harold Cox noted shortly before his request to interview witnesses was denied, "All we know is that Broderick and Mears have given us various printed statements, but so far as we are officially aware they may have invented the whole."[63]

While the members of the Bryce Commission had no real idea whether or not the stories that they endorsed were true, they gave the official stamp to a set of highly sensationalistic tales produced for foreign and domestic consumption. Indeed, the role of the committee was not to establish the truth of atrocities but to assure their credibility. The original versions of the anonymous depositions upon which the committees findings were based have never been found in the Home Office, where they were to be placed. Furthermore, the committee was asked to claim far greater familiarity with the evidence than it actually had, and, as Cox discovered, several of the barristers who allegedly took evidence from refugees denied having done so or had very different accounts of the credibility of witnesses than what the secretaries reported to the committee.[64] The commission was in essence called upon to conduct a mock inquiry that would substitute the good name of Lord Bryce for the thousands of missing names of the anonymous victims whose stories appeared in the pages of the report.

The report was timed for simultaneous publication in Britain and the United States and created an immediate sensation when it appeared in May 1915. The balance between the mundane and the hair-raising in the report gave it an air of judiciousness that seemed to lend credibility to what might otherwise have been unbelievable tales. "It is quite possible," the authors intoned, "that in some cases where the body of a Belgian or a French woman is reported as lying in the roadside pierced with bayonet wounds or hanging from a tree, or else as lying gashed and mutilated in a cottage kitchen or bedroom, the woman in question gave some provocation."[65] This combination of dispassionate authorial voice and horrifying description gave the Bryce Report an air of seeming impartiality while corroborating the most sensationalistic allegations against the German army. Hundreds of letters, newspaper articles, and reports confirmed that the flat, dispassionate writing style, the official seal, and the good name of Lord Bryce had convinced the world of German barbarism. As Charles Masterman, the director of British propaganda, wrote to Bryce, "Your report has *swept* America. As you probably know even the most skeptical declare themselves converted, just because it is signed by you!"[66]

The Bryce Report itself is a tour de force in the genre of inquirial writing. The use of barristers to examine witnesses gave credence to the idea that not a single story was reported that would not hold up in "any court in England." Throughout the process of compiling the report, the integrity of the members of the committee was sedulously protected by the official secretaries who supplied the processed data. The committee members had only to exclude stories that they found to be questionable and organize the remainder into the report. In its use of detail and its assertion that the victims of outrage "harboured no hatred or resentment towards the Germans," the report claimed a scrupulous and punctilious attention to facts and a disregard of any evidence born of emotion. A profusive use of numbers, ages, and situations and a tendency to highlight those particulars that were not known thus gave the report the impression of an exact, dispassionate, and uembroidered relation of facts. According to the *Appendix*, a three-hundred-page compendium of depositions and other documents given in evidence to support the claims of the report, "In all cases [the depositions] are given as nearly as possible . . . in the exact words of the witness. . . . In every case the name and description of the witness are given in the original depositions and in copies which have been furnished to us by H.M. Government. The originals remain in the custody of the Home Department, where they will be available in case of need, for reference after the conclusion of the war."[67] The rhetoric of scientific method, the indisputable reliability of the examiners and the committee, and the evocation of the binding power of the sworn statement assured readers that what they read was the unmediated experience of the victims of German atrocities. Just as the authority of the examiners substituted for the names of the victims, the prestige of the committee rendered superfluous any necessity for public discrimination in evaluating the evidence.

The reception of the Bryce Report was stunning. Its release coincided with the sinking of the *Lusitania,* adding a dramatic and emotional piece of evidence to its studied accusations of German barbarism. According to a confidential cabinet document tabulating the response to the Bryce Report in the United States, "Even in papers hostile to the Allies, there is not the slightest attempt to impugn the correctness of the facts alleged. Lord Bryce's prestige in America put skepticism out of the question."[68]

Although the government could never hope to control the prolific and irrepressible genre of atrocity propaganda, it could lend it legitimacy. A legal discourse endorsed by men thus framed the case of sadistic violence against women, anchoring the sexualized rhetoric of war justification in the credibility of the courts, the government, and a committee of eminent experts. In the bureaucratic production of truth, women acted as narrative objects while the expertise of men substituted for any physical substantiation of the facts. The result was an official discourse at once lascivious, voyeuristic, and irrefutable.

By June 1915, Charles Masterman, the director of propaganda, estimated that his bureau at Wellington House had circulated "some 2 1/2 million copies of books, official publications, pamphlets, and speeches in 17 different languages" concerning the "rights and wrongs of the war"; and at this time the Bryce Report was already being circulated in ten different languages and would be further translated during the war.[69] Although the invasion of Belgium occurred in August 1914, the images of atrocity generated in the first months of the war remained a leitmotif of propaganda right up to the vociferous call to "hang the Kaiser" at the end of the conflict.[70] Even the publicist Robert Donald, a critic of Masterman, admitted in 1917 that Wellington House had "made good use of outrages" and "brought out clearly the great moral issues raised by the war."[71] In his 1917 report on propaganda, Donald warmly recommended continuing such efforts by "placing before the public in neutral countries accounts of every fresh outrage committed by the enemy, presenting the narrative in popular form, and by speedier methods than those now practiced."[72] Although propaganda changed dramatically over the course of the war, atrocity stories remained a persistent theme even as they were regarded with increasing irony by soldiers, pacifists, and those weary citizens eager to end the war.[73]

Indeed, one of the tragedies of the British effort to manufacture truth is the way authentic suffering was rendered suspect by fabricated tales. As Ruth Harris has pointed out in her study of French rape narratives, propaganda reduced women's actual experiences to a generic and voyeuristic sub-genre of war propaganda.[74] The deceptive methods and questionable stories employed by such highly regarded authorities as the Bryce Committee would cast doubt on the authenticity of suffering. Most importantly perhaps, rape narratives helped undermine pacifist opposition, making the position of antiwar feminists particularly untenable. "I do not enjoy having my country in the Pontius-Pilate-like attitude of neutrality," complained Theodore Roosevelt to Bryce after reading the report. "As for Jane Addams and the other well-meaning women who plead for peace without even daring to protest against the infamous wrongs, the infamies worse than death which their sisters in France and Belgium have suffered, I lack the patience to speak of them."[75] This was precisely the sort of response that British authorities had hoped for.

The Crown's prosecution of Kate Hume and the official commission of the Bryce Report illustrate the ways the government was forced to deal with the increasingly important control of information in the early years of the war. What made the management of information so crucial was the fact that during the war nothing remained truly "unofficial." The British government was repeatedly held responsible for the words and actions of its citizens, its soldiers, and its newspapers, as well as for its officials abroad.[76] Since the success of the war effort seemed to depend on the belief that civilization itself was under threat, it was essential for officials to invest this threat with tangible meaning. Although the government entered the war committed to the political, legal, and diplomatic education of its people, the translation of these abstract ideas into physical terms held the key to the legitimation of the war. As East End MP Will Crooks explained to his working-class constituents, "The brutal murder of innocent folk in Belgium shows us what Germany would do. It is not a question of prosperity, conquest, or trade. We are fighting for liberty and for our homes."[77]

With the growing portrayal of German aggression as an attack on women and children, the lines between official and popular propaganda became blurred.[78] Newspapers and newspapermen, though subject to censorship, frequently evaded it, while journalists and newspaper proprietors acted in a variety of capacities within the administration and outside of it. Furthermore, the impression of the war that the British people absorbed came from the totality of images they received, the origins of which were often obscure. Private individuals and organizations borrowed from official images, just as officials compiled and made credible popular stories. The distinction between official and unofficial propaganda thus becomes considerably less important than the question of how those images were used to bolster the war effort.

The key to the popularity of Belgian atrocities among those promoting stern military action lay in the universal values with which they endowed the war. As the personal literally became political, the case of Belgium offered a way to explain the need for military action in private and sexual terms. "Britain is Fighting not only for Freedom in Europe," one recruiting poster proclaimed, "but to defend your mothers, wives, and sisters from the horrors of war."[79] The representation of the conflict in these highly gendered terms had significant international and domestic consequences. While atrocity stories helped raise money for charities aiding Belgian victims of war, facilitated the often difficult absorption of Belgian refugees into British homes, and worked as a rationale for those promoting American intervention, the questionable standards of inquiry used by the British helped turn Belgian women from objects of pity to objects of doubt in the postwar period.[80]

The domestic results of atrocity propaganda were equally significant. On one hand, atrocity stories enhanced the aura of heroism that surrounded the volunteer army and the men who bravely fought to protect women and children. On the other, they undermined any "excuse" civilians might have for opposing the war, seeking a negotiated peace, or choosing not to serve. Most poignantly, however, they provided an unanswerable rhetoric to those encouraging mothers and wives to send their men to war. Once these images saturated British political culture, some of their subversive implications would emerge. For now, though, we shall turn to their more immediate results.

CHAPTER TWO

THE MAKING OF TOMMY ATKINS

MASCULINITY, PROPAGANDA, AND THE TRIUMPH OF FAMILY VALUES

In Alfred Noyes's 1915 recruiting play *Rada,* the wife of a Belgian doctor and her twelve-year-old daughter are captives in their own home at the mercy of two German soldiers. Most of the drama's action is designed to reveal the brutality of the Germans, whose merriment includes forcing an old vicar and his cook to "dance naked round the dead body of his wife" and hanging a revolver from the Christmas tree.[1] In the final climactic scene of the play the German soldiers are ordered to hand Rada and her daughter over to be gang raped. Contemptuously Rada cries: "And war, they tell me, is a noble thing. It is the mother of heroic deeds, the nurse of honour, manhood."[2] Rather than allow her daughter to be ravished by the Germans, she locks herself and her child in the bedroom. The scene culminates with young Bettine, the innocent daughter, crying: "O British! British Come! Come Quickly, British!" as the Germans try to break down the bedroom door. The play ends when Rada shoots her daughter and herself to save them both from what is literally depicted as a fate worse than death. The British finally arrive, moments too late.[3]

In this play and hundreds of appeals like it, the plea for recruits, voiced in the cries of a young girl facing imminent violation in her own home and in the absence of her father, defined the terms upon which British men were purportedly going to war. The imperatives outlined in atrocity propaganda were making their way into recruiting productions, stimulating consciences and inviting the moral community to urge men to serve. In the cast of characters, which could be read literally or allegorically, Britain is depicted as the protective surrogate father. Crying out for "the British," instead of her natural protector, Bettine's symbolic appeal reveals the way recruiting propaganda promoted both the militarization and the domestication of British manhood, profoundly shaping the image of the army and the men within it.

For patriotic Britons the Great War offered an opportunity to win a cultural victory at home as well as a military victory abroad. As enlisting in the army became the supreme mark of loyalty, the British soldier was characterized as the embodiment of those moral values that defined British society.[4] "Tommy Atkins," the ideal-typical British soldier, was characteristically brave, cheerful, martial, and fair. "Our towns are full of lads in khaki," boasted the *Times*. "Billeted in schools, stables, and private houses, [they are] sturdy, bronzed, clean-looking fellows to a man, . . . impatient to fight . . . [and] given to sobriety and pure living."[5] Reasserting at once the virility of British manhood and its domesticity, war propaganda created an image of the common soldier that soon became a masculine ideal.

This image of Tommy Atkins departed considerably from its antecedents in the imperial poetry of Rudyard Kipling, who popularized the stock character in a series of poems about the Boer War.[6] While Kipling's Tommy Atkins was a cynical working-class soldier whose bravery and patriotism offset his vulgarity, the image of the common soldier in World War I was domesticated and refined. Traces of the older Tommy Atkins were certainly evident in music-hall songs, comic poetry, and popular cartoons, but during the war Tommy Atkins, and with him the image of the common soldier itself, went through a sort of apotheosis. "It is probable that . . . the general public will continue to think of the soldier as the man whose work it is to kill," complained the *Nineteenth Century* in an article on "The Happy Warrior," but the public would then have forgotten that "his chief function is to succour and protect; to risk his life for the sake of others."[7] Using similarly Christian rhetoric, the Reverend Alexander Irvine declared Tommy Atkins to be "England's standard-bearer" through whose eyes "millions of men and women and little children see the dawn of hope!" Imagining the words of this sacred soldier, Irvine addressed his listeners with a fictional speech from the mouth of Britain's archetypical warrior: "'I AM TOMMY ATKINS! The incarnation of England that was, and is, and is to be! I am the guardian of her honour, the avenger of her dead and the defender of her children! I am the agent of the Infinite, the forerunner of Demos and a righter of world wrongs. Above the din of battle I hear the voice of God. I know the Great White Comrade. He stands beside me as I do England's work.'"[8]

While Dr. Irvine's rhetoric no doubt provoked many a snigger at the camps where he preached, such language is significant because it reveals the masculine ideal British authorities wished to promote. Since Britain depended on a volunteer army until 1916, young men were subjected to a barrage of appeals imploring them to join up; once enlisted, they constituted a captive audience for ministers, officers, doctors, and other professionals intent upon delivering a moral message about the meaning of their service. Nowhere, however, is wishful thinking about the common soldier more evident than in the recruiting appeals designed to stir civilian hearts. On one hand, this propaganda regaled potential recruits with the desirable image of Tommy Atkins, the working-class soldier-hero to be emulated for his cheer, grit, bravery, and patriotism. On the other, it summoned up the specter of ruined Belgium and hinted darkly at the possibility of invasion—an invasion that would mean the rape and mutilation of British women and children. Although these images contrast starkly with one another, the specter of one always underlay the effusiveness of the other, subtly intensifying the level of obligation felt by men and their loved ones and licensing disparate members of the community to encourage men to enlist.

MANHOOD AND MILITARY OBLIGATION

The declaration of war on August 4, 1914, marked a sea change in the experience of young men accustomed to the relative freedom accorded to males in a liberal society. Although joining the army was voluntary during 1914 and 1915, social pressure to enlist was overwhelming, and little quarter was given to those who refused to join up. Whether a man's failure to enlist was attributed to effeminacy and cowardice or to overt disloyalty, during World War I the decision not to go to war was no longer regarded by most Britons as a choice compatible with loyal citizenship. A young unenlisted man in the autumn of 1914 could look forward to the sneers of his friends, the opprobrium of his football club, and even a curt dismissal from his job if he had not joined the army.[9] Patriotic trumpet calls and slurs upon his manhood would have followed him from his favorite music halls to a stroll through the park resonating in the lyrics of popular songs, the language of personal advertisements, and even, perhaps, upon the lips of his own mother, wife, or lover.[10] As Frank Ennor, a young bank clerk, wrote to his fiancée Lulu shortly before joining the First Grenadier Guards in 1916, "You cannot imagine what misery I have been through . . . but the time has come when all must go and I am not going to wait for conscription . . . I made my decision yesterday when walking through those fields with you and I know that you will secretly agree with my decision."[11]

Such sentiments are expressed repeatedly in soldier's memoirs, making up one of the most vivid memories of the early years of the war. William Orchard, writing to his father in Sussex about his reasons for joining up in 1914 explained that, "We are in the thick of it, large employers are sacking their young employees in order that they should be compelled to do their duty and enlist, and those who don't enlist for whatever reason are looked upon as funks and shirkers so you can imagine my feelings, as I can't bear to be thought a funk. . . . I told Phil . . . that I shouldn't join unless forced to but I simply *must*."[12]

Although invectives directed at young men were most effective in 1914 and 1915, when more than half of Britain's total wartime fighting forces were amassed under the voluntary system, they continued even after the institution of conscription in 1916.[13] In the hunt for "shirkers," the persecution of conscientious objectors, and the denunciation of those who failed to "do their bit," men of all social ranks experienced inordinate and often irresistible social, cultural, and political pressure to enlist. As the pacifist John W. Graham recalled, a man who refused to fight "had to have faith strong enough to see beyond public feeling of the time. . . . The women he knew cut his acquaintance. His mother and his brothers often jeered him at home. He was chosen by his employer to be dispensed with, and so left open to be punished for his refusal to serve. . . . 'Shirker,' 'coward,' 'dog,' were the words they were thought to deserve, when the Derby canvassers came to their workshops. . . ."[14] Only a khaki uniform or a missing limb could protect a young man on the home front from the ignominious brand of "coward" and the shrill taunts of strangers, friends, families, and texts. If the outward signs of the willingness to brave death—a uniform, a medal, a stump—had become the new symbols of masculinity, the potential mutilation of the male body was the price to be paid for the preservation of the masculine soul.[15] As A. Robert Saunders ironically put it, when reporting the condition of an injured friend, "Wallie is happier wounded and disfigured than home."[16]

Although a number of historians have argued that it was not moral pressure, propaganda, or war posters that drove men to enlist but a "sense of duty to their country," we cannot hope to understand what was meant at the time by "sense of duty" without analyzing the way it was expressed, identified, and embodied during the war.[17] Conscience, that ineffable manifestation of a socialized self governed by ideas of honor, family, and country, became the means by which masculine subjectivity was bound to military service. The inner sting that many men identified as an inescapable "sense of duty" cannot be separated from the cultural forces of "moral conscription." The archaic rhetoric of war posters, the sniping comments of young women, or the sanctimonious calls of parsons and teachers were simply external manifestations of an inner phenomenon. Inculcated in schools, social clubs, and boy's literature, ideas of appropriate male behavior defined both men's "sense of duty" and the language of recruiting, which worked in inextricable unison upon the thoughts and actions of young men. As one public-school boy wrote to another shortly before he enlisted, "I am really ashamed of you. To think that a great strong chap like you are, should, as yet, have done *nothing* for his country is really a shame. This is not only my opinion but that of all the O.U.s [graduates of Uppingham] . . . who *are doing something* . . . I really *do* think you are a slacker! . . . What you had better do is to *enlist at once*. . . . Soldiering is pleasant work. . . . Take it from me! . . . Now hurry up and get a job, for your country *needs* you. *Don't wait* for others to give you a lead!"[18]

Such earnest expressions of public-school enthusiasm vividly portray the social and cultural manifestations of "conscience" and the complex interaction between inner life and external pressure that, even years later, left many men unsure exactly why they had volunteered.[19] Writing from contemporary diaries, Major W. Hughes later mused on why men might have enlisted. Rejecting the idea that love for Belgium or France or any real hatred of Germany inspired men to go, he speculatively asks, "Was it because they believed it to be a duty and because the country was in danger, because their friends went, because the ladies sang 'We don't want to lose you but we think you ought to go,' because they expected honour and glory, or was it because of the change that it promised, the chance of a break in a monotonous existence?" Major Hughes does not offer an answer to this question. Like Peter Simkins, who has rendered the most complete perusal of war diaries on this subject, Hughes suggests, "It would be interesting to find out but I think very many would find it hard to say."[20]

Given the abstract nature of "duty" and the multiplicity of forces that drew or pushed men toward enlistment, propagandistic renderings of the meaning of the war became all the more important in providing an official justification for a wide variety of personal motives. Though to the young public-school boy quoted above, duty to one's country was sufficient reason for an "Old Uppinghamian" to join up, polemicists consistently countered anticipated reluctance to enlist with an appeal to the defense of the family. If men joined out of "duty" to their country, the nature of that duty and the significance of that country was often expressed in terms of the home. "There is something infinitely greater and more enduring which is emerging already out of this great conflict," declared Lloyd George at the Queen's Hall, "a new patriotism, richer, nobler, and more exalted than the old. . . . I see amongst all classes . . . a new recognition that the honour of the country does not depend merely on the maintenance of its glory in the stricken field, but also in protecting its homes from distress."[21] In drawing attention to the relationship between "patriotism" and protecting "homes from distress," Lloyd George evoked those prolific images that tended to define the European conflict in personal and domestic terms. The issues at stake in the war were not merely nationalistic; they cut to the very heart of the values Britons held most dear.

By focusing on Belgian atrocities and hinting at the possible perpetration of similar deeds in Britain, recruiters offered compelling reasons for all citizens to participate in the enlistment drive. "Meetings necessarily touch a small proportion; in particular the women of the people whose influence on the men will turn the scale," noted an observant amateur recruiter. "The one sure and swift way to impress them is by pictures, at every post office and public house, at every shop window and gatepost, at the entrance to all factories and workshops, let bold clear picture posters be displayed showing what has happened to those conquered by Germany. . . ."[22] As recruiters focused on the humanitarian causes of the war and warned a receptive public of Britain's own vulnerability, it became increasingly difficult for ordinary men to decline to serve. Not only would failure to enlist imply a selfish disregard for the victims of German brutality, a careless dismissal of national honor, and an unwillingness to defend English homes, but it would also constitute a dramatic failure of British manhood. Such concerns had deep roots in Edwardian Britain.

Anna Davin has argued that anxiety over the poor performance of British troops in the Boer War of 1899–1902 resulted in a growing public concern about the stamina of the British race.[23] In part this concern manifested itself in worry over the deteriorating physical quality of potential recruits, yet it also reflected a series of moral reservations about the decadence, effeteness, and even potential effeminacy of British youth, accustomed to the leisure and prosperity of the modern age. In the years before the Great War, such concerns helped fuel an acrimonious debate over whether or not Britain should follow the lead of continental neighbors and adopt a policy of mandatory military service.[24] To many Liberals, conscription was an unacceptable encroachment on personal freedom, and implementing such a policy would mean nothing less than the wholesale betrayal of Britain's libertarian past. For a growing chorus of imperialists and conservatives, however, Britain's military preparedness, imperial power, and moral fortitude all required mandatory military service. While a number of military, strategic, and financial concerns underlay this debate, the impact of military service on masculine character became one of its battlegrounds. In his prewar pamphlet *The Briton's First Duty: The Case for Conscription*, George F. Shee, a moderate conscriptionist and "philosophic Liberal" concluded his plea for national service with the assurance to women that "the men of England will be better sons, better husbands, better brothers, and better fathers, by having given some part of their manhood to the service of their country."[25] And the conscriptionist Coulson Kernahan argued that compulsory military service would make "merely for manhood not militarism." "When it comes," he argued "it will not only mean robust manhood for the country, but a more real and virile Christianity."[26]

As recruiting propaganda evoked these prewar concerns, "defending the home" came to mean more than rescuing Belgium or preserving the domestic status quo but suggested also the rehabilitation of masculinity itself. The belief in the war as somehow "purifying" was intimately tied to the idea that military service would cleanse Britain of the vestiges of *fin de siècle* decadence and produce a regenerate manhood committed to ideals of duty, honor, chivalry, and family.[27] Rupert Brooke's famous metaphor for soldiers as "swimmers into cleanness leaping" is only one example of the early idea of the war as an avenue to ritual purification.[28] For the poet laureate, "Much suffering shall cleanse thee/ But thou through the flood/ Shalt win to salvation/ To Beauty through blood," while Lawrence Binyon, one of the *Times'* featured poets, went so far at to bless the "dear earth that bore us" for Britain would be "In the hour of peril purified. . . ."[29] Even the pacifist Vera Brittain, who "condemn[ed] War in theory most strongly," believed "wholesale murder" to be "preferable to atrophy and effeteness."[30]

In this spirit, Lloyd George defied Germany to "believe and to preach that we are a decadent and degenerate people." Reminding his indignant audience that "they proclaim that we are a non-heroic nation skulking behind our mahogany counters whilst we egg on more gallant races to their destruction," Lloyd George placed in the mouths of German critics the concerns of Edwardian conscriptionists who in the years preceding the war had voiced numerous doubts about British manhood and its ability and willingness to respond to a call to arms. Evoking a series of contrasts that compared the state of British manhood before the war with the regenerate masculinity of arms, Lloyd George, like a host of other observers, depicted the crisis as an inner battle against the corrupting influence of consumption and leisure as well as an external struggle against a hostile German adversary. Disclaiming the German vision of Britain as a thing of the past, Lloyd George answered the accusations by arguing that "The great flood of luxury and sloth which had submerged the land is receding, and a new Britain is appearing. We can see for the first time the fundamental things that matter in life, that have been obscured from our vision by the tropical growth of prosperity."[31]

The link between commercial luxury and emasculation—what the conservative critic J. H. Balfour Browne called "the limpness of our fibre at home"—runs throughout the language of recruiting at the beginning of the war.[32] "Happily, the great testing of the nation has come before the softness had gone too far," declared the Duty and Discipline movement, an organization devoted to patriotic child-rearing. For it would have been too late, "When the young manhood of the nation will be made up of the children who have looked upon themselves as entitled to go to the kinematograph every evening and to visit the sweet shop seven times a week; one trembles to think of the result."[33] Decrying the sentimentality that turns "flabby boys" into "muffs," the Duty and Discipline movement, like Lloyd George, Balfour Browne, and many other commentators on the state of British manhood, depicted the war as an event that could save the nation from the enervation, effeteness, and decadence, that threatened to undermine England's noble and chivalric past.

Nowhere is this attack on "decadence" more evident than in the wartime discourse over homosexuality. The association of homosexuality with "decadence," "effeminacy," and "effeteness" solidified in the late nineteenth century with the sensational trial of the playwright Oscar Wilde and the publication of several high-profile studies of "sexual inversion." No doubt bolstered by the lurid accounts of sexual perversity in Belgium, which put issues of sexuality at the center of public discourse, the war provided a convenient platform from which to drive home the domestic and international peril of this troubling "vice."[34] As Trevor Wilson has written, "A good many people . . . held that sexual 'laxity' went hand in hand with setbacks to the British cause . . . [and] that Britain's failures in the war were attributable to the 'vice' practiced by Oscar Wilde."[35] Not only did *The Manual of Military Law* set harsh penalties for any sexual contact between men, but sodomy was punishable by court martial, earning sentences of ten years to life in military prison.[36] While Robert Graves suggests that homosexual attachments occurred at the front among perfectly competent officers and men, the popular association of homosexuality with effeminacy underlay contemporary hysteria over "decadence," since it seemed to preclude the sort of masculine hardiness necessary to wage war.[37] These tensions erupted in particularly flamboyant fashion in 1918 with a libel suit involving a production of Oscar Wilde's risque play *Salome*. During the trial, right-wing MP Pemberton Billing claimed that a black book containing the names of 47,000 sexual perverts, including a former prime minister, was in the possession of German agents who were using it to threaten national security.[38] While Billing suggested that possible blackmail put the nation at risk, the extent of the hysteria makes sense only within a context in which national security appeared to be inextrica-

bly linked to masculinity and where heterosexual virility and national
welfare had already been welded together in the public mind.[39]

Indeed, the linking of national danger with failed manliness was a
chronic theme in war propaganda, which frequently depicted the righting
of world politics in terms of the enforcement of gender roles. On September 5, 1914, the *Brighton Herald* published a letter that asked Brighton
women "to make trouser wearers—supposed men *enlist*."[40] The letter was
followed by another from "An Indignant British Matron" which suggested
that "every English women learn how to load and use a revolver for her
own defense. As I see hundreds of cowardly male curs (I cannot call them
men) perambulating the streets daily, apparently ignoring their obligation
to their country . . . I think it would be wise for women to try and help
themselves, so that when England is invaded they could at least account
for one foe less, and save their own honour, and they might be able to hide
their young males behind their petticoats."[41] The rhetoric of the "Indignant British Matron" raised the specter of a newly empowered womanhood inspired to defend itself in the face of a male abandonment of the
essential properties of masculinity. As men became "so called . . . men,"
"cowardly male curs," and "trouser wearers—supposed men," these letters
raised the vision of a shamefully emasculated youth groping for protection behind a woman's petticoats. Playing on such logic, Lady Maxwell
declared that men should "come out and fight and not sit by the fire and
spin," while advocates of women's work complained that male shop attendants were "serving out lace ribbons . . . instead of serving bullets to
the Germans."[42]

Within the wartime vocabulary of gender definitions, men were those
who protected; women those who required protection. Unenlisted men,
existing among those who were being protected, were ineluctably feminized by virtue of their place behind the lines. Thus, the mistress of a Girl
Scout troop in Bath rudely suggested to E. A. Brookes, an unenlisted railway porter, that "Seeing . . . you cannot be a man not to join the army. We
offer you an invitation to join our Girl Scouts as washer up."[43] Symbolically stripped of his gender identity and even his human identity, outcasts
like the Bath railway porter gained a pariah status distinct from that of
enemy aliens only in that their flaw lay in the will rather than the blood.
If, as Paul Fussell and others claim, soldiers rejected these images, women
very often did not. Miss Dorothy E. Higgins, a volunteer nurse serving in
France, wrote to her father invidiously comparing the unenlisted men
back home to a wounded French boy whose only desire was to get well so
that he would be *"bon pour aller en front."*[44] "I expect that you have been
fearfully busy with all the recruiting . . ." wrote Miss Higgins in disgust. "I
call it rubbish Raymond Snowshall claiming to be the sole support of his

mother. She is a perfectly able bodied woman. . . . I am awfully glad Young's application [for military exemption] was refused: he is an idle useless lout who ought to have gone ages ago. . . . I too long for Hunter and Archie Bosson to go: they are but cucumbers of the ground in Alford. What about the Hildreth boy? Is he still gibbering with fright? Such people make me sick when one sees the life out here."[45]

Miss Higgins's own privileged position as a woman at the front gives her a basis from which to attack the cowards back home and to extol both the heroic French boy and the merits of female labor. In her next letter to her father she urged him to "get women to work for you." As she declared confidently, "If French women can do it . . . *extremely* well as they *are* doing, I'm sure *Englishwomen* can do it even better. It is wonderful here how the women are doing the men's work . . . I know it seems very extraordinary and topsy turvy . . . but still these are topsy turvy days and one must try to do one's best to fit in and use the materials at hand. Now do cheer up and make up your mind to get anyone you can, to do the work, even if you hire a batch of Hun prisoners and have to shepherd them yourself with a 12 bore."[46] This self-assured advice from a daughter proud of her work, of her soldierly uniform, and of the striking ability of women to do men's work, to a miserable father attempting to carry on at home, highlights the wartime reversal of gender roles so perceptively identified by Sandra Gilbert, Susan Kent, and Margaret Higonnet.[47] Yet it also shows the way representations of manly courage and cowardice entered women's vocabulary and the profound implications it had for the way women evaluated their men and themselves.

In their lavishing of affection upon soldiers, the message of patriotic women was that sexual hierarchy could be preserved only by men willing to volunteer for the front. As soldiers were exalted as supermen and women assumed their male civilian roles, the slacker, the conscientious objector, or the man out of uniform was threatened with becoming a sort of mock woman—despised, disenfranchised, and powerless. In a culture where the label of "woman" could be regarded as an insult, reassigning the taunt of femininity was thus a way of demonstrating that fear and frailty were no longer the province of women, but belonged instead to the realm of the unenlisted man. As one personal advertisement in the *Times* tauntingly announced, "Englishwoman undertakes to Form and Equip a Regiment of Women for the Firing Line if lawn tennis and cricketing young men will agree to act as Red Cross nurses in such a Regiment."[48]

Women's divesting of their own femininity and reinvesting it upon men is most literally expressed in the presenting of petticoats to unenlisted civilians. As veteran Charles Heinson remembered it, women would drape their underclothing across the streets "for young men to wear instead of khaki."[49] In a sort of forced gesture of psychological cross-dressing, the petticoat was not only offered as the alternative to the khaki uniform but implied that a woman had liberated herself from the cumbersome garment that was the implicit dress of any man not in khaki.[50]

Such practices were both deeply conservative and potentially subversive. Not only were they shameless attempts to force young men into rigidly defined sex roles, but they offered women a rare opportunity to critique masculinity and impugn the character of men. The feminist journal *Common Cause* fulminated over a 1914 *Times* ad that requested "Petticoats for all able-bodied youth in this country who have not yet joined the navy or army."[51] "No thank you!" the journal replied, "An unmanly man is not fit to wear a woman's clothes. It is time men learnt that a strong capable woman is not necessarily 'virile,' nor a feeble man woman-like."[52] A year later, feminists were able to answer such insulting rhetoric even more pointedly. Responding to *Punch's* suggestion that "Shirkers should . . . disguise themselves as women," since it "ought not to be difficult," A. E. Parsons tartly retorted that a "shirker" shopping for women's clothes in the "World's Emporium" would find Red Cross active-service outfits, doctor's uniforms, ammunition-makers' attire, and the clothes of women drivers and women tram conductors, all of which would be "too wide across the shoulders" for a male slacker.[53]

Despite such subversive potential, many propagandists seemed unable to resist playing on male anxieties about gender identity. A recruiting poster captioned "Will You Go or Must I?" blatantly exploited the threat of sex role reversal to drive home the case for Irish enlistment.[54] Avoiding a campaign that called upon hostile Irishmen to defend England, the director of Irish recruiting, Headley Le Bas, instead encouraged men to defend their women and their own sense of honor and manhood.[55] In the poster a beautiful young woman shows herself ready to take up arms in place of her shamefaced lover as Belgium burns in the background. The implication of the message is that only in the righting of gender roles at home can men hope to be effective in remedying a travesty against the family abroad. Although the question may be posed ironically, the rifle in the woman's hand directly links the masculinization of women with men's failure to enlist. In the poster, burning Belgium across the water, a nuclear family on the Irish shore, and the Amazonian woman in the foreground link the triple consequences of non-enlistment: Belgium will suffer, the Irish family will become vulnerable, and women will have to play the part of men.

This poster was apparently designed to stimulate anxiety about the mutability of gender categories. The idea that the failure of a man to act like a man might result in a woman threatening to fill his role cast doubt upon the virility of the civilian and implied that manliness lay in the will to act rather than in a particular sexed body. Like the sending of petticoats to unenlisted men, this poster suggested that the war was as much a fight for the reclamation of manhood at home as a battle for the defense of womanhood abroad. Indeed, the two were intimately related. Only in a nation where every man responded to his masculine duty to serve could the army hope to raise the divisions necessary to defeat a foreign aggressor. And only in such a nation could men expect the respect and compliance of women whose roles were becoming alarmingly mutable as the war dragged on. The relationship between the position of women and the enlistment of men was tellingly explained by Cathcart Wason, MP, during an acrimonious conscription debate in 1915. "There is no room in the present state of civilization," Wason thundered, "for short-haired women who will not make a home and long-haired men who will not defend it."[56]

DOMESTICITY AND MARTIAL VIRTUE

Although the rehabilitation of masculinity seemed to be at the top of the propagandist agenda, it was masculinity of a particular kind, centering on loyalty to the state and the family. In linking military service to a man's place in the family or his relationship to women, propagandists tried to domesticate and define British manhood by distinguishing it from wanton, phallocentric German barbarism. According to propagandist images, the purpose of the expeditionary force was to save British national honor by restoring the political order, the gender order, and the social order in the raped and brutalized country of Belgium. The three central characters in this simplified history were Germany, England, and Belgium, depicted most frequently as the brutal militarist, the chivalric rescuer, and the suffering woman. In this propagandistic family psychodrama, the "Hun" became a multivalent image of masculinity gone awry. Publicists not only depicted the Germans as violating womanhood by the act of rape, but as attacking the female body in the ritual amputation of women's breasts.[57] They not only envisioned the enemy bayonetting babies, but they represented him as cutting off the hands of children—a gesture interpreted as a direct attack on the military future of the invaded nation.[58] And finally, they not only depicted the Germans as bursting into homes, separating men from women, and terrorizing the family, but as foul creatures defecating on dinner tables and finally burning to the ground the home itself.[59] As the investigator J. H. Morgan pessimistically declared, "between the German trooper who dips a baby's head into scalding water in order to get more coffee from its mother [and] the commandant who at the point of the bayonet thrusts a living screen of priests, old men, and women with babes at the breast between his own troops and those of the enemy there is a difference of degree rather than kind."[60]

While violence against women and the family lay at the heart of this vision, it was interwoven with a variety of other imperial, industrial, and modernist fears. The rape of Belgium was about the blurring of boundaries—not only the crossing of a border but the failure to protect one aspect of life from another, to secure the private from the public sphere. Although the implications of Prussianism were measured in terms of the breakdown of the family, they also represented the vision of an industrial, an imperial, and a moral order gone awry—an imaginative nightmare in which lawless barbarism seemed to take control of the technological means of destruction.[61] If the war was being waged to subject these dark forces to the rule of law, its representation as an avenue to ritual purification becomes far more comprehensible. The Germans were not just an ordinary enemy: they represented modernity, industry, and the family gone deeply awry under the efficient direction of an autocratic government immune to the problems of democratic war.

This multivalent image of Germany had profound repercussions for the forging of British national identity, since it allowed for the unequivocal celebration of armed conflict as a remedy to both international and domestic ills. Indeed, recruiting propaganda offers crucial insight into the minds of middle-class enthusiasts attempting to create a political nation out of the rough-hewn men who would bear the brunt of the war. In the context of an expanding democracy facing a war without conscription—that is, without the political means to compel the actions of its subjects—war propaganda offers a view into the kind of nation British authorities were trying to create. For raising a volunteer army to fight in the trenches is but an extreme version of one of the principle problems of democracy: how to compel subjects to conform when the available means of coercion are circumscribed by law. As Lloyd George remarked to Welsh recruiters with perhaps a hint of wistfulness, "The days have gone by when the rulers of the people could issue a proclamation and say 'we have declared war upon such-and-such a country, and it is your duty to fight, to subscribe.'" Instead, "The people want to know the reasons why, if they are to make sacrifices. Fortunately, the more thorough their acquaintance with the causes of this war the greater will be the sacrifices that they will be prepared to make. After all, conviction is essential to confidence, confidence is nine parts of courage. If we want valiant troops, we must have men rallying to the flag imbued with the idea that they are going forth in a holy war, to do battle for justice and right."[62]

Recruiters thus depicted the war as an event staged to restore rightful sovereignty in Belgium, to return lawful fathers to the head of their homes, and to save women and children from the horrific consequences of a violent usurpation of paternal authority. As the case of Belgium was rhetorically elided with the potential invasion of Britain, the appeal to men's chivalry became part of a masculine ethic grounded in the protection of the British home and the defense of the principle of domesticity abroad. The Parliamentary Recruiting Committee thus reassuringly reminded women that "When we say to our men, 'Your Country Needs You,' we do not mean that Parliament, or the Government, or Lord Kitchener, or the King, or Mr. Asquith needs them. It is Britain—British cottage homes, British women and children, peaceful fields and villages—that need them."[63]

If German masculinity was characterized by the destructive behavior of men whose physical lusts were divorced from any affective relationship to the women in their midst, British masculinity was presented as civilian manhood, realized in armed service and motivated and restrained by the thought of its women. In attempting to account for the different tactics of the British and German forces, C. Sheridan Jones thus explained that "the English officer . . . makes way in the street or the railway car for a lady, maybe offers her his seat or holds open the door . . . and is always ready to show her courtesy. But the cultured Prussian practices none of these absurdities. Watch them in the cafes of Berlin, and you will see them shoulder women on one side, or brush past them and tread on their feet. The Prussian officer has read his Nietzsche and has been told that 'women are birds, beasts, or cats—or, at the best cows!' And he treats them accordingly. And as with women, so with all things that appear weak or helpless or defenseless."[64]

This contrast is telling. The representation of the chivalric Englishman became so pervasive on the home front that the idea that the British soldier could pose a danger to women was almost entirely written out of the popular conception of the military.[65] One of Kitchener's first public instructions to troops, meant as a warning against venereal disease, was to: "resist both temptations ['wine and women'] and while treating all women with courtesy, [to] avoid any intimacy."[66] And at the suggestion of a female reader that girls should be kept away from military barracks, the popular newspaper *John Bull* lashed out with the indignant assertion that "unless Mr. Thomas Atkins is very different in his morals abroad" from what he seemed to be at home, such "censorious insinuations" were practically libelous. According to *John Bull*, a nun responsible for the care of a number of girls in France, "brought them for safety at night to the British trenches and placed them under the protection of British soldiers." While the French correspondent who reported this incident regarded it as "a wonderful tribute . . . to the honour of every Englishman," *John Bull* declared that the soldiers were simply "good average samples of decent-living honourable Britishers and that it is an infamous outrage on the name of Britons for parsons, peeping Toms, and puritans in petticoats to warn parents and guardians to keep their womenfolk in doors after sunset, lest the soldiers should molest them or lead them into temptation."[67]

Although feminists protested against Kitchener's classification of women as a "temptation" and continued to warn of the dangers even friendly soldiers posed to unsupervised girls, their fears remained on the margins of a widespread popular discourse that regarded the British soldier as the wholesome savior of innocent women, far more likely to be injuriously seduced himself than to do the female sex any physical or moral harm.[68] This image of the Tommy as at once manly and gentle, sexually attractive and morally restrained, militarized and domesticated lies at the heart of the vision of masculine citizenship war propagandists wished to promote. "The real Tommy Atkins . . . who nurses French babies, [and] scrubs his landlady's table, marches to battle singing music hall songs," declared the socialist writer Robert Blatchford. "Some tell us England is decadent, that the British are played out. But the nation which can turn out men like Tommy Atkins by the hundred thousand has not come yet to the top of its form."[69]

As the soldier or officer in khaki gained almost a cult status on the homefront, he was proclaimed by the press and the public to be both an oracle of truth, and a preserver of all those things upon which British life depended. Captain Martin Hardie, a field censor, noted that "Nearly every letter from the B.E.F. is sacred. . . . Its opinions [are] quoted to friends of the recipient and by them passed on to others."[70] Indeed even the Home Office seemed to share this adulatory attitude, exempting uniformed soldiers from such security measures as registering in hotels since the khaki uniform itself carried with it the implicit trust of the nation at large.[71]

This effusive attitude towards soldiers was more than shared by young women on the home front. Virtually everywhere they went, uniformed men were accosted by flirtatious girls suffering from "khaki fever." As one writer recalled, "When quite ordinary men donned khaki they became in the eyes of a number of foolish young women objects to be pestered with attention that very few of them desired."[72] Jessie Pope, a popular wartime poet, exemplified such attitudes when she declared in her 1915 poem "Rose" that "To-day, the sound in wind and limb, Don't flutter Rose one tittle," for "Her maiden ardor cleaves to him, / Who's proved that he is brittle. / Who buys her an engagement ring / And finds her kind and kissing, / Must have one member in a sling / Or, preferably, missing."[73] Extolling such paragons as "the khaki clad cherub," or "the one-legged soldier-man"—a hero whom the girls say is "no end a duck"—Pope's patriotic advocacy of the wounded soldier exemplifies both the adulation enjoyed by soldiers on the home front and the tone-deafness many men would complain of encountering among civilians with no real knowledge of the front lines.[74]

Regardless of their attitude toward the civilians who worshiped them, men were not given complete liberty to enjoy these attentions. That the image of the Tommy was meant to constrain the actions of young men is evident when viewed within the context of a series of moves directed at the regulation of male behavior during the war. The attempt to curb professional sports in Britain, to radically restrict licensing hours in pubs, and to anathematize the leisure and sexual activities of men of military age, was part of an effort to redefine masculine behavior, binding single men to the family and the state.[75] The publicist F. E. Smith, for example, exhorted young men to "put dalliance off for a fitter time," commenting on the shameful behavior of unenlisted men who were to be seen strolling with girls in "places of resort."[76] Denouncing both the football fields of the North and the leisure gardens of the South, Smith sardonically speculated that the "thousands, and thousands of able-bodied, unattached young men, nearly all of them with girls [are] waiting . . . till the horrors that have been and are being perpetuated in Belgium and France are repeated in England." As Smith forbodingly warned, "During the process of Germanization the people of the United Kingdom, as conscripts under the German warlords and citizens under German Governors, would have learned too late that it might have been better to choose the path of righteousness, of duty and patriotism, however stony the road, rather than the soft way of dishonour and leisurely ease."[77]

Such criticisms cut across class lines. Not only were working men discouraged from drinking and sport, but wealthy men were characterized as effete "Cuthberts," interested only in playing tennis and enjoying the selfish leisure money could provide.[78] In this spirit Captain Tom Sherwood, who described himself as "just an ordinary Tommy Atkins," characterized "shirkers" as men of casual patriotism who cheered on the troops and then "return to their whiskeys and sodas and wonder if their ties suit them" and "their trousers are creased."[79] And J. H. Balfour Browne, deploring the continuation of male leisure while defenseless Belgian women suffered at the hands of the Germans, disgustedly insisted that "the part of our young men is not—as some think—to loaf; but to defend their country."[80]

Appeals that combined the civic obligation of men with their domestic loyalties were also part of a bipartisan attempt to define national duty in propaganda along familial and communitarian lines. Posters, pamphlets, and speeches repeatedly appealed to men as fathers, as sons, as brothers, as sweethearts, or, as in the case of the neighborhood Pals Batallions, as members of an organic local community, where eligible young men enlisted together as "pals." Although a large body of propaganda evoked the excitement and pleasure of martial life, as the war progressed appeals to duty and honor were increasingly and explicitly tied to the avowed need to protect women and the home.[81] It is no anomaly that the question famously posed to the conscientious objector Lytton Strachey by the Hampstead draft tribunal was, "What would you do if you saw a German soldier trying to rape your sister?"[82] And it is not entirely surprising, given the predominance of such rhetoric, that the militant pacifist Guy A. Aldred should have boasted, much to the annoyance of his patriotic countryman, that "if the Germans came into London and outraged the women and children, he would refuse to take up the rifle in their defense."[83]

Indeed the issue of familial obligation was taken so seriously that one of the crises precipitating Asquith's fall from power in 1916 was the perception that he was about to renege on an ill-advised pledge he had made the previous year to call up all single men before married men would be asked to serve.[84] And ultimately the justification for extending conscription to married men in April 1916—three months after single men were subject to compulsion—rested at least in part on the idea that no home would be safe unless the rapacious German was stopped at the gate. In the words of "One Clear Call," a highly promoted recruiting pamphlet, British soldiers were fighting to defend "national honour," "Belgium" and "our womenfolk and little ones" from "the Tyrant of the Universe."[85] As recruiters promoted a patriotic notion of masculinity that rested on loyalty to family, women, and community, however, military and domestic duty subtlely became one, narrowing men's range of acceptable action and implicating women in the raising of recruits.

CHAPTER THREE

REDRAWING THE BOUNDARIES
OF THE PRIVATE SPHERE

PATRIOTIC MOTHERHOOD AND THE
RAISING OF KITCHENER'S ARMIES

In the early months of the war a woman who signed herself "sad sweet-heart" wrote to the "editoress" of a penny woman's magazine that claimed to be the favorite paper of a million homes. "[W]e have been so happy until this dreadful war broke out, and my dear one is to join his regiment and go and fight," the correspondent wrote. "I feel my heart will break, and as though I can't let him go. I am certain he will never return to me. I am torn to pieces with grief and sadness. . . . Tears come into my sweetheart's eyes when I beg of him not to go, and this makes things harder for me to bear."[1] The editor, known to her readers for her sympathy, answered the letter in a conversational write-in column called "Heart to Heart Chats." "Dear lassie," she admonished, "I . . . want to make you see how wrongly you are behaving. Instead of imploring your sweetheart to shirk his duty, you should have done your best to urge him to fulfill his duty in the spirit of a true British soldier. . . . You could have done so much to uplift him and send him away with a heart full of hope and courage. . . . Remember, dear, that although we women can't go and fight for our country, there is much that we can do at home. One of the things is to cheer our dear ones—husbands, sweethearts, fathers, and brothers—and send them off to their calling with brave, noble hearts."[2]

The response of "sad sweetheart" to the outbreak of the war was to preserve her domestic happiness and to keep her man safe from death. Yet what would have been considered a natural reaction during peacetime was in time of war a wrongful inversion of feminine duty. In a conflict defined in terms of the safety of home and family, the sacrifice of sons and lovers became a form of military service for women and a domestic duty essential to the waging of war. While the specter of the rape of Belgium eroded men's civic choice, it sanctioned women to persuade and hearten those men who many believed stood as the only bulwark against German aggression. Recruiters, politicians, and journalists relentlessly exhorted women to send their men to war, assuring them of the national danger and personal shame that would fall upon any man—and his womenfolk—should he refuse to enlist.[3] "The spirit of the men of a family depends in no small measure on the spirit of its women," declared Major Leonard Darwin as he implored girls not to discourage their men from enlisting, "and on the spirit of the women may, therefore, depend the fate of the country."[4]

Such ideas, promoted widely in the press and in recruiting propaganda, had broad implications for the way many women and girls came to understand their own worth in time of war. While many ordinary women never nursed soldiers at the front, labored in dangerous munitions factories, or served in the women's auxiliary corps, they carried on at home with no less desire than their more famous sisters to seek personal validation for their sacrifices. As propagandists reminded these women that "The Kitchen" was "The Key to Victory," and that she who saved two slices of bread helped "Defeat the U-Boat," mundane domestic tasks acquired a new military significance.[5] Nowhere is this transformation more clear than in the ideology surrounding motherhood.[6] Although women could not serve in combat, they could plausibly argue that they played a key role in the shaping, raising, and recruiting of those who would. "Your breasts have suckled a lion brood / The bravest of the brave . . . ," the jingoistic tabloid *John Bull* reminded women; "But your sons must fight, lest ye be shamed / By the woman-defiling foe,"

> Kiss them, fondle them, send them forth,
>   To stand in the battle's van.
> Then lift your eyes to the star-lit skies,
>   And thank God ye have mothered man.[7]

Given this unhappy imperative, it is not surprising that publicists assured women, particularly mothers, that theirs was a priceless contribution, demonstrating a bravery and patriotism second only to the heroism of those who had volunteered for the front. Even more significantly, though, is the way women themselves latched onto this rhetoric to encourage one another in their patriotic duty. In an editorial addressed to "The Mothers of England," the editor of *Mother and Home* argued that by sending sons to war "with a faith that only a mother can instill . . . you are as much fighting as are your soldier and sailor sons."[8] And *The Girl's Own Paper* proudly reminded its readers that "Where patriotism is, women must be. A nation is the home. . . . A man takes counsel with his wife, he obeys his mother. . . . Here we have the whole plan and superstructure of the nation."[9] Ironically, as conservative publicists inspired mothers to demonstrate such heroic patriotism, they inadvertently provided women with a usable language with which to lay claim to the war. The results of this campaign would be contentious indeed.

PATRIOTIC MOTHERHOOD

As patriotic sources increasingly depicted soldiering as a domestic duty performed on behalf of the women and children of Britain and their counterparts in Belgium, they correspondingly presented mothering as a military duty essential to the prosecution of the war. Indeed, one of the most difficult tasks recruiters faced was to persuade mothers to give up their sons, and they appealed continually to women's boundless sense of duty in order to do so. Echoing scores of similar productions, a poem printed in the Conservative *Primrose League Gazette* reminded mothers that,

> Never a word must hinder
>   Never a hand must stay,
> Never a lip must falter,
>   That cheers them on their way.
> Mothers whose hearts are breaking,
>   Who sorrow and pain have known
> How will ye answer England
>   If ye give England not her own?[10]

In exchange for such wrenching requests, publicists praised women for their heroic sacrifices and reminded them of their patriotic obligations during what was rapidly becoming a total war. "Many an English mother has had to grieve for her brave lad fallen in battle, still she has not seen her home in flames nor heard her little ones screaming with terror when struck down by cruel hands," the British Mothers Union reminded its members.[11] Appealing to mothers to "*GIVE YOUR SONS,*" the representative of the union declared, "Not enough men are sent out, and this is largely because not enough mothers say to their boys as one did lately: '*My boy, I don't want you to go, but if I were you I should go.*'"[12]

Ironically, the price demanded for the security of home and children was the sacrifice of adult sons. With the number of underage boys in the army, the dichotomy between children and soldiers must have seemed strangely inapt to some anxious mothers.[13] Equally skeptical must have been those parents who were financially dependent on their sons but ineligible for the meager separation allowances offered to support married men's families.[14] Asquith callously alluded to such reluctant parents when he denounced "selfish fathers" and "tyrannical mothers who . . . being hard and selfish by nature, have literally forbidden their sons to enlist," thus exposing them to "the immediate criticism of their comrades-in-arms, and to something very like a moral stigma for the rest of life."[15] Of course, such threats did not stop at least one formidable matron from telling a dismayed recruiting officer that she would rather have "one live son" than a "dozen dead heroes."[16] Despite its painful ramifications, however, the appeal to mothers by women's groups, the government, and the press, as well as the actual sacrifices—willing or not—made by millions of mothers all over Britain, would give women a profound language with which to claim a stake in the war.

The link between motherhood and military strength was, of course, hardly novel. As Anna Davin has argued, eugenicists and pro-natalists at the turn of the century were obsessed with the relationship between faulty child-rearing and Britain's poor performance in the Boer War, where they believed that weak, undersized recruits showed the signs of inexpert mothering.[17] Significantly, prewar feminists deployed almost identical logic, though for very different purposes. Linking motherhood to the spilling of blood on the battlefield, feminists like Olive Schreiner used the intimate connection between mothers and soldiers to make a compelling case for female pacifism.[18] "Men have made boomerangs, bows, swords, or guns," observed Schreiner in her influential tract *Women and Labour.* "Our relation to war is far more intimate, personal, and indissoluble. . . . We have made the men who destroy and were destroyed! We have in all ages produced, at enormous cost, the primal munition of war. . . ."[19]

Although Schreiner's imagery remained a staple of pacifist thought throughout the conflict, the language of motherhood was increasingly appropriated by patriotic women who used the idea of women's stake in the bodies of their sons to claim recognition for their own vicarious service on the battlefield. Not only did feminists draw attention to the role of women in giving birth to soldiers in order to refute anti-suffrage arguments, but mothers increasingly came to regard themselves as a sort of parallel army, sharing the sacrifices of their sons at the front.[20] "Men have become fighters and women have become soldiers," declared the philanthropist Mrs. Alec Tweedie, a reader of *Common Cause,* who lost her own son in 1917. "Not only did women to start with give them birth . . . but [they sought to] hearten and spur them on to work from the moment war broke out. There was no shirking. The boys whose rearing has cost these women long years of toil and anxiety . . . were yielded up with a heart-pang and a face smile. And having thus surrendered their own blood to the country, the women turned to see what could be done at home in the same cause with female brain and body."[21]

While suffragists had frequently argued that mothers, like soldiers, risked their lives for the nation, the Great War gave urgency and plausibility to such claims. In the late nineteenth century, giving birth was still a risky, often fatal business, undertaken without antiseptics or effective ways to stem postpartum bleeding. Patriotic mothers like Mrs. Alec Tweedie insisted that the death of a soldier was shared by the mother who had risked her life to bear him. Indeed, for both Tweedie and Schreiner, the origin of the son in the mother's body gave her a fundamental stake in his death upon the battlefield. While to Schreiner the squandering of mothers' sons was a reason for women to oppose war, for Tweedie it became the basis on which to claim a sort of military equality.[22] In Tweedie's reasoning, the son was more than the product of the mother's labor; he was a corporeal extension of herself. In yielding up their sons, mothers, in Tweedie's mind, "surrendered their own blood," a sacrifice for which she believed women deserved hereditary honors passed down through the female line.[23]

The articulation of a form of female military service performed through the body of a son was thus a common way for women to claim a stake in the sacrifices of the fighting forces. As the *Girl's Own Paper* put it in an article on "Mothers and their Boys," "The mother lives every battle with her boy and more. . . . With the boy goes the mother—you cannot separate them."[24] And a *Times* poem addressed "To Women" echoed these sentiments, reminding women that, "For you too to battle go / . . . And not a shot comes blind with death / . . . but invisibly it tore and entered first a woman's breast."[25] Such articulations of the indivisible relationship of mother and son were significant because they endowed women with an authority bequeathed by the sacrifice of their men. To Margaret Peterson, men must heed those women who had "given their all / Husbands and sons to the battle, lest the faith of an Empire fall":

> O ye who might have been soldiers, and yet have
>   stood aside,
> What is your place in this kingdom for which our

men have died?
Shall ye share in the day of triumph the peace that
     dawns afar,
Ye who have hidden your manhood under a coward's
     star?

Now, by the joy of women when Love walks light
     upon the earth,
And by the mother courage that fought to give you
     birth,
Throw back these doubts that hold you, stand forth
     and play your parts,
Lest shame for having loved you wake in the
     women's hearts . . . [26]

In such formulations, women are not only child-bearers but also sol-
dier-bearers, recasting motherhood as a form of national service comparable to the production of arms or the shedding of blood.[27] "Of the
women are born the men needed for the fighting line" declared Mrs. Hudson Pile in what would become commonplace logic. "No mother's son of
ours, we hope, could be so mean and cowardly as to shirk his just share in
this life and death struggle. . . . To those who have shouldered no task, let
the women of England show that they hold them in contempt as unworthy of their mothers or their race."[28] Like Peterson, Mrs. Pile assumed that
soldiers' mothers' stake in the war effort validated their expression of contempt for those who refused to enlist. Their production of sons and their
moral encouragement of men to serve were thus tasks of military importance that allowed mothers to claim some of the patriotic cache of the
heroic soldier as well as to share in the language of indispensability enjoyed by the female munitions worker. Indeed, by 1916 Olive Schreiner's
distinction between the product of male labor—"boomerangs, bows,
swords, or guns"—and the product of female labor had become largely
empty. With the passage of the Munitions Acts, which facilitated the entry
of women into war industries, women made both the arms and the men.[29]
As the pacifist poet Mary Gabrielle Collins lamented:

Their hands should minister unto the
     flame of life,
     their fingers guide
The rosy teat, swelling with milk,
To the eager mouth of the suckling babe . . .

     But now,

Their hands, their fingers
Are coarsened in munitions factories . . .
Are bruised against the law,
     "kill, kill!" . . .[30]

Although Collins's poem is a pacifist diatribe that plays on the contradiction Schreiner evoked in her opposition of motherhood and war, the parallel between the manufacture of arms and the making of men was often articulated with a striking lack of irony. In *Goodbye to All That*, Robert Graves cites a letter written to the *Morning Post* by an anonymous reader calling herself a "Little Mother." In the letter, the Little Mother professed to articulate the views of the anti-pacifist women of Britain. "[W]e women, will tolerate no such cry as 'Peace! Peace!,'" the Little Mother solemnly declared, "We women pass on the human ammunition of 'only sons' to fill up the gaps, so that when the 'common soldier' looks back before going 'over the top' he may see the women of the British race at his heels, reliable, dependable, uncomplaining."[31]

Although some feminists have expressed skepticism about Graves's source, the Little Mother's letter is actually highly typical of a female rhetoric prevalent during the early years of the war. Equating "only sons" with "human ammunition," the Little Mother rhetorically transforms patriotic women into both the producers of arms and virtual soldiers active in the lethal deployment of the product of the womb. Decrying those pacifists who "disgrace their sacred trust of motherhood," the Little Mother instead grounded her case for women's worth in the valorization of military service and the experience of maternal loss.

The connection between motherhood and warfare, however, was not articulated only in the sacrifice of grown sons. If the vital link between mother and son gave women a rhetorical claim to the experience of battle, many authorities presented the nurturing and raising of soldiers as a useful alternative to military service itself. What Olive Schreiner ironically termed "the primal munition of war" would be referred to quite literally in some accounts of women's patriotic duty.

Bearing Arms versus Bearing Children

One of the few women nominated for military honors during the war was Mrs. J. G. Paterson, a noted rearer of soldiers and "the only woman authorized to fly the recruiting officer's ribbons."[32] Mrs. Paterson was a member of Lord Meath's Duty and Discipline movement, an organization devoted to improving the health and patriotism of those children who would make up the armies of the future. She gained recognition during the war for her successful efforts to bring undersized working-class recruits up to military standards, and although Mrs. Paterson was denied honors in 1917, she was commended by Lord Haldane and the queen for her uniquely female form of recruiting.

Mrs. Paterson became involved in recruiting well before the war when she and her husband discovered two working-class boys fighting outside their Surrey home. Instead of breaking up the fight, the pair watched on "impartially" as Mr. Paterson instructed one youth in the "use of his left." The Patersons subsequently befriended the boys and worked indefatigably to persuade them to enlist. Mrs. Paterson, however, had a special place in her heart for her first recruit—a "baker's boy" who had assisted her in 1908 when her infant daughter's pram stuck in a rut and, to her great alarm, almost overturned. Not long after, Mrs. Paterson took the heroic lad to enlist at St. George's barracks where, much to her disappointment, he was rejected as medically unfit for military service. As she later related to the *Daily Mail,* "Having put our lips to the cup, we were not prepared to see it dashed from our lips without a struggle."[33] Instead, Mrs. Paterson took the boy home and fattened him up, putting the finishing touches onto his physique by taking him for a holiday to the Norfolk coast. "On our return we rushed him up to the barracks without a minutes delay, and his expansion had been such that he passed with flying colours. The other day he came home on leave . . . a smart, straight, nimble, self respecting soldier in whom you would not recognize the uncouth lad of 6 months before."[34] From that moment onward, Mrs. Paterson opened her home to lads who needed feeding and exercise, and she worked diligently to bring the youth of her neighborhood up to military standards.

To Mrs. Paterson, the distinction between a lady recruiter and the recruiting sergeant was that his duty ended with the acceptance or rejection of the recruit, whereas hers lay in the physical and moral formation of a suitable soldier. On one hand, Mrs. Paterson's story is about the civilizing process and the way the proper exercise of feminine influence, class patronage, and military service could transform a working-class lout into a useful citizen-soldier. On the other hand, the working-class boys who appear in Mrs. Paterson's list of "successes" seem oddly like fatted calves. They are literally fed and exercised for the sole purpose of being sent to the army. Against the expense and effort of this project, Mrs. Paterson weighed "the intrinsic satisfaction of helping these good lads to help themselves, and of helping in a tiny way his Majesty's Army, which needs them and will make men of them—and which moreover, helps us women to sleep soundly in our beds."[35]

Although women claimed a stake in military service through their production of "the primal munition" of war, many women were dissatisfied with this vicarious form of military service. Contemporaries commented on the keen desire of women to go to the front as nurses, ambulance drivers, or later in the auxiliary military services. The *Times* noted that "the mothers, sisters, and wives of officers and men are offering—no begging—to be allowed to go to the front," while one female diarist, writing of life in London, observed that, "Educated girls are showing their feelings in different ways. . . . Many are wild to learn Red Cross First Aid and above all bandaging. . . . Girls say they are determined to get to the Front somehow. . . ."[36] Indeed, Rose Macaulay's envious lamentation in "Many Sisters to Many Brothers," "Oh its you that have the luck out there in the blood and muck," has become a famous expression of womanly longing and is emblematic of the feeling of being left behind and left out that was experienced by many women at home.[37] As the press, official propaganda, and the stories of the elderly glorified the soldier, sanctified the war, and glamorized the experience of combat, many women became increasingly frustrated with their duties behind the firing line. This frustration led, with surprising frequency, to demands for female combatant service. "We mothers of England, mothers of the Empire, will never see the land of our fathers trampled underfoot," declared the redoubtable Mrs. Alec Tweedie. "We will fight if necessary. Shed our blood if necessary, just as our fathers, brothers, husbands, and sons have shed theirs."[38] Mrs. Tweedie was by no means the first woman to make such a proposal.[39] Not only did sporting women discuss female military service, but the *Ladies Field* instructed women on defensive tactics and provided advice on the best way to fight an invading army.[40] At least one suffrage organization debated the merits of forming a women's militia, and articles about girls who had tried to join the forces and the story of Miss Flora Sandes, an Englishwoman who served as a sergeant in the Serbian army, were clipped and saved in women's diaries with remarkable frequency.[41] According to the *Daily Sketch*, "Every day our Mrs. Gossip receives a bundle of letters . . . from girls who want to fight . . . One meets her at every turn, scornful of her knitting, bitter, even, as she reviews her progress in a superficial course of instruction in first aid to the wounded. 'What is the use of a great hulking creature like me sitting here rolling bandages and winding wool?' She demands. 'Why can't they let us train and do some real work? They've taken Tony with his weak chest and Jerry who faints if he cuts his finger. I could knock the spots off them both at any game you like to mention. Why shouldn't I beat them at potting Germans?'"[42]

Contrasting with ironic suggestions that used the threat of armed women to shame men into battle, these proposals arose instead from a consciousness among women of their own eternally inferior status in a state where the combat soldier stood as the pinnacle of citizenship. "Miss

Gladys Davidson, one of Lancashire's best rifle shots . . . wants to fight in the trenches," noted the column. "[A]t Blackburn yesterday she advocated the formation of a women's regiment offering her services as an expert sniper on the battlefield. Miss Davidson regards the reservation of military duties to men as a great injustice. Not only is she anxious to fight, but she has expressed her willingness to sacrifice her luxuriant growth of auburn hair if permission is given immediately for the formation of a woman's regiment."[43] Miss Davidson's significant offer to give up her "crowning glory"—in some sense to unsex herself—is emblematic of the burden of femininity in a time of the extreme valorization of a set of practices monopolized by men. As one "superfluous woman" asked, "Why should I drag out a safe, uninteresting life here . . . while men give up their full and useful careers to defend me? Why can't I, a superfluous spinster, go and defend the busy father of families and the highly trained professional men? I don't seem to be much of a national treasure now. I shall be much less one after the war, when 'three women to every man' no longer is a correct estimate of the superfluous female element of the country."[44]

Against these sporadic proposals, the mothering of soldiers was frequently advocated as the alternative to military service for women. "What would Lord Kitchener say if he had time and inclination to explain his opposition to the formation of a corps of Amazons?" asked Mrs. Gossip, responding to "Girls who want to be in the Fighting Line." "There is a reply which will satisfy the rebellious girl who can shoot and ride and thrills at the sound of a bugle or the sight of a mounting Union Jack. It is this. Women must be kept out of battle, not because they are the nation's weakness, but because they are its strength. Again and again many men go out to battle and fall, yet their nation will rise again. But destroy women, and that nation is crippled for centuries."[45] In Mrs. Gossip's equation, women needed to be kept from battle so that they might replace the decimated nation after the loss of its men. The soldiering of the army and the repopulation of the nation thus became the central patriotic functions of women unable to serve in the army themselves. Yet this advice claimed an even more intimate relation to war as the columnist suggested that the nurturing of babies could be regarded as a sort of vicarious form of killing uniquely accessible to women.

In the same article, Mrs. Gossip related the satisfying story of how one "young Amazon" had overcome her desire to fight in the war. "One girl I know who was worrying herself haggard over the impossibility of getting out to fight has the advantage of owning a wise father. 'You can't go sniping at Germans,' he explained to her, 'but see what you can do in the way of building up a future army!'" According to Mrs. Gossip, the advice of the father promised to make the girl even more militarily useful than her brother. "That daughter is now keenly interested in the welfare of six British slum babies, and thanks to her efforts, there will probably be six rickety 'rejects' less in 17 years time. Her lieutenant brother complains that he can't claim to have put out of action an equal number of Germans."[46] What is significant about this episode is the direct juxtaposition of the killing of Germans and the nurturing of babies. Mrs. Gossip posed the latter duty as a consolation for women's inability to accomplish the former, yet she implied that the girl's responsibility for future kills might be more numerous and useful than the direct hostile actions of her officer brother.

With the deployment of a rhetoric of mothering that constructed nurturing as a comparable duty to soldiering, it becomes evident why many separation allowance recipients believed that they were being paid by the state for the civic function of motherhood.[47] On one hand, the mothers of young children were ostensibly one of the central resources that Britain was fighting to defend. On the other, the mothers of sons were the suppliers of that "primal munition" of war without which home defense and national honor would be impossible to maintain. It is not surprising that Mother's Day was first organized in Great Britain during World War I. According to Mr. T. A. Whitehead, an airplane manufacturer from Richmond who sponsored the event, it was to be "a recognition of what is due to the mothers of the Empire."[48] As posters such as "Go! It's YOUR DUTY, Lad!" and "Women of Britain, Say GO!," addressed an appeal to women that in many ways echoed the calls to arms directed at men, the sending of men to battle became the womanly equivalent of enlistment itself.[49] Indeed, women who refused to let their men go could be vulnerable to shameful imputations not wholly unlike those that faced men. As the editor of *Women's World* reminded her readers in a specially chosen poem, "'Weak, Cowards, Hysterical' be said of others / NEVER OF SOLDIER'S WIVES OR SOLDIER'S MOTHERS!"[50] The moral pressure directed at men was thus not unique, and while many women took the issues of the war to heart and willingly sent their men to battle, they too were under tremendous public pressure to offer lives for their country. Despite this hortatory atmosphere, however, the concept of patriotic motherhood often left women in a difficult and highly ambiguous position.

A Double-Edged Sword

In 1918 the National War Aims Committee commissioned Mary Martindale to write "One English Woman to Another," a pamphlet meant to address complaints from army censors that reports of food shortages in

England were demoralizing the troops.[51] The pamphlet made its plea for
fortitude by reminding women that men were sacrificing life and limb for
them. In the alleged words of a soldier who did not "lose" but "gave" his
arm "for us women, for our children, for our homes . . . 'Everything shall
be given that we can find to give, to keep *you* safe from the awful horrors
of an enemy invasion.' That is their view," declared Martindale, "But this
tremendous war is not going to be won only on the battlefields; it is with
us women also that victory lies." Encouraging stoicism, morale, and a
"fight to the finish," Martindale told women that "In the first and last resort, all springs from the heart of the woman. If a woman's heart is strong,
she will pour her courage into the soul of every man who goes out to do
battle. If a woman's heart grows feeble, or her hand writes 'grousing' messages to the Front, she takes the heart out of the boys. They will stick anything as long as they know that the dear ones at home can carry on."[52]
Martindale's advice highlights the difficult and contradictory position of
women in wielding the rhetoric of war. If men, as Martindale graphically
reminded women, sustained bloody amputations to protect women from
the horrors of an enemy invasion, the stoic courage she endorsed pitted
the wholeness of the male body against the sanctity of the female one.
Martindale's implicit dichotomy is a late articulation of an idea reiterated
in war propaganda for four long years. Not only did early propagandistic
sources claim that the war was being fought on behalf of women—"You
have smitten ogres blind / When the fair princess cried out to you," one
early poem claimed—but the morality of the war itself was persistently
laid at the feet of women.[53] In the words of the *Recruiting Times,* "The devotion of women everywhere has sanctified our cause, as the blood of heroes and martyrs has consecrated it."[54] Such ideas, however, were never
straightforward and uncomplicated.

Although journalists and politicians almost universally praised female
sacrifice on behalf of the war effort, female patriotism met with an am-
bivalent reception even as a variety of sources encouraged superhuman
acts of stoicism on the part of mothers and wives. This tension is evident
in the journalist Michael MacDonagh's account of his discomfort at meeting in the flesh the type of "Spartan mother" idealized in propaganda
sources. "I have met the Spartan mother who grieves not for her son killed
in the war but glories in his fate. Calling on her to-day to give her my con-
dolences on the loss of her son, aged 18, who has fallen in battle, she told
me she felt no grief, only pride that a boy of hers should have died for his
country, and I could see that her pride was all the more intense for the
deep love she bore him. I wonder are there many mothers like her. Such
stoicism appears to me almost unnatural."[55] While the attitude of Mc-
Donagh's friend echoed those sentiments advocated by patriotic oracles

ranging from *John Bull* to the bishop of London (who claimed that had he "a dozen sons, each in [his] love alike" he would rather have "eleven die nobly for their country than one voluptuously surfeit out of action,") her fortitude could not but seem "unnatural" to a flesh and blood observer.[56] The question of how to encourage mothers and wives to give their loved ones without making a mockery of the natural affection between the sexes was thus a problem repeatedly faced by recruiting authorities and became a recurrent theme in Coulson Kernahan's 1915 memoir, *The Experiences of a Recruiting Officer.*

In Kernahan's narrative, the painstaking attempt to distinguish right from wrong uses of feminine influence does not focus primarily on women's patriotic intentions or even upon the utility of their actions, but on the degree to which their patriotic efforts can be accommodated in an idealized paradigm of subordinate femininity. Early in his narrative Kernahan relates the story of his experience with female hops pickers in rural Sussex. Kernahan paints the bucolic hoppers in idyllic terms, generated by his appreciation for their deferential and mildly eroticized patriotism and their willingness to do what they're told. Like the women he denounces later in his narrative, the hops pickers use their taunts to gather recruits. The harassment of a lad named Harry excites his warm admiration: "'Come on, Harry,' some bright eyed, clean-complectioned and bonnie lass would say . . . 'Come on, Harry, all the officer says is true. My brother's gone and my cousin's gone, and the boy I'm going to marry is a soldier. We only wish we were a man ourselves—don't we, girls?—that we could have a go at them murdering Germans. Show you're a man, Harry. We shall all be proud of you if you do, for we don't want, any of us—do we, girls?—to have a man who isn't a man, and won't do his duty to his king and country to-day.'"[57]

What emerges most forcefully in Kernahan's analysis of feminine behavior is that whether the women he meets work to aid recruiting or to hinder it is less important to him than the acceptability of their conduct as women. Though Kernahan in no way rejects female recruiting, he demonstrates a persistent fear that women with no legitimate connection to the men they send might be using enlistment for the ends of personal gain. Drawing elaborate distinctions between the proper and improper use of feminine influence, Kernahan reveals a number of the prejudices and anxieties endemic to the discourse of recruiting. If a woman offered her man with a conjugal or maternal reserve, if it was done without any compromise of feminine sweetness, and if it was done with deference to himself and a respect for male and official authority, Kernahan is able to depict the act in an aura of romantic heroism. As Kernahan proudly describes the scene, "the others, old, middle aged, and young, less ready of speech but no less ready in patriotism, would for the most part add their word. 'that's right Ada! . . . Do as she says, Harry, and prove you're a man . . . ' 'Show 'im that we hoppers are as patriotic as the rest, Harry, and we'll all be proud,' would come from another girl, while possibly a young buxom woman would dive deep into her bodice for a picture of her 'soldier chap' or a very old woman would proudly produce a photograph of her 'five soldier sons. . . . '"[58] Kernahan's narrative, which moves from the apparent relation of an actual incident to the admission of its fablelike quality, lauds the very rhetorical behavior that he and others—in a different context—were likely to revile and decry.

For Kernahan, female recruiting was beneficial when it was imbued with the noble sacrifice of a mother or the erotic sweetness of a lover and was wholly unacceptable when performed with the militant energy and independence of a suffragette or lady reformer. A typical example of his displeasure can be found when the brother of one of the hoppers must be told *not* to enlist because of his sister's illness. When the all-knowing Kernahan arrives at his shop, however, he finds "a tall, handsome lad, white-faced and trembling behind the counter, looking at a lady with a heavy double chin and pince-nez perched on a high-hooked nose. She was richly clad in furs, and was rating the young man roundly. 'You ought to be ashamed of yourself skulking there behind a counter, a strong, big fellow like you!' The boy—he was only just eighteen, I afterwards heard—gazed agonizedly at the two red-cheeked girls, who were giggling vulgarly at another counter, and he made a reply of some sort. . . ."[59]

The messages delivered to Harry and the shop boy by the "bonnie" hopper and the woman of wealth are essentially the same, revealing the degree to which Kernahan's judgment of female recruiting is based not upon content but upon style. Those women who ask his advice are ubiquitously sweet, beautiful, refined, and sensible, whereas those who presume to instruct him of his duty or to act without his counsel are duly ugly, selfish, coarse, officious, and do more harm than good. The stereotypes depicted in Kernahan's stories, prevalent in much material on women recruiters, make up a prescriptive formula for what women's role in recruiting should be—a formula that invariably broke down when recruiting rhetoric was deployed by women themselves. In the ideal relationship, women were supposed to be reluctant to let their men go but anxious for the men to want to go. When men showed reluctance and women demonstrated enthusiasm, this balance was undermined, bringing criticism upon women for doing what in many contexts was represented as their patriotic duty.

Indeed, as women wielded the language of patriotism to underscore their contributions to the war, they became trapped by the inherent irony of a propaganda campaign that drew on the vulnerability of womanhood and yet exhorted mothers, wives, and lovers to bravely sacrifice their men. If women blessed the cause, fortified their men, and provided the pretext for fighting in the first place, their approbation gained a sinister and misanthropic twist as propagandists continually quoted expressions of feminine courage reminiscent of the savage patriotism of the Roman matron.[60] For every woman like the cowardly mother who told Kernahan that "I'd rather have one live son than a dozen dead heroes," sources quoted many more that expressed the sentiment of Kernahan's wife who agreed that it was "Better a son's life lost for his country / Than a coward saved at the expense of his honour and his manhood."[61] It is impossible to say which sentiments dominated consciousness during the war, but the impression carefully promoted by patriotic sources implied that it was the latter. As the *Spectator* confidently declared, "No [English] woman has cried in agony that the future of the world might go hang so long as her husband or her son was safe."[62]

This is the double-edged moral of a story MP Will Crooks tells of an incident that allegedly took place while he was among his working class constituents in the East End of London. Crooks was walking down Commercial Road with a young fellow in khaki freshly back from the front, when the soldier saw an old chum. "Why, Bert," he said, "Not in khaki? You're not joined up?" "Naw!" Bert replied. "I ain't such a fool." And Bert went on to argue against the war.[63] The soldier had to go, but Crooks remained and, purposely pitching his voice loudly "to attract the attention of passers-by," he shouted, "Do you understand that it is the likes of him, doing what he is doing, that enables the likes of you to be where you are in safety? You are not willing to do your bit to stop the Kaiser from murdering women and children." By this time a number of women (about fifty, according to Crooks) were standing around listening. "There was no need for me to say any more," Crooks declared, as "I heard the women calling 'leave him to us Mr. Crooks, leave him to us.'"[64]

In many ways the episode demonstrates the complexity surrounding the use of women in the coercion of men. The pamphlet itself is a propagandist tract written by a working-class politician stoking the determination of East Enders to "fight to the finish." The Tommy and the shirker are archetypal figures whose moral position in the community depends upon the intervention of an old politician and the coercion of a group of women moved to action by Crook's account of the enslavement of the women and girls of Lille.[65] The reader never hears the fate of the shirker and is left to imagine the actions of the women. Yet the moral of the story is that a man who refuses to fight for his women abroad will be sacrificed to them at home.

This impression emerged repeatedly in representations of the relationship between mothers and sons. In Allan Monkhouse's play *The Shamed Life* the protagonist, Claude, discovers that his mother, who appeared to be holding him back, was only shielding him from the recognition of his own cowardice.[66] As Claude explains to Isabel, a beautiful young girl with a beau at the front, "My mother thinks I'm a coward. I suppose I am. She dreads it for me. For herself too, I daresay. But she shields me D'you see?"[67] To Isabel, Claude's cowardice is incomprehensible—"dead is better than feeding hens"—but she is unable to persuade him to enlist until the news of the death of her fiancé arrives.[68] Although at the end of the play, the women triumph over the man by sending him to join up, the response of the beleaguered Claude echoes the sentiments expressed by those pressured by women to enlist. In Claude's comments, Isabel herself becomes like a weapon forcing him to a certain death: "You're a high and mighty person with a lover at war. You're hard. You're like steel. . . ."[69] Although Claude's mother attempts to protect him from revealing his cowardice while Isabel wishes to convince him that "it is better to die a hero young than to live a long mean life," their messages are the same.[70] In this story, both the woman who tells the man to go and the one who pretends to hold him back have a contempt for cowardice and a strong desire to see Claude enlist even if it should mean his death. In this context, it is clear why Claude angrily declares of women, "You force us to it. You hound us on."[71]

Like the character of Claude in *The Shamed Life*, many men internalized the idea that they were fighting the war, if not to protect their women, so that their women might be proud of them when they returned. Thomas Macmillan, a clerk from Glasgow who enlisted in November 1914, related that once he had made his decision to enlist his mother "confessed she felt greatly relieved at the thought that somebody else's son would not have to fight for her and hers."[72] And P. T. Bryant wrote to Mrs. L. Hayman, his former Bible class teacher in Brighton, that he joined up because he wanted to "be worthy of his so worthy mother."[73] As Bryant expressed it: "It seems one horrible blood feud the whole world over and yet when we look back at our peaceful homes we think they are well worth fighting for."[74] The shame of not having fought was also a concern of men who wished to hold up their heads in public and to make their families proud of them when they returned. As one soldier told his wife, "Your face seems to be always with me lately. I sometimes say why do I go through with this. I wouldn't stick the way I am doing now in civil life for 2 pounds a day but you must never be ashamed of your hubby in years to come and I must be able to stay in England and not be afraid to look everyone straight in the face, knowing I have done my bit."[75]

Although many men accepted the idea that they were fighting for a cause best expressed by the image of a safe home and clung to the belief that they were protecting their families and their women, others became increasingly resentful of sentimentalized and coercive propaganda motifs. Thomas Macmillan relates a typical anecdote of the soldiers' growing irony toward a war justification based upon family values. "It happened frequently 'on the field' after the completion of an unpleasant job-of-work, that my comrades would turn to each other and ask in derision: 'Daddy what did you do in the Great War?'"[76] To this question there were a number of caustic responses, each reflecting the growing irony in some quarters regarding the imagery that saturated the home front. Robert Smillie, the head of the Scottish Miner's Union, responded to this poster with the terse answer: "I tried to stop the bloody thing my child."[77] And H. G. Wells, who opposed "ridiculous placards and street corner insults" as a means of recruiting, later "laughed to think of that recruiting poster and all the men who must have been lured into the army . . . and afterwards despised by their children for not being conscientious objectors."[78] The collector John Keeble has speculated that such posters may have been defaced by graffiti, an assessment echoed by Macmillan, who remembers that "Many of the replies are unprintable, but they provoked such wild merriment that the uncongenial task often proved a blessing in disguise."[79]

In a milieu characterized by the experience of loss, suffering, and bereavement, it is understandable why many mothers believed that they shared with their soldier sons the brunt of the war. Indeed, this faith may have even offered some psychological consolation. Women who had lost sons were no doubt desperate to find some meaning in the sacrifice they had made.[80] Furthermore, the language of patriotic motherhood offered easy words of consolation for those unsure of how to comfort friends, relatives, or compatriots smarting under an unbearable loss. The social pressure upon women to raise brave and soldierly sons and fear of the scorn that might fall upon those they loved no doubt also fed into mothers' response to patriotic appeals. Whatever the motive, the strategic use of what was a widely shared (and generally approved) rhetoric during the war would become, as Graves's mocking disapproval of the "Little Mother" reveals, highly suspect later on. Although mothers received sympathy for their plight, such patriotic language became increasingly problematic as it was articulated by sweethearts and strangers whose enthusiasm for recruiting was much more tenuously grounded in personal pain. If bearing soldiers gave women a certain sacrificial claim, loving soldiers met with a very different response, leading women into one of the most problematic articulations of feminine patriotism ever to be encountered.

PART II

SHAMING RITUALS
AND SEXUAL IDENTITY

Chapter Four

The Order of the
White Feather

On August 30, 1914, Admiral Charles Penrose Fitzgerald deputized thirty women in Folkstone to hand out white feathers to men not in uniform. The purpose of this gesture was to shame "every young 'slacker' found loafing about" and to remind those "deaf or indifferent to their country's need" that "British soldiers are fighting and dying across the channel."[1] Fitzgerald's estimation of the power of these women was enormous. He warned the men of Folkstone that there was "a danger awaiting them far more terrible than anything they can meet in battle," for if they were found "idling and loafing tomorrow" they would be publicly humiliated by a lady with a white feather.[2]

Paramilitary bands of women known as "The Order of the White Feather" or "The White Feather Brigade" captured the imagination of numerous observers and even enjoyed a moment of semi-official sanction at the beginning of the war. According to the *Chatham News,* "An amusing, novel, and forceful method of obtaining recruits for Lord Kitchener's Army was demonstrated at Deal on Tuesday when the town crier paraded the streets and crying with the dignity of his ancient calling, gave forth the startling announcement—'Oyez! Oyez!! Oyez!!! The White Feather Brigade! Ladies wanted to present the young men of Deal and Walmer . . . the Order of the White Feather for shirking their duty in not coming forward to uphold the Union Jack of Old England! God save the King.'"[3] Numerous women responded to the cry and began to comb the city placing white feathers in the lapels and hat-bands of men wearing civilian clothes.[4] The practice was widely imitated by women all over the country and continued long after conscription was instated in 1916, creating one of the most persistent memories of the home front during the war.[5] Dr. M. Yearsley is one of many diarists who recalled that "young girls of all ages and styles of beauty, but particularly those of the type called 'Flappers,' were parading the streets offering white feathers to young men in mufti, with a fine disregard of discrimination. . . . It is an established fact," Yearsley insisted, that "one of these inconsequent children offered her emblem of cowardice to a young man on leave who had just been awarded the V.C."[6]

If patriotic motherhood made a plausible case for the military and imperial centrality of women's domestic work, the practice of white-feather-giving instead carried the sexual power of women into the public sphere. On street corners, in omnibuses, and at places of resort, the white-feather women reminded men that women were abroad, that their eyes were everywhere, and that men had better conform to the strictures of patriotism or risk public exposure for the private crime of cowardice.[7] With interrogation, insults, or a silent gesture, the white-feather women and their loquacious sisters stripped the epaulets of masculinity from their unlucky foe. As one disconsolate reader wrote to the *Times*, "I have volunteered but they would not look at me. There must be a large government badge for the disqualified. Until we receive this, in Whitehall and great streets, . . . the only badge we have [is] the WHITE FEATHER."[8]

Despite initial enthusiasm, using women to shame men into enlistment would ultimately produce two rather problematic consequences. On one hand it undermined the government's credibility by making it appear to foreign and domestic observers that Britain was "begging for recruits."[9] To large sectors of the press, voluntarism itself symbolized the ineffectiveness of the Liberal government and led to a series of claims, loudly articulated in the Northcliffe press, that the people wished to be commanded rather than persuaded and that the country needed to be "told what to do."[10] The occasional transvestitism of the state for the purpose of recruiting appeared to be the ultimate symbol of the government's weak, vulnerable and passive attitude to the problem of enlistment.

If these tactics seemed to testify to the impotence of the liberal state, however, they had precisely the opposite effect on the image of women.[11] While propaganda was meant to persuade women to use their influence to secure more recruits, many women seized upon these appeals as license to arbitrate male behavior and to demonstrate their own superior bravery and patriotism. As women and soldiers encountered each other on the streets, the rhetoric of voluntary recruiting began to backfire—and not entirely by accident. This chapter examines the context in which white-feather-giving flourished, what it meant to women, and why it ultimately helped bring the whole edifice of voluntary recruiting crashing down.

THE SOCIAL HISTORY OF A GESTURE

If on one level the order of the white feather was meant to guarantee a form of masculine behavior that would obviate the need for compulsion, on another level it was the *reductio ad absurdum* of the recruiting methods favored by the liberal state. When Admiral Penrose Fitzgerald mounted the bandstand at Folkstone, he initiated a practice meant as much to embarrass the government as to shame young men. From his memoirs, an autobiographical justification of the principles of the National Service League, we know that Fitzgerald was a Conservative conscriptionist with no love for "the effeminate hypocracy" of voluntary recruiting.[12] Denouncing Lord Haldane's army reforms, the Liberal principle of voluntary enlistment, and the humiliating methods required to raise an army under voluntarism, Fitzgerald mockingly describes the raising of an East Surrey Territorial regiment before the war by offering lady staffers a free pair of gloves for each recruit.[13] Despite the fanfare, which included a fox terrier wearing a recruiting badge and territorials on bicycles, "'the great silent courage of the British' failed by thirty-two men, to furnish the required quota."[14] As Fitzgerald sourly notes, "England expects every man to do his duty. And if he won't, the Minister of War will send a lady to kiss him and a fox terrier to entice him."[15]

On one level, Fitzgerald's account is simply an amusing story by a pro-conscription propagandist, yet on another it offers some insight into the psychology of a Conservative forced by the limitations of the law to function within a voluntary system of which he entirely disapproved. Men like Fitzgerald and Lord Northcliffe recruited with relish, instigating and fanning some of the most outlandish forms of feminine display, yet on another level their mocking manipulation of gender was the ultimate attack upon their Liberal adversaries. Not only was the practice of white-feather-giving—widely publicized by Northcliffe—ridiculed in both the domestic and foreign press to the mortification of the Asquith government, but the *Labour Leader* and several Liberal MPs actually endorsed conscription on the grounds that it was preferable to a voluntary scheme that involved such feminine taunts.[16] As one official at the Ministry of Information lamented, "The *Times* writes that recruiting is deteriorating, that intimidation and flattery are employed alternately resulting in scandals. The inciting to enlist through young girls, the presentation of white feathers (symbols of cowardice in England) by excited women, are only surface signs of the national degeneration. . . . Clearly the Government is thereby trying to burden others with the unpopularity they will not take upon themselves."[17]

Although the practice of white-feather-giving could be justified as an aid to recruiting, it also worked as a parody of the very institutions it was supposed to promote and drew upon women an avalanche of criticism for turning voluntary recruiting into an embarrassing farce. As late as 1964, Gordon Watkins, the producer of a BBC series celebrating the fiftieth anniversary of the Great War, reflected these attitudes when he issued an advertisement soliciting responses from white-feather women and the men they had shamed. In the ad, Mr. Watkins tauntingly suggested that "I doubt if any of these women will be brazen enough to admit it now." The BBC was inundated with responses from men who had received white feathers, but the reply from women to an advertisement that proclaimed its intention to "deal with the lunatic fringe which existed at home during part of the war" was so low that I have found only two letters in the collection from women who admit to having bestowed white feathers.[18] Responses from men who received white feathers and from women who saw them given, however, should not be dismissed out of hand because of the reticence of the givers or the recipients' temporal distance from the war.[19] As Mr. Watkins's tone suggests and many of the letters corroborate, claiming to have given a white feather during the 1914–18 war was by the 1960s a highly embarrassing and shameful admission.[20] Mrs. Thyra Mitchell, one of the two women who did write in, found herself in the *Daily Mirror* hailed as a self-proclaimed "chump," and although the tone of the article was more one of astonishment over the admission than hostility toward Mrs. Mitchell, such notoriety is not necessarily of the sort many women would have wished for.[21]

Because of women's later reluctance to admit that they participated in the white-feather campaign, their motivations remain both suggestive and mysterious. On one hand, these women were clearly acting on the same patriotic impulses elicited by propaganda and through popular culture. The ubiquitous celebration of the soldier and denigration of the unenlisted man created a milieu in which the young male civilian was fair game for any sort of public humiliation. Many women reported feeling anger and contempt for unenlisted men, stemming both from larger cultural attitudes (which depicted unenlisted men as "cowards" and "shirkers") and, in many cases, from personal experiences of the loss of their own male friends and relatives. Mrs. Thyra Mitchell recalled that she gave a white feather to her acquaintance Jack Mills because she "was very angry" and "felt he should be doing his bit."[22] For women who had sent loved ones to fight, the sight of an unenlisted man was often particularly galling, especially since the army was continually short of men, endangering those already at the front.

As an unusually provocative form of patriotism, however, white-feather-giving may also have had more transgressive motives. Officer T. A.

Lowe loved getting white feathers to display in the trenches, especially
since he and his friends "sometimes . . . got off with the 'feather girls,'
often quite young and pretty."[23] Providing a coy patriotic cover for flirtatious encounters, it is possible that this disdainful gesture had some sexual appeal as well. Indeed, while eyewitness accounts suggest that old
women and even men were capable of bestowing feathers, the gesture is
most commonly remembered as an insult leveled by young women self-
confidently traversing public spaces such as market squares, cafes, and the
theater district of the West End. Sometimes described as "flappers," these
women seemed to display the brash modernity of "new" women for
whom the experience of war afforded a taste of unprecedented independence.[24] Their attacks upon manhood can perhaps be read as a display of
their own uncharacteristic upper hand in a world where patriotic women
trumped "cowardly" men and where handsome servicemen in "civvies"
were sometimes available for the asking.

Although the internal motives of the white-feather women are speculative, patriotic messages, romantic literature, and sheer bravado all contributed to fanning a risky activity that, to some young women, seems to
have been irresistible. The most haunting evidence, however, has been left
by those who received or witnessed the giving of this terrible emblem, and
it is from these narratives that we begin to piece together a picture of what
might aptly be termed "propaganda in action."

While both male and female witnesses tell of strangers and loved ones
who received white feathers, it is still a memory that inspires shock, dis-
belief, and misunderstanding. Not only have military historians insisted
on the "ineffectiveness" of the white-feather campaign, but its connota-
tions are so shameful that contrary to all evidence, social historians have
attributed it only to the wealthy classes, while feminist historians have attempted to deny its widespread existence altogether.[25] Its prevalence, its
broad social distribution, and above all its wrenching effect upon the actions of those who received this blow are nevertheless well documented in
the memories of both men and women who wrote to the BBC. "Whilst in
East India Dock Road, Poplar, I was handed a white feather by a . . . lady,
with some remarks from her about cowards," recalled T. O. Cunningham,
"I told her where she got off in no uncertain terms, then made my way to
Woodstock Road Recruiting Office and joined the Middlesex Regiment."[26] While the white feather was probably not solely responsible for a
man's decision to enlist, in a disproportionate number of cases (even
when the gesture was highly resented) men went to the recruiting office
directly after the incident.[27] C. G. Byrne enlisted two days after receiving
feathers from two different girls in Portsmouth, though he was not yet fif-
teen years old. Although Byrne was unsure whether the white feathers had

a direct impact upon his decision to enlist, he reflects that "my life was governed by those few days of self analysis and decisions, which were undoubtedly fanned by the gift of those feathers."[28]

Veteran Francis Almond offers some insight into the psychology of such an insult. "The idea spread like a virulent disease," Almond recalls. "It is doubtful if it ever gained a recruit. The act seemed to be more retaliatory than anything else. Some of the recipients were already in the service, just walking around town in their 'civvies.' But the pain, and acute embarrassment of the infliction 'He was given a white feather.' A lie, once uttered, is never wholly overtaken. White Feather—what a thing to live down."[29] Emphasizing both its ineffectiveness and its terrible effect, Almond gets at the heart of the stain that could only be removed by enlisting. Despite his denial of the efficacy of the gesture, its emotional significance is clear when he describes his own feelings upon being mocked by group of working class women while home on leave. "I passed a group of 2 or 3 middle aged women with shawls over their heads, gossiping at the end of Parliament street. As I went by, one of them exclaimed 'Ee—he ought to be in't Army—he did a' all' [sic] I was glad when I had passed out of earshot. But thank goodness, that tragic emblem of cowardice, the horrible white feather, never came my way."[30]

The horror expressed by Almond at the mere thought of receiving a white feather many, many years later in part explains why the BBC's call for accounts of the white feather became in almost every case a vindication of the recipients' bravery, patriotism, and willingness to serve, and as a belated retort to insulting women who could never be recovered. Most recipients who were not medically unfit or conscientious objectors thus begin their narratives by relating their own contributions to the war, their regiments, where they were wounded and, in the case of some underage men who did not enlist, their service in later wars. C. B. Abraham's letter is typical: "I was in the 12th London Regiment (the Rangers) and volunteered for foreign service. . . . We were in the Front line in the second battle of Ypres and had a very rough time. . . . [I]n August 1915 a few of us were given 45 hours leave. . . . The next morning I put my best grey suit on, and was passing along Barking opposite East Ham Town Hall, when suddenly something stuck in my chest, it was the pin of the white feather, as I looked the young woman was running away, so I chased after her but lost her in the crowd, perhaps it was a good thing I did."[31]

Many letters written to the BBC relate the wrenching stories of overaged men, young boys, fathers of families, and the medically disabled who joined or tried to join the army out of the fear of receiving the white feather. Mrs. J. UpJohn vividly recalled the day her father received a white feather while coming home from work in Westminster: "I was only six years old at the time, but I can remember the occasion well, as it was one of the only times I remember my father crying. But that night he came home and cried his heart out. My father was no coward but he had been reluctant to leave his little family, my mother, my sister of three, and I. My mother had been very ill, with the shock of her dear brother, being killed at the Dardanelles [Mrs. UpJohn's mother miscarried as a result of 'the fatal telegram']. . . . So you can see that it was through circumstances, and not cowardice that my father was still in civilian clothes. . . . [H]e joined up soon after. I never forgot how upset he was, poor dad he was never a coward, though he had his faults like all of us. . . ."[32] Mrs. UpJohn, like many female respondents, begins her letter to the BBC by declaring that she had never given a feather and then relating an incident in which she sedulously protects the honor of the recipient. Mrs. UpJohn's letter was followed by yet another written specifically to reiterate the fact that her father was "no coward," showing the lasting significance of these categories to the generation that fought in the war and the sensitivity of many women to imputations against the men they loved.

Despite these wrenching narratives, men who received white feathers were not always passive victims. Harry Taylor of Essex remembers that his father, who was wounded at the retreat from Mons and gassed at Ypres, was handed a white feather in the Market Place at Chutorfield by a young woman who "in return received a sharp slap in the face for her trouble."[33] And when P. W. Bassatt of Staffordshire was presented with a white feather in October 1915 he "smacked the female's face that surprised her, I just been refused for the 3rd time."[34] Numerous letters testify to the fact that the white-feather women were subject to insults, slaps, and rudeness before they were embarrassed with a display of the signs of battle they had so foolishly missed. "In those days there was a part of Clarence Pier call the 'Bull Ring' and we used to go there to try and get a girl," recalled Mr. J. Jones, who was presented with a white feather while home on medical leave after being wounded in France. "I saw a girl I liked and tried to get talking to her but she didn't seem interested and then I saw her talking to another soldier. So . . . I said 'you spoke to him why can't you speak to me?' She replied 'I don't speak to toy soldiers only those with guts, so you'd better have this' and gave me a white feather."[35] Jones promptly slapped her in the face whereupon her friend, a local dockworker, challenged him to a fight. "I opened my tunic and pulled up my shirt and showed my wound and told them I had only just come out of hospital after having been to France and done my bit. The bloke apologized . . . and the girl just ran off."[36]

Although he is wearing a newly issued uniform, the girl rejects Jones as a suitor because the pristine condition of his clothes leads her to believe he has not yet been to the front—an apparent deficiency that renders him an undesirable object of love, unworthy even of address. The tale is one of many about women's inability to read men, their attention to superficial detail, and their failure to tell a hero from a coward, even if this distinction should literally hit them in the face. The slapping, silencing, or shaming of the white feather women were standard means of vindication and were perceived as justified by the act itself, opening up a number of questions about the significance of this gesture. A woman who gave a white feather in essence put herself outside the laws of chivalry. If, as Coulson Kernahan described them, these women were "no gentlemen," "female cads," "blackguards" and the like, the gendering of their heinous activity in masculine terms also made them subject to masculine forms of reprisal such as insults and physical abuse.[37] That women who gave out white feathers asked for and deserved such treatment was readily accepted even by middle-class commentators who believed that these activities placed women so far outside the bounds of propriety that they no longer deserved even the politeness that regulated intercourse between the sexes.

Indeed, a former munitions worker, Alfred G. Allen, remembers an incident where the reprisal meted out to a white feather woman transgressed both chivalric behavior and social deference. He had enlisted in August 1914 but his mother had reported him as underage, leading to his discharge. His friends were killed in action, and wishing to do war related work, he signed on at the munitions factory in Walthamstow. According to Allen, he and his friend Christopher Crow were attacked by a white-feather woman in 1915. Although the incident left Allen "too shocked to move," his workmate "roared like a wanton bull as she took hold of his lapel, whilst he with a vicious blow struck her wrist upwards." The band of her wrist watch snapped and "a beautiful small gold watch flew yards into the air to eventually land with a crunching smash to the pavement. She retaliated with a terrific smack with her other hand on my mates face. People seemed to gather round from nowhere. Pandemonium soon reigned as voices were raised in abuse and argument before the woman was finally led away by the . . . discomfited young lieutenant [who was accompanying her]. She was shouting at the top of her voice 'If the cap fits, wear it!' . . . An elderly woman who knew me removed the white feather from my lapel and ground it under her foot."[38]

While the white feather itself was usually bestowed by a young woman of any class, an embarrassing taunt, a loud reproach, or a public upbraiding was as likely to be wielded by a spinsterly busybody as by a provocative flapper. Such women were sometimes associated with what were considered to be the worst aspects of the suffrage movement. Sylvia Pankhurst claims that members of the militantly pro-war WSPU roamed public parks distributing white feathers and while there is no evidence that any other suffrage organization was directly involved in this practice, feminists were not above reproaching unenlisted men.[39] When Dr. M. Yearsley clashed with such a lady on his way to a dinner party, he immediately classified her with the givers of white feathers and used her misguided recruiting speech as a basis from which to attack her case for the vote. According to Yearsley, "In the bus . . . sitting by the door was an aggressive looking lady of uncertain age, evidently a suffragette, as she carried a copy of *Votes for Women*. A little higher up were three lads in khaki. Suddenly she addressed me in a loud voice. 'Are you not ashamed of yourself, standing there in evening dress? . . . Why aren't you *doing* something for your country, a fine young man like you? Look at these splendid fellows in khaki,'—here the splendid fellows in khaki blushed furiously— 'Doing their duty, whilst you play the coward.'"[40] According to Yearsley "there was more of the same sort and I waited until she was out of breath. . . . Then I said, 'Madam, firstly I am a hospital surgeon and I see a certain number of wounded. Secondly, I am drilling recruits two day a week and have just done two hours of it, as you might have gathered from the husky state of my voice. Thirdly, I am unfortunate enough to be well over age.'"[41] After the woman muttered an apology and "cast a vicious glance at the splendid fellows, who were openly sniggering," Yearsley touched the *Votes for Women* in her hand and "gave her the knock-out blow: 'Before you obtain *that*, madam, you have much to learn, including how to restrain yourself and the folly of judging by appearances.' She left the bus . . . and I sank into her seat, with a sigh of contentment."[42]

The uninvited taunt from a woman in a public place and the chagrin of the woman upon realizing her mistake are the stuff of men's recollection of women's profound lack of penetration. Each of these narratives seeks a rhetorical revenge, wrought after the fact, upon the woman who attempted shame and embarrass the man who wrote in. For Yearsley, the woman's ill-informed recruiting effort was an ample basis from which to attack her judgment, her continence, and her fitness for the vote. With the prevalence of such negative perceptions, why did so many women subject themselves to insults and physical abuse by pursuing an activity that was almost universally reviled and decried?

"WOMEN OF BRITAIN SAY—'GO!'"

It is important to remember that the white-feather campaign originated within a system of voluntary recruiting that vociferously called upon women to send men to war. Until the institution of conscription in 1916, recruiting propaganda relied heavily upon a patriotic appeal that welded masculinity to military service and branded the unenlisted civilian as a coward beneath contempt. Women not only functioned in this campaign as the direct voice of conscience, but appeared more subtly as the objects soldiers fought to defend, the rewards only heroes dared to desire, and as the specter of what a man might become were he to "show the white feather" and fail in his duty. Gendered conceptions of patriotism thus implicated women in defining the parameters of male citizenship while endowing women's traditional domestic, maternal, and sexual roles with an openly expressed importance to the military state.[43]

As early as August 1914, personal advertisements appearing in the *Times* accused unenlisted men of cowardice and effeminacy in the name of presumed female acquaintances.[44] We have no idea whether these taunts were actually written by women, but even those advertisements that clearly were not—such as the productions of the Parliamentary Recruiting Committee—nevertheless implicated women in a recruiting rhetoric that hinged on a masculine sexual identity policed by women and the humiliating threat of appearing unmanly.[45] "It will not be very long before every woman in the country will be looking 'coward' at every man she sees at home," the *Times* forbodingly warned. For the writer "has talked with six women, varying in station from servant-maid to marchioness, all of whom have asked why so many young and active men are seen around who do not appear to be doing anything about going to war."[46]

Recruiters, legally bared from resorting to conscription until the enactment of National Service in 1916, put much thought into the motivation of young men, appealing both to threatened masculinity and to sexual desire as means of persuasion. In this way, Henry Arthur Jones was using commonplace logic when he declared that "The English girl who will not know the man—lover, brother, or friend—that cannot show an overwhelming reason for not taking up arms—that girl will do her duty and will give good help to her country."[47]

The incitement to such tactics was by no means unusual especially during the first two years of the war. One recruiting leaflet addressed to "MOTHERS!" and "SWEETHEARTS" reminded mothers of Belgian atrocities and warned sweethearts that, "If you cannot persuade him to answer his Country's Call and protect you now *Discharge him* as unfit!"[48] A poster designed for the Lord Mayor of London put the same message even more bluntly. Addressing "The Young Women of London," the mayor asked: "Is your 'Best Boy' wearing Khaki? If not don't *YOU THINK* he should be? If he does not think that you and your country are worth fighting for—do you think he is *worthy* of you? Don't pity the girl who is alone—her young man is probably a soldier—fighting for her and her country—and for *You*. If your young man neglects his duty to his King and Country, the time may come when he will *Neglect You*. Think it over—then ask him to JOIN THE ARMY *TO DAY!*"[49]

In this way, while "Women of Britain" were told to "Say Go!" something as private as female sexuality took on a military significance at the expense of all those unenlisted men who appeared reluctant to defend it. While this poster and others like it were criticized in Parliament and in the feminist press for their blatant manipulation of gender, the state had nevertheless assumed the guise of a woman for the purpose of recruiting.[50] This propagandistic turn implicated women's most intimate domestic and sexual relationships in the raising of the new armies. According to the *Times:* "Many correspondents point out that lectures are not the best means of reaching the workingman and that all-important recruiting agency, his sister or sweetheart."[51] Instead, one such correspondent suggested in a metaphor that melded women and recruiting posters: "Show their eyes." In this way propaganda, both in the deployment of gendered images and in its ability to instigate female behavior, turned women themselves into a form of propaganda. Ideal-typical notions of masculinity and femininity were key to this process since they represented both the traditional values that the British were apparently fighting to defend and the modes of gendered behavior that seemed necessary to successfully wage war.[52] What came as more of a shock to many observers, however, was that many women in turn donned the mantle of the state as they used their own physical and rhetorical power in the service of the crown.

Although propagandists like Admiral Fitzgerald, Lord Esher, and Arthur Conan Doyle urged women to shun men out of uniform, to show contempt for the unenlisted, and even to hand out white feathers to men wearing mufti, the authorities showed almost universal horror when women actually practiced what many publicists themselves had preached. In the same lecture in which he exhorted the girls of the Women's League of Honour to send their men to war, Major Leonard Darwin made clear that he was "very far from admiring those women who go up to young men in the street . . . and abuse them for not enlisting, a proceeding which requires no courage on the woman's part, but merely a complete absence of modesty."[53] And the recruiting sergeant Coulson Kernahan, ordinarily a vigorous advocate of female recruiting, warned women that "the sending or offering of white feathers, so far from witnessing to your patriotism, witnesses only to the fact that you are unpardonably ignorant, vulgar, and impertinent."[54] Clearly, a rhetorical taunt and the threat of an emblem like the white feather were ideally meant to obviate the need of actually handing one out; indeed, that women heeded these calls was not necessarily the intention of those propagandists who made double-edged appeals to such unlikely groups as "The Young Women of London."

The discrepancy between the behavior of women apparently necessitated by the war and a sense of womanliness that transcended necessity, propelled contradictory observations on women's role in recruiting, and placed white-feather-giving outside the boundaries of acceptability, as a sort of emblem of all that was wrong with female patriotism. The *Times* correspondent Michael MacDonagh was horrified when, going home in a tramcar one night, he witnessed the presentation of white feathers. "The victims were two young men who were rudely disturbed from their reading of the evening paper by the attack of three young women. 'Why don't you fellows enlist? Your King and Country want you. We don't.' One of the girls was a pretty wench. She dishonoured one of the young men, as she thought, by sticking a white feather in his buttonhole, and a look of contempt spoiled for a moment her lovely face."[55] Although MacDonagh worked for a journal complicitous in prompting women to acts of patriotic disdain, he was nevertheless deeply troubled as he witnessed a practice entirely in keeping with the sentiments endorsed by such respected authorities as the Lord Mayor of London. As they parodied the rhetoric of propaganda posters, the actions of these young women turned a ubiquitous call to arms into a monstrous distortion of femininity. Spoiling her pretty face with a look of contempt, the girl becomes emblematic of an act that marred what should be lovely as it perverted the sentiments of both courtship and war.

MacDonagh's reservations were shared by a wide variety of observers, particularly when the victim was already enlisted. J. P. Cope remembered the fury of his wife when a similar incident took place while he took her to tea at the Mikado Cafe on Long Row. Mrs. Cope had been disinfecting her husband's uniform and thus he was wearing civilian clothes when "3 young ladies passed me and placed 3 white feathers in my hand." According to Mr. Cope, "I said to her look what them girls gave me as I did not know what they was for." His wife immediately accosted them and "they told her I ought to be in khaki out in France." Deftly turning the tables, Mrs. Cope told them "they ought to be in a Munitions Factory making Ammunition for the Soldiers to defend themselves."[56] Ordering the girls to return to Long Row the next day, Mrs. Cope turned their misguided accusations into an embarrassing retort: "the next day we went down I had my khaki on then with all my Decorations . . . we met them . . . and told them to give me the feathers back but they was too ashamed to do so we left them and went in the cafe and sat down they followed us and told my wife they would pay for our teas my wife told them that my Husband would pay for us as it would be an Insult to take their money they little knew what I had gone through in the first year of war always wet through from frost snow rain wounded at Neuve Chappel and how many battles I had been in I was wounded 2 and gassed 2 . . ."[57] Mrs. Cope's display of her husband in full regimental attire and her challenge to the women to give back the white feathers become the means by which she casts aspersion upon the wielders of shame. Like the wife of another "Old Contemptible" (who asked a white-feather woman, "have you a Husband in the Army? I don't suppose you have with a face like you have"), Mrs. Cope spurned the insightless women who "little knew" what her husband "had gone through in the first year of war."[58]

Despite receiving much implicit encouragement from propaganda and press sources, the white-feather women endured the scorn of flesh and blood observers ranging from Coulson Kernahan to Mrs. Cope. If they persisted in their patriotic feather-giving under such inauspicious circumstances, the act itself must have offered some gratification. Indeed, to decipher the attraction of white-feather-giving for those who literally or rhetorically wielded this remarkable taunt, we must turn to the romantic popular culture offered to patriotic men and women seeking entertainment on the homefront.

SEXUAL SELECTION AND IMPERIAL ORDER

The inspiration for the use of the white feather and its significance in the construction of masculine honor and feminine disdain were borrowed from *The Four Feathers,* a popular imperial adventure by A. E. W. Mason first published in 1902.[59] In the novel, Harry Feversham, a young military officer who cannot stand the thought of battle, resigns his commission upon learning that he is to be sent to the Sudan on active duty.[60] Suspecting the cowardly motives behind his resignation, three of Harry's comrades send him white feathers, thus forcing him to confront the devastating truth of his own martial inadequacy. The emotional climax of the novel comes when Harry must offer an explanation of the incident to his fiancée Ethne. As the narrator dramatically explains, "the dreadful thing for so many years dreadfully anticipated had at last befallen him. He was known for a coward."[61] After returning her engagement ring, Ethne breaks a white ostrich feather from her fan and returns it to Feversham along with the three original feathers. As the narrator explains, "The thing which she had done was cruel no doubt, but . . . [s]he was tortured with humiliation and pain. . . . Their lips had touched . . . she recalled with horror."[62]

This final act of humiliation at the hands of the woman he loves spurs Harry to redeem himself—a redemption possible only in the spilling of blood. Upon leaving Ethne, Harry embarks on a trek to the Sudan to save his former friends from rebellious Dervishes who have refused to submit to colonial rule. In Africa, his symbolic passage to manhood occurs when Harry sinks his untried dagger into the body of an Arab, infusing his sanguinary quest for personal courage with visceral phallic imagery. "A brown clotted rust dulled the whole length of the blade, and often . . . he had taken the knife from his breast and stared at it . . . and clutched it close to him like a thing of comfort. . . . He ran his fingers over the rough rust upon the blade, and the weapon spoke to him and bade him take heart. . . ."[63] In this extraordinary passage, the knife becomes almost a surrogate woman to be "clutched close to him" and to "speak to him" and "bid him to take heart." As Harry caresses the dried blood of his victim—a testimony and proof of manhood encrusted on the very blade of his knife—the novel's juxtaposition of sex and empire begins to emerge, vividly highlighting a number of cultural assumptions that underlay the bestowal of the white feather of cowardice.

In the novel, imperialism and sexuality are intimately related since the masculine traits needed to satisfy the woman are the same as those required in the conquest of empire. After rescuing his comrades from the clutches of Dervishes, proving his willingness to kill and his indifference to danger and death, Harry's redemption is complete, and he is able to return the feathers and reclaim his bride. Upon Harry's heroic return, Ethne treasures his redeemed white feather "because it was no longer a symbol of cowardice but a symbol of cowardice atoned."[64] The mock order of the white feather becomes instead the true badge of courage, as Harry's atonement allows for the rehabilitation of his name and his reintegration into the society of his friends, his family, and the woman he loves.

As both the symbol of Harry's humiliation and the instrument of his redemption, the white feather endows womanly scorn with rich creative possibilities. For wartime enthusiasts, the objective of giving a white feather was not only to shame a man but to change him as well, and, as numerous men later testified, it could be wielded with a certain amount of patriotic self-righteousness by those would-be Ethnes who regarded a slacker as an affront to the ideal of manhood itself. A. M. Woodward perfectly summed up this attitude when she wrote to the *Times* to remind women that "there is a wider duty than making garments. . . . Young men must be persuaded to think what this war really means. . . . So I am commencing a little missionary work. To-morrow I mean to give a leaflet to every man who is apparently a possible recruit. I shall watch for them on the tram, in the street, at cricket and tennis grounds, at the theater, at the restaurant; and I hope that the little single appeal 'from the women of England' will at least rouse their thought and will possibly help them to act."[65] While leaflets, rather than feathers, were Woodward's symbolic medium, her faith in the creative power of womanly censure is abundantly clear. If Woodward compared herself to a missionary, such evangelism often had decidedly sexual overtones as well. In a sort of inversion of 'khaki fever,' scorning a coward can be read as the other side of loving a hero—a potentially transformative demonstration of that female patriotism so seductively displayed by Mason's heroine.[66]

Indeed, the imperial and sexual assumptions evident in *The Four Feathers* pervaded both the language of patriotic femininity and the ideal of romantic love during the war. If courage was the key to both sexual selection and the conquest of empire, women's imperial and eugenic task was to love a soldier and scorn a coward. As the *Girl's Own Paper* solemnly explained, "Women will forgive almost anything in a man except cowardice and treason. . . . Not only is this feeling instinctive, but it comes to her through long years of human evolution. . . . With hearts full but tranquil souls, women can send forth their sons, their husbands, their sweethearts, their protectors, to danger or to death—to anything saving halting and dishonour. A great Admiral put it neatly when he said 'victory was won by the woman behind the man behind the gun.'"[67] In the suggestion that both women and war demanded the same qualities of a man, female sexuality became central to contemporary understanding of the forging of martial identity. "The soul's armour is never well set to the heart unless a woman's hand has braced it," the Mother's Union warned, "and it is only when she braces it loosely that the honour of manhood fails."[68]

During the war, female journalists, music-hall entertainers, and an array of patriotic publicists of both sexes popularized these sentiments by articulating women's military purpose in terms of their sexual and moral power over men. When the Baroness Orczy, author of *The Scarlet Pimpernel,* called for the "First Hundred Thousand" female recruiters to join her "Active Service League" in 1914, she made explicit the logic latent in such patriotic acts of feminine disdain.[69] "Women and Girls of England—Your hour has come!," the baroness declared. "The great hour when to the question . . . 'what can I do?' your country has at last given an answer: . . . 'I want your men, your sweethearts, your brothers, your sons, your friends. . . .'" Advising women to "use your influence" so that men "[will] respond one and all," the baroness reminded women that although they could not "shoulder a rifle" they could actually serve their country "in the way she needs most."[70] The baroness posed the influencing of men as literally a form of "active service" for women and offered a military style badge and a place on the League's "Roll of Honour" to any woman or girl who pledged to, "persuade every man I know to offer his service . . . and never to be seen in public with any man who being in every way fit and free . . . has refused to respond to his country's call."[71] The baroness succeeded in enrolling 20,000 women and for her efforts received a letter of commendation from the king.[72] Yet Orczy was merely one of a multitude of commentators who bade women to persuade their men to enlist and to scorn those who refused.

To Orczy, the withdrawing of the feminine body—in the refusal to be seen in public with a man out of uniform—worked in conjunction with moral coercion to isolate the man who refused to enlist. Her assumption seems to have been that what persuasion and female patriotism could not achieve, sexual desire and public shame could. If the presence of women was contingent upon the wearing of a uniform, the purpose of the league was to assure that the signs of military and sexual prowess would be worn together or not at all.

As patriotic women's groups posed the raising of recruits as a form of military service for women—a patriotic duty comparable, according to the Baroness Orczy, to "shouldering a rifle"—popular singers, writers, and artists represented the soldier-hero as a romantic ideal worthy of a woman's love and hopeful of her body. Highlighting the distinction between the sexually attractive recruit and the contemptible slacker, female music-hall stars such as Vesta Tilly and Clara Butt became famous for their sexualized recruiting songs and their erotic impact upon enlistment.[73] At venues ranging from local music halls to the carnivalesque recruiting rallies of Horatio Bottomley, the alleged contingency of love upon war dominated the period of voluntary recruiting, turning military service itself into a sort of national aphrodisiac.[74] In the most famous recruiting song of the war, women explained that, "[N]ow your country calls you / To play your part in war / And no matter what befalls you / We shall love you all the more . . ."

> Oh, we don't want to lose you / But we think you ought to go, . . . / We shall want you and miss you, / But with all our might and main / We shall cheer you, thank you, kiss you, / When you come back again.[75]

In the song, women offer their love and kisses as men's reward for going to war; yet in many music-hall songs, the sexual implications of soldiering were even more explicit. In "I'll Make a Man out of You," popularized by Gwendoline Brogden in *The Passing Show*, the artiste enthusiastically proclaimed to the audience her "perfect dream of a recruiting scheme . . . If only all the girls would do as I do / I believe that we could manage it alone. / For I turn all suitors from me but the sailor and the Tommy, / I've an army of my own."

On Saturday I'm willing, if you'll only take the shilling, / To make a man out of you. / I teach the tenderfoot to face the powder, / That gives an added lustre to my skin, . . . / It makes you almost proud to be a woman, / When you make a strapping soldier of a kid. / And he says "You put me through it and I didn't want to do it / But you made me love you so I did."[76]

The use of double entendres—in this instance comparing making a man face gunpowder to a woman applying face powder—played with the idea of the eroticism of war and its stimulating effect on female sexuality. In making a soldier the woman makes a man, and in making a man she conversely creates a soldier; this transformative power is itself a source of erotic pleasure as the singer flaunts her ability to counter a man's volition by stimulating his desire. As the song puts it: "You put me through it and I didn't want to do it / But you made me love you so I did."

Female entertainers themselves frequently tried to recruit men from the audience in the highly patriotic atmosphere of the music hall.[77] Major D. K. Patterson, an "Old Contemptible" home on leave in 1915, went to the Royal Hippodrome in Belfast where a comedienne sang "We Don't Want to Lose You" directly to him. The mirth of the company surprised the vocalist who, much to Major Patterson's satisfaction, burst into tears upon being told that he was already in the army.[78]

The longing to transform men into soldiers and the eroticism of martial prowess was as evident in popular women's fiction as in bawdy music-hall lyrics.[79] In September 1914 *Women's World* began a serial called "A Soldier's Wife," which ran with the sensational advertisement: "Amy Had Married the Only Coward in France." Through a mistake, Amy believes that she was saved from a fire by Jules and marries him instead of her true savior, Jack. After marrying Jules, Amy discovers her mistake. To the humiliation of Amy and Jules's mother, "a gallant old lady who loved her son to the point of adoration [but] loved her country and her son's honour better," Jules deserts from the French army. The two women, however, finally persuade Jules to rejoin his regiment at the front, where he shows his bravery and saves his marriage in the single act of performing well as a soldier.

Similar motifs appeared in popular women's literature even after the institution of conscription in 1916. In August 1917, for example, *Women at Home* magazine published a romantic story by M. McD. Bodkin, KC called "The White Feather." In the story, Molly Burton, "a bright, pretty, warm hearted little girl and as brave as another" accidentally gives a white feather to a recipient of the Victoria Cross.[80] Molly is intensely drawn to posters "urging young men to join their comrades in the trenches, to fight for England and liberty against the ravishers and murders in Flanders. Shirkers and slackers awakened her utmost scorn . . . 'If I were a man' she said, 'I would go at first call. I would not have other men out fighting for me while I skulked at home amongst the women.'"[81]

Molly is troubled by the presence in her neighborhood of "a splendid figure of a man" "lazing around Brighton" while "illustrated posters proclaimed that every man was needed at the Front."[82] Finally able to stand it no longer, she gives "the handsome coward" a white feather snipped from her favorite hat. The culmination of the story, and the fruition of its sexual and military motif, comes when Molly is invited to a grand ball "for a military angel . . . Robert Courtney, most illustrious of Victoria Cross heroes [who] has been residing anonymously at Brighton for nearly a fortnight."[83] Predictably, "the hero of the Victoria Cross was her slacker, still wearing the White Feather." The story culminates in the conflation of romantic and martial masculinity in the person of the hero. As the narrator explains, Captain Courtney "waltzed as he fought, superbly." In the final passage of the story he "caught her close in his arms, half resisting, wholly yielding, and kissed her on the lips. When she emerged panting and blushing from the close embrace without a word more spoken on either side, they were engaged. Captain Courtney was no slacker in love or war!"[84]

Although "The White Feather" is unusual in presenting a positive view of the practice of handing out white feathers relatively late in the war, it may offer some insight into the way women envisioned this practice themselves. The story was published in a popular woman's magazine and is adamant in its depiction of Molly as a brave, enticing, and patriotic girl whose nationalistic gesture sets her on the path of adventure and romance. In linking patriotism and romantic imagination, the story offers some insight into why the categories of courage and cowardice, which became the foundation of women's romantic war literature, seemed to have inspired patriotic action in an assortment of women during the war. In a context in which waging war was regarded as the single most important civic task, the paradigm of courage and cowardice made it possible for women to envision national service in sexual terms. In turning women's romantic fantasies into public duty, a variety of stories, songs, and patriotic appeals promised women a vicarious attachment to the front through the honor of the men they inspired, while elevating such amusements as the selection of beaux into tasks of national and imperial importance. This romantic aspect of white-feather-giving comes across with remarkable vividness in a variety of accounts written by men who received feathers during the war. Bill Lawrence, writing from an old people's home in Warwickshire many years later, remembered being upbraided by a lady milliner on a train for not offering his seat to a wounded soldier. "I got up straight away . . . and took my trousers down so far, I had a thick pad of cotton wool and a bandage I had had a *very* severe wound in the back . . .

it was a bit smaller than a wallnut and all jagged edged and poisoned." Mr. Lawrence warned the woman that if he'd "been a nasty tempered man he may have got what they call a smack in the gab," but quickly notes that "she was a very good friend afterward." Leaving the girl to manage the store, the woman took Mr. Lawrence to her room, "put a bottle of whiskey [at] the side of the bed took [off] all clothes and got in bed and said do as you like you earned it . . ."[85]

While Lawrence's tale of patriotic female sexuality is seen through the eyes of a man (and at a distance from the war that endows it with the complications of postwar oral history), he is not unique among those who remember a decidedly erotic dimension to female recruiting. About a year after the war had begun, Mr. H. Symonds was listening to a ginger-haired girl giving a recruiting speech at Hyde Park Corner. He was seventeen at the time but eager to go, "so when ginger gently tucked a white duck feather into my button-hole I went off to the recruiting office and, putting two years on my age, joined up." Symonds saw nothing unusual in this incident, yet he did believe that the experience was unique in one respect: "I believe I am the only recipient of a feather, who had it taken back by the giver and was given a kiss in return!" Three or four days later "in uniform, I again stood in Hyde Park and listened to 'Ginger' she recognized me and in front of the crowd round her stand she came up to me and asked for the return of her feather. Amidst mixed cheering and booing I handed it to her. She had tears in her eyes as she kissed me and said 'God Bless.'"[86] Symonds's account of the receipt of his white feather is quite rare. His ability to exchange the white feather for the kiss of a lovely woman turns what men generally regarded as a hostile taunt into an erotic event that won the bestower admiration and inspired the recipient to enlist willingly. As Symonds explains, "Few people realize that those women who gave feathers were not just flighty empty-heads, but had a far deeper insight into *mysterious man* than is generally supposed. I was wounded twice but never regretted the quietly given push from a girl that sent me to the recruiting station."[87]

Although white-feather-giving is generally remembered as an event that excited enormous hostility, it is possible that women like Ginger received a certain amount of now-forgotten encouragement. Not only did both the official and the unofficial productions of the voluntary recruiting movement brandish female sexuality as a means of shaming men into uniform, but popular fiction, musical theater, and advice literature frequently asserted the military efficacy of sexual desire even after conscription made such incentives redundant. Those few women who have since commented on their recruiting activities remember feeling an anger toward men who appeared to be shirking their duty entirely in keeping with the sentiments expressed in vast sections of the press as well as by scores of patriotic Britons. Caroline Rennles, a young munitions worker during the war, admitted that if she "saw a chap out in the street," she'd say, "Why arn't you in the army?" Indeed, she would taunt her unenlisted male colleagues at Woolwich Arsenal because the sight of them drove her "mad." "I used to call them all white-livered whatsonames I could lay my tongue to."[88] Within a social context in which people displayed extreme hostility toward conscientious objectors, shirkers, and those regarded as cowards, and in which few propagandists shied away from employing women to make these points, the white-feather campaign should not come as an entire surprise, despite the criticism it intermittently provoked.[89]

Like the passion among civilians for souvenirs, relics, and news from the front, women's inability to fight seemed to find compensation in a desire to make men fight and to possess and love a man who had been to the front. John Graham remembered an imprisoned conscientious objector whose wife refused to visit him but instead wrote letters of reproach because of his failure to enlist.[90] And Ronald W. Crawley recalls receiving daily white feathers from his firm's female typist. Though Crawley was underage he "finally got fed up" and joined the army "going out to the terrible battle of the Somme within 6 months."[91] The spirit of such harassment is summed up in a poem called "Fall In!" by Harold Begbie. Sent by a girl named Phyllis to her friend Walter Bone, the poem asked,

> What will you lack, sonny, what will you lack
>   When the girls line up the street,
> Shouting their love to the lads come back
>   From the Foe they rushed to beat?
> Will you send a strangled cheer to the sky
>   And grin till your cheeks are red?
> But what will you lack when your mate goes by
>   With a girl who cuts you dead? . . . [92]

To this vision of emasculation and "lack," Phyllis asked Walter what he thought of the poem and commented herself that "I think it's fine like all his books."[93] If such comments were the logical outcome of a rhetoric that stressed the patriotic power of feminine censure, they nevertheless had a startling ability to cut two ways.[94]

White Feathers and Wounded Men

For men resentful of the paradigm of courage and cowardice manifested in the marked distinction between the man in uniform and the supposed coward in mufti, masculinity was more than a series of external symbols; it was part of the essence of a man who had served or been willing to serve as a soldier or officer at the front. Women's reading of the signs of manhood relied on that external emblem of courage—the military uniform. Though exemption badges, medical certificates, and armbands were meant to protect exempted civilians from feminine taunts, men frequently complained that these signs of good will were invisible to those patriotic women whose only measure of a man was the fabric of his clothes.[95] Not only did women sometimes mistake "starred" men for "shirkers," but in incidents that caused still more outrage, they inadvertently bestowed their tokens of shame upon wounded men recuperating in civilian dress—a mistake that may have occurred as late as 1918.[96]

The ironic contrast between the authentic bravery of men who fought and women's sartorial reading of male courage thus fills narrative accounts of the white feather campaign, endowing this descriptive medium with rich retributive possibilities. "A gallant young officer was recently decorated with the V.C. by the King at Buckingham Palace," recounted Michael MacDonagh in his war diary. "Later on the same day he changed into mufti and was sitting smoking a cigarette in Hyde Park when girls came up to him and jeeringly handed him a white feather. He accepted the feather without a word and . . . put it with his V.C. It is said he remarked to a friend that he was probably the only man who ever received on the same day the two outstanding emblems of bravery and cowardice—the V.C. and the white feather. Within a week he had returned to the front and made the Great Sacrifice."[97] In stories like MacDonagh's, women recruiters not only miss the signs of masculine prowess—an exemption badge, a stump, or a wound—but in the most famous emblem of their wrongheaded activities they are unable even to distinguish courage from cowardice, the very feminine discrimination upon which the eugenic health of the nation was supposed to depend. The official symbol of courage is bestowed by the king at the palace, while the feminine symbol of cowardice is bestowed by a group of girls in the park; they are both orders, and the presentation of one mocks the bestowal of the other. Recounting the tale thus avenges the gesture as the shame cast upon the soldier is thrown back upon the women who are narratively and morally hoist on their own petard.

As women used the uniform to identify the soldierly spirit and manly will inherent in every British Tommy, soldiers, military rejects, and conscientious objectors all began instead to assert personal suffering as the locus of true manhood. The language of the khaki uniform thus became highly ironic. As women, intoxicated with that enthusiasm for soldiers known as "khaki fever," saw in the glamour of the uniform the mark of a true soldier, men home from the front regarded this superficial remnant as only a vulgar symbol of the signs of manhood written on the body. P. C. S. Vince of Surrey remembered the vast discrepancy between the external emblems of military service and the hidden wounds of battle to which civilians, particularly women, seemed almost incomprehensibly blind. Vince was wounded on April 24, 1917, and was given a white feather while waiting to be admitted to Roehampton hospital to be fitted for an artificial leg. "Having on my overcoat and my stump covered up, I did no more but stand up on my good leg and put my stump right into her face, and her reaction was awful and she did no more than flew off the tram."[98]

While women read manhood in terms of the wearing of a uniform, accounts like Vince's spoke of brave soldiers, wounded men, and recipients of the Victoria Cross whom women mistakenly branded as cowards because they were out of uniform. Yet as men noted, if a uniform could be taken off the wounds of battle could not. These hidden scars—clothed and covered in the romance of a uniform or the ignominious attire of civilian clothes—were the indelible marks of manhood etched deeply into the bodies and consciousness of those who fought. In stories like these the uniform becomes to the body what language is to meaning—an inadequate approximation of a vast complex of suffering that women, irretrievably fixated by surfaces, fabrics, and colors, could never comprehend. Emblematic of the civilian lack of understanding for what lay beneath the khaki uniform, the actions of women became a narrative medium with which to eloquently display men's hidden suffering. As Reuben W. Farrow recalled in an almost metaphoric event, "a woman scornfully asked a young man in a tram car 'why are *you* shirking your duty?' He quietly withdrew from his pocket a handless stump and showed it to her! In confusion she tried to apologize—and quickly left the car."[99] In this incident and others like it, the silent response of the Tommy hints at the idea that the scarred body itself was simply a physical sign of the even deeper scars that could only be understood by those who knew the horrors of the front.[100] If a man's clothes seemed to hide the meaning of battle written on his body, the body itself could show only an approximation of what he had been through as a soldier—a point made with particular force by Roderick Nicholson and a fellow veteran of Gallipoli who, accosted by two white feather women, "unscrewed their dummy hands" and threw them into the women's shopping baskets.[101]

For those men who remembered the white-feather campaign, however, hidden wounds were not just soldiers' wounds but included also the psychological scars receiving a white feather left upon many men who did not wish to fight. The advent of the white-feather women thus appeared to MacDonagh to be "almost as terrible to the young male who has no stomach for fighting as an enemy army with banners—and guns. At the sight of them he is glad of the chance of being able to hide anyhow his diminished head."[102] In this rhetorical turn, the emotional wounds inflicted by women at home mimic the physical wounds inflicted by the enemy in battle. Although MacDonagh is speaking figuratively, such metaphorical language took a quite literal form in the recollections of many men who survived the war.

Veteran G. Backhaus told the BBC the story of two friends of his who received white feathers claiming that, "Unfortunately both the men I know who suffered that terrible [fate] died because of it."[103] Relating the story of how his underage cousin had enlisted as a result of female taunts and was "blew to pieces" and how an overage friend of his "died of madness" as a direct consequence of these insults, Backhaus makes it clear that women, rather than the enemy, were responsible for these tragic deaths. As Backhaus concludes, in terms reminiscent of those used to describe death in the trenches, "the look in his eye has haunted me ever since. . . . The cruelty of that white feather business needs exposing."[104]

Backhaus's impression is not exceptional. Ernest Barnby also believed that such a gesture resulted in the premature loss of his brother who, in spite of his Derby armband, "was presented with a white feather by some scatty female and as a result was seized by a depression which developed into tuberculosis which killed him."[105] And Granville Bradshaw bitterly claimed that his friend Basil Hallam, who was famous for his song "Gilbert the Filbert the Colonel of the Nuts," was de facto killed by white feather women. According to Bradshaw, the two men were walking down Shaftesbury Avenue after Hallam's show when "we were both surrounded by young, stupid, and screaming girls who stuck white feathers into the lapels of our coats. When we extricated ourselves Basil said 'I shall go and join-up immediately' . . . I heard a few weeks later that my friend Basil Hallam had joined the paratroops and in his first decent with a parachute it failed to open. He was killed and he died during the afternoon."[106] In these accounts, the emasculating attacks of women on the domestic front are comparable to the eviscerating assault of the enemy in battle. Insofar as the fear of one prompted men to brave the other, women and the enemy in some sense become one.

As the cultural landscape encompassing the white feather campaign was gradually overshadowed by the seriousness of the war, public officials, returning soldiers, and a variety of other responsible citizens increasingly saw this feminine affront as an outrageous disruption of public order rather than as an even marginally legitimate means of coaxing men to the colors. In 1915 Cathcart Wason, MP, warned the Home Secretary that state employees were being "subjected to insolence and provocation at the hands of some advertising young women presenting them with white feathers" and inquired whether he would authorize the arrest of "such persons" for "acting in a manner likely to create a breach of the peace."[107] While the Home Secretary dismissed this request, its lavish rhetoric suggests a sense of outrage that would only continue to grow as the war progressed. By 1916 changes in recruiting had distanced white feather giving from what rationale it once possessed. Not only would passage of the National Service Bill end official recruiting appeals, but rising casualties and the induction of large numbers of men into the army meant that women who continued to upbraid men out of uniform did so without official sanction and at increasing risk of making mistakes.

While formal recruiting appeals would end with conscription, however, public hostility toward unenlisted men in no way subsided. The press singled out conscientious objectors and pacifists for special attack, while the practice of white feather giving continued intermittently into 1918, nourished by an increasingly bitter atmosphere of suspicion towards those apparently unwilling to "do their bit."[108] Despite this widely shared contempt for unenlisted men, however, the practice of shaming cowards might have had a more gender-specific fascination as well. Commenting on the psychological legacy of white-feather-giving, Virginia Woolf noted that "External observation would suggest that a man still feels it a peculiar insult to be taunted with cowardice by a woman in much the same way that a woman feels it a peculiar insult to be taunted with unchastity by a man."[109] If, as Woolf suggests, the practice of shaming a man should be understood as the moral equivalent of such sexual harassment, the war might have offered a rare retaliatory opportunity to women who wished to thrust back upon men a taunt equivalent to ones they had experienced themselves.[110]

The thrill and risk involved with committing this transgressive act might also have beckoned some of its practitioners. Often associated with the ultra-nationalist followers of Mrs. Pankhurst, white-feather-giving may possibly have offered some of the same gratifications as suffragette militancy. Like suffrage violence, white-feather-giving allowed women to discard the restrictions imposed by Victorian sex roles. As suffragette Margaret Haig recalled, "for me, and for many other young women like me, militant suffrage was the very salt of life. . . . It gave us release of energy, it gave us that sense of being of some use in the scheme of things. . . . It gave us scope . . . , and it gave us what normal healthy youth craves— adventure and excitement."[111] While this link is purely speculative, the aspect of thrill-seeking, the romantic allure of undertaking a "just" act at the risk of personal injury, and the longing to hurl back upon men the sort of deprecating public taunts that women had long experienced when walk-

ing out unaccompanied may all have contributed to this remarkable manifestation of female patriotism. While many contemporaries noted that
this practice was by no means universal and that women were often as indignant about it as men, the white feather gave its practitioners a rare
power over their victims and underscored the fact that sex alone was an
inadequate marker of manhood, morality, or citizenship—points not so
different from those pressed by conscriptionists, feminists, and others
with increasing vigor as the war dragged on.

CHAPTER FIVE

CONSCRIPTION, CONSCIENCE, AND THE TRAVAILS OF MALE CITIZENSHIP

On October 12, 1915, Edith Cavell, a British nurse tending Allied and German wounded in Brussels, was executed before a German firing squad for smuggling Allied prisoners into neutral Holland. According to accounts of her death, the execution was particularly shocking. The firing squad allegedly missed their mark when Miss Cavell fainted and the execution was carried out by a German officer who shot several rounds from his revolver into her prostrate body.[1] Brand Whitlock, the American ambassador to Belgium, pleaded in vain for clemency and only a few hours before her execution the Spanish ambassador, the Marquis de Villalobar, implored the Germans to commute the sentence, exclaiming: "Oh, come now! It's a woman. You can't shoot a woman like that."[2] These heart-rending and futile efforts made the enemy's merciless sentence appear even more revolting. As Herr Zimmermann, the kaiser's undersecretary for foreign affairs put it, "I know no law in the world which makes distinction between the sexes."[3] The Germans refused even to surrender Cavell's body, which was purportedly (and in retrospect rather appropriately) buried in Brussels wrapped only in newspaper.[4]

Although Cavell was undoubtedly guilty, the press dwelt little on this fact. Cavell's sex, her occupation, and her exemplary reputation as a clergyman's daughter carrying out humanitarian duties in a foreign country charged the event with an emotional impact carried by few other incidents. Her memorial service drew hundreds of grieving nurses to St. Paul's Cathedral, where she was honored by the prime minister and the Queen Mother and commended for her bravery in the line of duty.[5] The murder of Edith Cavell had become a national symbol—but a symbol that worked in more ways than one.

The execution of Edith Cavell was immediately seized upon as a graphic demonstration of the need for more recruits. Echoing Edmund Burke's homage to Marie Antoinette, the vicar of St. Paul's declared that "if ever a challenge rang out to the chivalry of our young men . . . it is surely to be heard in the dastardly execution of an Englishwoman at the hands of an enemy. . . . By this crowning tragedy of cowardice, the enemy has murdered not only a woman in cold blood, they have also murdered chivalry. So far as the nation is concerned, what will be the answer of those 'nearly two million of unmarried men' who could enlist without disaster to the munitions supply . . . ? If chivalry and manhood are not extinct in them they will mark their answers as one man."[6]

If the murder of Edith Cavell became the quintessential symbol of Germany's violation of womanhood, however, her courage in the line of duty also made her an example to the young manhood of the country. As Asquith marveled during a parliamentary debate over National Service, "What year in history had done more to justify our faith in the manhood and womanhood of our people? It has brought us . . . the imperishable story of the last hours of Edith Cavell facing a worse ordeal than the battlefield. . . . She has taught the bravest man amongst us a supreme lesson of courage."[7] A wreath in her honor was laid at the foot of Nelson's column and, as one observer wrote, "the seamen and officers who had died . . . [at Trafalgar] welcomed her, as it seemed, to their company."[8] Recruiting meetings were held around the base of Nelson's column in full view of Cavell's wreath. In her native village in Norfolk every eligible young man allegedly joined the next day, and her image became a staple of recruiting rhetoric during the remainder of the voluntary effort.[9] That effort, however, was not to last long.

Indeed, the murder of Edith Cavell is just the most potent reminder of how the rhetoric of voluntary recruiting ultimately played into its own demise. If, on one hand, the challenge of Cavell's execution "rang out to our young men of military age not yet enlisted," what would happen if they should fail to heed this call? And what of those men whose sense of chivalry and honor was not sufficient to cause them to obey the "voice from the grave—the voice of Nurse Edith Cavell" as one man?[10]

MANLY DUTY AND THE
PARADOX OF FREE WILL

The execution of Edith Cavell took place during Britain's deepening re-cruiting crisis. Despite the growing call for "military preparedness" among Conservatives before the war, Asquith's Liberal government maintained a strong aversion to the sort of intrusive and potentially unpopular mea-sures that would have been necessary to raise and finance a large con-scripted army.[11] While the enthusiastic enlistment of thousands of young men at the outbreak of hostilities allowed the Liberal administration to proclaim voluntarism a success, this complacency began to change during the second year of the war. Not only did mounting casualties begin to take their toll on the British forces, but most localities in the United Kingdom had, by mid-1915, exhausted their supplies of young men willing to sign up voluntarily for foreign service.[12] Increasingly embarrassing advertise-ments directed at hesitant young "slackers" along with aggressive calls for conscription in the Northcliffe press began to revive debate over this con-troversial subject.[13] In May, anxiety over supplying the army with recruits and a serious munitions shortage, which seemed to be crippling the fight-ing capacity of the military, forced Asquith to form a coalition govern-ment to deal with the worsening crisis. The inclusion of conscriptionists in the new cabinet and Lloyd George's conversion to the cause of manda-tory National Service as the new Minister of Munitions put the issue of compulsion back onto the agenda of national politics.

While conscriptionists argued that mandatory military service was es-sential to fostering both national defense and a sense of civic responsibil-ity, defenders of voluntarism feared that to impose conscription would destroy national unity and provoke labor protests. In early September the Trades Unions Congress had come out strongly against conscription, and during the parliamentary debates over National Service, Irish members had assured the government that such a measure would meet "determined and deadly" opposition in Ireland.[14] Liberals hoped to avoid such divisive-ness by appealing to a set of transcendent common values, including the sanctity of family, nation, and manly honor, to inspire all eligible Britons to take up arms voluntarily. Recruiters could then enforce through moral awakening what many Conservatives believed could only be achieved by physical force—a large, efficient, and morally regenerate continental army. As long as Liberals held political power and voluntarism remained the law, conscriptionists had little choice but to join hands with their former an-tagonists and rely upon the forces of persuasion to raise Britain's armies.

As one Conservative confided to his diary, "going on tour with little-navyites, traducers of the Army and peace-at-any price men to raise recruits and explain the war to the people" seemed rather anomalous; yet, as he accurately declared, "we have certainly done it whole-heatedly."[15]

What is ironic about the language of voluntary recruiting, however, is that during the war the very terms required to defend this liberty would ultimately contribute to the rationale for its abandonment. To those who rejected the idea of conscription, the difference between a volunteer and a conscript army was the moral superiority of the volunteer himself. When asked by his disgruntled employer why he did not support conscription, the Reverend A. B. Maitland explained that "The only single men who could be excused are those with married men's responsibilities, the rest are either cowards or ghouls and therefore no good to either a conscript or a voluntary system."[16] Arthur Conan Doyle agreed with this prognosis, declaring "shame, shame, shame on the man who fails his country in her hour of need! I could not think that the service of such a man was of any avail. Let the country be served by free men, and let them deal with the coward or sluggard who flinches."[17] Conscriptionists, of course, had nothing but contempt for the much quoted idea that "one volunteer is worth three pressed men." "The Voluntarists seem to forget that all law and Government rests ultimately upon force," noted Ellis J. Griffith of Anglesey. "No one has yet suggested that voluntarism should apply to taxation, or that one gladly offered sovereign is more efficacious to meet the public expenditure than three conscript sovereigns. . . ."[18] Yet the moral issues that surrounded voluntarism remained crucial to the libertarian case.

In choosing to enlist, the volunteer, according to contemporary theorists, had gone through an inner transformation, one that enlightened him to the duties of citizenship and grounded his defense of the nation in moral conviction rather than physical force. According to the Liberal journal the *Nation*, an organ that stood at the forefront of the intellectual defense of voluntarism, "The full reality of anything beyond the daily round of private life is grasped with an effort . . . but when it is grasped, the most limited of average men has stepped beyond himself and won a moral and intellectual advance. It is this same process which the speeches and advertisements and posters are daily conducting to fill the ranks of our voluntary army. . . . [T]he process itself, so far from being objectionable, is the normal process, and ultimately the only defensible process, by which the citizen can be led to do his duty as a member of society."[19]

To the authors of this apologia, voluntary recruiting not only uplifted the individual but validated the cause. "'Moral compulsion,' means the raising of a free army, which has been educated to give the best of its manhood to a cause which deserves its sacrifices. Physical compulsion would embody the same men without an understanding of the cause, and it might be used with equal success for any cause, however debased. . . . We cling to [voluntarism] both for its impotence to do evil and its power to do good."[20]

Liberal faith in the difference between a volunteer and a conscript army was so profound that on the eve of conscription the government worried that the men in the trenches would not accept their conscripted colleagues. In a speech delivered to introduce the Derby plan, Asquith pointed out that, "in existing circumstances the status of a compelled man in the field will be anything but pleasant. . . . [A] mark will certainly be placed against the compelled man by the man who went freely. Nor will the matter stop here. Throughout all time a distinction will be drawn between the men of whom it will be said that they needed no legal spur to make them do their duty, and the men who did not come forward till they were actually obliged." [21] Although Asquith's ominous predictions were clearly evoked for rhetorical effect in a final attempt to elicit voluntary recruits, these concerns were taken seriously enough to be considered by the government while it debated the implications of conscription. In a cabinet document entitled "Can Compulsory Be Combined With Voluntary Service?," Lord Curzon presented the "views of some hundreds of soldiers of all ranks, from Generals to N.C.O's and men" on the question of whether "the men who had volunteered would despise and ostracize those who might join under compulsion."[22] The response of a brigadier-general commanding an infantry brigade is typical: "My own opinion is that the British soldier, New Army, Regular, or Territorial, will have no great feelings about how a man is produced for the 'front,' as long as he is produced."[23] Yet for many defenders of voluntarism, particularly early on in the war, getting men to the front was only one goal of voluntary recruiting.

Both Liberals and Conservatives agreed that men's willingness to fight for their country was a sign of the moral quality of the individual and the nation. Where they differed markedly, however, was in the initial reluctance of many Liberals to resort to force, should persuasion break down. This attachment to free will was, of course, not limited to Liberals alone. Not only did organized labor strongly oppose compulsion of any sort, but even Conservatives were inclined to share a more general belief in the moral superiority of the man who voluntarily chose to serve. The Unionist Arthur Steel Maitland, for example, continually insisted to his colleagues on the Parliamentary Recruiting Committee that an "inquisitorial" canvass should be avoided, objecting that it might put undue pressure on men to enlist.[24] While this might seem an odd reservation for the most prominent Unionist representative of the county's official recruiting body, Maitland's squeamishness about the use of coercion in recruiting made sense within a broadly liberal paradigm that regarded free will as central to the constitution of a patriotic and moral citizenry. Not only did Britain distinguish its own political culture from that of Germany, where a conscripted army symbolized the lack of freedom of the German people, but a surprising number of leaders from both parties believed that Britain's moral superiority could be read in its recruiting numbers. As the Unionist leader Andrew Bonar Law insisted in December 1914, the voluntary system "has not failed here. We have got so far, and I am sure we shall get, all the men we need."[25]

What might explain this bipartisan confluence of opinion early on in the war is the fact that many recruiting enthusiasts defended voluntary recruiting not because it preserved personal freedom but because it was a symbolic act of citizenship, emblematic of an inner transformation far more significant that merely joining the army. To the bishop of Northampton, "The breakdown of the voluntary system would mean the British Empire's proudest boast was false and unfounded."[26] The Liberal MP G. N. Barnes passionately agreed: "I refuse to believe that voluntaryism is going to fail us, because to believe that would be almost tantamount to believing in the moral bankruptcy of the nation."[27] And the highly patriotic *Standard Recruiter* explained to those soliciting volunteers that "What we really aim at is awakening . . . the young men of Britain . . . to a properly informed sense of their obligations, responsibilities, and duties, as well as privileges as citizens. . . . Make a citizen today, and, if he be eligible, you have a recruit. In a hundred ways I have found the work lies in making citizens."[28]

This idea of "making citizens" was crucial to the conceptualization of a volunteer army. What voluntary recruiting did that conscription could not do was to act as a mark of inner conversion, signifying the loyal sentiments of those who had joined and assuring observers that external actions were accompanied by inner transformation. It was these sentiments that lay behind an elaborate campaign to distribute khaki armbands to those rejected for military service. In order to distinguish men refused on medical grounds from those who had not volunteered at all, observers believed that the government ought to offer an outward sign to those denied the right to serve through no fault of their own.[29] While armbands were meant to protect the medically unfit from civilian harassment, their more ominous purpose was to place ever more pressure on those who wilfully refused to go. As Headley Le Bas explained, "take two men standing behind a shop counter, one may have been rejected as medically unfit, the other may be as sound as a bell and shirking serving his country, but how is it possible to tell the difference between the two?"[30] Le Bas, whose advertising agency was charged with much government recruiting work, saw the plan as an invaluable aid to enlistment: "If the man who is unfit was wearing the armlet the other man would have to enlist, public opinion would compel him to do so."[31] The *Recruiting Times* fully concurred: the armlets would "supply an unmistakable sign by which the willing can be picked out from the unwilling. The young man who has offered his services, possibly repeatedly, but in vain, will be able to show that it is no fault of his that he is not in the ranks. The 'slacker' and the shirker will be marked."[32]

What the armlet campaign reveals is that demarking the willing from the unwilling had become a moral issue of central importance. To Lord Northcliffe, owner of the *Times* and the *Daily Mail*, armbands promised to prevent the "gross injustice that is inflicted on such people as . . . my chauffeur Pine, who is an ex-soldier, lamed for life . . . [by] a cannon ball" but who was "loudly abused by a company of soldiers" for being unenlisted.[33] The logic of the campaign suggested that as long as a man had put himself at the disposal of the government, that man, though rejected, invalided out of service, or placed in non-combatant work, deserved to be free of harassment on the home front. Yet it also had a more sinister side. Although the purported rationale for the armband campaign was to protect men like Northcliffe's chauffeur Pine, it also implied that those who refused to serve deserved to weather the full brunt of public opinion. A man who failed to serve was no longer simply exercising the freedom of choice guaranteed under a liberal regime, but risked encountering an angry citizenry that would "make his life a burden" until he agreed to enlist. Under these circumstances, it is understandable why even the pacifist Independent Labour Party declared compulsion to be preferable to "the general hunting and harrying of young men now taking place."[34] For although British men had a legal right not to volunteer, military service was increasingly becoming the litmus test of loyalty, citizenship, and manhood itself.

Although Liberals had once championed diversity of thought, the danger of conscription was precisely its inability to guarantee anything but the bodily compliance of the man produced to serve. In a nation obsessed by a fear of spies and "the enemy within," signing up became the only symbolic act that could mark the will of the inner man.[35] It was in this moral and transformative capacity, rather than in the idea of a right to choose, that many Liberals eventually defended the principle of voluntarism. As the *Nation* argued in its defense of "moral compulsion," the "dullest and least imaginative man who has in the long run responded to the broad appeals of a poster, or even the rough taunts of his fellows, has performed a moral action. . . . He has consciously said to himself that it is better to face the bullets than to be justly branded as coward or a 'slacker.' He has in the end seen, however slowly or stupidly or reluctantly, that he has a duty. . . . The man who is literally compelled is, . . . in so far as he merely obeys compulsion, no man at all, but an organism which performs certain physical acts under physical pressure. The genuine conscript . . . marches in the ranks precisely as the requisitioned horse trots in the commissarial train."[36]

The Liberal stake in voluntary recruiting, however, was political as well as moral. The early months of the war became a crucible in which to test the efficiency of the Liberal government in a time of crisis. Enlistment was read as a sign that men had grasped the issues of the war and as a validation of the principles that the Liberal government stood for. If voluntarism worked, Liberalism would have passed a crucial test in its own eyes and in the eyes of conscriptionists.[37] With the moral authority of the government at stake, the terms that recruiting authorities were willing to use to educate the democracy began to expand.

Imperatives of Gender

Exploiting the gendered images circulating in the press and popular rumor, both the defenders and opponents of voluntarism drew increasingly upon a propaganda campaign that would tolerate no argument. "The causes of the war are only of moment to us, at this stage, in that we gain more strength in our arms and more iron in our souls by a knowledge that it is for all that is honourable and sacred for which we fight," argued Arthur Conan Doyle. "It is not words and phrases that we need, but men, men—and always more men. If words can bring the men then they are of avail. . . ."[38] The nature of these "causes" and the meaning of these "words" was evident to anyone who could read the tales of atrocities that saturated the news. Embodying this idea, the Parliamentary Recruiting Committee asked the women of Britain if they understood "that for every man who is kept back from service now, there is so much the greater danger of our homes being burned and laid waste? Let the women think of what has happened in Belgium. Towns and villages have been destroyed by fire and sword, women and children outraged and killed, mothers separated from their children, and wives from their husbands, not knowing whether they are dead or alive. . . ."[39]

By defining men's deepest familial commitments as the very concerns that lay at the heart of the war, anti-conscriptionists hoped to vindicate the voluntary system and win a symbolic triumph for Liberal military policy over the foreboding premonitions of Tory conscriptionists. As long as voluntary recruiting was the sole legal method of obtaining men, patriotic Conservatives had little choice but to go along with this campaign and contributed rhetorically, morally, and artistically to a form of recruiting that depended on internal motivation rather than physical force for its success. The gendered campaign, however, cut both ways since it delegitimated any refusal to serve in the eyes of voluntarists and conscriptionists alike. As Arthur Kitson would later declare in a scathing denunciation of conscientious objectors aimed at British labor, "*THE HUNS* are fighting to enslave the world! . . . They intend to make *your daughters* their harlots, as they have already made the young women and girls of the invaded districts of France and Belgium!" Excoriating the cowardice of men who had refused to serve and drawing on the authority of the Bryce Report, Kitson reminded British workmen that the Germans "believe in crucifying women, in raping young girls to death, in hacking off babies' limbs, and impaling them on their lances . . . in inoculating disease into the blood of POWs, in pouring oil over old men and women and setting them on fire, in raping mothers in the presence of their children, and daughters in the presence of their mothers, and innumerable horrors too filthy to publish!"[40]

If presenting the war as a crusade fought on behalf of women and children was meant to obviate the need for compulsion, it also presented a moral imperative that, if ignored, implicitly justified the raising of an army by any means possible. As the bishop of London declared on Germany's highly publicized execution of Edith Cavell, "this will settle the matter, once for all, about recruiting in Great Britain. . . . There will be no need now of compulsion."[41] The bishop's mock advocacy of voluntarism implied that avenging this brutal death was the only conceivable moral choice a man could make. The idea that there would be "no need now of compulsion" was based not on a validation of free will but on the assumption that any man worth the name would be so revolted by this crime against English womanhood that he would voluntarily enlist.[42]

The bishop of London was not alone in the use of such reasoning, though similar logic could lead to quite different conclusions about the need for compulsion. Writing to the mother of a dead comrade, Sergeant Major Healy of the Royal Fusiliers commented that, "Nobody is more sorry than myself to see conscription come into vogue for I appreciate to the full the value of a voluntary system and understand fully that it has been a thing for a Britisher to rightfully boast about." He nevertheless concluded that "if the men will not come forward of their own accord, then, we must put sentimentality in the background and make them do their bit. I have, like thousands more seen some very horrible and revolting sights in France and Belgium and when I was on leave, I was disgusted to note how little thousands of young men, or at least, men of military age, appreciated the danger of our not defeating the Hun. . . . I feel our position pretty keenly and as I am a married man and have children, I know to the full, what to expect, should the devils get into England."[43] Although Major Healy went on to comment on the unlikelihood of such an event, the mere specter of an attack upon the family seemed to justify the abandonment of free choice and to render incontestable the claim upon men of military age. As a prominent Scottish Liberal lamented in December 1914, "I meet many good Liberals in Midlothian and elsewhere who are prone to take the view that we pacifists made a mistake and the Jingos were right all along."[44] And W. Llewelyn Williams, a vociferous anti-conscriptionist, could not help angrily observing in February 1916 how many Liberals had abandoned voluntarism in order to follow those MPs "clad in the irresistible khaki garb" and vote for conscription.[45] This defection is far less surprising, however, when we examine the degree to which the language of voluntarism had lost its libertarian core.

The contrast between Maitland's desire to avoid all undue pressure, and the tactics advocated by the *Nation* in its support of "moral compulsion" reveal how much anti-conscriptionists had conceded in their advocacy of a man's choice. The faith Liberals had placed in free choice meshed poorly with the system of absolute values fostered by the war. According to the *Nation*, the central principle of Liberalism was that public opinion itself would gravitate toward the general good with better instinct than any system that depended upon dictation from above. But once the public good became a matter of general agreement among those in power, "public opinion" was no longer a moralizing force but only a symbol of public concurrence with official doctrine. As "an independent liberal" explained in an anonymous biography justifying Lloyd George's conversion to conscription,

> Mr. Asquith and Mr. Balfour held strongly that we ought, as long as possible, to stand by the voluntary principle, not only because of its moral grandeur and the sublime spectacle that was offered to the world in the spontaneous free-will offering of British manhood on the altar of patriotism, but also because it was in harmony with our traditions and spirit as a nation and gave promise of meeting our needs. . . . Mr. Lloyd George, on the other hand, while admitting what voluntarism had done, felt strongly that the system was most unfair in its incidence.[46]

In the idea of the "moral grandeur" and the "sublime spectacle" of free will, it is clear that voluntarism had become an aesthetic principle rather than an avenue of real choice. In Lloyd George's reservations—and in Asquith and Balfour's tacit concurrence with the stipulation that voluntarism should be used "as long as possible"—it becomes clear that many politicians had come to favor voluntarism only so long as it did not include the right to decline to serve in the army. To choose to serve was a splendid and noble thing, but the choice not to serve would be met with force. As one advocate of voluntarism inauspiciously explained, "The voluntary system does not mean liberty to give or to withhold service. . . . Its success depends upon the universal recognition of a universal duty."[47] And Asquith himself pointedly reminded men in 1915 that "If they do not come voluntarily, they will be fetched, or rather, they will not be fetched in Lord Derby's mild and pleasant way, but by the stern methods of legal as opposed to moral compulsion."[48]

The gradual turning away from voluntarism during the second year of the war was primarily a move of expedition by the leaders of a country engaged in a war of attrition. The theorization of a temporary relinquishment of rights in order ever after to preserve rights meshed well with the fear of a totalitarian Germany bent upon conquest. Yet, as we shall see, this intellectual move would have subtle implications for the meaning of citizenship. With the re-theorization of liberty as a principle that could be defended in the abstract even as individual rights were eroded, it became clear that many Liberals had lost faith in the inner man. As J. A. Hobson gravely commented, "Liberty" had become a "war economy," and conscription itself was no less than "a rude formal withdrawal" of the government's "faith" in its citizenry.[49]

The rather unconvincing insistence that voluntarism was "working," like the *Nation*'s defense of "moral compulsion," implied that the validation of voluntarism would come only from its ability to put an army in the field. Repeatedly, defenders of voluntarism in the press and in Parliament concede that they would be willing to resort to conscription were there no other way to win the war.[50] Indeed, pacifists alone seemed to have a consistent stance from which to argue against conscription and they would pay dearly for their beliefs.[51]

THE BURDENS OF CONSCIENCE

The gendered discourse of war justification and the notion of patriotic masculinity that it validated undermined public faith in the power of the individual to make a judgment at once legitimate, moral, and pacific, greatly facilitating the passage of the Military Service Act in January 1916. Although conscientious objection remained a legal ground for non-enlistment even after the enactment of conscription, the actual treatment of conscientious objectors, many of whom were jailed for their beliefs, shows the degree to which the majority of Britons had lost faith in the idea of a moral code whose dictates lay outside the interests of the war.[52] Indeed, as the burdens of conscience shifted from the individual to the state, this illusive moral indicator received increasingly bad press. Not only had conscientious objectors "incurred the odium of all public spirited people," but a series of speakers in Manchester captured the attitude of many Britons when they declared that conscience was "rot," "a synonym for self-ishness," and "a cowardly refuge for shirkers."[53] J. A. Seddon claimed to represent the sentiments of workingmen when he argued that "we trades unionists regard the conscientious objectors as national blacklegs."[54] And Lord Derby showed a similar lack of faith in individual conscience when he attempted to sell the tribunal system by arguing that it would allow a man to rely "not on his own conscience but on a tribunal to decide his best course in view of his personal responsibilities."[55]

Asquith's heavily moral rhetoric at the outbreak of the conflict and the validation of the war in terms of crimes against women and the family claimed for the war a discursive space that encompassed all manifestations of moral sentiment.[56] While those involved in the voluntary recruiting campaign drew upon these images to make their case, many Liberals began to accept the idea that military service was the legitimate basis for mascu-line citizenship—even as they insisted that such service must be freely given. "I lately wrote to three papers suggesting that the vote should in fu-ture be limited to those who have shown themselves ready to fight," wrote one advocate of voluntarism. "Though . . . he who wants a chance to help rule must be ready to fight," he added comfortingly, such a plan "also al-lows the man who doesn't want to help to rule to refuse to fight."[57] These ideas were, of course, far more frequently endorsed by Conservatives, but the habits of mind that made such utterances possible were shared by a wide variety of patriots, deeply undermining the position of those men with strong (and legal) objections to performing military service.[58]

As voluntary recruiting began to break down—due initially to a reset-ting of the physical standards for enlistment by the War Office—those who attempted to operate the voluntary system began to lose faith in the educability of the potential recruit and his ability to arrive at the single correct decision regarding his life. Not only did Arthur Henderson, the leader of the Labour Party, come out in support of conscription, but in August the government began to compile a National Register to survey every man and woman in the country between the ages of sixteen and sixty-five in order to ascertain his or her willingness and ability to per-form national service. To the horror of the nation, the Register revealed two million eligible young men in non-essential industries who had not yet enlisted.[59] Although the government denied that the register was a prelude to conscription, evading it was a criminal act and the information it provided proved highly useful both to Derby canvassers and later to conscription authorities. Named for the conscriptionist earl of Derby, who was appointed Director General of Recruiting in October 1915, the

Derby scheme used thousands of volunteers, working off the National Register, to canvass virtually every eligible young man in the nation. Under the Derby scheme recruiting began to pick up considerably, but Derby's successes were deceptive. Many of the men who attested under the Derby plan were married men who, noting an earlier "pledge" by Asquith to induct all single men before married men would be called up, hoped that they could delay their call-ups by agreeing to serve when needed. Indeed, Asquith's "pledge" probably sent more men to the registry office than to the recruiting office, and despite Derby's successes the voluntary method offered little hope for raising the seventy divisions Kitchener requested at the end of 1915.[60]

Furthermore, Derby canvassers soon discovered a reservoir of unwilling bachelors who, as Asquith put it, preferred to be "dragged by the scruff of their necks," than to enlist voluntarily—despite the alleged odium that was to fall upon the conscripted man.[61] To patriotic supporters of the war, whether advocates or critics of conscription, such obstinacy seemed mystifying, particularly in light of the massive campaign that had been undertaken to explain the morality and necessity of the war. As the publicist F. E. Smith testily declared, "The fact that we are committed to this struggle; that the ministers of the crown and both houses of parliament are satisfied that there was no other way for us unless we were prepared to incur the contempt and hatred of the World; the fact that the entire Press of the United Kingdom . . . has told us that we have taken the only course open to men of honour and spirit, ought to be enough to satisfy any Briton."[62]

The libertarian defense of voluntarism on the grounds of personal freedom had little chance in such a context. The *Nation* had evoked the power of public opinion to assure the justice of the war, yet even this bastion of Liberalism labeled those who refused to enlist as "cowards" and "slackers," lacking in imagination. Although the *Nation* lay the right to judge in the hands of the individual, it also maintained a certainty in its own access to the single definition of moral action. The failure of young men to enlist was no longer a demonstration of the public's "impotence to do wrong" but instead became a moment of truth undermining Liberal faith in male conscience and justifying a number of coercive measures designed to enforce the ends of the army and the state.

As a single validating idea—the prosecution of the war—replaced the old Liberal tolerance for difference in the realm of thought, conscience, and action, wartime patriots redrew the boundaries of the political nation. Distinguishing the believer from the non-believer and dictating the characteristics that constituted the true Briton, publicists and politicians defined male citizenship along rigid, patriotic lines. Britain's "two nations" were no longer the rich and the poor, but the proponents of war and the advocates of peace. Once an idealized notion of patriotic masculinity came to define acceptable male behavior, voluntarism lost its practical use. Since the act of enlisting became, at least symbolically, the inceptive moment of citizenship, it was rhetorically impossible to be a young man of military age, a loyal British subject, and unenlisted. This tautology completely undermined the rhetorical basis of voluntary recruiting and abandoned the parliamentary defense of voluntarism to a few principled opponents whose protests went unheeded until the end of the war.[63] While the Labour Party remained technically opposed to conscription, there were ultimately no Labour resignations over the issue which seemed to carry the tacit support of a number of MPs who, like their leader Arthur Henderson, became convinced that there was no other way to supply the army. Furthermore, with the defeat of Lloyd George's draconian proposal to institute "industrial compulsion" to secure Britain's munitions supply, many trade unions were willing to concede the necessity of military conscription. At a large meeting of labor organizations in Birmingham, held in support of the Derby plan, a unanimously carried resolution stated that "Failing a satisfactory response from all classes it will not be possible for trades unionism further to oppose compulsory methods."[64]

By the end of January 1916, the first Military Service Act had passed through Parliament with overwhelming bipartisan support.[65] Despite the sustained opposition of some trade unions, the outrage of virtually all pacifist intellectuals, and Sir John Simon's dramatic resignation from the cabinet, there was surprisingly little protest of the government's unprecedented move to conscription.[66] Indeed, many men and women from all classes had come to believe that the voluntary system was unfair in sacrificing the best and the brightest while leaving the self-interested unscathed. As Coulson Kernahan complained, "It is when some manly, clean-living young fellow, the idol, possibly . . . of a widowed mother, of his own accord comes forward to say that she and he recognize it is his duty to enlist and is enlisted and sent out possibly to his death, while such scoundrels as that I have described, turn with foul language away, to remain in craven safety at home, and probably to play their part in breeding the next generation of English men and English women, that I feel most sick at heart. . . ."[67]

Industrial conscription had been defeated and no attempt was made to apply conscription in Ireland, quelling some of the most serious reservations about National Service. Furthermore, the impact of conscription on troop morale was highly beneficial, since the men at the front could now expect a steady flow of reinforcements. These beneficial results made it increasingly difficult for opponents of conscription to voice their continued opposition without appearing unpatriotic and disloyal. Since the first Military Service Bill applied conscription only to single men, many married men and women saw it as a way to preserve their families rather than as an aggressive assault on their domestic well-being. Once general conscription was instituted in May, the country had already become used to the idea of mandatory call-ups.

Nothing is perhaps more crucial to explaining both the parliamentary consensus and the general public acceptance of conscription than the belief that Britain was fighting a righteous war to defend civilization from an evil foe. In a war defined in such black-and-white terms, the duty of every man to fight for the nation, the family, and civilization itself seemed apparent, delegitimizing any difference of opinion and vilifying those courageous enough to oppose the war or any of the means being adopted to fight it with efficiency. Members of the pacifist ILP were routinely denounced as "white-livered curs," "bloody pro-Germans," "friends of the Kaiser," and "Traitors to our country," while conscientious objectors were subject to physical abuse ranging from imprisonment to lynching.[68] At Lyndhurst, wounded soldiers at the military hospital brutally attacked conscientious objectors, who were "punched and pelted, knocked down and kicked and sneered at by hundreds of soldiers and civilians." According to one survivor, "Two of us . . . were thrown over a bridge into a river, a drop of about 14 feet, and afterwards pelted and knocked down. . . ." Similar incidents occurred elsewhere in the country. At Lyme Regis "a number of women and girls" incited a "riot" against conscientious objectors. "Afterwards the men who had suffered from it were punished for it on the grounds that they had irritated some soldiers. . . ." A similar riot occurred at the Work Centre at Knutsford, "the culmination of growing friction between C.O.s and the hooligans of the town. . . ." According to witnesses, "A crowd occupied the streets around the Centre and knocked down and kicked and broke the heads and tore the clothes and smashed the bicycles" of the conscientious objectors. "Eighteen wounded men were treated that night in the hospital. . . . One policeman told a man lying battered and helpless on the road that he was 'to get into his kennel. . . .'"[69]

The unitary model of acceptable behavior and thought fostered by the war had clearly begun to undermine some of the basic tenets of liberalism itself. While Liberals had initially maintained that it was the freedom of choice that humanized the British cause, many began to believe that if people refused to fight for their liberties they would have to be forced to be free. As Conservatives and Liberals united in the attempt to create a uniform, homogeneous, and civically minded citizenry, the political distinctions so apparent before the war gave way to a new set of salient categories that redrew the boundaries of the political nation around the indisputable bipartisan image of patriotic service and the protection of the home. "It is a splendid reflection on the influence of family life that it is the married men who measure and accept their responsibilities with conspicuous readiness," declared the *Spectator* with admiration. "They have learned that a home is a thing worth fighting for. . . . One is almost tempted to say that these are the men who alone have an indefeasible qualification for a vote; these are the men, however poor their homes may be, who have that 'stake in the country' of which it used to be fashionable for politicians to talk."[70] In this moral context, pacifists and conscientious objectors became national pariahs. Even more than the "slackers" and "shirkers" before them, those who persisted in resisting military service, even after it became legally enforceable, were suspected of disloyalty that would ultimately cost them the vote.

Indeed, to some Britons, conscription itself implied a failure of masculine citizenship. The archbishop of Glasgow insisted that men who had not volunteered would be "disgraced by compulsion," while a contributor to the working-class newspaper read in Salford scolded "shirkers" and reminded them that "In a time of unexampled national danger when the lives of the children, women and your fellow-countrymen are in peril," you have been guided by "cranks and faddists and ignorant, hare-brained chatterers of the peace at any price fantasy."[71]

[Y]ou lost one chance of learning what a vigorous manhood means. . . . In no other country would you be tolerated as you are here. You would be dragged from your holes like rats and held up to the [execration] of an outraged people. . . . [W]e mark our reprobation of your meanness and cowardice by shunning you as creatures without honour or courage and branding you as traitors to the land of your birth, deserving not less, but more ignominy than so many German spies. You have been appealed to . . . graciously, forcibly, beseechingly and you have turned down every entreaty. Now it remains for the State to make you realize what power it possesses to compel you to recognize and discharge the first of all great national duties.[72]

While Liberal and Labour MPs prevailed in amending the Military Service Bill to preserve the highly controversial right of conscientious objectors to present their pleas for exemption to draft tribunals, most ordinary Britons seemed to believe that "conshies" deserved to rot in prison or be shot. As one anti-conscriptionist angrily wrote in 1915, "Conscription and Democracy are . . . twin brother tyrants born together in France in the 1790s. . . . They know in their hearts that the coward or the convinced pacifist will be no use in a fight, but they are angry to see him refuse their will. They cannot make a sheep fight, but they can drill it and put it in uniform and say 'serve it right' if it is killed. . . ."[73] Pacifist meetings were routinely broken up by marauding soldiers, and even working men and women participated in heaping scorn upon those who they believed had disloyally refused to serve.[74] As Robert Roberts remembered it, "the rapidly rising casualty figures, the appearance of thousands of Belgian refugees, the many atrocity stories, together with innumerable letters like the one cited from our local press finally turned simple patriotism into something much more grim and ugly."[75] The patriotic language that denounced unenlisted men and turned the willingness to serve into a litmus test of loyalty and good citizenship would nevertheless have unexpected beneficiaries as well.

In the Trail of the Hun

Broken pledges, treaties torn,
Your first page of war adorn.
We on fouler things must look
Who read further in that book.
Where you made – the deed was fine! –
Women screen your firing-line;
Villages burned down to dust;
Torture, murder, bestial lust,
Filth too foul for printer's ink,
Crimes from which the apes would shrink.
Strange the offerings that you press
On the God of Righteousness!

—BARRY PAIN.

There were many proved instances of Germans using women and children as battle-screens.

1) "In the Trail of the Hun." During the war, the Germans were alleged to have used women and children as human shields to prevent Allied soldiers from firing. The poem in the upper left corner is typical of wartime verse that recorded such events: "Broken pledges, treaties torn,/ Your first page of war adorn./ We on fouler things must look/ Who read further in that book./ Where you made – the deed was fine!–/ Women screen your firing-line;/ Villages burned down to dust;/ Torture, murder, bestial lust,/ Filth too foul for printer's ink,/ Crimes from which the apes would shrink./ Strange the offers that you press/ On the God of Righteousness!" (*War Illustrated* [1915])

2) "Remember Belgium Enlist To-Day" Parliamentary Recruiting Committee (1915). British soldiers were frequently represented as a bulwark protecting the imperiled family. In this poster, the soldier marks a zone of safety toward which woman, child, and baby flee their burning Belgian village. (Imperial War Museum, London Q33161)

3) Edmund J. Sullivan, "The Gentle German." Sullivan's cartoon reflects the rumor that Germans bayoneted Belgian babies. The wings suggest that the impaled child is now heavenbound. (From *The Kaiser's Garland* [1915])

FOR THE GLORY OF IRELAND

BELGIUM

'WILL YOU GO OR MUST I'?

left   4) "*Serve* your Country *or* Wear THIS." The woman in the upstairs window is hanging out a petticoat for unenlisted males to wear in lieu of military uniform. The photograph suggests that working-class women were also capable of putting pressure on men to enlist. (From the *Daily Chronicle*'s weekly periodical, the *War Budget*)

above   5) "For the GLORY of IRELAND 'WILL YOU GO or MUST I'?" Irish Recruiting (1914). (Imperial War Museum, London Q80367)

6) British sailor bids farewell to his family. (Courtesy Hulton/Archive)

7) "GO! It's Your Duty Lad Join Today" [1914]. This recruiting poster depicts a patriotic mother admonishing her civilian son to join up. (Imperial War Museum, London Q70864)

8) E. V. Kealey, "Women of Britain Say—*GO!*" Parliamentary Recruiting Committee (1915). (Imperial War Museum, London Q46428)

9) Saville Lumley, "Daddy, what did *YOU* do in the Great War?" Parliamentary Recruiting Committee (1915). (Imperial War Museum, London Q33122)

10) "The Defenders of Europe." A patriotic tableau at the Alhambra Theater from the very successful revue *Not Likely*. (From the *Tatler*, September 1914)

11) Uniformed British soldiers marching in the street for a recruitment drive. (Courtesy Hulton/Archive)

12) Woman giving a recruiting speech in Trafalgar Square, London, August 1915. (Courtesy Hulton/Archive)

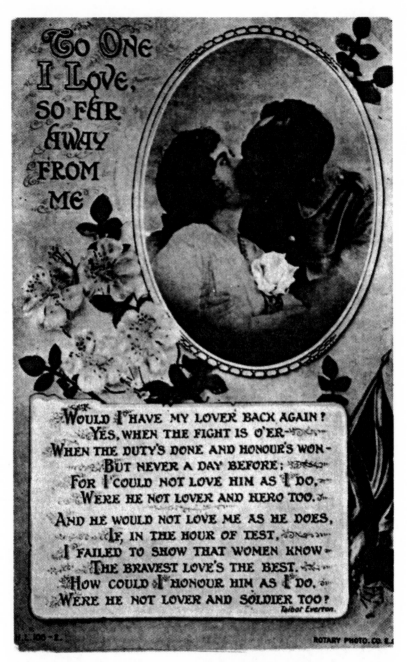

13) "To One I Love So Far Away From Me." An example of the sort of romantic postcard that might have been mailed to a lover at the front. (Courtesy Mansell/Timepix)

C.O. IN PRISON
THE IDEAL.

14) "International Brotherhood." Drawing produced by conscientious objectors depicting the moral ideal of the CO in prison. In contrast to the militant image of a female Britannia, conscientious objectors favored this image of "International Brotherhood" as a naked youth. (No-Conscription Fellowship [1917])

15) "The Vulgarity of Voluntarism." This German cartoon was reproduced in the *Bystander* to show enemy impressions of the voluntary recruiting campaign. According to the caption, "Kitchener is represented . . . as compelled to recruit Suffragettes in place of the reluctant male. Such cartoons derive their inspiration from the British newspapers, which persist in deriding British youth, despite the fact that a million and a quarter of them have answered the call to arms." The article endorsed conscription on the grounds of its dignity and manliness. (From the *Bystander* [1914])

May.21.1914

16) Mrs. Pankhurst arrested at the gates of Buckingham Palace shortly before the outbreak of World War I. (Museum of London, 2624)

17) Women's "Right to Serve" procession passing through Piccadilly Circus on July 17, 1915. The parade was staged by Mrs. Pankhurst to demonstrate women's willingness to sign up for munitions work. (Museum of London 15350)

18) "General" Flora Drummond and Lloyd George at a meeting of women war workers in Manchester, 1918. (Museum of London 13486)

19) "ON HER Their Lives Depend" Ministry of Munitions (1917). (Imperial War Museum, London Q79989)

20) A suffragette dressed as the "Spirit of Ruined Belgium" marching past the houses of Parliament. Women in allegorical costume lead the women's "Right to Serve" procession, organized by the suffragettes on July 17, 1915. (Museum of London 15352)

CHAPTER SIX

REINVENTING WOMANHOOD

SUFFRAGETTES AND THE GREAT WAR FOR CITIZENSHIP

The summer of 1917 witnessed a remarkable reversal of fortunes. Mrs. Emmeline Pankhurst, the head of Britain's militant suffragette movement, boarded a ship destined for Norway to begin an overland trip to Petrograd where she was to persuade the women of Russia to stand behind the Kerensky government and to stay in the war. Mrs. Pankhurst, jailed countless times for a violent campaign that included church-burning, picture-slashing, window-breaking, one public suicide, and a vicious heckling campaign against Liberal politicians, had, until 1914, been known primarily for her theatrical use of militancy and the precise organization of stunning parades to draw attention to the bitter injustice of women's disenfranchisement. As the head of the Women's Social and Political Union and leader of the militant suffragettes, Mrs. Pankhurst had endured life as a political prisoner in British jails, where she suffered the physical torture of force feeding and the emotional persecution of a press united in its horror of female violence.[1] Yet on this June day in 1917, she, along with her working-class accomplice Jessie Kenney, was headed on a mission to Russia with the blessing of the British authorities and the fond tidings of the Seamen's and Firemen's Union, which admired Mrs. Pankhurst's patriotism and appreciated her promise to aid the widows and orphans of sailors lost at sea.[2]

Mrs. Pankhurst's were not the only fortunes whose reversal was thrown into relief on that day. Traveling from London to Aberdeen on the same train as Mrs. Pankhurst was the former head of the British Labour Party, James Ramsay MacDonald. Unlike the ultra-nationalist Mrs. Pankhurst, Ramsay MacDonald was traveling to Russia to encourage the revolutionary government and the people of Russia to seek a negotiated peace and a speedy end to the war. Because MacDonald was a socialist and a pacifist, his passport was granted reluctantly by the government and was issued only after Sir George Buchanan, the British ambassador to Russia, suggested that the Russians desired to hear from the left as well as the right wing of British labor.[3]

Mrs. Pankhurst was not only aware of Ramsay MacDonald's presence, but she had disdainfully requested her own passport out of the conviction that "we represent the true feeling of the British people about the war much more accurately than Mr. Ramsay MacDonald."[4] She need not have worried about such bad impressions. When it was time to depart, the sailors belonging to the Seamen's and Firemen's Union refused to set sail with MacDonald aboard. Havelock Wilson, the head of the union, had ordered the rank and file to refuse passage to the notorious pacifist, and Captain Tupper, who had warmly greeted Mrs. Pankhurst, enforced this embarrassing prohibition because of MacDonald's alleged inability at a recent Labour meeting to explain how the widows of U-boat victims would be compensated without extracting reparations from Germany.[5] As Ramsay MacDonald ignominiously disembarked under the escort of the very workingmen he was alleged to represent, Mrs. Pankhurst and Jessie Kenney, dressed with the taste, expense, and respectability of well-heeled bourgeois ladies, waved with satisfaction from the ship's deck, thanking Captain Tupper and his men for their courtesy and relishing the humiliation of Mr. MacDonald.[6]

What are we to make of this odd clash on the docks of Aberdeen? The shifting fortunes of Mrs. Pankhurst and Ramsay MacDonald beautifully illustrate the way British women—particularly organized feminists— were able to take control of the discourse, drama, and spectacle of war to serve their own ends and further the campaign for female citizenship.[7] At a moment when women undertook war work in unprecedented numbers and when even the most ardent critics of women's suffrage acknowledged the heroic sacrifices of mothers and wives, feminists made explicit the link between national service and female citizenship. Nowhere is this exhibition more evident than in the activities of the newly rehabilitated Pankhursts and their militant followers. Indeed, the Women's Social and Political Union (WSPU) and the nationalist wing of Millicent Fawcett's constitutionalist National Union of Women's Suffrage Societies (NU) were able to accomplish more with their patriotic support of the war than had been possible in the many years of constitutional and militant struggle in times of peace. This chapter examines the way organized feminists, particularly former militants, used the war to demolish the anti-suffrage argument piece by piece and to build a new and powerful case for women's enfranchisement.

In the years following the Great War, scholars of women's suffrage and many former suffragists themselves took it as axiomatic that the extraordinary service women rendered during the war ultimately won them the right to vote.[8] Indeed, so widely was this interpretation accepted that even today most studies of women's suffrage end with the outbreak of war in 1914, despite the fact that it was not until February 1918 that the Representation of the People Bill was signed into law, breaking the sex barrier and granting the vote to women over thirty. While it has become customary in recent years to challenge this received wisdom, my own findings suggest that the enfranchisement of women was indeed granted as a reward for loyal service but that such service alone did not win women the vote.[9] Making the case for female enfranchisement took more than the patriotic activities of Mrs. Pankhurst and like-minded women. It also depended on the actions of male opponents of the war like Ramsay MacDonald, whose much scorned dissent cast a shadow over the public perception of maleness as a sufficient qualification for citizenship. As we shall see, it was in a context in which loyal service, patriotic sentiment, and British blood came to seem more important than manhood, majority, or property that the public began to understand women's war service as part of an irrefutable claim to citizenship.

THE SPECTACLE OF FEMINIST NATIONALISM

The declaration of war in August 1914 ushered in a much heralded truce between suffragists and the government. The WSPU and the NU both agreed to abandon agitation for the vote, and in exchange the government released suffragettes imprisoned in British jails and granted the amnesty that would allow Christabel Pankhurst, Mrs. Pankhurst's militant daughter, to return from Paris where she had been evading arrest.[10] It is here that most histories of the suffrage movement end; yet, in many ways an account of the final struggle for votes for women should commence rather than conclude with the outbreak of war.

The first days of the war were an upsetting and chaotic time for suffragists, particularly since most prewar suffrage organizations were avowedly pacifist.[11] Even the militant WSPU, which had scandalized the country with a campaign of unrestrained vandalism and self-starvation, had been strictly ordered by Mrs. Pankhurst to stop short of taking the lives of others. The outbreak of war was thus greeted with horror by women's organizations, several of which remained committed to pacifist or neutral policies throughout the conflict. In the first wartime issue of the *Suffragette*, Christabel Pankhurst, the editor of the WSPU organ, declared that the war was no less than "God's vengeance upon the people who held women in subjection," and Millicent Garrett Fawcett, the head of Britain's largest suffrage organization, was actually speaking at a peace rally when war was declared.[12] Nevertheless, the WSPU leadership, half the NU leadership, and a significant portion of the rank and file in both organizations met the British declaration of war with patriotic ardor and soon began to exploit the conflagration for its feminist and political possibilities.[13]

This sudden repudiation of pacifism by many prominent suffragists was the result of shrewd political considerations and a reassuring belief in the moral basis of the war.[14] Mrs. Fawcett received a stinging letter in August 1914 from Lord Robert Cecil, a leading supporter of women's suffrage, declaring that pacifist activity would compromise women's claim to the vote.[15] Biographer Sylvia Pankhurst has speculated that her mother's conversion might have been precipitated by similar considerations, for "none knew better the abuse and ostracism which would fall on any who dared stand for Peace."[16] The publicity given to atrocities also endowed the war with a moral purpose resonant to British feminists. Susan Kingsley Kent has shown that the representation of the war in terms of sexual violence against women gave feminists a profound stake in the defeat of Germany and helped to justify female participation in Britain's war effort.[17] As the pacifist Maude Royden sadly conceded, "there was no question of opposition to the war itself within the great Suffrage organizations, since the vast majority of their members believed that the war had been forced upon us and was, on our part, a battle against a militarist ideal."[18] This stance did not, however, signify abandonment of older feminist claims.

To accept the commonly held idea that women's suffrage agitation was dropped for the duration of the war is to take the rhetoric of the truce with the government far too literally. As the *Anti-Suffrage Review* rightly observed, rather than abandon their agitation for the vote, British feminists simply re-articulated their demand for citizenship in demonstrative professions of loyalty that subtly undercut anti-suffrage arguments. When suffragette Louisa Garret Anderson became chief surgeon at a military hospital in Paris, her eighty-year-old mother shrewdly noted that "If you succeed you will put the Cause forward a hundred years."[19] While Mrs.

Fawcett's NU committed itself to organizing patriotic relief work that would prove women "worthy of citizenship whether our claim is recognized or not," the WSPU began a flamboyant campaign of recruiting rallies, patriotic meetings, and foreign propaganda all of which highlighted the essential role of women in achieving military victory.[20] "The WSPU has been the Downing St. of the Women's Movement," explained Mrs. Pankhurst, justifying this particularly aggressive course of action, "and it is no more to be expected that our organizations should now . . . take to knitting than that Mr. Asquith should set his ministers to making army boots or uniforms."[21]

As hunger-striking suffragettes were released from jail, many were horrified to learn that their leadership had committed the WSPU to a vigorous pro-war campaign.[22] How precisely the WSPU leadership decided on this course of action so shortly after Christabel's apocalyptic denunciation of war is difficult to determine, but by September 1914 Christabel was delivering patriotic speeches to audiences in London and in October she embarked on a six-month "mission" to North America where she addressed crowds in New York, Washington, Chicago, Indianapolis, Minneapolis, and Canada on the German menace and the necessity of entering the war on the side of the Allies. Having taken top honors in International Law at Manchester University, Christabel was equipped to speak on foreign policy and delivered major speeches around the United States that shocked audiences with their jingoistic defense of the British cause, their unmeasured abuse of Germany and the German people, and their complete disregard of Wilson's admonition not to engage in partisan debate.[23] The pacifist Edith Ellis, who was also in America at the time, heard Christabel speak in New York and wrote to her husband that "it was all buttering of the Americans and vilifying of the Kaiser . . . I had hard work to keep my tongue, but I did, when I heard people all round me call her Joan of Arc."[24] German agents regarded Christabel's patriotic speaking with so much alarm that they offered Ellis "huge sums of money" to follow her around the United States refuting her arguments. And Mrs. Raymond Bacon, president of the New York State Women's Suffrage Association, actually refused to receive Christabel upon learning of her unabashedly pro-Ally position. Neither the attention of German agents nor the disapproval of American feminists quelled Christabel's partisan rhetoric.[25]

More than arrant war-mongering, Christabel's speeches were a direct refutation of the anti-suffrage case as it had been articulated so often before the war. Nowhere is this more evident than in her famous Carnegie Hall speech, delivered to a capacity crowd in New York City on October 24, 1914. While the *New York Tribune* admiringly described her as "a pink-cheeked slip of a girl with fluffy yellow hair in a gown of white satin and pale green chiffon," her speech was anything but mild.[26] As she explained to her audience, "you must not suppose that because the suffragettes fight the British Government for the sake of the vote, and because we have refused to allow the Government to crush our movement by imprisonment and torture, you must not suppose that on that account the suffragettes are not patriotic. Good Heaven! Why should we fight for British citizenship if we don't highly prize it?"[27]

Indeed, for Christabel Pankhurst, the war between Britain and Germany was simply a continuation of the fight for freedom that suffragettes had waged against the authorities in their own country. "Germany has adopted as her national religion the theory that might is right," Christabel explained. "Now, I am a militant. That is not to say that I prefer war to peace; but it is to say that when people want to govern me by physical force and not by the moral force of justice, then I am prepared to defy their physical force to the very death. . . ."[28] In Christabel's deeply allegorical interpretation of the war, Belgium was "a Suffragette country" beset by Germany which was a "male nation."[29] The issues at stake in the conflict— and for which Britain had gone to war—were to defeat the principle of "Might is Right" and reestablish a world in which law reigned over physical force. In this way the suffragette repudiation of the physical force argument as a bar to women's enfranchisement was ineluctably linked to the issues that lay at the heart of Britain's stated war aims. If "Might is Right" was wrong for Germany and needed to be met with international force, then it was equally wrong for the British authorities to throw suffragettes in jail and to force women to submit to a state of virtual conquest in which voteless women were subject to laws that they had no role in making.[30]

While the very spectacle of Christabel's presence in such prestigious venues as Carnegie Hall and the London Opera House undermined the easy dismissal of women's role in defending the state, her speeches themselves were also lawyerly exercises meant to reveal the stupidity and injustice of the anti-suffrage position. What Christabel's speeches did was to highlight the international and imperial centrality of women in an age in which the case against suffrage had rested on women's marginal role in waging war. "Sooner or later this war will end in victory, and when that day comes women who are paying their share of the price . . . will insist upon being brought into equal partnership as enfranchised citizens of this country," declared Christabel at the London Opera House. "The events of this time are proof that even in the province of national defense, even in the province of Imperial policy, the women's council is needed as well as the men's."[31] Refuting the "physical force" argument, which denied the validity of women's claim to citizenship by arguing that all political power should rest in the hands of those who wielded force, Christabel showed, first, that this principle was antithetical to everything that Britain claimed to stand for and, second, that women's capacity for forceful international action was far from negligible—a point that the militants of the WSPU would demonstrate again and again throughout the war.

While Christabel was on tour in the United States, her mother was at home traveling the country delivering flamboyant recruiting speeches. As one tabloid joked in 1914, the WSPU "had declared war on the Kaiser."[32] Mrs. Pankhurst appeared at recruiting rallies with military officers and public officials, stirring the hearts of her young listeners with her charismatic call to arms. "Much as I love peace, I believe there are times when it is right to fight," declared Mrs. Pankhurst at the Kingsway Hall. "And I say to young men: There are women to-day who never thought to envy men their manhood, but who would, at least for this purpose, be glad to be men (Cheers)."[33] According to Sylvia Pankhurst, who unlike her mother and eldest sister remained a committed pacifist throughout the war, "Mrs. Pankhurst toured the country making recruiting speeches. Her supporters handed out white feathers to every young man they encountered wearing civilian dress, and bobbed up at Hyde Park meetings with placards [reading] 'Intern them All.'"[34] Mrs. Pankhurst traveled tirelessly to address patriotic meetings in London, Manchester, Brighton, Folkstone, Hastings, Bradford, Birmingham, Leiscester, Plymouth, Exeter, Glasgow, Liverpool, Sheffield, Huddersfield, and Edinburgh (to name only a few of the cities on her exhaustive recruiting tour) and was greeted with enthusiastic cries of "Votes for Women" as she pleaded with men to do their "Duty to the Nation."[35]

The specter of German atrocities greatly enhanced women's authority to speak to men in this way. "There are people who say, 'What right have women to talk to men about fighting for their country, since women are not, according to the custom of civilization, called upon to fight?'" quipped Mrs. Pankhurst at a 1914 recruiting rally in Liverpool. "It is only by an accident that British women on British soil are not now enduring the horrors endured by the women of France, the women of Belgium, and the women of Serbia." Reminding men of their self-imposed monopoly on defense, Mrs. Pankhurst insisted that, "The least . . . men can do is . . . to redeem [their] word to women, and to . . . do [their] best, to save the mothers, the wives and the daughters of Great Britain from outrages too horrible to even think of."[36] WSPU stalwart "General" Flora Drummond put the case even more forcefully: "We, as a fighting force of women, feel that we have the right to ask men to fight for freedom," she declared at a rally for workingmen held in the Blackburn Town Hall. "I cannot conceive how it is that there are to-day men of military age who can calmly sit and read about the atrocities that are being committed and then do nothing. There are some of you who say there would be no difference if we were under German rule. Then why don't you take a ticket for Berlin and go there! It is certainly not for you to remain in the midst of your British brothers here and try to permeate them with your own feeling of discontent and your own preference for Germany. Those of you who do that in industrial and other circles are nothing more nor less than a catspaw of the Kaiser."[37]

For many, the WSPU's enthusiastic turn to military recruiting and their merciless advocacy of draconian conscription policies in the pages of the *Suffragette* seemed a betrayal of the feminist cause. "When I first read in the press that Mrs. Pankhurst and Christabel were returning to England for a recruiting campaign I wept," lamented Sylvia Pankhurst. "To me this seemed a tragic betrayal of the great movement to bring the mother-half of the race into the councils of nations. 'Women would stand for peace!' How often, how often had they and all of us averred it!"[38] Mrs. Pankhurst, however, defended such work as being of the utmost national importance. "I'm not nursing soldiers," she explained disparagingly. "We have always worked in a national way, so we are doing everything we can to help recruiting and make it possible for more men to go and fight."[39] Indeed her feelings on these issues were so strong that when Sylvia staged an anti-conscription rally at Trafalgar Square in 1915, Emmeline publicly repudiated her daughter's "foolish unpatriotic conduct" and, in a particularly cutting line, cabled: "Regret I cannot prevent use of the name."[40]

Emmeline and Christabel were not the only ones who felt this way. Sylvia's meeting was broken up by angry soldiers who threw paint and rotten fruit at the speakers and violently forced the demonstrators to disperse; the patriot Pankhursts clearly had a far more secure platform than their pacifist kinswoman.[41] Yet why would Mrs. Pankhurst side with riotous soldiers over her own daughter and how could she turn her back on years of feminist opposition to warfare? The answer lies in the manner an initially popular war could be harnessed to the case for female citizenship. Every recruiting speech was a public spectacle, highlighting women's extraordinary patriotism and pointing out the deficiency of those men who had not enlisted.[42] Indeed, many WSPU recruiting speeches made much of the fact that as militant women, suffragettes were particularly entitled to urge men to fight. "We militant women understand so clearly and well how the man of an age for military service feels at this time," Christabel declared. "He is wondering if it is really his duty to take his life in his hands and go out there to war. The militants all, at one time or another, had a choice to make which was not so very different from that . . ."[43] Despite its empathetic tone, the speaker made clear that militant women had bravely risked their lives to win the very political freedoms that some men now shied away from defending.

Although some suffragists endorsed women's role in military recruiting, the WSPU's unabashed enthusiasm was unique.[44] "There is much nobility in fighting, there is more in giving up our best-beloved for our country; there is very little nobility and surely very much impertinence in using the kind of power which some call 'women's influence' to urge strangers to enlist," declared the feminist journal *Common Cause* in 1915.[45] Similarly, the *Vote* reminded women that, "In the past, we have bitterly resented the lectures on our duties which have been inflicted upon us by men. We think men will equally resent being 'inspired' . . . by us to a course of action for which they feel no sense of vocation."[46] Despite these misgivings among feminists, the popular press had nothing but admiration for the Pankhursts' new avocation and concurred fully with their patriotic sentiments. The Tory tabloid *John Bull* wished "Good luck" to Mrs. Pankhurst, actress Clara Butt, and other women whose "splendid work" was "coaxing thousands to the colours," while memoirist J. C. Carlie remembered with pleasure the way Mrs. Pankhurst had come to Folkstone to speak "not as a militant suffragette but as a whole-hearted advocate of the war."[47]

By orchestrating such spectacles, the Pankhursts put together a highly visible and marketable platform from which to proclaim women's civic worth. Speaking at venues ranging from opera houses to municipal halls, the Pankhursts' rallies took the form of public entertainment. "Christabel Pankhurst . . . has come back radiant from exile," commented the *Manchester Guardian*. "She had a most affectionate welcome [at the London Opera House] appearing alone on the huge stage with an olive green curtain as the background and a barrier of bouquets at her feet. . . . The flags of the Allies decorated the room, and a women's band played national airs."[48] Sometimes appearing with stars like Clara Butt and patriotic speaker Horatio Bottomley, the Pankhursts filled large meeting halls to capacity and were able to raise sizable amounts of money for their patriotic causes.[49] Indeed, thanks to their militant past, the Pankhursts were already celebrities and their name was ineluctably associated with the campaign for women's votes. The beautiful Christabel, flitting back and forth between London and Paris, was the diva of the suffrage movement, while her mother, a mesmerizing speaker, went on numerous missions abroad to promote the British cause. Although the Pankhursts formally suspended suffrage propaganda in August 1914, their radiant displays of feminist patriotism foregrounded the importance of female citizenship to national security and undercut those who denied women the vote on the grounds of their military inutility.

WSPU recruiting activities were also part of a larger feminist plan for national reorganization that would grant women boundless new opportunities. While Mrs. Pankhurst and Christabel never tired of pointing out that the men of France and Belgium had failed to protect their women from the horrors of war—belying the idea that women rested comfortably behind the lines—they were equally determined to send men to the front so that women could assume new wartime roles. As Flora Drummond put it, "We are not going to stop home and weep but to stay at home and WORK, while you do the fighting."[50] The WSPU would make this demand with particular force in their speeches, their publications, and in the realm of public spectacle.

Christabel returned home from America in March 1915, and in April the *Suffragette* reappeared as a jingoistic pro-war paper. In October the journal was re-christened *Britannia* and "like a bride changing her name," explicitly dedicated to "King, Country and Freedom." Scholars have generally taken this change as confirmation that the Pankhursts abandoned feminism for a paranoid nationalism that echoed the worst excesses of the Tory press. To Sylvia Pankhurst, "The WSPU . . . had now entirely departed from the Suffrage movement. Giving its energies wholly to the prosecution of the war, it rushed to a furious extreme, its chauvinism unexampled among all the other women's societies . . . Christabel demanded the military conscription of men, and the industrial conscription of women. . . . In flamboyant terms she called also for the internment of all people of enemy race . . . and for more complete and ruthless enforcement of the blockade of enemy and neutral nations. . . . So furious was her attack that, in its over-fervent support of the National War Policy, *Britannia* was many times raided by the police, and experienced greater difficulty in appearing than had befallen the *Suffragette*."[51] Sylvia's description is indisputably accurate, yet for all its jingoism, the WSPU remained a decidedly feminist organization. Despite being harassed by Liberal authorities for partisan attacks on the government's handling of the war effort, the Pankhursts succeeded in getting the attention of those who counted—the king, Lord Northcliffe, and Lloyd George—while they continued to use their public prominence to articulate the case for female citizenship.

Nowhere is this more evident than in the great procession for women's work organized by the WSPU in July 1915. In the summer of 1915, Minister of Munitions David Lloyd George received a letter from the king suggesting he use the Pankhursts to organize women in support of the war. By July, Lloyd George had secretly given Mrs. Pankhurst £2,000 to arrange a gigantic procession of women prepared to undertake war work. Echoing the dramatic prewar marches demanding the vote, the Pankhursts' parade symbolically linked the woman's movement with a spectacular pageant of patriotism. This is perhaps the key event in the rehabilitation of the Pankhursts, and much to the fury of more moderate women's groups, it would put them on the map as the official voice of women for much of the war.[52] Indeed, the £2,000 subsidy was only the beginning of the contributions the WSPU would receive from the generous hand of Lloyd George, first as Minister of Munitions and later as prime minister.[53] Although some scholars have dismissed the WSPU's war feminism as irrelevant, press coverage and official patronage gave the Pankhursts a public prominence that they expertly manipulated to demonstrate women's worthiness for the vote.[54]

The Pankhursts' parade was held at a moment when thousands of working-class women were unemployed and had no hope of finding jobs without a relaxation of union restrictions against unskilled labor. Columns of thirty thousand women demanding the right to work marched down London's Embankment accompanied by ninety brass bands and a dramatic "Pageant of the Allies." According to the *Observer*, a hundred thousand spectators lined the route from Westminster to Blackfriars and "the processionists almost overwhelmed those in charge" in their eagerness to sign up for war work.[55] The parade was led by young women in Grecian robes carrying Allied flags, while the "place of honour" in this tableaux vivant was given to Belgium. "The soul of that martyred but unconquerable land was vividly typified by a tall, slender lady dressed in mourning," wrote Michael McDonagh in his war diary. "She carried aloft the flag of her country, torn and tattered but still beautiful in its colours of black, yellow, and red. She walked barefoot through the slush of the roadways—heavy rain having fallen earlier—and on her delicately chiseled face there was an expression of pride and sorrow and devotion, all of a high degree."[56] Singing patriotic songs like "Tipperary" and carrying banners reading, "Women's Battle Cry is Work, Work, Work" and "Shells Made by a Wife may Save her Husband's Life," the seemingly endless procession of women was made all the more poignant by the rain, braved without complaint by the female marchers. As the *Daily Mail* reported, "It was not merely a cheerful but a conquering spirit."[57] "To call it historic—this procession of wives and mothers, matrons and girls all demanding the right to serve—is not enough," agreed the *Daily Chronicle*. "It is the first time in history that the womanhood of England, or, indeed, of any country, has made so simple, so spontaneous, so overwhelming a manifestation of it's dauntless and undivided spirit. Even the rain seemed but a deliberate test of the hardihood and endurance of the women. But the test became a triumph. Organized as an army, the procession never faltered in its purpose."[58]

Although the Ministry of Munitions was still unable to offer employment to the thousands of women who signed registers testifying to their willingness to enter factories, the procession demonstrated to the nation women's willingness to work, undercutting any excuse men had for staying at home and giving Lloyd George the leverage he needed to pressure unions into relaxing rules for unskilled labor.[59] While socialist women were deeply disturbed by the prospect of women becoming "blacklegs," the WSPU had no such qualms, reveling in the unquestioning display of female loyalty and its disturbing contrast with selfish and disloyal "closed shop" attitudes of male trade unionists.[60] "The reason the women are not getting skilled training today is that it has been . . . opposed by the organized skilled workmen," Mrs. Pankhurst later reminded an audience at the London Pavilion. "Yes, there is opposition there, opposition and prejudice of a kind almost intolerable in time of peace, but which is something like treachery and traitorism in time of war. . . . We hear of strikes and riots among men. Well . . . what if women lost patience and began to riot—not for more money, not in order to have easier conditions, but because they were not allowed to work at the time of their country's need."[61]

Following the march, Mrs. Pankhurst and her deputation were received by Winston Churchill and Lloyd George, who enthusiastically addressed the crowd: without women "victory will tarry," Lloyd George proclaimed admiringly, "and a victory which tarries means a victory whose footprints are footprints of blood." In her own speech, Mrs. Pankhurst declared that "Women are going to work. They are going to save the men in the trenches. Let us all unite in giving three cheers for the Army and Navy. Three cheers for the good old country that we mean to save."[62] The next day her parade shared coverage in the daily press with news of striking Welsh miners, highlighting the loyalty of women at a moment when male trade unionists appeared to be less than reliable.[63]

In addition to casting the Pankhursts as the organizers of patriotic British womanhood, the march allowed the WSPU leadership to claim an undeserved status as representatives of female munitions workers—a position of enormous strategic advantage and one used to fuel the WSPU's dramatic industrial campaign. While Christabel and Emmeline traveled the lecture circuit persuading men and nations to do their duty, Christabel's devotee Annie Kenney, a former factory worker, traversed the country calling for a Balkan war and lecturing on the Serbian question, and "General" Flora Drummond toured the Clyde, Tyneside, and the Welsh mining districts quelling industrial unrest and helping to break strikes in the most radical parts of the country. In all these activities, the WSPU publicly and spectacularly drew attention both to women's patriotism and to the need of men to be persuaded by women to do their duty whether that duty was to enlist, to repudiate strikes, or to allow women to take their places in factories and workshops. As Christabel declared with hyperbolic intensity, "Everything which militates against the British Empire becoming a military camp until victory is assured is treason. . . . Ministers who are feeble should be treated as Enemies of the People. . . . No conscription, forsooth! We are all conscripts. . . ."[64]

COMPARATIVE PATRIOTISM

If the Pankhursts used the war to subvert the "physical force" argument against women's suffrage, they nevertheless accepted more and more of its premises as the conflict dragged on. Not only did they stake their claim to citizenship on women's military indispensability, but they undercut the notion of manhood suffrage by impugning the civic worth of those men who failed to defend the state. While scholars have traditionally recognized the importance of munitions girls, military nurses, and other female workers whose patriotic endeavors helped win women the vote, what has been less apparent is the way the granting of women's suffrage occurred in a context where male as well as female citizenship was being reexamined. As we have seen, "slackers," pacifists, and conscientious objectors were given little quarter on the home front. By engaging in a sort of comparative patriotism, the WSPU exploited press coverage and public podiums alike to proclaim nationalistic women to be better citizens than cowardly, Liberal, pacifist, or foreign men. In addition to turning female patriotism into public spectacle, the WSPU united with the girl on the street and the Tory press to expose "disloyalty" where ever it occurred—particularly when the disloyal elements were male and enfranchised. Not only were WSPU supporters to be found among the white-feather girls, but the public pronouncements of the WSPU leadership flaunted the cowardice of unenlisted males, culminating in Mrs. Pankhurst's shocking repudiation of the female franchise until a "soldier's vote" was secured to rescue the nation from "slackers" and conscientious objectors.[65]

Mrs. Pankhurst's highly publicized reversal occurred in August 1916 at a moment when franchise reform was being increasingly discussed in the press and Parliament. Because soldiers forfeited their residential qualifications by leaving home, virtually all enlisted men were disenfranchised as soon as they joined the army. As we shall see, this injustice was deeply upsetting to patriotic Britons who, by the spring of 1916, were demanding franchise and registration reforms that would grant returning soldiers a broad new political voice. While moderate suffrage organizations heatedly opposed any expansion of the franchise that did not include women, the WSPU believed that the linking of women's suffrage with the soldier's vote was nothing but a Liberal ruse to sink both measures.[66] "Mr. Asquith insults as well as injures women when he tries to use them as catspaws to prevent the best men in the country from recording a vote," editorialized

Britannia, "while any and every crank, coward or traitor, is to be free to vote as usual and indeed with more power than usual because of the disenfranchisement of the brave and patriotic men of the Army and Navy."[67] Sending a diehard anti-suffragist, Commander Bellairs, to the House of Commons to declare that *her* organization did not want the vote if it meant that soldiers would be "dished" and the country would be in the electoral hands of disloyal civilian males, Mrs. Pankhurst and the WSPU won plaudits from Conservatives while incurring the wrath of all other suffrage organizations.[68]

Mrs. Pankhurst's gesture, however, must be looked at for what it was—part of the larger theatrics of patriotism, calculated to embarrass Asquith and to silence those who had begun to grumble about the "selfishness" of women as soon as electoral reform appeared again on the national agenda. Its shock value was significant, but while Mrs. Pankhurst's statements could offset criticism of women's motives for undertaking patriotic work, they in no way impeded the legislative progress of women's suffrage. Despite the anger of other feminists, by March 1917 Mrs. Pankhurst had returned to active suffrage agitation, accompanying the Joint Women's Suffrage Committee on its procession to 10 Downing Street where she lobbied Lloyd George on behalf of the female franchise.[69]

Self-renunciatory displays like the Bellairs incident were deeply political and contributed to the image of right-wing feminism that the WSPU wished to project at a moment when Tory sentiments were enjoying much public support. The WSPU loathed the Liberal leadership, which not only failed to support women's suffrage in the prewar years but which they held responsible for the policy of "force feeding" that had ruined the health of so many militants.[70] Suffragettes alledgedly threw a hatchet at Asquith during a 1912 visit to Dublin, and in February 1917 Mrs. Pankhurst attended a conspiracy trial in Derby to deny charges that the WSPU had spent £300 trying to assassinate Lloyd George.[71] While Mrs. Pankhurst and Lloyd George had clearly made their peace by 1915, the WSPU's vendetta against the Liberal administration had in no way subsided. Using their attack on the Liberal government to show women's political and military savvy, the WSPU laid Britain's martial mishaps at the feet of male electors. Our "duty is to do our share of the fighting by crusading against inertia, weakness, compromise, treachery even, on the part of the so-called leaders of the nation," declared *Britannia* menacingly. "If we had political power we should have done that long ago. To the men civilians who also are protected by the heroes of the Army and Navy we as British women deliver this challenge 'Be loyal to your protectors—to the men whose living bodies are your shield and defense and put leaders worthy of the name in the place of those mis-leaders whose unfitness for their high office has been so tragically proven!'"[72]

The Pankhursts relentlessly compared their own right-wing ideas about rationing, martial law, conscription, and the treatment of aliens to the pusillanimous policies of the Liberal authorities. As Mrs. Pankhurst wryly reminded one audience, "I will tell you who is to blame if things are not as they ought to be. It is you enfranchised men . . . (cheers and laughs)."[73] Following such statements with public wreath-layings at Joan of Arc's shrine, calls for martial law and industrial conscription, and an ever more strident advocacy of a ruthless blockade policy against Germany, the WSPU established a Conservative, tough-minded, pro-war feminism that brandished militant women as better citizens than Liberal men.[74] The Liberal-dominated government took these attacks seriously enough to raid the WSPU offices repeatedly and to shut down its press under the Defense of the Realm Act, but the Pankhursts proved difficult to silence.[75] After Asquith's resignation in December 1916, WSPU stalwarts followed him on an organized heckling campaign, shouting "Wait and see!" (a deprecatory allusion to his "business as usual" war policy), and stalked, insulted, and harassed influential Liberals in a sort of nationalistic charivari directed against ministers whom they considered insufficiently zealous in pursuit of the war.[76] Such tactics made the Pankhursts the darlings of the powerful Northcliffe press, whose owner, Alfred Harmsworth, not only suggested putting Christabel in the War Cabinet for her tough stance on the blockade, but endorsed her political career on the grounds that she "has brains," "is a lady," and her looks will "have power over the men in the House."[77] Such sentiments were shared by a number of other patriotic authorities including Lloyd George, Conservative editor Leo Maxse, and possibly even Commander Lord Kitchener, who gratifyingly approved "The Great Scourge," Christabel's prewar diatribe against venereal disease, for distribution to the troops.[78]

Once Lloyd George successfully ousted the reviled Asquith in December 1916, the WSPU's principled opposition to the female franchise melted away. "The shipwreck of Women's Suffrage . . . would be a blow in the face and a stab in the heart of women who in manifold ways have toiled in the nation's interest and are now counting the minutes that must pass before they gain the vote which is precious, above all, as a means of serving their country," declared *Britannia* passionately in April 1917.[79] Indeed, by the time Asquith fell from grace and proposals on women's suffrage were under consideration by a legislative committee, the Pankhursts' point had been made with graphic clarity: suffragettes put soldiers above themselves, "slackers," conscientious objectors, and cowards were unfit to vote, and women were loyal citizens whose enfranchisement would serve the nation.

While the WSPU used female patriotism as a foil against which to mea-sure the claims of "unpatriotic" men, they also exploited a national racial hysteria to further their political ends. With the outbreak of war in 1914, Britain plunged into a state of anti-German paranoia that manifested it-self in such irrational acts as the internment of German governesses, the dismissal of foreign waiters, and the wholesale sacking and looting of East End butcher shops—many German-owned—following the sinking of the Lusitania.[80] While aliens had been ineligible to vote in parliamentary or municipal elections since the 1880s, naturalized male subjects possessed the franchise, a privilege deeply galling to female suffragists of British birth.[81] Taking advantage of this ugly moment in the nation's racial his-tory, the WSPU placed itself at the forefront of the anti-alien campaign to highlight the idea that British blood, rather than masculine gender, car-ried the seeds of civic well-being. "The Bosch is really made in a different way from the rest of us," insisted Christabel. He is "the enemy of mankind, . . . sub-human, and of a different species."[82] In a complex array of activities, ranging from investigating seances to expose pro-German spirits, to a vicious defamation campaign against Lord Haldane (who had once made the mistake of calling Germany his "spiritual home"), the WSPU picked up on themes prevalent in the tabloid press to launch a feminist anti-German campaign demanding that blood take precedence over sex in designating the full rights of citizenship.[83] "British citizenship has been going for far too cheap," argued Christabel in a call for the revo-cation naturalization certificates, "except where British born women are concerned. . . . British women have not secured delivery of the vote. But any German spy, any German financier, any German merchant or other advance guard of the Kaiser's Army, has been free to acquire British citi-zenship [with] a few years residence . . . and a five pound note. . . . If British men are not strong enough in numbers, in intelligence and energy to keep the nation going, then the right people to be 'naturalized' as British citizens . . . are British women!"[84]

Nowhere are these prejudices and their implications more evident than in the great parade held on July 22, 1916, to protest overly generous nat-uralization laws and to display women's patriotic support of the war.[85] Marking the anniversary of the Great Parade for Women's Work held in London the previous year, the giant Women's War Procession reveals the consolidation of right-wing causes that had become part of the WSPU platform. The main themes of the parade were a call for the return of Aus-tralia's jingoistic Premier Hughes for service in an Imperial War Cabinet, a lavish display of female munitions workers (chanting and playing "gong-like" notes on their shells), a repudiation of compromise peace, and a call for the revocation of naturalization certificates and the internment of all enemy aliens. Carrying banners reading "We Want Hughes," "Our Duty Towards The Dead is to Fight Until the Complete Defeat of the Enemy," and a tableau of Minerva supporting a flag-draped portrait of Kitchener, who had drowned earlier that year in a U-boat attack, the militaristic and xenophobic nature of the parade was unmistakable. So was the enthusiasm of the crowd and the Tory press. To the *Globe*, the demand for Hughes showed that "women are proving themselves not only patriots in their actions, but politically shrewd in their judgement on the conduct of war," while the *Morning Post* insisted that "never . . . has there been more . . . sympathy between demonstrators and onlookers."[86] While all conceded that the enthusiastic munitions girls calling for the return of Hughes were the favorites of the crowd (receiving boisterous cheers from wounded Tommies and armless Australian soldiers alike), members of the crowd were most likely to join the parade behind banners "demanding firmer measures with aliens."[87]

The procession received a cool reception in several moderate feminist papers. Nina Boyle was disgusted to see it heralded in the press as a great "suffragist effort," and instead found "the whole thing . . . revolting alike to good breeding and common honesty."[88] But the response of the *Lady's Pictorial* was far more typical: "These women of England were urging their countrymen and sisters to go forward to victory, to achieve peace without compromise, to keep Britain for the British," declared the paper approvingly. "[T]hey know that victory can only be secured by making unceasing and unselfish effort now."[89]

Not surprisingly, the Pankhursts and Lloyd George, who once again received them, were delighted with this spectacular display of patriotic ardor by women of British blood. By calling attention to the alien question and using women war workers to do so, the parade staged a dramatic contrast between women's loyal sense of civic obligation and the disquieting fact that men of "enemy race" could vote in Britain. While naturalized subjects did retain their right to vote, the constant impugning of their loyalty in the popular press, in Parliament, among rioting East Enders, and within some of the nation's premier feminist organizations helped to undermine further public faith in the logic of a franchise grounded in gender, property, and legal definitions of something as emotional as nationality. "To men of alien birth have been given honours, places in the Privy Council, titles, [and] public positions of all sorts which have been rigorously denied to the Florence Nightingales of our land—women not only of British birth, but of proven and magnificent loyalty," explained Christabel. "It is a question of defending our citizenship from adulteration."[90] As the Pankhursts played upon stereotypic notions of the "German race" to exalt the true-blue credentials of British blood and British birth, they gave their spectators yet another reason to rethink the enfranchisement of women, who more than anyone else were "guardians of the race."

Such graphic demonstrations of female loyalty were not restricted to what Christabel dramatically called "the London Front."[91] "General" Flora Drummond's strike-breaking campaign in the industrial North and West defined patriotic female citizenship in opposition to the potential disloyalty of British workingmen and took this message to the farthest reaches of the nation. In January 1916, the WSPU inaugurated an ambitious "anti-bolshevik campaign" in Scotland, the north of England, and in the Welsh mining districts.[92] Financed by large subscriptions to its "Win the War" fund (and a covert £15,000 grant from Lloyd George), the WSPU commenced a tour of industrial centers that soon spread over the country, involving the organization's entire leadership.[93] From the perspective of the Ministry of Munitions, such a campaign must have come none too soon. By 1916, British authorities were troubled by increasing levels of industrial action, particularly in Scotland. The "Red Clyde," as it was known, was a hotbed of radicalism, pacifism, and strong antiwar sentiment. Located in the heart of Glasgow's shipbuilding district, the Red Clyde was the seat of worker discontent over rising prices, intensifying work conditions, and the abandonment of prewar labor regulations. This radical atmosphere fostered serious strikes, rent boycotts, and even "soviets" by the war's end.[94] It was to these and other problem spots that the WSPU sent the indomitable Flora Drummond to quell industrial unrest and to establish the place of women on the side of bourgeois order, patriotic vigor, and military victory.

Mrs. Drummond would typically arrive at a coal pit or factory gate, often under the escort of loyal female workers, mount a soap box, cart, chair, or other handy podium and begin railing against the men—particularly shop stewards—for their disloyalty to their comrades in arms.[95] At the Fairfield shipyard on the Clyde, Mrs. Drummond spoke to an audience of over four thousand men in February 1916 on their duty not to strike in wartime. As she explained in an interview with the *Glasgow Bulletin*, "We women suffragists have buried the hatchet. . . . [W]e have set aside everything but the fact that Britain is at war, and that Britain must win. So we feel that we have a right to appeal to other people who have grievances, such as the Clyde workers and the Welsh miners, to bury THEIR hatchets too. . . . We come to the men simply as British women trying to do OUR bit for our country and appeal to them as British men to do THEIR bit by working all together until Germany is beaten."[96] Astonished commentators remarked with wonder on the fact that she was not torn limb from limb. One "Old Sandy," from whom she was trying to rent a lorry to be used as a speaking podium, initially refused, saying, "Why, they'll murder you . . . and smash my wagon."[97] While most attributed her safety to the fact she was a woman, at least part of it had to do with the female shock troops she often traveled with. At a pit in the Rhondda Valley in Wales, Mrs. Drummond was railing against pacifism and Ramsay MacDonald when a "Pacifist leader jumped up . . . and tried to take the platform from me. . . . Instantly some of the women present closed round me, and they pushed that fighting Pacifist clean down the bank and out of the way. So he lost his standing and his prestige at the same time."[98]

Mrs. Drummond was not the only WSPU orator who benefited from such support. Christabel was speaking to a large audience of northern workers in St. Andrew's Hall, Glasgow, in 1918 about her organization's militant opposition to a compromise peace, when a group of pacifist workers started to sing the "Red Flag" and drown her out. Instantly, loyal munitions girls from the Georgetown works responded, singing "Rule Britannia" even more loudly than the male workers. According to the *Empire News,* "these young women . . . with brothers and fathers at the front, were straining . . . at the leash." Soon the girls, "unable to restrain their indignation longer, leaped from their places, and like a troop of lancers, went clean through the pacifists. It was a wild, weird scene. . . . There was one lady who was a regular master of fistcuffs. [It later turned out she had been taking jiu-jitsu lessons.] One big beefy-looking shirker tried to punch her, but she ducked and his arm went nowhere and the lady's fist just got the place it was meant to, and he collapsed at her feet, gobbling and groaning." Finally policemen were called in "and swept out the stragglers. . . . But a vendetta has been proclaimed. No quarter is to be given by women to shirkers."[99]

Though numbers are difficult to ascertain, such sentiments seem to have been shared by more than a handful of munitionettes. The WSPU counted munitions workers among their most loyal paper sellers and collected significant sums of money from them for the Women's Party—the WSPU's political party launched in 1917 in anticipation of the female franchise. In March 1918, munitions girls in Coventry and Birmingham gave the WSPU Women's Party £880 followed by the public presentation of a shell filled with an additional £1,520. Female Clyde workers contributed £1,335 and the wives of Seamen's and Firemen's Union members produced a small model torpedo boat with £100 and the promise of £400 more. During that particular drive, the Women's Party raised over £8,000 for its political causes.[100]

The attraction of the Women's Party for some female industrial workers may have had to do with the lavish attention they received from a leadership tireless in visiting factories and workshops to proclaim the superiority of the female labor force.[101] According to Christabel, women industrial workers eschewed strike activity and were far more loyal, reliable, and efficient than their male colleagues. Encouraging women to attend union meetings in order to combat the propaganda of the shop stewards, *Britannia* made much of the anti-bolshevik position of female munitions workers and touted Christabel herself as a sort of right-wing Mary Macarthur with her own following of Tory industrial workers.[102] As one home-made banner held by munitions girls proudly proclaimed, "The Only Time We'll Strike is When We Strike the Kaiser."[103] Whether such sentiments were typical or not, the WSPU's objective was to paint a picture of the loyal female worker and to contrast it with the entrenched image of the male shirker, the male striker, or the male pacifist—tropes that had already gained currency in the press and Parliament. As Christabel declared to female munitions workers at Woolwich Arsenal, "These miserable creatures threaten to strike. Well, if they do go out lock the gates on them and never let them back. (Applause.) . . . Comb them out. . . . Keep women in the factories and send these 'skilled' workers to the Western Front. . . . The men who talk of peace by negotiation have lost . . . any idea of what it is to be a British citizen." They are "foxes without tails—men who disgrace their manhood and have lost their souls. They do not resent the Germanization of England, because they are Germans already."[104]

Somewhat surprisingly, observers regarded the Pankhursts' industrial campaign as a success; in fact, the testimony of contemporaries suggests that Mrs. Pankhurst, Flora Drummond, and Annie Kenney succeeded on a number of occasions in shaming men out of their demands and persuading them to return to work. "Mrs. Flora Drummond, one of the foremost leaders of the Women's Social and Political Union, is a present doing very useful work," declared the *Western Mail* in October 1917. "She has established herself in South Wales, and has set herself the task of dissipating Labour unrest, heartening those who are lukewarm in the prosecution of the war, and striving to maintain the civil population at the pitch of determination necessary to achieve a complete measure of success in the great conflict which is absolutely essential to succeeding generations in this country." Drawing attention to an industrial dispute settled by the WSPU in Gwaun-cae-Gurwen, Mrs. Drummond told the reporter that "if the women were left to deal with these false pacifists a firm hand would be used."[105] While Sylvia Pankhurst traveled to the same mines and factories to encourage men to strike for better wages, the WSPU leadership reaped more tangible rewards for quelling industrial unrest. In fact, Lloyd George decided, on these grounds, to give Christabel the coveted "coupon" of coalition endorsement when she contested the seat for Smethwick in the 1918 election. As he wrote to Conservative Leader Andrew Bonar Law, the WSPU leadership had been "extraordinarily useful to the Government, especially in the industrial districts where there has been so much trouble these last two very trying years. They have fought the Bolshevist and Pacifist element with great skill, and I know that especially in Glasgow and South Wales their intervention produced remarkable results."[106] Bonar Law agreed and persuaded the Unionist candidate Major S. N. Thompson to withdraw from the contest, leaving Christabel as the favorite to win Smethwick against the Labour Party candidate J. E. Davison.

Christabel's popularity with female munitions workers was not entirely surprising. Not only did she appeal to their patriotism, inspire them with her rhetoric about sex equality, and encourage their sense of pride in their accomplishments, but she spoke up forcefully against their dismissal and demobilization and praised them for the very thing the public at large was inclined to criticize them for: namely their taste in finery and their desire to transcend their class.[107] As she wrote in her anti-Marxist pamphlet *Industrial Salvation*, "The I.L.P. lecturer works himself up into a frenzy in his efforts to incite the working woman to the class war. He tries to rouse her to class jealousy by his denunciation of the 'employers wife in her silk dress.' But the working woman simply and calmly adheres to her determination, not to prevent the employer's wife from having a silk dress, but to have a silk dress too! . . . The working woman who spends her earnings on silk dresses, silk stockings, shapely shoes, fine underwear, fur coats, pretty hats, and all the rest of it are far better social reformers than all the men's Socialist or Labour organizations rolled into one."[108]

What the Pankhursts attempted to do in this odd array of public activities was to rewrite the gendered basis of citizenship. If citizenship had once been based on manhood, majority, and property—and could be held by naturalized Britons as well as true-born Englishmen—the Pankhursts took advantage of this Tory moment to suggest that loyal service, patriotic sentiment, and British blood might be safer underpinnings for the nation, and that patriotism, rather than sex, ought to be the foundation of the parliamentary vote. In an atmosphere where the disenfranchisement of conscientious objectors was discussed in the press, where the franchise would be extended to boys as young as nineteen if they had seen active service, and where "enemy aliens" could be interned in concentration camps (and thus disenfranchised) regardless of their naturalization status, the WSPU's claim to the vote was increasingly based on the true-blue credentials of loyalty, patriotism, and British blood—attributes that, as Mrs. Pankhurst never tired of pointing out, women demonstrated more deeply and profoundly than men.

The contrast between male cowardice and female militancy was one that Mrs. Pankhurst would make with dramatic clarity on her trip to Russia in 1917.[109] Mrs. Pankhurst embarked on her "mission" at the very moment when the Women's Clause of the Representation of the People Bill was being debated in the House of Commons. Publicly demanding passage of "the Bill, the whole Bill and nothing but the Bill" before she left, Mrs. Pankhurst's mission to Russia became a theatrical display of comparative patriotism, legitimating women's claim to a vote being renegotiated on the basis of patriotic service. Not only did the voyage begin with the humiliation of her pacifist rival Ramsay MacDonald, but Mrs. Pankhurst's "mission" culminated in her extraordinary relationship with the Russian Women's Battalion of Death—a living symbol of female patriotism and male inadequacy.

From a diplomatic standpoint, Mrs. Pankhurst's visit could not be considered a tremendous success. On her arrival in Russia, she basked in the adulation of the Conservative press, was visited by princes and princesses, and had the future Czech president Thomas Masaryk virtually at her disposal, yet the volatility of the Russian situation prevented her from speaking to large crowds of female factory workers, particularly since she refused on principle to relinquish her bourgeois clothing. Although she took tea with Russian premier Alexander Kerensky, Mrs. Pankhurst soon discovered that she could do little to bolster his support and came to feel that he was an ineffective leader who might with advantage be replaced by the Czar.[110] Despite their grandiose plans, she and Miss Kenney could do nothing to save Russia and were finally persuaded by Masaryk to flee the Bolshevik Revolution, which they had been so disappointingly unable to prevent.

Not surprisingly, Mrs. Pankhurst's "mission" made its greatest impression not in Russia but in England, where her correspondence and photographs brought home dramatic images of female military service. The so-called Battalions of Death were organized by the Russian provisional government to shame deserting men by using the spectacle of female combatants to humiliate soldiers into rejoining their units. While this extraordinary gesture seems to have meant little to peasant deserters, it meant a great deal to British feminists and Mrs. Pankhurst spent much of her time in Russia reviewing the Women's Batallion of Death and socializing with its commander, Maria Leont'evna Botchkareva, and her adjutant, Mademoiselle Scridlova. The relationship between Mrs. Pankhurst and Madame Botchkareva is one of the war's stranger feminist moments. Botchkareva was a Siberian butcher's daughter whose husband had been killed in battle. Upon his death, she enlisted in the infantry and by showing bravery in the face of mass desertions—she took two trenches—was given command of a combat unit. After returning wounded from the front, she was decorated with the St. George's Cross and chosen to command the Russian Women's Batallion of Death.[111]

If the Battalion of Death seemed to illustrate women's capacity to excel under fire, its true significance was far more ironic. Not only did the poorly trained women sustain enormous casualties, but the formation of the battalions themselves was a cynical effort to shame Russian men rather than an earnest attempt to repel German soldiers. "Cowards, Traitors, Judases," declared the battalion's manifesto, "We come to die by your side."[112] Mrs. Pankhurst herself exclaimed at the way women's "tender bodies" were subjected to gunfire because men were too cowardly to serve and made much of Botchkareva's wounded and shattered recruits as they convalesced in hospital, yet she and Miss Kenney were wholly seduced by the Battalions of Death. Madame Botchkareva returned regularly from the front with tales of combat that ignited the imaginations of Pankhurst, Kenney, and readers of the *Britannia* in England—"The greatest thing in history since Joan of Arc," proclaimed Mrs. Pankhurst enthusiastically.[113] Intoxicated with the glamour of female combat units, Pankhurst herself enjoyed a place at center stage during drills and parades when the short-haired women were blessed by Orthodox priests while proudly marching in their smart military uniforms. Yet despite its ostentatious—and almost comic—theatricality, the image of Mrs. Pankhurst reviewing the troops in her enormous hats and Edwardian furs serves as a reminder of how deeply the claim to citizenship was intertwined with the symbolics of military service.[114]

The WSPU attempted to show that even in a world in which suffrage was based on physical force, women would make better citizens than men. By fighting Bolshevism in Russia and at home, the WSPU leadership highlighted the militaristic and conservative nature of women and made the case for women's suffrage as "a necessary war measure."[115] Pointing out that unenlisted men rested behind the lines protected by the army, that conscientious objectors had the right to vote, and that a pusillanimous Liberal government had dragged its feet on conscription, rationing, and industrial compulsion, the WSPU made a mockery of civilian manhood. "Too many of our men civilians have shown themselves to be lacking the INSIGHT and INTUITION as well as the MORAL COURAGE necessary for the war against German intrigue and treachery," fulminated *Britannia,* in an article advocating women's votes. "The great prewar bogey of the anti-Suffragists was that Woman's Suffrage would be a national danger because women . . . did not understand the questions of diplomacy and national defense. . . . That is not the truth!"[116] Such sentiments would come to fruition in the formation of the Woman's Party.

Upon Mrs. Pankhurst's return from Russia in late 1917, the WSPU leadership announced that it would change the name of its organization to the Women's Party and challenge the old male parties by courting the women's vote on a platform of "Victory, National Security and Progress."[117] The Women's Party platform set out an ambitious plan combining military efficiency with feminist reform. Warning of the danger of a premature peace, they proclaimed that the chief cry of the Women's Party would be "Down with pacifism everywhere," and assured women that it was with the Women's Party, rather than the Labour Party, that the good of the country rested.[118] In a platform calling for strict rationing, central direction of industry, and "efficient and loyal public service," the Women's Party advocated "ridding all Government Departments of officials having enemy blood or connections, and of all officials who have pacifist and pro German leanings or have displayed lack of the necessary zeal and competence." Calling for a coordinated Allied command, "Britain for the British," and no surrender of power to "any so-called League . . . of Nations," the Women's Party advocated amending naturalization laws "to prevent Germans and their allies from acquiring British nationality." On Ireland they were strict Unionists.[119]

Appended to this xenophobic platform, however, were a series of remarkably progressive proposals. In exchange for worker control of industry—which the Women's Party adamantly opposed—it endorsed shorter hours and better working conditions. It was on "Special Women's Questions," however, that the Women's Party diverged most forcefully from the popular Tory line it adopted on questions of military efficiency and national security. Rather than endorse a Conservative maternalist position on women, the former WSPU leadership advocated "equal pay for equal work," equal marriage and divorce laws, maternity and infant welfare, national health and education, and state-subsidized housing—complete with communal kitchens, central heating, and cooperative housekeeping to relieve women of the drudgery of housework.[120] As an alternative to Marxism, the party promoted a new type of "Industrial Salvation," based on consumption, leisure, and the "abolition of the proletariat," which would be raised to middle-class status by the Women's Party's progressive reforms.[121]

The Women's Party was inaugurated to rave reviews from the Tory press and became an object of scorn among Labour loyalists, moderate women's organizations, and the trade unionist Mary Macarthur, who was smeared by Christabel as a "hun-loving" pacifist and Bolshevik.[122] Yet, in the context of the war, this conservative feminism was not without logic. Despite their jingoistic stance, the Pankhursts and their colleagues worked relentlessly to publicize women's contributions to the war effort and to demolish the idea that maleness alone rendered an adult Briton worthy of the vote. Furthermore, the nationalist rhetoric with which they framed the case for female citizenship was not, as some historians and contemporaries assumed, incompatible with feminism. The nationalist feminism articulated by the Pankhursts shows that a feminist agenda could be tacked onto many different politics. Indeed, the Pankhursts were not so much a feminist anomaly as the feminists most in tune with the cultural climate of wartime Britain and it was their vision of the meaning of citizenship that was to be most fully realized in the momentous legislation that granted women the vote.[123] Even as they alienated former colleagues in the women's movement, they acquired the backing of an odd assortment of new allies, ranging from right-wing press barons to conservative munitionettes. Lloyd George himself celebrated the suffrage victory with Mrs. Pankhurst at an intimate breakfast at 10 Downing Street.[124] Such scenes make sense only if we recognize that the Pankhursts' retreat from militancy did not constitute an "abandonment of suffrage agitation," but simply a shrewd change in tactics—one that paralleled the similar patriotic refashioning of the National Union. If the Pankhursts' methods were unusual, it will become apparent that their patriotic logic was not.

PART III

THE CULTURAL CONSTRUCTION
OF THE LAW

Chapter Seven

The Power of Sacrifice

"Physical Force" and Women's Work

Mabel Lethbridge was only seventeen years old at the time of the accident that would change her life. In 1916 she "lied to her mother" about the type of work she planned to do and "lied about her age" to get into the munitions factory. Historian David Mitchell tells the story from a rare interview with her "nearly fifty years and forty five operations later." After working in the factory at Hayes, near London, for less than a week, "she volunteered to work one of the antiquated 'monkey machines' that forced a mixture of amatol and TNT down into the 18-pounder shell cases. Four girls hauled on a rope to raise a massive weight (the 'beater') and then, at a signal, let it drop on the mixture, until it was packed tight." Although the Ministry of Munitions had condemned this dangerous way of handling TNT, the new machines had not yet arrived at the works, and Miss Lethbridge and her friends were forced to continue filling shells in a manner that had already resulted in numerous accidents. "Toward the end of her shift, as Mabel gave the signal to lower and the 'beater' descended on yet another shell, there was a frightful explosion. The workers were blown to bits or burned alive, and she was the sole survivor. Appallingly wounded, she was unconscious for ten days; her left leg was amputated, and surgeons cut and stitched and grafted away at her shattered body." She was awarded the Order of the British Empire for her bravery, but it must have been poor consolation for the loss of that limb.[1]

In a context in which female war workers could sustain such horrific wounds, the logic of much anti-suffrage argumentation began to unravel.

Despite the nationalistic displays orchestrated by the Pankhursts and other patriotic women, the most fundamental argument for denying women the vote remained one of "physical force." While 1916 saw a series of noteworthy "conversions" to the idea of women's suffrage, a committed phalanx of "Antis" vocally opposed any expansion of the female franchise when the idea of legislative reform was introduced later that year. Drawing upon quickly deteriorating prewar logic, Antis asserted that women did not deserve the parliamentary vote because their place was "in the home," they were "of no use in war," and they lacked the capacity to use "physical force," upon which both domestic law and international diplomacy ultimately rested. Since women's "nature" prevented them from bearing arms, they were not entitled to the same rights and privileges as male electors, who could be called upon at any time to sacrifice their lives for the state. To Antis, this claim upon men was the bedrock of citizenship.

During the war, however, women's groups and individual women alike began to undercut the physical-force argument in three dramatic ways. The first and most spectacular was the demand made by a small but vocal group of women for the right to bear arms. The second related assault involved highlighting the heroic self-sacrifice of women under fire, particularly doctors and nurses who, like Edith Cavell, had sacrificed their lives for a patriotic cause as willingly and bravely as any man in the field. The final and most important was the recognition among all sectors of society that female war workers, who fought the enemy from behind the lines at considerable personal cost, bore a claim to the vote indistinguishable from that of their male colleagues. The work of these women was not only significant in its own right, but greatly facilitated the suffrage case by captivating public opinion and undercutting anti-suffrage argumentation on its own terms. Indeed, the Pankhursts were not as anomalous as they might at first appear. As we shall see, Britain's mainstream suffragists too lost no opportunity to promote, publicize, and exploit for political ends the heroic activity of the "Women of Britain."

"Arms and the Woman"

Female armed service had rarely been more seriously discussed by women than at the moment when invasion appeared possible and the horrors of war seemed to lie at Britain's threshold. Numerous women insisted upon their willingness to serve at the front, declaring a desire to fight and if need be to die for their country. In 1914, *Votes for Women*, the official organ of the United Suffragists, published a series of articles and letters on whether a women's militia should be formed for home defense. Published under the telling heading "Should Women Shoot?," the debate grew out of a dispute between Emmeline Pethick Lawrence, the pacifist leader of the United Suffragists, and the Honorable Evelina Haverfield, one of the organization's most vigorous proponents of patriotic action, over Haverfield's proposal to form a Women's Volunteer Rifle Corps.

Emmeline Pethick Lawrence was a former militant who remained committed to antiwar feminism. Endorsing an international feminist pacifism, she spoke at Carnegie Hall in New York, only a week after Christabel Pankhurst, on "women's work in stopping war."[2] She remained deeply opposed to women bearing arms and discouraged feminists from joining a Women's Volunteer Rifle Corps. Evelina Haverfield was cut from a different piece of cloth. Mrs. Haverfield was the daughter of a British peer who had accompanied her husband to the Boer War, where she made herself indispensable by supplying his regiment with remounts collected off the veldt. As an expert horsewoman, she was useful not only to the British army but later to the militant suffragettes for whom she paraded on horseback dressed in full Joan of Arc armor before she was imprisoned in 1910 for rushing the houses of Parliament. With the outbreak of war in 1914, she founded the Women's Emergency Corps, to replace men in a variety of occupations, and later founded the Women's Volunteer Reserve— a paramilitary organization that performed militarily useful work as well as drilling, parading, and marching in uniform. Unable to satisfy her thirst for action at home, Mrs. Haverfield eventually joined Dr. Elsie Inglis's Scottish Women's Hospitals as director of transportation—a post from which she resigned following accusations that she imposed overly harsh discipline on her orderlies and ambulance women.[3]

Those readers who responded affirmatively to the question "Should Women Shoot?" believed that a women's defense force might be the only shield between British women and the sort of wholesale sexual violence experienced in Belgium. "What has been the result of being helpless, inefficient, and weak?" asked Lena Ashwell. "Surely horror of indescribable and fearful proportions. . . . [P]erhaps it is better to die fighting than to be the passive victims of mutilations and worse than mutilations."[4] Indeed, news of the invasion of Belgium and the German threat to the channel ports meant that many Britons took the possibility of invasion more seriously than they had at any time since the Napoleonic Wars.[5] Women particularly were terrorized by reports of atrocities and were those most likely to encounter the Belgian refugees who flooded England carrying stories of war, homelessness, and devastation. Noting that British women who were caught resisting an invading enemy could be treated as *francs tireurs* and summarily executed under the rules of war, women like Mrs. Haverfield and Mrs. Dawson Scott supported the formation of recognized women's militias that would function similarly to the Territorial forces raised for home defense.[6] While controversy prevented Mrs. Haverfield from arming her volunteers, she and her followers insisted that drill practice was essential to "train women for their own defense in the last extremity" and that "if women made themselves really efficient they would be recognized when the time came."[7]

Many women were, of course, horrified by these arguments. Mrs. Hertha Ayrton, for example, pointed out that women not only risked their lives every time they brought a child into the world, but suggested that if suffragists took up arms they would, "acquiesce in the suggestion . . . that the rights of citizenship can only be granted to those who kill."[8] While many women opposed Mrs. Haverfield's suggestion for its impracticality, for the impossibility of gaining the government recognition essential to transforming armed women into recognized "regular" reserves, and for its wholesale abandonment of women's larger pacifist commitment, to women like Mrs. Haverfield, Mrs. Dawson Scott, and Mrs. Alec Tweedie the bearing of arms held a particular allure as the ultimate symbol of female equality.[9] "Women are being appealed to every day in the Press to send out their sons and brothers and friends," commented Miss Olive Hockin. "It seems to me impossible for a suffragist to do this and to stand aloof in feminine superiority, saying that she is too pure and spiritual to fight herself, and therefore her male relations must do it for her."[10]

While Mrs. Haverfield denied any intention to engage the enemy except in the event of invasion, the marching and drilling of uniformed women and the adoption of military "rank" gained an astonishing popularity among women on the homefront, despite scathing ridicule. Numerous "church bazaar" corps sprung up all over England, much to the annoyance of those who disliked the spectacle of women "playing soldier." As Violet Markham disparagingly put it, women seemed to be adopting the khaki uniforms and military titles of "men who have fallen on the bloodstained fields of Flanders or in the trenches of Galliopli," and Gladys Medwin went so far as to ask whether these "pseudo-superwomen" had been able to "gird on manhood at a moment's notice."[11] Yet to enthusiasts like "Colonel" Bertha Aikin, commander of the Active Service Girl's Cadet Corps, such organizations were useful on the home front and kept young girls productively employed: "Our motto is—'be strong and very courageous.'"[12] Foreshadowing the popularity of women's volunteer police forces and women's auxiliary military services, such uniformed paramilitary organizations demonstrated women's passionate desire to be recognized as servants of the state and their wish to sport the "sacred khaki" that had come to symbolize citizenship itself.[13]

It is perhaps for these reasons that Sergeant Flora Sandes gained such popularity with Britain's female public. No one brought home women's willingness to face danger more dramatically than Sandes, whose noted exploits with the Serbian army seemed to serve as proof that women could operate effectively on the field of battle.[14] The forty-year-old daughter of a Suffolk vicar attached to a Serbian hospital unit, Sandes unexpectedly became a combatant in October 1915 during a retreat when her commanding officer, wishing to retain all competent personnel, inducted her into the Serbian army so that she would not be sent back from the advancing Bulgarians. In August 1916, Sandes was given command of a platoon during a withering campaign in which the Serbian Second Regiment was reduced from three thousand to five hundred men. Sandes was not seriously wounded until November 1916, when her arm and leg were pierced with shrapnel during a battle in Macedonia. In the hospital, she was decorated with the Kara George Star—the most coveted decoration in the Serbian army—and promoted to Sergeant Major. Eventually she was sent to England, where she achieved fantastic success as a fundraiser for the Serbian army. Despite her success in London, she returned to the front in time to help recapture Serbia from the enemy in the great offensive of September 1918.

Flora Sandes was turned into a heroine both by the Serbs—who valued her fundraising skill and her ability to wrangle uniforms from the British authorities—and the many British women who tucked news of her exploits into scrapbooks and diaries. She also became a role model for women who dreamed of the right to serve and who were perhaps emboldened by her success to offer their services to the state. "Rather than let the old country go under, the women of the Empire would be willing, aye more than willing to take a place in the firing line," declared Mrs. Alec Tweedie, who lost her own son in 1917. "Give [women] a chance of the trenches . . . if our country wants us we shall go to fight. The writer is ready to form a Women's Battalion, the moment it becomes necessary for women to fill that fighting breach. Women have done more for their country than handle a rifle, and thousands of us are ready to do that too."[15] Such offers were, of course, roundly declined by military authorities, yet the spectacle of women's willingness to fight, to serve, to work, and to die for the war effort had a powerful effect on feminists' ability to justify their claim to citizenship. As "General" Flora Drummond was able to point out in 1918, women's absence from the fighting line had nothing to do with their unwillingness to serve but only with the government's unwillingness to consider women's offer. Lord Kitchener, Mrs. Drummond declared, had evidence that "thousands of women had offered to go into the trenches, and the reason why they were not there was because they were not permitted."[16]

In a context in which the willingness to serve counted for almost as much as service itself, women's ability to make a plausible claim regarding their willingness to fight was an issue of at least rhetorical importance. "I see mischief ahead in Girl Guides, in Leagues of Honour, and in this very Women's Emergency Corps," wrote one discomfited anti-suffrage commentator, while another deplored the attempt to make patriotism the "trade-mark" of suffragism and denounced the "offer of a notorious Suffragist lady to raise a battalion of fighting women," adding that such women were likely to be "shot and bayonetted" by the enemy or to "take advantage of their sex so as to put the enemy's soldiers into an unfair and impossible position. . . ."[17] Because only one British woman saw actual combat in World War I (although several succeeded in enlisting only to be unmasked at the front), the achievements of women like Mrs. Evelina Haverfield and Flora Sandes are largely symbolic—but their symbolism was significant in showing that a vocal handful of British feminists did not flinch at the idea of bearing arms and that even those opposed to such measures took the arguments of their opponents seriously.

With the suffragettes' militant campaign, women's capacity for violent action had been graphically brought home. The idea of armed female service was but a step beyond the capacity for terrorist violence that few would have thought possible before the Pankhursts unleashed their militant campaign for the vote.[18] Eleanore Rathbone, while repudiating the use of arms by women, nevertheless believed that women "have as much right to risk their lives in the service of their country as men" and in an unusual concession reminded constitutionalists that "The militant suffragists have at least demonstrated the courage and endurance of women under physical suffering. I believe that many National Union women would welcome eagerly the opportunity of proving that they are as ready as the militants to face danger. . . ."[19] Her challenge would be more than met by the unarmed women who braved shell fire in medical units throughout Europe.

"Bravery & Devotion under Fire"
Medical Service and Personal Risk

As World War I progressed, the language used to describe the significance of going to war subtly changed in emphasis. While at the beginning of the war, praise for soldiers emphasized their bravery, their sprit, and their prowess in battle, by 1916 the apotheosis of the Tommy centered on his willingness to make the "Great Sacrifice." This subtle shift from an emphasis on the ability to kill to reverence for a willingness to die put women's claim to comparable service on much firmer ground. Dr. Elsie Inglis, Dr. Louisa Garrett Anderson, nurse Edith Cavell, and a host of lesser-known women who served as nurses, doctors, orderlies, stretcher bearers, and drivers at the front illustrated women's bravery in the face of physical danger.

If to most Britons the idea of women bearing arms had an eccentric im- plausibility about it, sacrifice and suffering did not. Atrocity propaganda, which emphasized the rape and murder of women and children, was seized upon by feminists who wished to dispute the fallacy that, in war, women rested comfortably behind the lines. Zeppelin raids on London and costal towns and the sinking of passenger liners only brought home further the fact that even British women were vulnerable to enemy action.[20] While giv- ing birth to "future soldiers," under often dangerous hygienic conditions, or being brutalized by a murderous enemy certainly illustrated that women spilled blood in the name of war, both these arguments cast women as victims with little agency in risking their lives. The work of women at the front was therefore significant in demonstrating women's ability to make the same sort of willing, patriotic sacrifice as men who vol- unteered for the army. No organization built its reputation for patriotism on such heroic self-sacrifice more effectively that the National Union, which raised the astronomical sum of £500,000 to support fourteen all-fe- male hospital units under the efficient direction of Dr. Elsie Inglis.[21]

Dr. Inglis was a graduate of the University of Edinburgh Medical School and a founder of the Scottish Women's Suffrage Federation. She offered her services to the War Office at the beginning of the conflict but, like many other women doctors, was unceremoniously told to "go home and sit still."[22] Because of the sexism of the British authorities, British medical women wishing to serve in combat zones frequently enlisted with the French, Belgian, Russian, or Serbian Red Cross, for whom dire necessity outweighed any preference for male doctors. Treating dangerous fever epi- demics as well as harrowing war wounds, British women doctors frequently found themselves overwhelmed by the medical needs of defeated armies moving through impoverished regions in central and eastern Europe. While the NU established one permanent hospital behind the French lines, most of the other units "moved from place to place, working at Calais, Corsica, Troyes, Salonica, and numerous towns in Serbia, Russia and Roumania."[23] Ironically, the prejudice of the British authorities meant that the NU hospi- tal units performed much more dangerous service than they would have done otherwise. Both the Serb and the Russian armies were severely beaten, subjecting the British medical women to dangerous retreats. While advanc- ing armies had the power to keep medical personnel behind the battle lines, retreating armies were often followed by their medical units, which risked being overrun, shelled, or taken prisoner by the enemy at any time. Katherine Hodges North, an ambulance driver with the Scottish Women's Hospital (whose transport was under the direction of Evelina Haverfield), describes a terrifying retreat from advancing Bulgarian troops in Roumania in October 1916. "All the time we were going we heard guns nearer and nearer. . . ."

[J]ust over the hill the shells were bursting and flames from the burning town and oil wells could be seen. Two or three shells burst over us while we waited. Then the order was given to get on, *retreat*, and all the soldiers had to go first. We were the last of all and when we'd got about a quarter of a mile our (blasted) car stopped and wouldn't budge, so with great calmness! With shells coming nearer and nearer, we cleaned the plugs, oiled various bits and eventually . . . she started. . . . It was getting towards sunset, there was a scarlet sky, a vast undulating plain ahead, behind us the crash of ever nearing guns and the long lines of soldiers coming wearily back. Again orders to move, and again we kept to the last and it began to pour. Off we went, and I shall always see that sinister plain and the rain and the grey ghostlike figures of the soldiers and guns retreating.[24]

Such bravery inspired intense admiration. "It is extraordinary how the women endure hardships," wrote the prefect of Constanza in a widely quoted comment on the Scottish Women's Hospitals. "They refuse help, and carry the wounded themselves. They work like navvies. No wonder England is a great country if the women are like that."[25] Indeed, Dr. Inglis became the first women to be awarded the Serbian Order of the White Eagle, presented by the crown prince for her decision to stay with wounded Serbian soldiers even as her hospital was being overrun by the enemy during the retreat through Dobrudja.[26] Inglis died of advanced cancer shortly after she had successfully evacuated her wounded troops from Archangel in a heroic escape aided by the British authorities. Much to the pride of the NU, which ran frequent stories on the Scottish Women's Hospitals in *Common Cause*, Dr. Inglis was buried on November 29, 1917, with full military honors at St. Giles Cathedral, Edinburgh. Her heroism and death received significant and adulatory coverage in the London, Scottish, and provincial press, where Elsie Inglis had become a household name. According to the *Lancet*, Britain's premier medical journal, Dr. Inglis represented the "conquest of bravery over terror, sanitation over muck, and order over chaos. . . . Elsie Inglis gave her life for her country and its Allies as truly as any soldier in the trenches has ever done. . . ."[27]

The achievements of Dr. Elsie Inglis and the many other women who risked their lives at the front would be put to good use by Britain's suffragists. Mrs. Arncliffe Sennett, president of the Northern Men's Federation of Women's Suffrage, loudly objected during a patriotic meeting in 1916, when Horatio Bottomley praised female war service but denounced suffrage agitation. Despite the hisses of uniformed women, Mrs. Sennett stymied Bottomley by inquiring whether he knew that "nearly all those organizations he has extolled were initiated, formed and are chiefly run by suffragists, who want their rights? Does he know that the Scottish Units were equipped, financed, and sent out to the war zone by Mrs. Fawcett's organization?"[28] Similarly, *Common Cause*, when commenting on Lord Charles Beresford's proposal to bestow the vote on every volunteer who had risked his life for his country, asked about the qualifications of "the hundreds of women who are serving at the front, and risking their lives in nursing deadly fevers, and who have in many instances been exposed to shell fire as well as the soldiers." Moreover, the writer pointed out, "for every woman who is accepted for service abroad there are probably dozens who have volunteered . . . ," not to mention the "multitudes of women who risk their lives . . . and die in thousands in order to give birth to the men who serve the state."[29]

Such claims were important given the negative publicity women received for the pacifist activity of several prominent members of the NU leadership. The National Union was Britain's largest suffrage society and also its most divided, comprising between five and six hundred affiliated chapters and representing fifty-two thousand members all over the country.[30] The NU, like many suffrage organizations, was deeply split between nationalists who believed that women must make fighting Germany a patriotic priority, and pacifists who still believed feminism and militarism to be incompatible. At the outset of war Mrs. Fawcett took the bold stand of informing all NU members that they should now consider themselves to be members of the "Women's Active Service League"—a title adopted to mark the ostensible end of suffrage agitation.[31] While the rank-and-file membership for the most part seemed to concur with such patriotic intentions, a number of prominent NU leaders, including Catherine Marshall, Helena Swanwick, and Maude Royden, continued to agitate against the war. Few suffrage organizations managed to keep these differences submerged for long, and with the exception of Sylvia Pankhurst's unyieldingly pacifist *Women's Dreadnought* and Christabel's uncompromisingly jingoistic *Britannia,* the pages of most women's suffrage journals accommodated sharp disagreement over issues of war, pacifism, and patriotism. As Sylvia Pankhurst wistfully put it, "the profound divergences of opinion on war and peace had been shown to know no sex."[32]

Initially Mrs. Fawcett attempted to keep together her pacifist and nationalist wings by committing the NU to relief work, which was both a patriotic necessity and decidedly nonviolent. This uneasy compromise was shattered by the request of several NU leaders for passports to attend an International Women's Peace Meeting at the Hague. Though most British delegates were denied passports for Holland by unsympathetic British authorities (ostensibly looking out for the women's safety in hostile waters), many *Common Cause* readers regarded the overture—and subsequent pacifist activity—as treason plain and simple.[33] "Let the pacifists . . . contemplate the result achieved by Peace Conferences," hissed Adela M. Spon. "Must they not admit that they have merely enabled the Huns to steal the march on their more honourable and humane enemies? I think it is greatly to be deplored that The Common Cause . . . should be used as an organ for airing principles that the great majority of Englishwomen look upon as offensive and traitorous to that greater common cause—the defense of this realm of Great Britain against its enemies."[34] Indeed, French feminists had refused to attend the Hague Conference at all and Madame Veronne, a prominent French suffragist, had unexpectedly denounced any pacifist overtures while Belgium and parts of France were occupied by Germany.[35]

Many *Common Cause* readers shared these sentiments. In the autumn of 1914, a pacifist letter by Nora O'Shea calling for a speedy end to hostilities received a torrent of angry responses. "I can think of nothing which would cause men more greatly (and reasonably) to mistrust our judgement in national action than feminine agitation for premature peace," wrote Agatha M. Richardson from Dublin, while Ellen Capman declared that, "If suffragists are at this crisis going to advocate an 'early cessation of hostilities,' it will only prove the Antis are right in arguing that women are unfit to form an opinion on Imperial matters." Moreover, she added, "it will alienate the sympathies of many women . . . who are utterly opposed to such a short sighted and suicidal policy as that of the pacifists."[36] Hostile reactions to the Women's Peace Meeting at the Hague were, if anything, even more fierce. Dr. Ethyl Smyth wrote to the *Morning Post* enclosing her reply to a solicitation made on behalf of the peace conference: "Whether you realize it or not, you are playing the game of Germany, and for that reason are traitors. As one of a family of soldiers I am ashamed that such literature should have passed my doors."[37] Such sentiments were echoed over and over by rank-and-file members in the pages of *Common Cause*, despite a running and articulate disagreement presented by the pacifist members of the NU leadership. As Jane Ellen Harrison wrote after being misquoted by the antiwar writer C. K. Ogden, "I believe the present war to be both necessary and just."[38] Similarly, Marion Chadwick, defending the pacifists, nevertheless observed that "very few Suffragists desire the war to cease until Belgium is cleared from her oppressors," while Harriet Powell reminded fellow suffragists that Germany was "a nation fighting against civilization, with hands dipped in the blood of Europe, branded with the brand of Cain." Why, she asked, would pacifists like Isabel Ashby "urge Suffragists to make no war munitions for their husbands, their lovers, and their sons, who are pouring out their blood in the trenches? Does she wish our men to die defenseless?"[39]

With a shrewd eye to politics in Westminster and to the attitude of the press, Mrs. Fawcett, the experienced Liberal leader of the NU, believed that the association of feminism with pacifism at that moment would be irretrievably damaging to the cause of women's suffrage.[40] Already, the increasingly acrimonious debates in the pages of *Common Cause* had given the ultra-patriotic Pankhursts the opportunity to seize public opinion and denounce their old rivals as nefarious peace-mongers. Worse still, the pacifist activities of the NU leadership and the Women's Peace Meeting at the Hague were the staple news items in the *Anti-Suffrage Review* and other conservative journals and an embarrassment to many patriotic rank and file members who were becoming disgusted with the "disloyal pacifism" of the dissenters. In the face of scathing press reports and uncontrollable dissent within the ranks, Mrs. Fawcett finally purged the leadership of its pacifist elements by orchestrating a resignation over the issues of whether or not the NU would send two official delegates to the Hague.[41] Despite deep and lingering bitterness, *Common Cause* emerged trumpeting the invaluable aid women had given to the war effort. The Bryce Report appeared just in time to further vindicate the anti-pacifist position taken by the majority leadership, and the NU executive embraced a shrewd patriotic feminism with calculating vigor.[42] As the *Anti-Suffrage Review* rather aptly attested, "They sew and knit comforts for the soldiers, but with such a perpetual running accompaniment of suffragist self-laudation that they might as well embroider the sacred name of Mrs. Pankhurst or Mrs. Fawcett on every sock and every muffler, so as to give notice to the soldiers as well as to the country . . . that Suffragism alone has the trademark of thoughtful and benevolent patriotism."[43]

The *Anti-Suffrage Review* had reason for complaint. Not only was Dr. Inglis being lionized as a heroine, but other medical women were also capturing the hearts and headlines of Great Britain. The former militant Dr. Louisa Garret Anderson and her medical partner Dr. Flora Murray succeed first in Paris and then in a convalescent hospital in London to become one of the most successful medical teams of the war. Much to the fury of the *Anti-Suffrage Review,* Drs. Murray and Anderson tried to convert their patients to a pro-suffrage position by wearing the suffragette colors of purple, white, and green, displaying the militant motto—"Deeds not Words"—prominently in the hospital, and proselytizing to the wounded about the justice of women's suffrage.[44]

While exceptional women like Drs. Inglis and Garret Anderson received much publicity, hundreds of ordinary middle class women like Vera Brittain saw service abroad as nurses and orderlies stationed close to or on the front lines.[45] Subject to shell fire, wounds, and a participant's view of the war, many of these young women took pride in the danger and importance of their work, which was vividly brought home by the relatively new medium of snapshot photography.[46] Yet the sacrifice of one woman would make more of an impact on the national psyche than the service of all other medical women combined. That women was, of course, nurse Edith Cavell, whose dramatic execution in 1915 by a German firing squad made the world gasp.

In death, this obscure, middle aged spinster became an international superstar, the quintessential martyr to "German barbarism," and an evocative symbol of the Allied cause. As we have seen, Edith Cavell was a British nurse, shot for smuggling Allied prisoners out of occupied Belgium—a capital offense under the laws of war. She was also the very embodiment of acceptable female patriotism. As a nurse ministering to the sick and wounded, Cavell glowed with the idealized aura of nurturing femininity, while discreetly offering practical and essential assistance to her country. It was thus with horror that the British learned she had been shot for treason by the enemy in an act of seeming barbarism that is perhaps more shocking for its propagandistic ineptitude than for its revelations about the German capacity for violence against women. Cavell's arrest, her languishing stay in a damp jail cell, the futile pleas for clemency, and the bravery and dignity of her dying words were all well known. Her death itself was narratively reenacted again and again in newspapers, books, and pictures, becoming a regular feature of the notoriously tasteless "Crimes of Germany" calender series as well as in lurid atrocity postcards. A small, unfinished net purse, crocheted while she sat on death row, is still preserved like a holy relic in the archives of the Imperial War Museum—testament to a time when all she touched seemed vaguely sacred.[47]

Despite the almost universal adulation of Cavell and the inordinate horror at her death, her symbolism was itself deeply contested. While pacifists claimed her dying words—"Patriotism is not enough"—as the final vindication of their repudiation of warfare, military authorities busily used her execution as the centerpiece of a last-ditch recruiting campaign designed to stave off (or, failing that, to vindicate) conscription.[48] Meanwhile, feminists claimed Cavell as one of their own, harnessing her death to the cause of women's suffrage and using it to foreground women's capacity for militarily useful action and their willingness to die for their country. In an article tellingly entitled "Justice for Women or Sentimental Cant," *Votes for*

Women claimed that "Miss Cavell . . . has had her actions and her memory insulted and degraded by every sort of sentimental misrepresentation." Deploring the characterization of the fifty-year-old Cavell as a "girl" and the implication that Cavell was naively unaware of the gravity of her offense, the author insisted that "What Miss Cavell did she did with her eyes open . . . she died in the holy conviction that she had done right. Is it not intolerable [to suggest that she was] the victim of the tragedy instead of its heroine? . . . [S]he knew very well what penalty she incurred and would have been ashamed to shirk it on grounds of sex."[49]

Ironically, the feminist implications of Cavell's death were most trenchantly brought out by George Bernard Shaw, who provocatively observed that "if she had come back alive to demand the political rights granted to the meanest men, and had broken a shop window to compel attention to her claim, she would have been mobbed and insulted and subjected to gross physical violence." To Shaw, this irony left Britons with two options. Either "enfranchise her sex in recognition of her proof of its valour" or acknowledge "that Edith Cavell's sacrifice has been rejected by her country." As *Votes for Women* pointedly asked, "Throughout all the years in which women . . . have demanded the vote has any attempt been made to exclude unchivalrous men? The meanest men, as Mr. Shaw points out, are able to vote: why not women?"[50]

Like women who wished to bear arms, women who risked injury or death became an important part of both feminist panegyric and suffrage argumentation.[51] This bravery didn't slip the notice of the general public. Not only did the *Times History of the World War* devote an issue to women's work that highlighted the Scottish Women's Hospitals, but in 1916 the king ordered that the military medal could be awarded to women who had shown "bravery and devotion under fire." "This," commented the *Daily Telegraph,* "is a most significant and gratifying act. It is an indication of the changed attitude of women themselves to war, and also of the nation towards women who . . . render conspicuous service during hostilities. . . . 'The Commander-in-Chief in the Field' is practically enjoined not to overlook women . . . who serve the state."[52]

Such recognition of women's heroism under fire, and the attention it received in the press, once again deeply discomfited the stalwarts of the *Anti-Suffrage Review.* Griselda Cheape deplored the way suffragists seemed to be making "strong headway with the unthinking public. . . . 'Look!' they exclaim, 'what the women have done. Look! At Serbia, at Miss Elsie Inglis.'" Yet, as she weakly insisted, women would always be the "auxiliary sex" since the use of German prisoners to carry stretchers showed that the physical force argument still held strong.[53] Such arguments carried little weight. Elsie Inglis, anticipating such comments, refused to work with male personnel despite official pleas to spare women from the most dangerous types of transport work. Not only did suffragists continually emphasize the daring self-sacrifice of women who gave up their lives, but such reasoning began to make headway even in the houses of Parliament. Asquith attributed his "conversion" to women's suffrage to the heroic actions of women like Edith Cavell, who had "taught the bravest man amongst us a supreme lesson of courage," and Haldane battled a last-ditch effort by Lord Loreburn to derail women's suffrage in the House of Lords by pointing out that "Women are taking a tremendous part in this war. They are sacrificing their health, their lungs. . . . A good many have died. There have been women, like Edith Cavell, whose names will not be forgotten, women who have died under shell fire, died under bombardment, died by bullet wounds just the same as men have died."[54]

"Tommy's Sister"

Ultimately, however, the argument against women's suffrage was most powerfully subverted by those women whose work at home made it possible for Britain to wage war and whose service to the country was indistinguishable from that of their male colleagues. If women serving on the battlelines helped to undermine the physical force argument, women war workers undercut traditional ideas about "women's place." As even Mrs. Despard's journal the *Vote* could not resist pointing out, "Women's place . . . is no longer the home. . . . It is the battlefield, the farm, the factory, the shop. . . ."[55]

The role of women war workers in winning the vote has been deeply contested, largely because of the age limitation that in the end excluded women in their twenties (who made up the majority of the nearly one million female munitions workers) from the very vote their heroic work was supposed to have won. Yet women's war work was a major catalyst to change, for its jolting of expectations about women, for its placement of women at the center of the war machine, and for the effacement of difference between "male" and "female" roles that lay at the heart of anti-suffrage arguments.[56] With conscription and the implementation of the Munitions Acts, which eased restrictions on unskilled labor, 1916 saw the increasing replacement of male with female workers at home. The surprise of seeing women in munitions factories, as conductors on trams, as police constables, and in a variety of other activities that required efficiency, strength, and masculine dress startled people and resulted in tremendous public interest in women's roles and extensive praise for the "splendid women" who were making it possible to carry on at home.

Of course, women in Edwardian Britain had always done inordinately hot, heavy, dangerous, and dirty work. Backbreaking laundry work, relentless piecework, unsafe factory operations, filthy rag collecting, and humiliating domestic service were all part of the ill paid, relentless, and meager lot of England's poor. With the outbreak of war in 1914, women of the upper classes inadvertently threw thousands of their working-class sisters out of work by patriotically denying themselves pretty hats, new frocks, delicate lace, and other "frivolous" finery that allowed poor seamstresses, textile workers, milliners and the like to eke out a living in sweated trades. So severe did female unemployment become in the opening months of the war, that Queen Mary joined forces with Mary Macarthur, the celebrated leader of the National Federation of Women Workers, to provide work for destitute women. The unlikely conjunction of "Mary R & Mary M" was widely remarked on, but succeeded at least in providing some low-paid needlework for laboring women.[57]

Women would receive further assistance from unexpected quarters. In May 1915, Lord Northcliffe, owner of the *Times* and the *Daily Mail,* broke the story of a "shell scandal," alleging that the Asquith government's desultory attitude toward the war had resulted in a shell shortage that left British soldiers unable to defend themselves. So great was the furor over these charges that it precipitated a political crisis and a new coalition government was formed, retaining Asquith as prime minister but offering cabinet posts to prominent representatives from all the major parties and establishing a Ministry of Munitions under the Welsh maverick David Lloyd George. As we have seen, Lloyd George was enthusiastic about the substitution of women for men in industry and, despite union opposition, began the campaign for "dilution" that fired off its first shots by engaging Mrs. Pankhurst to stage a giant procession in favor of women's work. The thousands of women—patriotic, desperate, or a bit of both— who signed the registers attesting to their willingness to work and the thousands more who daily flooded the offices of the WSPU with mail requesting information on how to serve signified to the country women's readiness to take on men's work. Armed with slogans like "Shells Made by a Wife may Save her Husband's Life," this willing female labor force made it increasingly difficult for trade unions to resist dilution, particularly as the Northcliffe press insisted that "substitution" was crucial to providing the shells and ammunition for vulnerable soldiers to defend themselves.

The substitution of women for men began to make a visual impact on the home front in the summer of 1915, and by 1916 the process was in full swing, facilitated greatly by the advent of conscription. It would be difficult to overemphasize the psychological and emotional significance of this change in visual culture. While women's work had previously been rendered "invisible" by its sheer commonplaceness, the re-gendering of visual idioms with a glimpse of ankle under unceremoniously short work skirts, small boots peeping from beneath dirty trousers, or a female face under a conductor's cap became magnets for the interested attention for passersby. Such jarring images would probably not have been tolerated in any other context. Yet the fury generated by the sight of an apparently healthy young man at work on the home front was so acute that it considerably mitigated the shock of seeing a woman laboring in his place. The astonishing sight of, say, a female milkman was thus rendered acceptable by the thought of the man she had released for service.

Accounts of the re-gendering of the homefront almost universally celebrate its sheer exuberant heterogeneity—a heterogeneity that was essential to the reevaluation of women's capabilities. Suffrage marches, which began to recommence in 1916 and 1917 following discussion of franchise reform, ostentatiously paraded women workers in a spectacle of diversity, competence, and patriotism. A march orchestrated by the Pankhursts in July 1916 carried icons commemorating the dead Kitchener, while munitions girls chanted "We want Hughes"—the ultra-imperialist Australian premier—as they "waved their hammers and spanners and their shining brass shell cases for Mr. Lloyd George to see."[58] A "great parade for women's suffrage" staged in March 1916 by the constitutionalists "took the form, of course, of a demonstration of the women war workers," explained Ray Strachey. "Almost all the women of the country were war-workers in one way or another, and there was no other form it could take. . . . [W]omen from seventy different trades . . . were on the platform, and the organizations supporting the meeting numbered over two million."[59] Finally, a massive suffrage deputation led by Mrs. Fawcett to 10 Downing Street in April 1917 not only included in its ranks Mrs. Pankhurst and representatives from over thirty other suffrage societies and affiliated organizations, but included actresses, agricultural workers, ambulance drivers, accountants, bacteriologists, bus conductors, bakers, civil servants, carpenters, dentists, dressmakers, doctors, electroplate workers, infant welfare workers, lamplighters, munitions workers, midwives, nurses, oxyacetylene welders, pit-brow workers, police women, poor-law guardians, railway women, silversmiths, textile workers, telephonists, van drivers, Voluntary Aid Detachment nurses, representatives of the Overseas Dominions, the Millicent Fawcett Hospital Units for Russia, the Scottish Women's Hospitals, and more in a virtual alphabet of women's newfound utility.[60]

Because the press was restricted in what it could print regarding operations at the front, journalists in search of good stories spent much time focusing on women's substitution for men on the home front—a subject that proved perennially popular with readers of both sexes. Indeed, women may never have been more popular in England than they were in 1916, and no one was more surprised than organized feminists so accustomed to weathering the wrath of the press and the public. "[B]y the middle of 1916 there was a universal chorus of praise for women," recalled Ray Strachey. "More than one well-known shipbuilder [said] publicly that he would be prepared to build the largest ironclads [with] women's labour alone. The newspapers, a little surprised, but very eloquent, took up all such remarks with enthusiasm and began to say that 'the nation is grateful to the women'—not realizing even yet that women WERE the nation just as much as the men were. And the women, a trifle dazzled by their unwonted popularity, their high wages, and their interesting new work, began to know what it was like to be made much of, and to have free scope for their abilities and powers."[61] While pacifist suffragists were dismayed to see women gain recognition over something as militaristic as war work, *Common Cause* and other suffrage journals were almost giddy with the inordinate praise of women, coming as it did at the very moment when rumblings were being heard about a modification of the franchise. "The day of women's supposed inferiority . . . has passed away . . . under the stress of war," declared the *Suffragette News Sheet*. Women had proved "able to do anything," and "that proof and its acknowledgment cannot soon be denied after the tornado of praises. . . . The eating of all those words would prove to be rather an indigestible meal."[62]

Among the plethora of occupations that provided the visual and rhetorical background for discussion of the women's vote, no craft was more widely attended to or more directly part of undermining the case against women's suffrage than munitions-making. Female munitions workers were feminists' most powerful retort to the "physical force" argument. As Angela Woollacott has written, munitions workers "were the first stage in the production line of death that ended at the front; they were well aware of the lethal nature of their manufactures and believed themselves to be essentially involved in the conduct of war." Fondly referred to as "munitionettes" or, even more tellingly, as "Tommy's sister," the munition girls "made the guns, shells, explosives, aircraft, and other materiel that 'made' the war."[63]

While home front panegyric preferred to emphasize the role of munitions girls in allowing the troops to defend themselves, at least some munitionettes took a much more aggressive view of their role. Indeed, it was not uncommon for the girls to attach notes to the shells, sometimes encouraging soldiers to kill the enemy. The self-identified "Detonator Plug Girl" fantasized about the "'dear little' detonator plug" she made that would send men "'to their last, long rest,'" while another girl casually commented to the *Sunday Times* that "lots of the girls whose men are out there want to do work that will help kill Germans and end the war."[64] Such sentiments even found their way into popular fiction. *The Englishwoman* published a one act play called *The Munitions Worker*, in which Tina, a dying explosives worker, refuses to take sick leave because God has told her to "go along and make shells for your country." Wishing to "help men at the front kill Germans," Tina refuses to abandon her post even though it means her certain death. As Angela Woollacott wryly notes, Tina's mentors "comfort themselves with the thought that Tina's spirit is 'the spirit of a whole nation soaring towards Heaven.'"[65]

If female munitions workers were very different from the nurses and ambulance drivers whose role was to succor and repair broken male bodies, they were similar in risking their lives for a patriotic cause. Hundreds of women died in munitions factories during World War I, and many more were maimed, poisoned, and plagued with a life of disability and ill health for their work. Frequently decorated with medals for bravery, these women were recognized as offering their lives for their country in a way not unlike that of Tommy Atkins himself. As Tina's doctor and factory matron put it once she had made her decision to continue making shells, she will "die as surely on the battlefield as any of our heroes."[66] Such panegyric clearly had a palliative and consoling purpose that grew out of the acknowledged danger of the occupation itself. Angela Woollacott has estimated that explosions may have accounted for upward of a thousand female deaths during the war, but because casualties were under-reported by munitions authorities, we have no complete statistical picture of how many women died or were injured in munitions plants.[67] What we know is sketchy at best, and much of it rests on personal accounts. In December 1916 a horrible explosion in the north of England killed 26 women workers and wounded 30 others.[68] At Gretna Green and Silverton in East London, a disastrous explosion and the ensuing fire took 69 lives and nearly spread across the Thames to ignite Woolwich Arsenal. In 1918 an explosion in the mixing house of a shell-filling factory near Nottingham sent up a huge mushroom cloud and killed 134 workers, including 25 women. Many more were wounded or asphyxiated. In addition to accidents and explosions brought on by the mishandling of high explosives, munitions works were the targets of zeppelin raids and bombing attacks, following which women were expected to resume their shifts immediately.[69] In solemn acknowledgment of such sacrifices, St. Paul's Cathedral held a service on April 20, 1918, for London munitions workers, playing the "Last Post" for those who had died.[70]

Perhaps the most serious consequence of munitions work, however, was not the danger of death or mutilation in an explosion, but the slow poisoning of women who worked with TNT. Known as "canary girls" because of their jaundiced yellow skin, female TNT workers sacrificed both health and beauty for patriotic work. One former munitions worker who worked at Woolwich Arsenal remembered that the TNT workers had a separate canteen because "everything they touched went yellow, chairs, tables, everything." And Lilian Miles, who handled the chemical tetryl, recalled that her black hair turned "practically green. . . . [Y]ou'd wash and wash and it didn't make no difference. It didn't come off. Your whole body was yellow."[71] According to Angela Woollacott, "for the women workers affected, their outward yellowness often meant miserable suffering, if not death." Yet they would return to their work again and again after short recuperative periods taken when skin rashes and swelling had made it too difficult for them to continue.[72] By 1916, the effect of TNT poisoning on workers was receiving some publicity. In the fall, two female physicians, Dr. Agnes Livingston and Dr. Barbara M. Cunningham, published an article in the *Lancet* demonstrating the dire health effect on women of TNT work. "An irritating rash, nausea, sore throats, and toxic jaundice are among the symptoms," they explained. Following their recommendations, authorities attempted to diminish the effects of TNT poisoning by giving girls a glass of milk or cocoa, ensuring that only those in their prime work with TNT and, in some factories, rotating them to less toxic work.[73] Yet for munitions girls themselves, and for the public absorbed with their plight, such sacrifices only enhanced the sense of comparability between their work and the work of their brothers at the front. "If I die, they can only say I have done my bit," were the dying words of twenty-year-old Florence Gleave to her father shortly before the girl succumbed to TNT poisoning. Tellingly, the newspaper that reported her death ran it under the caption "Rudheath Girl Dies for her Country."[74]

Perhaps none of these sacrifices would have mattered if women hadn't succeeded in satisfactorily performing the heavy industrial and skilled work from which they had so long been barred and that so few believed them to be capable of doing well. Nothing pleased suffragists so much as the praise of the quality and ability of these women—an issue of particular importance in a context in which appropriate wage levels for women were being hotly debated. At the outset of war, the idea of paying women workers equal wages was anathema to most employers, who believed that a "woman's work was never equal to a man's." Thanks to the indefatigable work of Mary Macarthur of the National Federation of Women Workers, supported by numerous feminist advocates of female workers, women won the same piece rates as men. But most women workers were paid on an hourly rate, and only the realization among male trade unionists that, without equal pay, female laborers would undercut them in a competitive market searching for cheap workers, did the concept of equal pay for equal work begin to take hold. While accepted by progressives in principal, women workers in practice still made only a fraction of what their male counterparts did, but these wages were still significantly higher that what they had been accustomed to, sometimes rising to more than two pounds per week—a princely sum by working-class female standards.[75] As one former munitions worker later described her changed circumstances,

> I was in domestic service and "hated every minute of it" when war broke out, earning £2 a month working from 6:00 A.M. to 9:00 P.M. So when the need came for women "war workers" my chance came to "out." I started on hand cutting shell fuses at the converted war works at the ACs Thames Ditton, Surrey. . . . We worked twelve hours a day apart from the journey morning at night at Kingston-upon-Thames. Believe me we were very ready for bed in those days, and as for wages I thought I was very well off earning five pounds a week. While at the ACs I remember a "zeppelin" got as far as London. We all had to go below ground. . . . (We were more afraid of the rats, big water ones, the works being alongside the river Thames near Hampton Court, than the zeppelin.)[76]

Despite their hard work under dangerous conditions, working hour after hour, usually on twelve-hour shifts, these high-spirited girls approached their leisure with great gusto. Because munitions girls were young and relatively wealthy, many observers remarked upon their penchant for dress, fur coats, cigarettes, and other flapperish consumer products that came to be associated with the female munitionettes. To Christabel Pankhurst, this taste for finery offered the key to amity between the classes, yet most of the press was inclined to be rather more censorious. Although authorities provided matrons to insure that no lace or frills crept onto the factory floor, attempted to provide temperant entertainment for girls, and engaged women's patrols, welfare workers, and female police to look out for the girls' morals, there was little they could do to combat the heady cultural atmosphere of the home front, especially when it was combined with money, alcohol, picture shows, dance halls, and the easy and convivial interaction between the sexes that had become customary among the young during war time. The first "flapper" was probably born during World War I on the factory floor and, as Angela Woollacott has pointed out, the munitionettes were regarded as the quintessential "Modern women."[77] Such transformation was hardly surprising. As trade unionist Mary Macarthur observed in response to one newspaper's disparagement of "Flaunting Flappers," "A girl who has to work all day in an office or factory, and to hang on her way home to a strap in a tram packed to suffocation, may lose something of her virginal shyness and diffidence, may not have eyes that are downcast and sedate, may even be hardly more alarmed by a bomb than her great-grandmother by a mouse."[78]

Despite such social innovation, suffragists found themselves with little to do in touting the contributions of female war workers; the press had latched onto them independently and drew precisely the conclusions that even the most ardent suffragist could have wished for. Emboldened by Lord Northcliffe's unexpected "conversion" to women's suffrage, which turned the *Times* and the *Daily Mail* from Anti to Suffragist newspapers, other journals began to follow suit. "[I]n the munitions factories, in the handling of heavy and often difficult machinery, and in adaptability and inventiveness and enthusiasm and steadfastness, their achievement has been astonishing," wrote H. G. Wells in the *Ladies Home Journal* of June 1916. "[I]t will be this superiority of our women . . . which has tipped the balance of this war. Those women have won the Vote. . . . The girls who have faced death and wounds so gallantly in our cordite factories . . . have killed forever the poor argument that women should not vote because they had no military value. Indeed, they have killed every argument against their subjection."[79] It was not only women's papers that lavished such praise. "The call to the Great adventure has come to both sexes," declared the *Daily Telegraph*. "The new female servants of the State are acting their part as patriots."[80] The *Glasgow Herald* meanwhile declared that "In literal truth, we are being saved by our women," while F. R. Heath, writing in the *Globe* in May 1916, proclaimed that "the women have now won their battle in the field, and . . . to continue to deny them the vote would be little short of monstrous."[81]

Feminists responded to such praise with mixed emotions. For pacifists, the terms upon which women's enfranchisement was being discussed was a bitter pill to swallow. Isabel Ashby sardonically commented on the discrepancy between the enthusiasm for pacifism and the endorsement of munitions-making in the pages of *Common Cause*, while Mary Macarthur sourly commented at a Women's Labour League Conference that "Although votes were denied to the mothers of men, it was now extremely likely the Government would concede them to the makers of machine-guns."[82] Yet most suffragists were intoxicated with the boost female war work was giving "the cause." "Our organizations remain unweakened and our belief in our cause . . . has only deepened in intensity during this time of trial," wrote a coalition of suffragists to Asquith in 1916. "If a new qualification is to be established based on services in the war, then the claim of women to a share in such a qualification cannot be ignored."[83] In all her correspondence with the Liberal administration demanding the vote, Mrs. Fawcett emphasized women's loyal contributions to the war effort, and

Asquith himself was forced to concede that "I recognize and appreciate the magnificent contribution which the women of the United Kingdom have made to the maintenance of our country's cause."[84] In May 1916 Mrs. Fawcett exuberantly reported to the NU membership that "if the citadel of Anti-suffragism has not already fallen, it is mined, and the garrison is not very far from capitulating. . . . From all parts of the country, evidence is constantly reaching our headquarters of Anti-suffragists dropping their opposition to the full citizenship of women, and assigning as the reason . . . the eagerness of women of all classes to take their share in the national burden and national sufferings caused by the war, coupled with the professional and industrial capacity of women, their adaptability, courage and endurance. These things have made a deep impression on the public mind, and have done more than anything else to produce the great change in public opinion on Women's Suffrage of which everyone is conscious."[85] As Ray Strachey would retrospectively conclude, "It was wildly illogical to be converted to women's suffrage because a girl who had been a good milliner could also be a good lift attendant; but so it was."[86]

Against this backdrop of praise and enthusiasm, the issue of franchise reform once again reared its head. The impetus came not from women, who had agreed to suspend agitation for the vote for the duration of the war, but from Conservative MPs who were deeply concerned over the disenfranchisement of soldiers at the front. Because Britain was due for a new election on the eve of war, the electoral register would have to be updated to ensure that soldiers and industrial workers would have a voice in reconstruction. Despite suffragists' truce with the government, most women's groups were unwilling to sit back quietly while the electoral register was amended to include new groups of men while holding firm on the exclusion of women. As Mrs. Fawcett warned, suffragists had "buried the hatchet, but they had marked the place where it was buried and were prepared if occasion arose to dig it up."[87] Suffragists, however, were in a far stronger position in 1916 than they had been before the war. Few people failed to notice that the war effort could not be maintained without the support of women, and 1916 had seen the movement of women into unprecedented roles in factories, on farms, and in public life that made clear the absolute essentiality of women in waging war.

CHAPTER EIGHT

VOTES FOR WHOM?

THE IDEOLOGICAL ORIGINS OF THE REPRESENTATION OF THE PEOPLE BILL

1917 had been a bad year for Mrs. Humphry Ward. Although her publishing career bounced back somewhat following Theodore Roosevelt's request that she write a stirring propaganda pamphlet for the American market, not even the luxurious research trips to the French front, the courtly attention of Britain's top generals, and the gala tours of munitions works could change the fact that the causes dearest to her heart, anti-suffrage and the career of her beloved son, Arnold, were faring badly in Parliament.[1] Furthermore, both her townhouse in Grosvenor Square and her country estate in Hertfordshire were let to the American novelist Edith Wharton, whose literary star—and literary income—had risen just as Mrs. Ward's was beginning to fall below the sum necessary to maintain her profligate family in genteel elegance.[2]

Despite such setbacks, the Conservative novelist was still the greatest asset of the National League for Opposing Women's Suffrage—a cause to which she had devoted endless energy since 1908.[3] Believing in the sanctity of womanhood, the elevated nature of women's "indirect" influence, and the proper role of women in local rather than national politics, Mrs. Humphry Ward bravely fought the sullying influence of the parliamentary vote with all the adamance that Christabel Pankhurst had battled "the Great Scourge." As one of the few eminent professional women who endorsed the "Anti" cause, Mrs. Ward paradoxically found herself the nationally renowned leader of an organization determined to return women to the domestic sphere. "There is something a little comic," Lord Robert Cecil aptly commented, "in the energy and the ability and the eloquence with which a writer like Mrs. Humphry Ward proclaims to the world that she ought not to be trusted with the franchise."[4]

Her protégé and fellow traveler was her son, Arnold. Despite bringing the family to near ruin with gambling debts incurred in London, Paris, Monaco, and Cairo, he remained loyal to his mother in his deep aversion to women's suffrage. Although Arnold Ward, MP, had been recalled from Parliament by his Unionist constituents for his shameless gaming and drinking, the wartime extension of Parliament (and the strategic intervention of his mother) left him temporarily in place to lead the fight against suffrage in the House of Commons. Taking leave from the army to do so—an absence enthusiastically granted by his regiment, which reviled him as an incompetent telltale, unfit for battle ("fat, uncountry, and a bad rider," was the withering assessment of one fellow officer)—Arnold presented himself at Westminster as a soldier-politician ready to champion the sexual underpinnings of the parliamentary vote.[5]

Indeed, he probably owed his mother as much. Her earnings as a writer provided the penniless Arnold with his sole source of income and her monthly payment to his creditors was all that kept him in the halls of Parliament rather than in the cell of a debtor's prison. Yet, despite his loyalty to the anti-suffrage cause, its fortunes sank in the lower house after a decisive debate on June 19, 1917, which resulted in a vote of 385 to 55 in favor of the women's suffrage clause of the Representation of the People Bill.[6] From then on, Arnold, his mother, and sundry other Antis including Lord James Bryce, the *Morning Post,* and an assortment of disgruntled Conservative peers would fight a rear-guard action without a driving logic, a solid organizational basis, or meaningful support in the country at large.[7] The coup de grâce to the Anti cause would come with a resounding defeat in the very bastion of conservatism itself. On January 10, 1918, the House of Lords voted 134 to 71 to approve the bill with the women's suffrage clause intact, thanks to what Mrs. Ward regarded as the nefarious "*volte face*" of Lord Curzon, who turned coat and enjoined Anti peers to abstain for the sake of national unity and peace with the lower house.[8] Mrs. Fawcett, who was sitting with Mrs. Ward outside the debating chamber, responded to her rival's horror-stricken exclamations by dryly observing, "That's what comes from trusting your men friends."[9] Despite a last-ditch attempt by diehard Antis to call for a national referendum on women's suffrage, the Representation of the People Bill, including the enfranchisement of female householders over the age of thirty, received royal assent on February 6, 1918, breaking the sex barrier and giving the vote to two-thirds of Britain's adult female population.[10]

To what turn of events did British women owe this change of fortune?[11] Despite the timing of the bill, both feminist and legislative historians have in recent years been quick to dismiss the idea that women's suffrage grew out of the patriotic service women rendered during the Great War. The former draw attention to the partial nature of the bill and to the fact that younger women—who had contributed the most to the war effort—were left out, emphasizing instead the hard work done by feminists in the prewar years to prepare politicians and the public to accept the female franchise.[12] Legislative historians, on the other hand, have tended to look at the bill as purely a product of party rivalry and political horse-trading with little to do with the prewar feminist movement or the Great War—both of which, they suggest, may actually have retarded women's suffrage.[13]

The Representation of the People Bill, however, was not simply the inevitable outcome of years of political wrangling (whether through Parliamentary politics or extra-parliamentary feminist agitation) but grew out of the cultural history of the war itself—a culture that suffragists, propagandists, Liberal and Tories, newspapermen, music hall stars, government ministers, striking workers, "conshies" and "shirkers," and the giddy young girls on the home front all helped to create. Indeed, the Reform Bill of 1918 was as much about defining manhood as about recognizing women, about honoring military service as about improving civilian life, and about codifying a system of punishment and rewards that grew out of the passion, hatred, and images of the Great War as about the democratization of the British electorate. While tempered and informed by party politics, liberal principals, and bureaucratic compromise, the Representation of the People Bill took up a number of discursive strands spun from wartime popular culture and wove them into law. Patterns of thought that had become second nature over three brutal years were codified and signed, irrevocably transforming Britain's electoral process. Sex and class, while never forgotten, became secondary to larger representations of loyalty, and a wartime conception of citizenship based on patriotism, service, and British blood fundamentally altered the masculine basis of the parliamentary vote.[14] Ironically, those most responsible for this change were not politicians and suffragists—though their manipulation of public discourse was crucial to shaping and selling the Bill—but the symbolically over-determined categories of "loyal women," "brave soldiers," and "contemptible slackers," out of whom the framers of the law made such liberal and effective use.

SOLDIERS INTO CITIZENS

The cultural underpinnings of the Representation of the People Bill are nowhere more evident than in the increasingly strident rumblings for a "soldier's vote" that began to emanate from Conservative circles in 1916. Although the 1918 Reform Bill is remembered primarily for enfranchising women, the actual impetus for the bill came from increasing discomfort over the inadvertent disenfranchisement of soldiers who had lost their votes due to stringent electoral residency requirements. While the Reform Bill of 1884 had virtually done away with formal property qualifications for the parliamentary vote, the residency requirement, which demanded that a man occupy the same lodgings for at least one year before qualifying for inclusion on the electoral register, effectively excluded both casual laborers and common soldiers, whose itinerant existence precluded them from inhabiting a stable domicile.[15] Further provisions barring renters of furnished lodgings, sons living at home, and multi-occupancy tenants created an additional bar for lower paid urban workers, including clerks, schoolmasters, and other poor white-collar workers who frequently resorted to cheap furnished lodgings in order to make ends meet.[16] On the eve of World War I, Britain, on paper, prided itself in having achieved virtual adult manhood suffrage, while in fact 40 percent of the adult male population was disenfranchised by virtue of electoral registration and occupancy requirements intentionally designed to prevent many of those allegedly enfranchised in 1884 from actually casting a ballot.[17]

The registration requirements, once so adamantly defended by Conservatives, would have profound consequences during the Great War. Not only did men who enlisted in the army lose their electoral qualification by moving out of their lodgings to join the British Expeditionary Forces, but male munitions workers who traveled to factories outside their home constituencies also lost the votes that they as a class had held since the Reform Bill of 1867 enfranchised urban workmen who were heads of households.[18] And thousands of working-class soldiers who now offered their lives for Britain had never qualified to vote at all, since occupancy and registration requirements primarily affected bachelors who did not yet own or rent their own homes.[19]

Given this history of offering votes with one hand while erecting barriers against the poor, the young, the unmarried, the transient and, of course, the female with the other, Sir Edward Carson's impassioned plea for the institution of a "soldier's vote" in 1916, came as a bolt from the blue. His democratic rallying cry was especially startling since Carson was a leading Conservative Unionist, the party that had been committed (since recovering from Disraeli's astounding about-face in 1867) to limiting rather than expanding democracy.[20] The Conservatives or "Tories" were traditionally the party of landed gentlemen who favored tariff protections advantageous to the countryside. By the twentieth century they also included members of the suburban and urban middle class who supported high military expenditure, the aggressive pursuit of empire, union with Ireland, reverence for the monarchy, and the maintenance of "tradition"—ideals, it would turn out, that appealed to many members of the working class as well.[21] While one characteristic of Conservatism was an inveterate distrust of democracy and the potential radicalism of the masses (who Tories believed would be lead by unscrupulous demagogues into demanding confiscatory taxation on wealth and property), Conservatives had also periodically embraced visionaries like Benjamin Disraeli, who believed that, moved by a love of the empire, the nation, and the crown, even the working classes might become loyal Tory voters.[22]

Sir Edward Carson's speech was thus surprising—and decidedly unwelcome to many members of his party—but not entirely without a driving logic. When Carson raised the issues of the "soldier's vote," he retreated from years of Conservative opposition to democratization but began to make real the wholly theoretical "physical force" argument that had played such a central role in prewar Conservative thought. During the early twentieth century, as we have seen, the "physical force" argument, which grounded male citizenship in the ability to wage war, gained tremendous purchase as an irrefutable case against women's suffrage.[23] As Anna Clark has noted, the opposition to women's suffrage subtly changed in emphasis during the period following the Boer War, taking into consideration increasing international competition and the counter-arguments of suffragists themselves. The idea that men would use their votes to protect the interests of women was refuted by feminists who exposed rape, wife beating, prostitution, and other forms of the sexual exploitation of women, which, they argued, showed that men had little legislative concern for the welfare of women. In the belligerent context of late-nineteenth-century imperial expansion, racial exploitation, and international rivalry, the breakdown of paternalistic Anti arguments led to a decisive move towards the brutal rationale of "physical force" as the unchallengeable basis of male hegemony.[24]

This argument, while carrying great weight in principle, was hideously misguided in its actual application since the vast majority of British soldiers before 1918 were in fact disenfranchised by virtue of the very electoral registration rules that caused such soul-searching during World War I. Indeed, while male politicians with no military experience pontificated about "physical force" as the basis of citizenship, the majority of Britain's soldiers, coming from the dregs of society and moving frequently with their regiments, were never permitted to cast a vote.[25] Theory and reality were completely at odds, and the unsavory class status of "Tommy Atkins" insured that few Conservatives, even during the Boer War, would spend much parliamentary capital trying to enfranchise him.[26] It was only with the apotheosis of the Tommy during World War I that the disenfranchisement of the common soldier began to cause such severe and widespread pangs of conscience among a Conservative party with apparently every reason to limit the size of the electorate.[27]

If theory and practice lived amicably enough in oblivious self-contradiction until 1916, why did Conservatives like Carson experience this sudden change of heart? I would suggest that there are three fundamental reasons, the first to do with politics, the second with perception, and the third with prejudice. On the eve of World War I, Britain was due for a new election. The Liberals had been in power since 1910—a situation of extreme frustration to Conservatives, who, thanks to the national crisis, were forced to postpone elections and line up behind their Liberal enemies in a patriotic show of national unity. To add insult to injury, Conservatives had long considered themselves to be the party of "military preparedness," advocating conscription, higher military expenditure, and aggressive imperial expansion with far more vigor than old guard Liberals pledged to lower taxes and greater personal liberty. Conservatives were also aware that in a wartime khaki election, they were likely to win seats and continually used the threat of an election to browbeat Asquith into considering reforms on Tory terms.[28] That those "Tory terms" should include the enfranchisement of foot soldiers, deck hands, and other lowly, half-caste, military personnel is one of the more astonishing results of Britain's heavily patriotic wartime culture. Like girls suffering from "khaki fever" (who had once disdainfully drawn their skirts aside to avoid being soiled by passing soldiers), the party of reaction fell head over heels for men in uniform—even if those uniforms were devoid of stripes and gold braid.

Not only did Carson suggest amending the electoral register to re-enfranchise those who had lost their votes as a result of military service, but he demanded the enfranchisement of *all* soldiers and sailors, including those who were well underage, whether they had been qualified to vote before the war or not.[29] For a party centrally concerned with preserving the "constitutional balance" and ensuring the dominance of men of property, such proposals were unprecedentedly radical. Men who had been ditch-diggers, factory operatives, errand boys, and beggars suddenly appeared to be incontrovertibly worthy of the parliamentary vote. As *Common Cause* pointed out, this call for a military service franchise challenged the constitutional basis of the electoral system and would enfranchise millions of men whom the Conservatives had considered unfit for the vote only a few years before. "'If a man is old enough to fight for me, he is old enough to vote for me,' cries Sir Edward Carson in red-hot enthusiasm; and nobody seems inclined to consider what this means." Expressing their "astonishment" that "even the solid Tory element hardly turns a hair," *Common Cause* indignantly reflected that, "many thousands of boys, fresh from school, now in the Navy, are supposed to have reached maturity, politically speaking . . . while their mothers who reared them and prepared them to . . . bear their part in Britain's defense are judged incompetent. . . . [A]ll parties have borne with great equanimity the spectacle of the British Constitution in the melting-pot; the men who posed as its staunchest supporters and champions are among the first and foremost to kindle and blow up the fire."[30] Such observations were not limited to feminist critics. Lord Bryce, a Liberal with decidedly elitist sentiments, would later reflect to his friend A.V. Dicey that "What was once the great Conservative Party has committed itself to the wildest revolutionary change by this Representation Act that England has seen since 1660," while the National Unionist Association feared that the sweeping reforms later proposed by the Speaker's Conference would enfranchise "the most unstable and emotional elements in the community, thereby increasing enormously the floating vote and the power of the demagogue."[31] Even ten years after the passage of the bill, David Close argues, older Conservatives believed the 1918 Reform Act had been a "blunder" and a "dangerous misfortune."[32]

What started Conservatives down this astonishing path of reform was their almost naive belief in the transformative power of military service, particularly during what was regarded as the quintessential "just war," waged for all that was dear to Britons. A sense of the moralizing influence of military life was, of course, nothing new to Edwardian conscriptionists. Both Mrs. J. G. Patterson and Colson Kernahan recommended a healthy dose of military service as the best antidote to a wasted youth, and George F. Shee had even declared that conscription would make men "better sons, better husbands, better brothers, and better fathers, by having given some part of their manhood to the service of their country."[33] Yet, the effusive representation of Tommy Atkins during the Great War seems to have taken this logic one step further, actually convincing Conservatives that a war that turned workers into soldiers also had the power to transform soldiers into citizens and erstwhile laborers into loyal Tory electors.[34]

This faith in the transmogrifying power of the military uniform is particularly evident in debates over the enfranchisement of soldiers. Lord Salisbury, for example, saw soldiers as a "reservoir of Conservative votes waiting to be tapped," and Lord Selborne, who dismissed the enfranchisement of teenage boys as "mischievous sentimentalism of the worst sort," nevertheless believed that Unionists supported the soldier's vote because they wished to "secure the votes of the men who have fought as a deliverance from the domination of the Trade Union influence." Referring to a Trades Union Congress resolution against conscription, Selborne declared that "the only men to save them from such folly will be the men who have fought. . . . I think these men will be an immense support to us for many years to come against radical and Liberal insanity in the matter of foreign policy, navy etc."[35]

Conservative confidence in the voting habits of soldiers was at least in part misplaced, Martin Pugh argues. "Lord Selborne's belief that experience in the trenches actually created support for peacetime military service turned out to be a pitiful delusion."[36] Yet for Sir Edward Carson and the many Tories, patriotic Labourites, and Lloyd George Liberals who agreed with him, giving the franchise "to the soldiers and sailors who are fighting our battles" was a simple act of justice. "That is the real property qualification—for what property would any man have in this country if it were not for the soldiers and sailors who are fighting our battles," Carson asked.[37] "[T]he men who . . . voluntarily or through the laws of this country, are ordered out to present themselves to be shot, and suffer what they do suffer in war, have a claim [to the franchise] paramount above everybody. . . . [W]e are not, in relation to these men, basing it at all upon anything like a property or residential qualification, but simply and solely upon the fact that they are the men who are preserving the lives and property of the people of this country."[38] As one observant listener adeptly commented, Carson was advocating "One gun, one vote!"[39] This line of argumentation, however, appealed to many more than just Conservatives. To Lloyd George, soldiers had a "right to a voice in choosing the government that sends them to peril and death," and both Liberals and Labour echoed the press and the public in their eagerness to extend the franchise to this worthy class of electors, as long as other deserving contributors to the war effort were not left out.[40] As we shall see, this last point would prove to be the Greek infantry lurking inside the Trojan horse of the "soldier's vote."

Certainly, not all Conservatives were pleased with this turn of events, particularly when the scope of reform was greatly expanded by an all-party "Speaker's Conference" convened in October 1916 to consider electoral reform. Unable to reach any consensus on registration and franchise reform in the coalition cabinet, the Liberal prime minister, Herbert Asquith, called upon the Speaker of the House of Commons, J. W. Lowthar, to appoint a bipartisan conference to consider the issue of electoral reform and to arrive at recommendations for a compromise solution. Recommending, in addition to a new military service register, universal manhood suffrage, a measure of women's suffrage, the end to plural voting, and proportional representation, the report flabbergasted Conservatives, especially since their own representatives had been present at the Conference table. Arthur Steel Maitland believed that the Conservative members of the Speaker's Conference had "really gone mad," while the *Unionist Agent's Journal* surmised that their representatives had been "'diddled' and 'hoodwinked' by Liberal trickery." Sir John Boraston wrote that he had yet to meet a Bradford Unionist "who does not consider that the Party has been sold to the Radical and Labour forces," and Unionist agents pessimistically surmised that they would lose 103 seats, even with the gains they expected to make through the soldier's vote.[41] Carson himself, no doubt chagrined by his role in launching such reforms, sponsored a petition, signed by over one hundred Unionist MPs, denouncing the Speaker's Conference and taking issue with such proposals as the liberalization of registration rules and the enfranchisement of large numbers of working-class civilians.[42] But to speak against recommended reforms that had become so closely tied to the soldier's vote was no longer politically possible in the celebratory atmosphere that exalted "Tommy Atkins" and linked the work of patriotic men and women to his welfare overseas. Even if not all Unionists believed in the moral glow of the Tommy and the political advantage of enfranchising him, they were unable to press their reservations without potentially sacrificing their position as the party of patriotism. As Walter Long wrote to Sir George Younger, "it would be absolutely fatal to the future of our Party" to resist reforms that would enfranchise "valiant servicemen and patriotic civilians."[43]

To Carson, who had opened up the Pandora's box of electoral reform, the fact that women's suffrage was being discussed at all was another horrifying trick of fate. Basing the right to vote on military service had at least seemed a safe way of insuring that women would be barred from any extension of the franchise. While a number of prominent Conservatives actually supported women's suffrage, and had a far better record on this issue than some of their Liberal counterparts, it was an issue traditionally unpopular with rank-and-file Conservative voters, and the Anti cause was one to which Curzon, Carson, and other prominent Unionists had pledged their names, their money, and their time.[44] The idea of a military service franchise thus seemed an attractive way of introducing reforms potentially advantageous to Tories (many of whom clearly believed that military life was a sure-fire instrument of Conservative conversion), while decisively repudiating the claims of women and other unsavory non-military personnel. "You can draw no comparison between any person claiming the franchise and the man who is risking his life and health in the trenches, and who is daily rendering himself likely to be shot on behalf of this country," Carson bellowed when the issue was first raised. "I do not believe there is any comparison between that and, say, the women's franchise question . . . it has nothing to do with this question, nothing whatever."[45] For Mrs. Humphry Ward, who actually succeeded in finding two thousand Anti women engaged in war work to sign a petition against the proposed reforms, "The true and ultimate sanctification of the Parliamentary vote becomes clearer than ever. It *is* physical force, the bone and blood of men! Everything else is subsidiary...."[46] And Sir Almoth Wright, seeing the logic of the "physical force" argument drain away, went so far as to declare that "a certain minimum personal vigour and muscular development [are] required to fit any individual to fight, and the same minimum should be required of the individual who aspires to the Parliamentary franchise—*even if it means debarring old men.*"[47] But the issue of women's suffrage was far more closely tied to the soldier's vote than many Antis cared to admit.

When the issue of franchise reform resurfaced, Mrs. Fawcett wrote to Asquith informing him that as long as only the registration process was repaired to re-enfranchise those who had lost their votes because of the war, suffragists would maintain their truce with the government and offer no objections. She also warned, however, that if any new class of elector was granted the franchise on the basis of war service, the case for women's suffrage must be considered as well—for no one had served more loyally, willingly, and heroically than women.[48] Her case had considerable merit. While Carson and his Tory sympathizers had proposed a soldier's franchise, Liberal and Labour politicians were unwilling to enfranchise soldiers and sailors without also securing the franchise of male workers who, like military personnel, had been disenfranchised because of the war and who not only worked for the war effort but were more likely to support one of the progressive parties.[49] If, for political reasons, the "soldier's vote" would have to ensure the enfranchisement of male munitions workers as well, what was the rationale for excluding women who had not only sacrificed loved ones but were working in virtually all the fields men were? "If you were to create a new ... military and naval franchise ... you would have to give a voice to all the other men," declared Asquith in August 1916. "Take the munitions workers. They have left their homes at the invitation of the State in large numbers; they have severed their old family ties and their old residential ties, and have gone into places hitherto unknown to them.... [T]hey are rendering equally important and effective service in the conduct of the War as are our soldiers and sailors." But his speech was particularly momentous in linking this class of claimants with another much more controversial group. As he famously put it, "the moment you begin a general enfranchisement on these lines of State service, you are brought face to face with another formidable proposition: What are you to do with the women?" Reiterating his long anti-suffrage credentials, Asquith went on to admit that "if we are going to bring in a new class of electors, on whatever ground of State service, ... we cannot possibly deny ... that during this War women of this country have rendered as effective service . . . as any other class of the community. It is true that they cannot fight, in the gross material sense of going out with rifles . . . but they fill our munition factories, they are doing the work which the men who are fighting had to perform before, they have taken their places, they are the servants of the State, and they have aided, in the most effective way, in the prosecution of the War."[50] While these arguments were never convincing to Antis, who repeatedly (and wholly inconsistently) declared that the vote should not be a "reward" for patriotic service, they touched a chord that seemed to harmonize with public feeling, even in local Unionist Associations, which by March 1916 were supporting women's suffrage at a rate of more than two to one.[51]

Under the rubric of a franchise based on militarily useful service, gender-based arguments unexpectedly began to crumble.[52] When the Speaker's Conference issued its report in January 1917, it recommended universal manhood suffrage, suffrage for female local government electors above the age of thirty or thirty-five (to ensure the numerical dominance of male electors), proportional representation, and a further redistribution of seats. With the exception of proportional representation, these major provisions held fast, though in the ensuing months of parliamentary debate there would be much room for fine-tuning the franchise to make it reflect even more perfectly the passions of the war.

In the final version of the Representation of the People Bill, the military service franchise not only enfranchised soldiers and sailors age twenty-one or above (providing them with provisions to use mail ballots or appoint proxies) but enfranchised boys of nineteen and twenty who had seen active service.[53] In addition to this combatants vote, the military service franchise included Red Cross personnel who had served abroad (including military nurses), women who had served abroad in the Woman's Auxiliary Army Corps, and merchant marines.[54] It did not, however, include munitions workers of either sex. Clearly, potential subjection to enemy fire, rather than status as a man or a war worker, had won out as the operative rationale behind the military service franchise. But, as legislators had to acknowledge, such criteria did not ipso facto exclude women and in 1918, 3,372 women proudly registered as military voters.[55] The age bar of thirty, of course, took away much of what the bill appeared to give to women, yet a new rationale was in operation, replacing the old notion of manhood as the primary qualification for the parliamentary vote.

But what of the munitions workers of whom Asquith and others had made so much? As we shall see, advocates of a restricted "servicemen's vote" won the franchise but lost the bill. Indeed, the military service franchise would constitute but one avenue to the vote, and additional franchise provisions within the Representation Act would ensure that male munitions workers and the majority of adult British women would find their way onto the electoral register even if they had not served abroad. As successful as they had been in limiting the military service franchise, Tories like Carson would discover that a wartime reform bill would have to include not just the men in the trenches but the women who bore them, and not just the soldiers who fought but the workmen who made them shells. Female munitions workers, as we shall see, would be deeply betrayed by the bill in an ironic twist of fate that made them the symbols of women's worthiness while using the age bar to deny them ballots. The Conservatives' most bitter and hard-fought amendment to the bill's proposed franchises, however, would not be the drive to limit working-class voters or even the attempt to exclude female voters, but a vindictive scramble to cast conscientious objectors from the garden of citizenship. The philosopher's stone of "service" would remain the driving force behind the bill, inexorably—but never completely—undermining the older logic of gender and class.

Expulsion from the Garden

On the surface, the widespread and principled acceptance of the "soldier's vote" should have irrevocably entrenched maleness as a fundamental qualification for the parliamentary vote. Yet the combination of political wrangling and public sentiment that demanded recognition for all those who loyally worked for victory opened up new breaches in the idea of manhood suffrage. Like the heroic women who managed miraculously to obtain a tiny piece of the military service vote, conscientious objectors would insure that ruptures in the masculine franchise could not easily be repaired. Indeed, at just the moment women were being included in a new franchise based on service, conscientious objectors were ingloriously having their right to vote snatched away by the very Parliament that had allowed for their military exemptions in the first place.

From the moment Liberals advocated and won conscientious exemptions in the Military Service Act of 1916, they incurred the bitter opposition of Conservative absolutists whose hostility to "soft options" would be re-waged—this time successfully—in the Representation of the People Bill. Primarily educated and middle class, most conscientious objectors had more in common with those trying to disenfranchise them than they did with the "errand boys" whom Carson proposed to honor with a military service vote. Their numbers—16,000 in all—make the vehemence of the quest to disenfranchise them even more remarkable.[56] Rarely, if ever, has so much parliamentary capital been spent to disenfranchise so few men. Given the relatively low impact the measure would have in practice, it was surprisingly hard fought between Liberals who believed that no man should be disenfranchised for exercising a legal prerogative granted by Parliament, and Conservatives who spat on the very name of any man who dared object on conscientious grounds to a war being fought over such sacred principles as liberty, freedom, and the safety of women and children. "[P]eople who refuse to risk their lives, and who have done nothing . . . to preserve the lives and liberties of their wives and children are not justified in claiming the advantages gained for them by the sacrifice of their fellow countrymen," argued Major Hunt in a speech that echoed the sentiment of many MPs. "They ought to go to a country where . . . outsiders, black, yellow, or any other colour can come in from anywhere and outrage women and murder children without protest."[57]

With conscription, the casual "shirker" was absorbed into the army, and only a small number of principled conscientious objectors remained to be subjected to such vindictive reproach. Yet for Tories—and the many members of the public, the press, and the nationalist wings of the other two parties who agreed with them—the fact that conscientious objectors could vote, while gallant men who volunteered for service abroad could not, was galling, unjust, and dangerous. Mrs. Pankhurst, at a votes-for-servicemen rally at the Albert Hall in October 1916, argued that soldiers had "proved their claim to the vote by making it possible to keep a country in which to vote" and asked whether "any woman could face the possibility of the affairs of the country being settled by conscientious objectors, passive resisters, and shirkers?"[58] And the *Times,* which advocated the release of "absolutist" conscientious objectors from prison, nevertheless insisted that "Men who, for whatever reason, persistently decline to do their duty as citizens place themselves permanently outside the community and have no title either to its protection or to the enjoyment of civil rights."[59] Such sentiments were echoed in Parliament by Mr. R. McNeill, the first to move disenfranchisement in the House of Commons, when he scornfully declared that conscientious objectors were "content . . . to enjoy the sweets of life out of the blood of their fellow creatures. . . . [I]s there anything unreasonable in Parliament and the Nation saying to those men, 'As a matter of concession . . . we have allowed you to stand out the fighting and when the fighting is over we will see that you stand out the voting?'"[60]

The motion to disenfranchise conscientious objectors followed directly on the decision to enfranchise soldiers and sailors, raising in Parliament an issue that had already been endorsed in sections of the press.[61] While an initial motion was defeated in June, thanks to application of government whips against the measure, growing clamor among Unionists politicians insured that this issue would not die so easily. In November a new amendment was

introduced by Sir George Younger, and practically before the debates had
begun, those who favored disenfranchisement gloated over the victory that
would surely ensue, now that the government, bowing to public pressure,
had agreed to leave the issue to a free vote. "What this country wants is that
this man, the conscientious objector, so called—shall not have the vote," declared Sir Clement Kinloch-Cooke confidently. "The Government on the last
occasion said that the conscientious objector should have the vote. To-night
we are going to try the issue. . . . We shall see a very different result."[62] Kinloch-Cooke was well justified in his smug assurance. On November 21, after
impassioned debate, the amendment passed 209 to 171, insuring that conscientious objectors and those court-martialed for refusing to obey orders
on the grounds of conscientious objection would be disenfranchised.[63] What
was even more telling was that ten Labour MPs (out of a parliamentary party
of only thirty-eight) and ten Liberals actually voted in favor of this Tory
amendment, while numerous Liberals abstained or left the debating chamber rather than be caught by their constituents "coddling the conscies."[64]

The measure was not without its eloquent opponents in both the House
of Commons and the House of Lords. Lord Hugh Cecil, one of the few
Conservatives willing to defend the rights of conscientious objectors, vig-
orously opposed the amendment, pointing out that it imposed a "retro-
spective penalty upon persons who have done nothing worse that avail
themselves of an exemption which Parliament themselves afforded
them."[65] Deploring the submission to "public opinion" that was now "in a
state of irritation" over the issue, Cecil condemned the idea that the state
should be empowered to punish a man for his opinions.[66] Lord Russell
likewise berated his colleagues in the House of Lords, deploring the faulty
logic that gave the vote "to the forger, to the thief, to the panderer, to the
bawd, to the white slave trafficker" but denied it "to the man whose offense
is that he has a conscience."[67] Many MPs who opposed disenfranchising
conscientious objectors, however, were at a loss for words when trying to
defend this much reviled group. Sir Edward Parrott, who spoke against the
amendment, nevertheless declared that, "I dislike the conscientious objector as much as any Member in the House. I think he suffers from apoplexy
of conscience, and that he is wrong-headed in his present views. . . ."[68] Mr.
Rowntree argued that disenfranchising the conscientious objector would
only enhance his influence and make him a martyr, while another MP suggested that it might be equally logical to disenfranchise the parents of conscientious objectors for bringing them up so poorly.[69] Even Lord Hugh
Cecil, the great defender of conscience, proclaimed the conscientious objectors to be "wrong with unsound judgement," but felt that it was unfair
to "punish people for erroneous opinions." Comparing the conscientious
objectors to Hindus and Muslims, he pointed out that "their religion is

foolish, and in some ways positively childish, but we respect them for practicing it, because it is their right to do so."[70] Finally, in a misdirected defensive gesture offered near the end of the final debate, Commander Wedgwood tried to take issue with the idea that "because these men are bad citizens, therefore they should have no vote."[71] With sentiments like these coming from their defenders in the Commons, it is not surprising that the Lord Chancellor would sardonically comment in the House of Lords that he "[did] not think there [would] be many found to drop a tear over the disenfranchisement of the conscientious objector."[72]

Liberal efforts on behalf of the conscientious objectors, however, were not insignificant. Over the objection of hardline Conservatives, they succeeded in passing further amendments that limited the duration of the disenfranchisement to the remainder of the war and a period of five years afterwards. Since the war officially ended in 1921, this meant the disenfranchisement would last only until 1926—far less than the twenty-year exile proposed by Captain Barnett when the issue of a time limit was first raised.[73] They also successfully argued that those COs engaged in militarily useful work, such as the Friends Ambulance Corps, should be exempted from disenfranchisement. Since the majority of conscientious objectors, including many Quakers, were content to assist the war effort as long as their work did not involve taking lives, this amendment reduced considerably the impact of the bill. Yet despite these curbs, the indignity of disenfranchisement was searing, and the debates over this question are deeply revealing about the meaning of conscientious objection and its impact on the constitutional framework of the new Reform Bill.

The conscientious objector, more than any other category of male subject, undermined the masculine nature of the franchise—a shift that could only have occurred once patriotic service itself had become the operative franchise qualification. As Kinloch-Cooke said in the House of Commons, "This Bill, I think the House will admit, is practically a sailors' and soldiers' Bill. . . . [It] was specially designed to give the men who have fought in the war the privilege of voting. If that be so, it cannot at the same time be justifiable to give votes to men who have refused to fight in the war . . . you cannot have it both ways."[74] Likewise, *Britannia* fulminated at the hypocrisy of a "soldiers' vote" if the conscientious objectors' vote was left intact, for such a situation would mean that "men do not vote on account of any service rendered to the state, but simply and solely because they happen to be males."[75] Becoming what we might call the "other" within a new binarism, based not upon sexual difference but upon differential service, conscientious objectors shifted the lines of debate from their traditional gendered entrenchments. Instead of the old "physical force" argument, in which a theoretical fighting male citizen foiled the defenseless and disenfranchised woman, wartime legislation established an actual military service franchise, replacing "defenseless" women with conscientious objectors as the symbolic and literal embodiment of the non-citizen.

A feminized representation of the conscientious objector also facilitated the substitution of "conshies" for women in the discourse of unworthiness that undergirded discussion of the vote. Often depicted as "hysterical" and "crankish" weaklings, conscientious objectors endured insults formerly reserved for radical suffragettes—insults no doubt encouraged by the collaboration between COs and the pacifist wing of the suffrage movement.[76] To one member of the House of Lords, conscientious objectors were generally "cranks, morbid, and on the verge of lunacy," while Sir George Cave explained that "many of them were of weak physique and . . . deficient in other ways."[77] One disgruntled Anti could not resist pointing out that while only a small percentage of women doing war work were suffragettes, "it is safe to infer that every pacifist and every no-conscriptionist is a suffragist."[78] Many observers also agreed that as a class, conscientious objectors compared very poorly with the patriotic women who were helping to win the war. Mrs. Pankhurst and her daughter Christabel never tired of pointing out that the home front was not populated by women alone but was teeming with men whose age, infirmity, or lack of patriotism insured that they were no more likely to see a battlefield that the most insulated women in Britain. Furthermore, while many women had expressed a desire to go to war—and were serving as ambulance drivers and hospital personnel, as well as in other dangerous fields—many men who were desperately needed at the front had chosen not to go because they had "conscientious objection" to military service.[79] Such arguments were by no means limited to feminist observers. Sir Clement Kinloch-Cooke tellingly argued that "The opposition to the women's franchise broke down on the ground that women had in our civil life taken the places of men who had gone to the war, that they have become war-workers." Yet, as he rightly pointed out, "to meet the case of women's enfranchisement, the Government came to a compromise. They fixed the female voting age at thirty, and by doing so, they excluded the majority of women who are working in the war." Under these circumstances, he asked "Why should these women be excluded and men of the same age who have refused the first obligation of citizenship, namely, to defend their home and country against the enemy, be included? . . . Such a step is neither just nor logical."[80]

Conscientious objectors also experienced a sort of civic emasculation as they were further stripped of one of the basic prerogatives of their sex—the vote—at the very moment their wives were receiving it. While men like Fenner Brockway, Lytton Strachey, Bertrand Russell, Clifford

Allen, Stephen Hobhouse, Philip Morrell, and Frederick Pethick-Lawrence were the most famous members of a cohort that weathered scorn, dismissal, and jail time for their opposition to the war, the indignities placed on lesser-known resisters must have been equally unbearable. The clause disenfranchising conscientious objectors explicitly allowed their wives to remain on the register, situating COs' new disempowerment directly in their own homes. While many conscientious objectors were unmarried, this provision insured that married COs would experience a political and domestic role reversal that would place them electorally beneath their wives. It also stressed the failure of unpatriotic men to measure up to the presumed loyalty of British women, casting them once again as a new class of outsiders.

A number of rhetorical habits that became second nature during the war made this change in the parameters of civic exclusion possible. While most unenlisted men (and a smattering of women) declared publicly that they were willing to go to war, and even wished to go, if only they were younger, fitter, qualified, or free to leave indispensable occupations, conscientious objectors conformed in neither action nor spirit to the masculine expectations imposed by the war. Indeed, their most unforgivable offense seems to have been adherence to a set of moral beliefs that were no longer tolerable to the nation at large. During a war in which the soldier was represented not as a killer but as a sacrificial agent willing to die to preserve the safety of women and children, it became possible for patriots to cast conscientious objectors as moral pariahs and enemies of the state. As McNeill declared to the House of Commons on June 26, 1917, "Either the whole community . . . is hopelessly in error over the rights and wrongs of this great struggle, or . . . the community is right and justified and this action of the conscientious objectors . . . has been . . . anarchic and practically subversive of the state."[81] Kinloch-Cooke heartily agreed. "[I]f all men had behaved like the conscientious objectors," he declared, the nation would be witnessing "hordes of Huns invading this country and crucifying our women and children."[82]

That conscientious objectors claimed "higher" ethical and religious reasons for opposing what was almost universally regarded as an ethical and religious war only fueled the odium of those who had little to hang onto but hatred and moral certainties. Under the system of absolute values fostered by the war, such opinions could not go unpunished. Indeed, the revulsion against the conscientious objector only escalated during the war, despite war weariness and longing for peace.[83] This anger played itself out in a final and highly popular lash of the whip—political disenfranchisement. In this visceral response, the conscientious objector was regarded as a sort of nonman who refused to conform to the expectations of his gender, the honor of his country, the values of his society, and the images of the war. While scholars have tended to assert the minimal effect of disenfranchisement, suggesting that it was easily evaded after the war, the lot of the conscientious objector was neither an easy nor a straightforward one.[84] Not only did they lose their votes until 1926, being re-enfranchised just two years before women were granted equal suffrage, but they were discriminated against in the civil service, could be denied promotions, and suffered the relentless persecution of veterans groups long after the rest of society had forgotten their sins.[85] While temporary disenfranchisement did not, perhaps, live up to the vindictive expectations of those like Lloyd George, who threateningly promised to make "the path of that class a hard one," it was essential to Tory reconciliation with what was an unprecedentedly radical franchise bill.[86] In this bill, service would trump all older franchise qualifications, yet its rationale would be strained to its fullest with the intractable case of women.

THE FEMALE FRANCHISE

What appeared to contemporaries a straightforward fact—that women were granted the vote as a result of patriotic service rendered during the Great War—has become a deeply contentious historical question. Thanks largely to the wholly logical observation that the women who performed the most crucial war service (working women aged nineteen to twenty-nine) did not actually receive the vote, scholars have begun to question the rationale behind a female franchise that left a multitude of patriotic women dangling, unrepresented below an age bar that it would take many of them years to surmount. This was not its only inequity.

Under the Representation of the People Act, women over thirty could qualify to vote under three different franchises: the military service franchise, the university franchise, and, accounting for the vast majority of female voters, the female franchise, which stipulated that a woman must be a local government elector or the wife of one in order to vote.[87] To qualify as a local government elector, a woman had to own or rent a dwelling valuable enough to be taxed as a "household." She could also inhabit unfurnished lodgings worth five pounds per year or more—a "democratic" provision that nevertheless excluded low-paid professional women like schoolmistresses, typists, and clerks who generally rented cheap furnished lodgings. Daughters living at home, mothers living with sons, widows who had lost their property, and domestic servants were also disqualified, since they did not rate as householders and did not pay their own rent.[88]

These restrictions so exasperated some women that they complained of being required to buy their votes for "the price of a husband or a van load of furniture"—an observation that had more than a grain of truth to it.[89] Whereas under the male franchise of the new Reform Bill *all* men over twenty-one years of age who had not been conscientious objectors, were not in prison, were not certified lunatics, were not aliens or vagrants, and did not live in a workhouse or an internment camp could vote as long as they had resided in a single constituency for a period of six months, women needed the same type of qualifications that had so effectively disenfranchised 40 percent of the male population in 1884.[90] How, then, do we reconcile the insistent view of contemporaries that women were enfranchised for "war service" with the actuality of what was a limited female franchise, debarring the young and the poor?

On one level, Parliament was able to enfranchise women on the basis of war service, while leaving disenfranchised thousands of those who had served, because of a tradition of symbolic suffrage, that stretched back into the nineteenth century and gave the inconsistencies of the female franchise an air of normalcy. Under a constitutional system in which principle and practice were often at odds, it was incongruous but not unacceptable to make female war workers the symbol of women's "fitness" for the vote, while being sure to erect barriers against a possible deluge of giddy young girls unrestrained by age, marriage, or responsibility for property. Indeed, for legislators accustomed to defending a male franchise on the basis of "physical force" while setting electoral qualifications that until 1918 prevented most soldiers from voting, this inconsistency in the female franchise was just another unavoidable example of the slippage between principle and politics. A new vision of women's service, yoked to an old image of women's nature, rationalized the inclusion of "women" as a general category in the franchise bill while justifying the exclusion of the youngest (and most industrious) third of the adult female population from the actual balloting.

As we have seen, by 1916 female war service was inspiring widespread "conversions" in formerly Anti journals like the *Times* and *Daily Mail*, and was becoming a cornerstone of suffrage argumentation in both the feminist and the Liberal press. "There is something like a general agreement that women have, by their magnificent service to the country in its need, added immeasurably to the proofs . . . that they are a reserve . . . which the nation neglects to its cost," declared the *Nation*, an organ long committed to female enfranchisement. "The doctors, the nurses, the relief workers, and the great army which hastened to replace male labour in field and factory did not suddenly develop their endurance, their unselfishness, their quick, adaptable intelligence. . . . The qualities hidden and diffused in time of peace, have suddenly been concentrated and illuminated by our hour of need. . . . The only theoretical argument which stood in the way was the doctrine that the State is based on physical force. We call that argument 'Prussianism' today."[91] This sense of a pervasive change in sentiment regarding women's suffrage was not just wishful thinking on the part of progressives. Not only had the powerful North-cliffe press declared its conversion to women's suffrage, but a host of other publications followed suit, declaring that the spectacle of female war service revealed women's now undeniable capacity for citizenship. "The magnificent way in which British women have rallied to their country's call . . . [has] added powerful new arguments to the already strong case for bestowing the parliamentary vote on women," exclaimed the *Chronicle* enthusiastically, while the writer John Galsworthy supported the female franchise by pointing out that "women have served as loyally as men and suffered more."[92] "There is no doubt that the war has had an enormous effect upon public opinion as far as [women's suffrage] is concerned," commented Lloyd George. "Women's work in the war has been a vital contribution to our success."[93]

As legislators could not fail to note, the change in sentiment evident in the press was paralleled by a similar shift in public opinion, demonstrated most graphically by the precipitous fall in the membership, financing, and organizational coherence of the Anti-Suffrage League, as well as by the dramatic swing among local Unionist Associations towards an endorsement of the female franchise.[94] When the war correspondent Henry Nevinson returned to England in July 1916, he discovered a "suffrage crisis in full blaze, but really promising for the first time," while a feminist reporter, covering the suffrage debates in the House of Commons in the spring of 1917, could not help noting that it was "the whole changing mental atmosphere of the crowd of men which was at once new and dramatic."[95]

Nowhere were these changes more vividly reflected than in the frequency and force with which arguments about female service began to make headway in the houses of Parliament, providing a rationale for the spate of conversions by former Anti MPs. Although historians have tended to dismiss the role of public opinion in shaping the Representation of the People Act, Parliament was a rhetorical community in which the success or failure of a bill could depend on the nature, quality, and persuasiveness of debate, which had to resonate with other legislators as well as with constituents.[96] Arnold Ward was denied the opportunity to stand for Parliament in 1918 because female Unionists were so enraged by his attempt to deprive them of their votes.[97] Indeed, speeches in the House of Commons could not be made without cost, explaining both the attention to public opinion among MPs and the extraordinary conversions to women's suffrage that occurred in midst of overwhelming press support for enfranchising women on the basis of their patriotic service. As one

Unionist admitted, many Conservatives disliked the Reform Bill but would not oppose it, "for fear of arousing the hostility of the electorate . . . especially the women who are thirsting for the vote."[98] Whether these conversions were "sincere" or not—and many historians suspect that they were not—by 1917 it had become politically expedient to praise women and customary to regard their patriotic work as a sign of their fitness for the vote.[99] Few politicians lost the opportunity to ingratiate themselves with their future constituents or to rationalize their otherwise inexplicable changes of heart with arguments that had come to seem commonsensical to most Britons. As Arthur Balfour wryly commented, the war had given a "very good excuse to a large number of excellent people, who had . . . been on the wrong side, to change their minds."[100]

The sheer inexorability of this line of argumentation was deeply infuriating to Antis and pacifists alike. Arnold Ward begged to be allowed to use the Anti-Suffrage Leagues's £5,000 reserve fund to stiffen the resolve of MPs who "are cowed by the attitude of the government and the press," while Helena Swanwick never forgave "the curious standard of values which resulted in British women being told that they were given the vote . . . not on account of their patient toil for ages as workers and mothers, not in virtue of their common humanity, nor because they had a peculiar contribution to make to political life, but because they helped carry on the war."[101] Yet for converts to the cause like Arthur Steel Maitland, Croydon Marks, and a spate of other politicians and MPs who spoke in the House of Commons, in the press, and at party meetings, "women had made good their cause by service."[102] As *Common Cause* could not fail to note, "The demand for the inclusion of women in the electorate rests now upon their proved service to the state."[103] The war had "changed the masculinist mind."

Rhetorical habits originating in the press, promoted by suffragists, and increasingly accepted by ordinary men and women thus powerfully shaped parliamentary debate over the issue of women's suffrage. Indeed, by the time the women's clause was being debated in the House of Commons, Anti arguments had come to seem increasingly outdated and foolish.[104] *Common Cause* could hardly contain its glee when Arnold Ward trotted out the discredited "physical force" argument while another misguided MP made the mistake of bringing in "the old 'pedestal,'" declaring that he "liked to see women upon it and 'not on a footing of equality.'"[105] While women's suffrage organizations could never be accused of counting their chickens, lobbying heavily before the commencement of debates in March and April and posting whips outside the doors of the House of Commons to prevent sympathetic MPs from leaving before the decisive vote count in June, many legislators believed that by the time the vote was taken, it was "absolutely clear that the fight [was] won."[106]

Such a foregone conclusion was by no means so certain in the House of Lords, a chamber in which Anti sentiment ran high and where hereditary peerages secured a certain immunity to public opinion, reflected in the candor of the debates. Indeed, when the inveterate anti-suffragist Lord Loreburn made his motion to strike the parliamentary franchise for women from the new Reform Bill, he knew he would find a deep reservoir of support.[107] Because of Britain's female majority, many Antis feared that the age limit of thirty would prove "merely a ficticious . . . artificial and temporary expedient" that would eventually hand power from "masculine" to "feminine" hands.[108] Although the age bar was bitterly resented in both Labour and feminist circles, it was politically essential to the passage of a bill that would have otherwise produced an electorate in which women vastly outnumbered men. Indeed, the demographic imbalance was not just a political issue but a deeply emotional one as well. "Women are the majority of the population now," Arthur Balfour sadly observed. "They will be, owing to the lamentable event of the past years, in a greater majority for years to come," while the duchess of Atholl opposed equal suffrage in 1924 because the preponderance of women on the register would be "largely due to . . . the fact that we lost 740,000 precious lives of men in the Great War. . . . To propose a great extension of this kind looks like taking advantage of the heroic sacrifice of those men."[109] Given such reservations, Mrs. Fawcett encouraged adultist suffragists to accept the compromise proposed by the Speaker's Conference. "Our policy should be to float our vessel on the tide that is now running strongly towards the success of our cause," she rationalized. "We never had such a good chance as at this moment."[110] While the age bar did much to reassure moderates in both Houses, the critics of women's suffrage regarded the enfranchisement of even "six million women voters," as an unprecedented "leap in the dark."[111] Had they know that the figure of six million was based on faulty census figures, and that not six but eight and a half million women would be enfranchised, they would no doubt have been even more alarmed.[112]

To Unionist Antis, Britain's military security and imperial health depended on the exclusion of women from parliamentary affairs. Not only were women allegedly "pacifist" by nature, but Unionist Antis believed that the enfranchisement of women in Australia had resulted in the defeat of conscription and that women would never be capable of a "fight to the finish" but would settle for an ignominious and inconclusive peace in order to get their men back. Indeed, Lord Curzon, President of the Anti Suffrage League and Conservative leader in the House of Lords, was certain that Australian women had "allowed their natural domestic desire to protect and recover their dear ones to over-ride the larger obligation of their duty to the State as a whole," while even the *Times* discouragingly asserted that

Australian women had "permitted their emotions to guide their pencils in the booths," while "reason and patriotism appealed to them in vain."[113]

The ability of pro-suffrage lords to defuse such arguments had much to do with the eloquence and actions of women outside the House. Anti lords, like their counterparts in the House of Commons, were deeply hampered by the fact that suffragette militancy—one of the most potent arguments against women's suffrage—had not only desisted but had been converted into pro-war loyalism. Furthermore, it was no longer acceptable to denigrate women publicly in a context where suffragists had made themselves synonymous with patriotism and where ordinary women had suffered and served. Virtually every Anti speech in Parliament conceded the excellence of British women and the importance of their service, causing one surprised suffragist to declare he was glad to hear "nothing of the 'shrieking sisterhood.'"[114] In fact, the specter of imperial irresponsibility—so central to the Anti case—was performatively refuted with each gesture of the high-profile WSPU, every heroic action of the massive NU, and each sacrifice made by ordinary British women engaged in acts of fervent patriotism. An irate Mrs. Ward marveled at the "cleverness" of Mrs. Pankhurst in so thoroughly associating her movement with the war effort, while the *Anti-Suffrage Review* begrudgingly admitted that Mrs. Pankhurst and Mrs. Fawcett were suffragists "for whom patriotism is still a living force."[115] Even an opportunity to make hay of women's "selfish" claim for the vote was undercut by Mrs. Pankhurst's refusal to accept women's suffrage without securing the soldiers' vote first—an act deeply infuriating to all other feminist groups, but one that deflected mounting criticism that women wished to put themselves forward ahead of soldiers.

Nothing could have been more galling—or awkward—to diehard opponents of women's suffrage than such conspicuous acts of patriotism. At the very moment Antis raised the issue of female pacifism, Mrs. Fawcett was busy purging the NU leadership of internationalists and declaring "talk of peace" to be "akin to treason"; at the same time Antis lamented the role of women in defeating Australian conscription, Mrs. Pankhurst was calling for martial law and Britain's white-feather girls were wreaking havoc on young unenlisted males; only weeks before the Lords worried themselves about women's inability to endorse a "fight to the finish," Christabel Pankhurst declared publicly that "before we conclude peace with Germany we must see . . . Hindenburg or Ludendorff . . . go to Marshall Foch bearing the white flag"; and at the very moment that Mrs. Humphry Ward was evoking the specter of the Russian Revolution as the first great experiment in universal suffrage to include women, Mrs. Pankhurst was in Petrograd reviewing the Russian Women's Battalion of Death, heartening the forces of reaction, and repudiating the evils of Bolshevism.[116] As Lord Willoughby de

Broke could not help observing, "to those who have any misgivings . . . I would refer your Lordships . . . to Mrs. Pankhurst and the Women's Party."

> Not long ago Mrs. Pankhurst and her Party published a very remarkable and from a Conservative point of view an exceedingly sound, document [for] national policy. This doctrine was so sound and so imperial that it even found favor in the *Globe* newspaper soon after Mr. Leo Maxse undertook the editorship. It is remarkable that the Women's Party is the only organized political Party which has put in the forefront of their program the maintenance of the union between Great Britain and Ireland . . . Mrs. Pankhurst also goes through the whole gamut which the Imperial Party . . . have most at heart, and therefore I do not think we need have many misgivings with regard to the actions that will be taken by . . . a certain type and quality of women in this country.[117]

The bishop of London, a recent "convert" to women's suffrage, agreed that the fears of Antis were greatly overblown. "When we read Mrs. Humphry Ward's pamphlet . . . we find a most terrible picture drawn by her of red ruin, to which the Revolution in Russia is absolute child's play. . . . It is said that it was the women's vote which defeated conscription [in Australia]. That is an entirely unproven assertion." Instead, the bishop of London refuted Lord Bryce's contention that women's suffrage had "done no good," pointing out the great boost it had given to age of consent laws, gambling suppression, temperance, and anti-pornography legislation, as well as women's support for imperial legislation curbing prostitution, the exploitation of native women, and the sale of drink to natives—causes long favored by the clergy and long hampered by male electors. As he put it, "I feel I shall have far greater power with six million women's votes behind me." Without the women's vote, "we should lose one of our best aids in the reconstruction of the world."[118]

If arguments about female pacifism, women's lack of imperial resolve, and their danger to military efficiency fell flat in a context where both prominent suffragists and ordinary women were daily making headlines with their patriotic bravery and their service to the state, lingering doubts about the "fitness" of young working-class women continued to haunt the debates. Thanks to the war, few critics still argued that women should be placed on a "pedestal" above the sullying arena of political action or paid work, but legislators continued to regard working-class women as ignorant, foolish, irresponsible, and potentially radical.[119] If female service was central to refuting specific anti-suffrage arguments, female nature still held terrors of its own—especially when that nature was young, single, uneducated, and propertyless. In Parliament, few wished to directly disparage the female industrial workers upon whom the country depended, yet the class from which they came was not above reproach.

Among the many hardships caused by the Great War was a severe servant shortage, as butlers, gardeners, and chauffeurs enlisted in the army, while maids flocked to better paid employment in munitions factories, where they made up part of the new female industrial class. Whether in aristocratic kitchens or on the factory floor, many Antis maintained a visceral, almost instinctive distrust of working women's ignorance and its potentially detrimental impact on British democracy. None felt this more keenly than Lord James Bryce, whose own *Report on Alleged German Outrages* was arguably designed to appeal to just such a constituency. "[T]he immense majority of women are not yet qualified by their way of life, by their knowledge, and by the interest that they take in public affairs, to use the vote to their advantage or to the advantage of the nation," declared Bryce. "Think . . . of the large class of domestic servants. Within ten miles of where we are meeting there are probably hundreds of thousands of cooks, housemaids, parlour maids, nursemaids, and those who are called 'tweenies,' who do not look at newspapers, and who know nothing at all about what is passing in the political world. We are proposing to give the vote to all of them."[120] Although the bill never threatened to enfranchise "tweenies" and other female domestics, many naysayers agreed that "the great mass of women whom you would enfranchise by this Bill will go more by sentiment than by reason," that young women would "invariably vote for the best looking candidate," and that "Not having any opinions of their own," single working women would be "easy victims of any representation which is made to them."[121] The imagined susceptibility of young working-class women to falacious representations, the manipulation of the press, and unscrupulous politicians—all the evils, in short, that Bryce disparagingly associated with American-style democracy, a democracy that he not only studied as a scholar but manipulated as a propagandist—now filled him with dread for Britain's political future.[122]

Because of lingering fears about female voters, it is no accident that gender remained a basic category of distinction in bestowing electoral qualifications, yet in the name of restricting women, Conservatives from both parties were able to reassuringly limit a number of other alarming electorates as well. For Tories particularly, the alluring cry of the "cheap loaf," the threatening prospect of "People's Budgets," and the temptation among "workers and their wives" to strike for better wages and to use the vote to improve their economic position, meant that the radicalism of the bill, in terms of male suffrage, would need to be offset somewhere.[123] By limiting the women's vote, legislators balanced a generous male franchise with a restrictive female one that would throw six million rate-paying wives into an electoral pool that included millions of unsavory young men who had never before exercised the vote. "[T]here is no part of the race in which I believe more than I do in the married women," intoned Lord Selborne as he pointed out the folly of blocking the women's clause. "Yet, by way of diminishing the risks of this experiment, the noble Marquess and his friends propose to leave in the young men and cut out the married women and women of property." Insisting that young men were unstable, radical and inclined to strike, Selborne admonished Antis not to disenfranchise "the greatest of all your elements of stability . . . the mothers of families, the married women."[124]

Underlying the illogical age restriction placed on women was also a more general distrust of the young. While the franchise had always debarred children, many Conservatives felt the age of majority (long set at twenty-one) was still deeply immature. Not only did critics like Selborne oppose extending the military service franchise to nineteen-year-old soldiers, but in the 1920s the Tory party went so far as to endorse an equal franchise that would set the voting age at twenty-five for both sexes.[125] Setting the age bar for women at thirty and making it contingent upon household status, thus not only limited the female electorate but limited an electorate made up of the young, the poor, the single, and the ill-educated, drawing upon prejudice against women in order to shore up the class and age nature of a franchise that was crumbling in the face of the soldiers' vote.

The hypocrisy of granting the vote on the basis of service while denying the franchise to women under thirty was, of course, not lost on contemporaries. Not only were many feminists outraged by the injustice of the age bar, but Antis deplored the fact that it undermined the whole professed rationale for granting women the vote. As Lord Curzon contemptuously remarked, "You are saying to the female war worker, 'we are much obliged to you for all you have done. You have rendered splendid and devoted services but you are young, and undisciplined, and immature; therefore, although soldiers of any age from nineteen to thirty may vote, you must not vote; you must wait a bit for more age and experience. . . . But meanwhile we are so grateful to you . . . that we propose to give the vote to your elder sister, to your mother, to your grandmother, and to your maiden aunt.'"[126]

The reason the age bar held fast despite its inconsistencies, however, did not just have to do with whom it kept disenfranchised but with whom it did enfranchise. On the level of principle, women were universally acclaimed for their war service, giving a rationale for why now, and not before, they could be recognized as citizens. On the level of politics, the age and property bar offered security to those who feared the more general radicalism of the bill. Local Unionist Associations eventually supported the Speakers Conference recommendations on women because the new female electorate had not only proved its patriotism but would be made up of the wives of rate-payers—a potentially conservative group with some stake in protecting the status quo. By enfranchising the taxed, the stable, the conservative, and the married women of each class, Conservatives could be sure that the new male electorate would be counterbalanced by a female electorate that—with luck—would simply add six million mature, propertied voters—voters who had proved their aversion to pacifism and their support for the war—to an electorate that for the first time would include nineteen-year-old boys and male domestic servants.

Enfranchising married women, many of them mothers, also helped to mitigate the logical inconsistencies of a franchise granted on the grounds of service. As Susan R. Grayzel has shown, motherhood remained a deeply reassuring marker of female identity throughout the Great War.[127] The fact that women had staked a claim as war workers by virtue of motherhood, sacrifice, and the blood of their sons allowed commentators to insist that such maternal service was the true basis on which women were granted the vote. As early as 1916, Lord Grey had urged the Speakers Conference to grant an extra vote to all men and women who had produced more than four children, since "they have rendered a service to the state without which the state could not continue to exist."[128] Using similar logic, suffragists addressing Asquith in 1916 reminded him of "the women who have given their husbands and sons ungrudgingly," while Mrs. Fawcett archly wrote in 1916, that "it is probably far easier to turn a shell case than to bring up a child. . . . '"[129] Indeed, Mrs. Fawcett retrospectively called the 1918 women's franchise a "motherhood franchise," an idea that provided a ready answer to those critical of the inconsistencies in the women's suffrage bill. Such logic emerged repeatedly among defenders of reform. In 1918, R. M. Wilson reminded readers of a pamphlet tellingly entitled *Wife: Mother: Voter* that, "Upon the plains of Ypres . . . our dead are sleeping, the sons of the Mothers of England who bore them and suffered for them. . . . Not men alone are sleeping there on the fields of France. Women too . . . have mingled their blood with the fallen on the stricken field."[130] As Lord Buckmaster passionately argued, "If women have not been called upon in large numbers to lay down their lives for the sake of their country, they have been called upon to bear the loss of lives far dearer than their own."[131]

Despite the age bar, however, women's suffrage might well have been defeated in the House of Lords—seriously and perhaps even fatally impeding the final passage of the bill—had not raw political considerations come into play.[132] Even Lord Curzon had to admit that "from the corner of its eye the public is keeping a watch on this Bill, and is noting what will happen in your Lordships' House."[133] As he pointedly asked in his dramatic appeal for abstentions, "are you prepared to embark upon a conflict with a majority of 350 in the House of Commons, of whom nearly 150 belong to the party to which most of your Lordships also belong?"[134] Most were not. For many peers, the memory of the Parliament Act, which severely curbed their veto powers, revealed just how damaging a direct confrontation with the lower house could be.[135] Whatever legislators thought of the arguments of their colleagues or the merits of women, they clearly realized that the public, the press, and the House of Commons had been swayed, and they felt powerless to oppose the inexorable rationale of a franchise bill based on patriotic service. Women's suffrage passed in the House of Lords by a vote of 134 to 71, with numerous abstentions, clearing the way for royal ascent on February 6, 1918. Women had finally obtained the parliamentary vote: not by throwing bombs but by making them; not by raising children but by sending them to die.

Epilogue

The ghost of Dr. Coulter was as prescient as he was comical, though by March 1916 it probably did not require a clairvoyant—much less an occult spirit—to predict the arrival of women's suffrage. The representation of the conflict in terms of the safety of the family had provided women with a usable language with which to lay claim to the war. In ways both innovative and traditional, patriotic women placed their sexual, reproductive, and moral power at the service of the military state. It was a stance for which they would reap unexpected—and no doubt bittersweet—political rewards. As women were, for the first time, entrusted to vote in parliamentary elections, it became evident just how potent the image of female patriotism had been. The spectacle of women engaged in backbreaking war work, the wrenching heroism of mothers and wives, and the image of barbarism abroad, which gave these efforts moral and social meaning, all revealed the depth to which women were implicated in war, justifying their claim to a national voice.

The specter of the family in peril, however, not only implicated women in the war effort, but produced a number of other unforeseen results. If men marched off secure in the belief that they protected women and children, the brutality of their own war experience led many to question these initial assumptions. Although the German occupation of Belgium was both violent and traumatic, the exaggerations of atrocity propaganda cast authentic suffering into doubt. Not only did the Germans deny the accusations that had been leveled against them, but a series of studies published in Britain and America after the war all argued that the propaganda was essentially false.[1] In many ways, this dispute over the imagery of the war challenged the legitimacy of the conflict itself. In the face of an event whose cost was measured in male lives, the suffering of the women and children of Belgium seemed not only trivial but untrue.

If war propaganda was later repudiated, it nevertheless facilitated a fundamental shift in the parameters of citizenship. The prewar conception of liberal citizenship celebrated diversity of thought while institutionalizing the male body as the site of political authority. Under the 1918 Reform Bill, the voter could inhabit a body of any sex, but the cost of physical diversity during the war was ideological conformity. Excluding those who had conscientiously opposed the war, legislators, as Lord Hugh Cecil recognized, decided to punish men for unpopular beliefs. At a moment when journalists, politicians, and sundry other patriotic citizens proclaimed support for the war to be the only acceptable political sentiment, the gender of political and social actors seemed to matter less. The apparent ideological unity of patriotic men and women had made sexual diversity no longer seem so threatening.

Ironically, nationalism rather than liberalism opened the door for feminist demands, yet nationalism never wholly measured up to its promises. Young female workers were not only barred from voting but were unceremoniously thrown out of jobs at the end of 1918. Without any electoral recourse, factory girls had little choice but to accept their lot and try as best they could to survive on the low-paid and demeaning labor they were forced to resume in the wake of demobilization.[2] With a bit of patience and a bit of luck, they would reach the age of thirty and perhaps marry a man in one of the lucrative metal trades they been driven from in late 1918, allowing them eventually to cast one of the votes that their service had been so rhetorically useful in achieving. Given these terms, though, it is no wonder that feminists have been inclined to disparage the bill.

The exclusion of young factory girls was not its only irony. Among the consequences of the women's franchise was a decided repudiation of the progressive roots of the suffrage movement. As Emmeline Pethick Lawrence noted with horror in 1919, "the newly enfranchised mothers of children flocked to the 'Make Germany Pay' candidate."[3] Enfranchised soldiers showed shocking apathy at the polls and did not materialize as a reliable phalanx of Tory voters.[4] Instead, women, about whom there had been so much hand wringing, turned into the loyal shock troops of the Conservative Party—perhaps in recognition of the fact that displays of patriotic service had gotten them what years of feminist agitation had not: the parliamentary vote.[5] The WSPU began its right-wing political campaign and in 1918 announced Christabel's plan to stand for Parliament as a Women's Party and Coalition candidate for the hotly contested seat of Smethwick—an election that she would no doubt have won, had women been granted the vote on the same terms as men.[6]

While Christabel's defeat precipitated a career change (first as the proprietor of a tea shop on the French Riviera and then as a traveling evangelist preaching the Second Coming of Christ), her mother died in 1928 while standing for Parliament as Conservative candidate for Whitechapel and St. George. This move to the right was foreshadowed when Mrs. Pankhurst and Flora Drummond joined forces with old comrades in the Women's Police Volunteers to help break the General Strike of 1926—an experience that later inspired Drummond to found the Women's Guild of Empire to combat strikes and communism.[7] The NU remained rather more respectable as a feminist organization, fighting on for ten years to achieve the equal franchise, finally granted in 1928. Despite anger within her organization over the age bar, Millicent Fawcett considered the passage of women's suffrage to be the greatest moment of her life. After sponsoring a celebration, where the Tory hymn "Jerusalem" was re-launched as the anthem of women's suffrage, Mrs. Fawcett retired triumphant.[8] Mrs. Humphry Ward was not so lucky. Apoplectic over Curzon's treachery, Mrs. Ward's health deteriorated as she worried about the fate of the nation in the hands of women voters and watched the Anti-Suffrage League's financial reserves go, not into a national referendum, but into a pension fund for aged nurses.[9] Lord Bryce shared her pessimism. After failing to secure a referendum on women's suffrage or to restore power to the House of Lords, he went on to write about the dangers of the press, propaganda, and an ill-educated electorate; apparently Bryce could not forget his "tweenie" or the horrors of American-style democracy, and may have lived to rue the day he collaborated with Wellington House.[10]

The conservative nature of the woman's vote, however, was sociological as well as ideological. Since only female householders and university graduates over the age of thirty were enfranchised, the women's vote was built on the very conservative guarantees Unionists had wished to secure.[11] It is nevertheless important not to overstate the propertied nature of the new female electorate. Millions of working-class wives whose husbands had steady work qualified to vote, just as their husbands had since 1867, but they must have felt the precariousness of their political position, as well as their economic welfare, with the rising tide of unemployment in the 1920s. Indeed, one is struck by the way property qualifications based on occupancy made any sudden change in a women's fortune, from widowhood to the decision to move in with a son or daughter, decisive in terms of her political voice. The only qualification that freed women from the need to qualify as local government electors (and therefore from the need for property) was the university franchise.[12] Ironically, despite legislators' praise of female service and their paeans to the institution of marriage, education (as feminists had always known) was a woman's only real security.

Despite its enormous significance, few feminists could have been unequivocally pleased with the bill. As the *Nation* contemptuously pointed out, legislators had settled on a property qualification for the woman's vote and "flesh and blood for men's."[13] Yet the significance of the 1918 Reform Bill went well beyond the limitations of the female franchise, for it had, for the first time, predicated full citizenship on something other than male gender. By shifting the parameters of debate from manhood to service, feminists, politicians, and the press destabilized the fundamental notion of a sex-based electorate. While cultural labels such as "hero," "shirker," "con-shie," and "heroine" often had more to do with stereotypic assumptions than with objective reality these wartime habits of thought rerouted the basic logic for awarding the vote.

NOTES

INTRODUCTION

1. "The Latest German Method, A Pacifist from the Spirit World," *Britannia*, March 17, 1916, p. 147.
2. *Britannia*, March 17, 1916, p. 150. These conversations took place over the course of two different seances.
3. For a wonderful account of this volatile moment in British history, see George Dangerfield, *The Strange Death of Liberal England* (New York: Perigree [1935], 1980). See also Brian Harrison, "The Act of Militancy: Violence and the Suffragettes, 1904–1914," in *Peaceable Kingdom* (Oxford: Oxford University Press, 1982), pp. 26–81. A provocative new interpretation of militant window-breaking can be found in Erika Rappaport, *Shopping for Pleasure: Women in the Making of London's West End* (Princeton: Princeton University Press, 2000), pp. 215–222.
4. While the passage of women's suffrage had looked hopeful in 1911, 1912, and 1913, on each occasion other agendas took priority over women's suffrage, and the government withdrew support or allowed measures to wither. Vocal and contemptuous opposition to women's suffrage could be heard in both houses of Parliament and in the press. While pro-suffrage opinion was gaining ground, thanks particularly to the efforts of constitutionalist feminists, the failure of even sympathetic lawmakers to treat the enfranchisement of women as a priority caused the militant suffragettes to step up their increasingly violent campaign of arson, vandalism, and sabotage. The experience of militancy, however, hardened lawmakers against the cause of women suffrage. For excellent accounts of the prewar movement, see Sophia A. van Wingerden, *The Women's Suffrage Movement in Britain, 1866–1928* (London: Macmillan, 1999), pp. 118- 153; Martin Pugh, *The March of Women: A Revisionist Analysis of the Campaign for Women's Suffrrage, 1866–1914* (Oxford: Oxford University Press, 2000). For an important cultural interpretation see Laura E. Nym Mayhall, "Creating the 'Suffragette Spirit': British Feminists and Historical Imagination," *Women's History Review* 4, no. 3 (1995).
5. There is a growing literature on gender and warfare that has brought out women's unique contributions to war efforts and the impact of such

participation on feminine identities, the position of women, and social reform. Notable recent works include Susan Kingsley Kent, *Making Peace: The Reconstruction of Gender in Interwar Britain* (Princeton: Princeton University Press, 1993); Angela Woollacott, *On Her Their Lives Depend: Munitions Workers in the Great War* (Berkeley: University of California Press, 1994); Margaret Randolph Higonnet, Jane Jenson, Sonya Michel, Margaret Collins Weitz, eds., *Behind the Lines: Gender and the Two World Wars* (New Haven: Yale University Press, 1987); Susan R. Grayzel, *Women's Identities at War: Gender, Motherhood, and Politics in Britain and France During the First World War* (Chapel Hill: University of North Carolina Press, 1999); Susan Pedersen, *Family, Dependence, and the Origins of the Welfare State: Britain and France, 1914–1945* (Cambridge: Cambridge University Press, 1993).

6. For a fascinating account of the extraordinary power embedded in "narratives of sexual danger," see Judith R. Walkowitz, *City of Dreadful Delight: Narratives of Sexual Danger in Late-Victorian London* (Chicago: University of Chicago Press, 1992).

7. I am therefore particularly indebted to several important exceptions to this rule. See Kent, *Making Peace;* Sandra Stanley Holton, *Feminism and Democracy: Women's Suffrage and Reform Politics in Britain, 1900–1918* (Cambridge: Cambridge University Press, 1986); Johanna Alberti, *Beyond Suffrage: Feminists in War and Peace, 1914–1928* (New York: St. Martin's Press, 1989); Martin Pugh, *Women and the Women's Movement in Britain, 1914–1959* (New York: Paragon, 1993); and van Wingerden, *The Women's Suffrage Movement.*

8. See, for example, Strachey, *The Cause,* pp. 348–349; E. Sylvia Pankhurst, *The Suffragette Movement: An Intimate Account of Persons and Ideals* (London: Longmans, 1931), pp. 607–608; Helen Fraser, *Women and War Work* (New York: G. A. Shaw,1918); Annie Kenney, *A Militant* (London: Routledge [1924] 1994), p. 271; Hilda C. Adshead, "Mrs. Buttletub Gets Her Vote," *Common Cause,* March 15, 1918, p. 649. Sylvia Pankhurst insisted that fear of renewed militancy was also decisive.

9. Holton, *Feminism and Democracy,* pp. 129–130. For an excellent discussion of the literature on the prewar suffrage movement see June Purvis and Sandra Stanley Holton, ed., *Votes for Women* (London: Routledge, 2000), pp. 1–12; Sandra Stanley Holton, "The Making of Suffrage History," in Purvis and Holton, pp. 13–33; Maroula Joannou and June Purvis, *The Women's Suffrage Movement: New Feminist Perspectives* (Manchester: Manchester University Press, 1998), pp. 1–14.

10. Sylvia Pankhurst's *Women's Dreadnought* and the *Suffragette News Sheet,* published by WSPU dissidents, were both strongly antiwar, but the latter paper clearly regarded women's war work as further proof of women's entitlement to citizenship. See, for example, *Suffragette News Sheet,* April 1916, pp. 1–2. The left-leaning Women's Freedom League suspended militancy for the duration of the war, but vowed to "keep the Suffrage flag

flying," stating that its organ, the *Vote*, would "publish . . . news that will be of interest to women who are determined to show that every service they render in this crisis is rendered as Suffragists, who still insist on their demand for recognition as citizens in their own country." *Vote*, August 14, 1914. Similarly, *Votes for Women*, the paper of the United Suffragists, showed a diverse range of opinions on the war, despite the editorship of pacifists Frederick and Emmeline Pethick Lawrence. Contributors to *Votes for Women* frequently used women's war service as evidence of their entitlement to the vote. See for example, *Votes for Women*, November 26, 1915. Many pacifist feminists lamented the fact that female citizenship was being demanded and conceded on such militaristic terms.

11. *Anti-Suffrage Review*, March 1915.

12. This is in part reaction to works published in the 1960s and 1970s by David Mitchell, Arthur Marwick, and others who made much of female militancy. While these scholars have been deprecated as "anti-feminist," their work remains extremely useful in tracing the parameters of women's wartime activities. David Mitchell has performed the additional service to women's history of leaving his considerable suffrage archive to the Museum of London, where it is accessible to scholars. See David Mitchell, *Women on the Warpath: The Story of Women of the First World War* (London: Jonathan Cape, 1968) and Arthur Marwick, *Women at War 1914-1918* (London: Croom Helm, 1977). For an important recent exception, see Jacqueline de Vries, "Gendering Patriotism: Emmeline and Christabel Pankhurst and World War One," in Sybil Oldfield, ed., *This Working-Day World: Women's Lives and Culture(s) in Britain 1914–1945* (London: Taylor & Francis, 1994), pp. 75–88.

13. See, for example, Claire M. Tylee, *The Great War and Women's Consciousness: Images of Militarism and Womanhood in Women's Writings, 1914–64* (Iowa City: University of Iowa Press, 1990); Jill Liddington, *The Road to Greenham Common: Feminism and Anti-Militarism since 1820* (Syracuse: University of Syracuse Press, 1989); Margaret Kamester and Jo Vellacott, eds., *Militarism versus Feminism: Writings on Women and War* (London: Virago, 1987); Jo Vellacott, "Feminist Consciousness and the First World War," *History Workshop Journal* 23 (Spring 1987), pp. 81–101; Joan Montgomery Byles, "Women's Experience of World War One: Suffragists, Pacifist and Poets," *Women's Studies International Forum* 8, no. 5 (1985), pp. 473- 487; Anne Wiltshire, *Most Dangerous Women: Feminist Peace Campaigners of the Great War* (London: Pandora,1985) and Alberti, *Beyond Suffrage*. Even June Purvis, whose work has splendidly illuminated the history of the WSPU, ends her rehabilitation of Christabel Pankhurst in 1914, making no mention of what might aptly be termed Christabel's "war feminism." June Purvis, "Christabel Pankhurst and the Women's Social and Political Union," in Joannou and Purvis, pp. 157–172.

14. Susan Kinglsey Kent, *Making Peace*; Cheryl Jorgensen-Earp, *"The Transfiguring Sword": The Just War of the Women's Social and Political Union*

(Tuscaloosa: University of Alabama Press, 1997), pp. 149–151; Lisa Tickner, *The Spectacle of Women: Imagery of the Suffrage Campaign, 1907–1914* (Chicago: University of Chicago Press, 1988), pp. 227–237; Holton, *Feminism and Democracy,* pp. 116–150.

15. Neal McCrillis, *The British Conservative Party in the Age of Universal Suffrage* (Columbus: Ohio State University Press, 1998), p. 18. For the most exact figures, see Martin Pugh, *Electoral Reform,* Appendix 10, p. 196. The number of women eligible to vote would probably have exceeded the 8,479,156 who actually registered.

16. Neal Blewett, "The Franchise in the United Kingdom, 1885–1918," *Past and Present* (December 1965), pp. 27–56. Martin Pugh's excellent *Electoral Reform in War and Peace* remains the most important book on the Reform Bill of 1918.

17. For useful methodological essays, see Lynn Hunt, ed., *The New Cultural History* (Berkeley: University of California Press, 1989) and Joan Wallach Scott, *Gender and the Politics of History* (New York: Columbia University Press, 1988).

18. An extraordinary number of works, many by literary historians, investigate the cultural history of gender and warfare. Among the most influential have been Sandra M. Gilbert, "Soldier's Heart: Literary Men, Literary Women, and the Great War," in Higonnet et al., eds., *Behind the Lines,* pp. 197–226 and Margaret R. Higonnet and Patrice Higonnet, "The Double Helix," in Higonnet et al., eds., *Behind the Lines,* pp. 31–47. Other notable works focusing on the cultural construction of gender in war are Helen M. Cooper et al., eds., *Arms and the Woman: War, Gender and Literary Representation* (Chapel Hill: University of North Carolina Press, 1989); Sharon Ouditt, *Fighting Forces, Writing Women: Identity and Ideology in the First World War* (London: Routledge, 1994); Jean Bethke Elshtain, *Women and War* (New York: Basic Books, 1987); Mirian Cooke and Angela Woollacott, eds., *Gendering War Talk* (Princeton: Princeton University Press, 1993). Recently, Susan Pedersen has raised the question of whether feminist historians have been too inclined to focus on culture and identities to the exclusion of other questions. For a provocative discussion of this issue, see Susan Pedersen, "The Future of Feminist History," *Perspectives* (October 2000), pp. 1; 20–25.

CHAPTER 1

1. "Terrible Death of a Dumfries Nurse," *Dumfries Standard,* September 16, 1914, p. 2. For accounts of the scandal see, "A Cruel Hoax," *Dumfries Standard,* September 19, 1914, p. 4; "Hume Case in Parliament," *Dumfries Standard,* September 26, 1914, p. 4; "The Nurse Hoax," *Dumfries Standard,* September 30, 1914, p. 2; "The Bogus Atrocity Story," *Dumfries Standard,* October 7, 1914, p. 4; "The Dumfries Hoax," *Daily*

Graphic, December 29, 1914, p. 8; "The Dumfries Nurse Hoax," *Daily Graphic,* December 30, 1914 p. 6; "The Reported German Cruelty to a Nurse," *Times,* September 30, 1914 p. 5; "Dumfries Atrocity Story," *Times,* December 7, 1914 p. 6; "The Dumfries Atrocity Hoax," *Times,* December 29, 1914, p. 3; "The Atrocity Hoax" *Times,* December 30, 1914, p. 5.

2. Committee on Alleged German Outrages, *Report of the Committee on Alleged German Outrages Appointed by His Majesty's Government* (London: H.M. Stationery Office, 1915).

3. "The Dumfries Nurse Hoax," *Daily Graphic,* December 30, 1914, p. 6.

4. "The Dumfries Atrocity Hoax," *Times,* December 29, 1914, p. 3.

5. Sir Otto Trevelyan to James Bryce, May 18, 1915, Bodleian Library, Oxford [hereafter Bodleian], Modern Manuscripts [hereafter MM], MS Bryce 18, fol. 72.

6. John Horne and Alan Kramer, who have spent years researching the German invasion of Belgium and have attempted to expose the brutal tactics of the German army in 1914, nevertheless acknowledge that, "In reality adult males were the chief victims. . . . Despite the double filler of the Home Office investigators and the [Bryce] committee itself, myth and hysteria coloured many of the witnesses statements used. The cumulative effect of the extracts . . . was one of random and widespread German sadism, especially towards women and children, which exceeded any possible reality." See John Horne and Alan Kramer, *German Atrocities, 1914: A History of Denial* (New Haven: Yale University Press, 2001), p. 234. For influential older accounts see, James Morgan Read, *Atrocity Propaganda 1914–1919* (New Haven: Yale University Press, 1941); Arthur Ponsonby, *Falsehood in War Time* (London: George Allen & Unwin, 1929).

7. William Le Queux, *German Atrocities: A Record of Shameless Deeds* (London [1914], pp. 45–121. For fascinating studies of the implications of such imagery see Susan Kingsley Kent, *Making Peace: The Reconstruction of Gender in Interwar Britain* (Princeton: Princeton University Press, 1993) and Judith R. Walkowitz, *City of Dreadful Delight: Narratives of Sexual Danger in Late-Victorian London* (Chicago: University of Chicago Press, 1992).

8. H. C. Peterson, *Propaganda for War: The Campaign Against American Neutrality, 1914–1917* (Norman: University of Oklahoma Press, 1939), p. 243.

9. See John Horne and Alan Kramer, "German 'Atrocities' and Franco-German Opinion, 1914: The Evidence of German Soldiers' Diaries," *Journal of Modern History* (March 1994), pp. 1–33. For a moving visual account see, Jay Winter, *The Experience of World War I* (New York: Oxford University Press, 1989).

10. Kent, *Making Peace,* pp. 23–26. For a fascinating account of the issue of veracity, see Trevor Wilson, "Lord Bryce's Investigation into Alleged German Atrocities in Belgium, 1914–1915," *Journal of Contemporary History* (July 1979), pp. 369–383.

11. See, for example, Sir Theodore A. Cook, *The Crimes of Germany* (London: The Field & Queen Ltd., n.d.), p. 11.

12. Cook, p. 11; Committee on Alleged German Outrages, *Evidence and Documents Laid Before the Committee on Alleged German Outrages: Being an Appendix to the Report of the Committee appointed by His Britannic Majesty's Government and presided over by The Right Hon. Viscount Bryce, O. M.* (London and New York: Macmillan Company for H.M. Stationery Office), p 82.

13. Charles W. Eliot to James Bryce, December 17, 1914, Bodleian, MM, MS Bryce USA 1, fol. 119.

14. *Times*, August 22, 1914, p. 7.

15. James Bryce to Albert Venn Dicey, August 20, 1914, Bodleian, MM, MS Bryce 4, fol. 72.

16. James Bryce to Albert Venn Dicey, October 28, 1915, Bodleian, MM, MS Bryce 4, fol. 92.

17. On the peace movement see Martin Caedel, *Pacifism in Britain 1914–1945: The Defining Faith* (Oxford: Oxford University Press, 1980) and Anne Wiltshire, *Most Dangerous Women: Feminist Peace Campaigners of the First World War* (London: Pandora Press, 1985).

18. Some of the following material is reproduced from Nicoletta F. Gullace, "Sexual Violence and Family Honor: British Propaganda and International Law during the First World War," *American Historical Review* (June 1997), pp. 714–747.

19. University of Oxford, Faculty of Modern History, *Why We Are at War*, 3rd ed. (Oxford: Clarendon Press, 1914), pp. 116–117. See also, *Times*, August 2, 1914, p. 5 and August 5, 1914, p. 7.

20. Belgian neutrality was also confirmed in 1870. For a discussion of the position of Belgian neutrality under international law, see Sir Augustus Oakes and R. B. Mowat, eds., *The Great Treaties of the Nineteenth Century* (Oxford: Clarendon Press, [1918], 1970), pp. 126–157; Bethmann Hollweg, "Interview With Sir Edward Goschen" (Berlin, August 4, 1914), quoted in A. P. Higgins, "The Law of Nations and the War," *Oxford Pamphlets* no. 24 (London: Oxford University Press, 1914) p. 13.

21. See, for example, Mrs. F. S. Boas, "Our Village and the War," Parliamentary Recruiting Committee [hereafter PRC] no. 33 (London: PRC, 1914–15), p. 2.

22. Oxford Faculty, *Why*, back cover; Parliamentary Recruiting Committee, "The Scrap of Paper," 1914, PRC posters no. 7 and 15, Department of Art [hereafter Art] Imperial War Museum, [hereafter IWM] IWM: pst:5083. PRC poster no. 17, intended for Scotland, read "A WEE 'SCRAP O' PAPER' IS BRITAIN'S BOND." Quoted in Philip Dutton, "Moving Images? The PRC's Poster Campaign, 1914–1916," *IWM Review*, no. 4 (1989), p. 48. I have also found the "scrap of paper" reproduced on postcards, collected among private memorabilia, and reprinted in a woman's magazine; *Times*, September 5, 1914, p. 10. Asquith and Andrew Bonar Law were the leaders.

23. Sir Edward Goschen to Sir Edward Grey, August 8, 1914, reprinted in Oxford Faculty, *Why*, p. 200.

24. See J. H. Morgan, *German Atrocities an Official Investigation*, (London: T. Fisher Unwin, 1916), p. 60 and Coleman Phillipson, *International Law and the Great War* (London: Fisher Unwin, 1915), p. 50.

25. See F. W. Mark and H. Leurie Hill, "When We Wound Up the Watch on the Rhine," (1914) or Asquith's request for war credits, *Times*, September 20, 1914, p. 4; August 7, 1914, p. 8.

26. For a classic account of the analogy between international and civil law in the early twentieth century, see H. Lauterpacht, *Private Law Sources and Analogies of International Law* (London: Longmans, Green & Co., 1927).

27. Arthur Conan Doyle, *To Arms!* (London: Hodder and Stoughton, 1914), p. 30. See also *Times*, September 20, 1914, p. 4.

28. David Lloyd George, "Through Terror to Triumph: An Appeal to the Nation," a speech delivered at the Queen's Hall, London, September, 19,1914, PRC no. 29 (London: PRC, 1914), pp. 4–6 in House of Lords Record Office, London [hereafter HLRO], LG/C/36/2.

29. David Lloyd George, "War Aims. Proposed Statement by the Prime Minister to Trade Unionists," extracts from the minutes of the War Cabinet on January 4, 1918, p. 5, in HLRO, LG/160/1/12.

30. G. W. Prothero, "Our Duty and Our Interest in the War," in *Tracts Relating to the European War 1914-*, issued by the Central Committee for National Patriotic Organizations (London: John Murray, 1914), p. 2.

31. The British Empire Union, "The Perils of Pacifism," no. 20 [1917], *Pamphlets and Leaflets* (London 1919), Imperial War Museum, London [hereafter IWM], 336.00 K.52496.

32. Coulson Kernahan, *The Experiences of a Recruiting Officer* (London: Hodder & Stoughton, 1915), p. 29.

33. *Times*, August 20, 1914, p. 4. For responses to Prothero's letter, see "Follow up to Dr. Prothero's Suggestion," *The Times*, August 21, 1914, p. 4.

34. This belief inspired a tremendous campaign by the middle and upper classes to educate "the people" in the origins of the war. See, for example, E. W. Wellington to Lord Northcliffe, August 28, 1914, British Library, London [hereafter BL], ADD 62326, fol.169.

35. *Times*, August 20, 1914, p 3.

36. Kernahan, p. 29.

37. *Times*, August 26, 1914, p. 7. On September 16, the *Times* extracted more extensively from the report that had been translated and released by the British Press Bureau the day before. *Times*, September 16, 1914. For Belgian complaints about British press coverage see, the correspondence between Jay Locock at the Foreign Office and F. H. Mitchell at the Press Bureau, September-October 1915, Public Record Office, London [hereafter PRO], HO 139/2, A 18, part iv.

38. Sir Edward Cook, *The Press in War Time* (London: Macmillan & Co., 1920); Kennedy Jones, *Fleet Street and Downing Street* (London: Hutchinson & Co., 1920).

39. Louis Raemaekers, "Germany's Pledged Word," *Raemaekers Cartoons* (London: Hodder & Stoughton, n.d.), p. 1 in IWM, Edith Cavell Collection, Box 114b.

40. Anon, "In the Trail of the Hun," *see illustrations.*

41. Belgium came to be almost ubiquitously depicted as a violated woman, bringing together the allegorical female representation of Liberty and the personified nation with the literal depiction of raped Belgian women.

42. "The Dumfries Atrocity Hoax," *Times,* December 29, 1914, p. 3.

43. The sources are innumerable; see, for example, Theodore Cook, *The Crimes of Germany: Being an Illustrated Synopsis of the Violation of International Law and of Humanity by the Armed Forces of the German Empire* (London: The Field and Queen [1917]); William Le Queux, *German Atrocities: A Record of Shameless Deeds* (London: George Newnes, 1914); W. N. Willis, *The Kaiser and his Barbarians* (London: The Anglo-Eastern Co. [1914]); The Parliamentary Recruiting Committee, "The Truth About German Atrocities," PRC no. 43 (London: PRC, 1915).

44. Phillipson, *International Law,* p. 184.

45. Morgan, *German Atrocities,* pp. 62–63.

46. Ernst Müller-Meiningen, *Who Are the Huns? the Law of Nations and its Breakers* (Berlin: Georg Reimer, 1915), p. vi.

47. "Atrocities in the Field," *Times,* September 10, 1914, p. 9.

48. "The Dumfries Hoax," *Daily Graphic,* December 29, 1914, p 8.

49. E. T. Cook to the Reverend Thomas Waugh, December 22, 1914, Public Record Office, Kew [hereafter PRO] HO 139/5.

50. Like the Foreign Office's later attempt to "verify" a corpse-conversion factory story fabricated in 1917, these incidents highlight the government's bid to bolster its domestic and international credibility while learning to govern by the idioms of the popular press. See "Miscellaneous General Files, 1917," April 1917, PRO, FO/395/147.

51. Cook, *Crimes of Germany,* pp. 6–7; See also Morgan *German Atrocities;* J. Corbell, "Four Postcard-Cartoons Relating to the Death of Nurse Cavell" (London: Inter-Art Co, n.d.), IWM, 345.21 K. 48954.

52. "British Troops at the Front," *Times,* September 12, 1914, p. 6.

53. Lord Selborne to the Editor, *Times,* September 15, 1914, p. 9.

54. *Times,* September 15, 1914, p. 9.

55. See "Parliamentary Debates," *Times,* August 27, 1914, p. 8.; M. D. Chalmers, "Letter to the Editor," *Times,* August 21, 1914, p. 9; Lord Selborne, "Letter to the Editor," *Times,* September 15, 1914, p. 9; "Parliamentary Debates," *Times,* September 15, 1914, p 10.

56. For an account of the failure of investigators to corroborate evidence see Wilson, "Lord Bryce's Investigation," p. 374.

57. Notes of Captain Martin Hardie, IWM, Department of Documents [hereafter Documents], Collection of Captain Martin Hardie, Item #7 writing tablet, November 15, 1915.

58. Quoted in Anthony Rhodes, *Propaganda: The Art of Persuasion in World War II* (New York: Chelsea House, 1976) p.139.

59. "War Office Memorandum," July 18, 1915, PRO, WO/ 32/ 4893.

60. See, for example, M. D. Chalmers to James Bryce, December 29, 1914 and Mears to Bryce, March 9, 1915 in Bodleian, MM, Add Bryce Papers, UB 57. For skepticism in the feminist press see, *Common Cause*, September 18, 1914; Millicent Garrett Fawcett, *Common Cause*, November 13, 1914, p. 534; James McKenzie to *Common Cause* March 12, 1915, pp. 757–8; *Common Cause*, March 19, 1915, p. 770. For a discussion of this problem see Wilson, "Lord Bryce's Investigation," p. 374.

61. Sir John Simon to James Bryce, December 4, 1914, Bodleian, ADD Bryce UB 57.

62. Trevor Wilson comes to a similar conclusion, although he is more inclined to feel that the Committee's larger goals outweighed its imprecision in reviewing the evidence. See Wilson, "Lord Bryce's Investigation," pp. 72–77.

63. Harold Cox to James Bryce, March 5, 1915, Bodleian, MM, ADD Bryce Papers, UB 57.

64. Harold Cox to James Bryce, March 1, 1915, Bodleian, MM, ADD Bryce Papers, UB 57.

65. Committee on Alleged German Outrages, *Report*, p. 40.

66. Charles Masterman to James Bryce, June 7, 1915, Bodleian UB 57 Bryce, 1915.

67. Committee on Alleged German Outrages, *Appendix*, p. 3.

68. "Cabinet Document," May 27, 1915 in Bodleian, MM, ADD Bryce Papers, UB 57.

69. See, for example, Charles Masterman, "Report of the Work of the Bureau Established for the Purpose of Laying Before Neutral Nations and the Dominions the Case of Great Britain and Her Allies," *Interim Report of the War Propaganda Bureau* (Wellington House, June 15,1915), p. 15, in PRO, INF/4/5. According to Bryce's biographer H. A. L. Fisher (who was himself a member of the committee), the Bryce Report was translated into twenty-seven languages. H. A. L. Fisher, *James Bryce*, vol. II (New York: Macmillan, 1927), p. 134.

70. Read, *Atrocity Propaganda*, pp. vii, 251–253. The persistence of atrocity propaganda is also evident in the publications of the National War Aims Committee set up toward the end of the war to combat war weariness among the domestic population. See, for example, National War Aims Committee, *Leaflets 1917–18*, BL,1854, e.5.

71. Robert Donald, *Report on Propaganda Arrangements* (London 1917), p. 3 in PRO, INF 4/4B.

72. Donald, *Report on Propaganda*, p. 7.

73. Read, *Atrocities,* pp. 223–233. See also conversation between Colonel Gibbons and Mr. Adams, August 16, 1917, HLRO, LG F/79/32, fol. 1.

74. Ruth Harris, "The 'Child of the Barbarian': Rape, Race and Nationalism in France During the First World War," *Past and Present,* November 1993, p. 174.

75. Theodore Roosevelt to James Bryce, May 29, 1915, Bodleian, MM, MS Bryce USA 9, fol. 218.

76. Attorney General's Office to Sir Stanley Buckmaster, October 23, 1914, PRO, HO 139/2.

77. Will Crooks, *The British Workman Defends his Home* (London: The Whitwell Press, 1917) pp. 6–7.

78. The distinction between "official" and "unofficial" propaganda is a main theme of the thorough and reliable account of official propaganda by Sanders and Taylor. See M. L. Sanders and Philip M. Taylor, *British Propaganda in the First World War, 1914–1918* (London: Macmillan, 1982).

79. Parliamentary Recruiting Committee, Poster no. 49 [1915]. The poster is depicted hanging prominently in the Parliamentary Recruiting Committee Offices at 12 Downing Street. Parliamentary Recruiting Committee, Minute Book no. 1, BL, ADD 54192. As well as serving as a recruiting poster, this motto was frequently reprinted on other Parliamentary Recruiting Committee paraphernalia.

80. British propaganda became the object of an isolationist postwar scholarship in the United States that regarded Americans as dupes of false atrocity stories. In the 1920s and 1930s many Americans regarded themselves as having been drawn into World War I by British cunning and falsehood. The classic study in this vein is Harold Laswell, *Propaganda Technique in the World War* (New York: Knopf, 1927).

CHAPTER 2

1. Alfred Noyes, *Rada: a Belgian Christmas Eve* (London: Methuen & Co., 1915), p. 17.

2. Noyes, p. 58.

3. Noyes, p. 64

4. For an excellent introduction to the recent literature on masculinity, see Joanna Bourke, *Dismembering the Male: Men's Bodies, Britain and the Great War* (Chicago: University of Chicago Press, 1996), pp. 11–30. For an insightful analysis of a similar phenomenon in the United States, see Nancy K. Bristow, *Making Men Moral: Social Engineering During the Great War* (New York: New York University Press, 1996), pp. 4–53.

5. *Times,* September 2, 1914, p. 4.

6. The original use of the name "Tommy Atkins" for the ideal-typical British soldier is not entirely clear. Robert Graves claims that the original Tommy Atkins was a Royal Welch Fusilier who fought in the War of

American Independence while others have suggested that "Tommy Atkins" was the name used on sample enlistment forms by Wellington's army. John Laffin, *Tommy Atkins: The Story of an English Soldier* (London: Cassell, 1966), pp. xi-xiii; Irving Howe, ed., *The Portable Kipling* (New York: Penguin, 1982), pp. 613–615; Robert Graves, *Good-Bye to All That* (New York: Doubleday, 1957), p. 83; R. J. Q. Adams and Philip Poirier, *The Conscription Controversy in Great Britain, 1900–1918* (Columbus: Ohio State University Press, 1987), p. 3.

7. "The Happy Warrior," *Nineteenth Century and After* vol. 76, no. 454 (December 1914), p. 1177.

8. Dr. Alexander Irvine, *God and Tommy Atkins* (London: Hutchinson, 1918), p. 125. The book is a collection of sermons given to recruits at military camps all over England.

9. In 1915 even the king participated in such rhetoric when he suggested levying a poll tax on male shop attendants to make them enlist. Lloyd George dismissed the idea. Stamfordham to Lloyd George, May 9, 1915, HLRO, LG/C/5/6/ fol. 21; Lloyd George to Stamfordham, May 11, 1915, HLRO, LG/C/5/6/ fol. 22.

10. These female taunts left a particularly vivid impression on those who served in the war. For a discussion of this theme, see Nicoletta F. Gullace, "White Feathers and Wounded Men: Female Patriotism and the Memory of the Great War," *Journal of British Studies* (April 1997), pp. 178-206. The most manipulative of these appeals could even be worded as a call from the dead. See, Anon., "In Flanders's Fields," found in IWM Documents, collection of Lieutenant Frank Ennor 86/28/1.

11. Frank H. Ennor to Kathleen, ND [1915], IWM Documents, 86/28/1/.

12. William Orchard to his father, September 1914, IWM Documents, 79/41/1.

13. John Osborne, *The Voluntary Recruiting Movement in Britain* (Ann Arbor: University Microfilms International, 1983), p. 2.

14. John W. Graham, M.A., *Conscription and Conscience: A History 1916–1919* (London: George Allen and Unwin, 1922), p. 30.

15. For a discussion of the relationship between dismemberment and masculinity during the Great War, see Bourke, *Dismembering the Male*, pp. 31–75.

16. A. Robert Sanders, *Journal*, January 18, 1915, IWM Documents, Collection of A. S. Robert Sanders.

17. Jay Winter, "Comment presented to the American Historical Association on: 'The Era of Total War: Gender, Sexuality, and the State 1914–1918.'" (Washington, D.C.: AHA annual meeting December 30, 1991), panel no 101. For an even more far-reaching critique of the importance of propaganda, see L. L. Farrar, Jr., "Nationalism in Wartime: Critiquing Conventional Wisdom," in Frans Coetzee and Marilyn Shevin-Coetzee, eds., *Authority, Identity and the Social History of the Great War* (Oxford: Berghahn Books, 1995), pp. 136–139. For an excellent discussion of the

importance of propaganda in shaping British attitudes, see Trevor Wilson, *The Myriad Faces of War* (Cambridge: Polity Press, 1986), pp. 731–47.

18. Peckham to Captain J. E. B. Gray, August 31, 1914, IWM Documents, Collection of J. E. B. Gray.

19. For a discussion of the attitudes of public school men, see Peter Parker, *The Old Lie: The Great War and the Public School Ethos* (London: Constable, 1987).

20. Major C. W. Hughes, *Diary* entry, September 2, 1914, p. 11, IWM Documents, 82/25/1; Peter Simkins, *Kitchener's Army: The Raising of the New Armies, 1914–1916* (Manchester: Manchester University Press, 1988), pp. 165–190.

21. Lloyd George, "Speech delivered at the Queen's Hall, London, September 19, 1914," p. 15 in HLRO, LG/L/36/2 fol. 30.

22. *Times*, August 31, 1914.

23. Anna Davin, "Imperialism and Motherhood," *History Workshop* no. 5 (Spring 1978), pp. 9- 65.

24. For a lucid study of this debate, see Adams and Poirier, *Conscription Controversy, passim.*

25. George F. Shee, *The Briton's First Duty* (London: Grant Richards, 1901), p. 252.

26. Coulson Kernahan, "Why I Support Lord Roberts," *Wesleyan Methodist Magazine* (March 1914), quoted in Coulson Kernahan, *The Experiences of a Recruiting Officer* (London: Hodder & Stoughton [1915]), p. 93.

27. "Our Married Recruits," *Daily Mail* (July 29, 1915), p. 1. The typical Tommy would have been young and unmarried but, as more married men entered the forces, there was increasing interest in representing the Tommy as a family man. *See illustrations.* For an excellent discussion of this theme, see Bourke, *Dismembering the Male,* pp. 163–167.

28. Quoted in Paul Fussell, *The Great War and Modern Memory* (Oxford: Oxford University Press, 1977), p. 301.

29. *Times*, August 8, 1914, p. 7; *Times*, August 11, 1914, p. 7.

30. Quoted in Lynn Layton, "Vera Brittain's Testament(s)" in Margaret Higonnet et al., eds., *Behind the Lines: Gender and the Two World Wars* (New Haven: Yale University Press, 1987), p. 74.

31. Lloyd George, "Queen's Hall Speech," p. 14–15. The derision toward the British was sometimes shared by the French who joked that, "Germany will fight to the last German and England to the last Frenchman." Lord Northcliffe to Sir Edward Carson, June 30, 1915, BL ADD 62158 vol. vi, fol. 129.

32. J. H. Balfour Browne, *War Problems* (London: Longmans, Green & Co., 1915), p. 88.

33. The Duty and Discipline Movement, *All Can Help: A Handbook for War-Time* (London: The Duty and Discipline Movement, 1915), p. 86.

34. See Susan Kingsley Kent, *Making Peace: The Reconstruction of Gender in Interwar Britain* (Princeton: Princeton University Press, 1993), pp.

41–42. For analysis of the imagined relationship between German atrocities and "deviant" sexuality, see Samuel Hynes, *A War Imagined: The First World War and English Culture* (London: Pimlico, 1992), pp. 223–224. A good introduction to early scientific writing on homosexuality is Havelock Ellis, *Psychology of Sex: A Manual for Students* (New York: Ray Long and Richard R. Smith, Inc., 1933), a concise anthology of Ellis's work on sexual psychology. While Ellis was highly progressive for his time, the tendency among Ellis and other experts to define "sexual inversion" as a "neurosis" may have reinforced contemporary prejudices.

35. Wilson, pp. 411–412. See also Hynes, *War Imagined*, pp. 16–17.

36. Hynes, *War imagined*, pp. 224–225.

37. Robert Graves, *Goodbye to All That* (New York: Doubleday [1929], 1957); Hynes, p. 225; Kent, pp. 41–42.

38. Marilyn Shevin-Coetzee and Franz Coetzee, eds., *World War I and European Society: A Sourcebook* (Lexington, MA: D. C. Heath, 1995), p. 181. For a full account of the trial see, Philip Hoare, *Oscar Wilde's Last Stand: Decadence, Conspiracy, and the Most Outrageous Trial of the Century* (New York: Arcade Publishing, 1997).

39. For a fascinating account of the trial see, Hynes, *War Imagined*, pp. 226–229.

40. "A Citizen's Army," *Brighton Herald*, September 5, 1914, p. 6.

41. "An Indignant British Matron," *Brighton Herald*, September 5, 1914, p. 6.

42. "Canvass for Kitchener," *Ladies Pictorial*, September 12, 1914, p. 384; *Standard Recruiter*, August 26, 1914, p. 6.

43. Scout Mistress, Bath Girl Scouts to Mr. E. A. Brookes, [n.d.], IWM Documents, Misc. Recruiting, K.44699.

44. Miss D. E. Higgins to her father, March 5, 1916, IWM, Documents, 86/73/1.

45. Miss D. E. Higgins to her father, March 5, 1916, IWM, Documents, 86/73/1.

46. Miss D. E. Higgins to her father, March 15, 1916, IWM, Documents, 86/73/1.

47. For fascinating discussions of gender role reversal, see Sandra Gilbert, "Soldier's Heart: Literary Men, Literary Women and the Great War," in Margaret Higonnet, et al., eds., *Behind the Lines: Gender and the Two World Wars* (New Haven: Yale University Press, 1987), p. 223; Kent *Making Peace*, ch. 2 and Margaret R. Higonnet and Patrice Higonnet, "The Double Helix," in Higonnet, et al., eds., *Behind the Lines*, pp. 31–47.

48. *Times*, August 31, 1914, p. 1.

49. Charles Heinson to BBC, May 15, 1964 BBC GW Hea-Hey fol 96. See also *Times*, August 31, 1914, p. 1; M. Yearsley, "Memoirs," IWM, DS/Misc/17, p. 19 and Osborne, *Voluntary Recruiting*, p. 176.

50. Anon., "British Women Flaunting Petticoats for Men who do not Volunteer." *See illustrations*. Many thanks to Nora Jones who helped me to identify this photo from the *Daily Chronicle* weekly publication, the *War*

Budget. For a splendid poetic and photographic record see Nora Jones and Liz Ward, eds., *The Forgotten Army: Women's Poetry of the First World War* (Beverley: Highgate Publications, Ltd., 1991).

51. *Times,* August 27, 1914, p. 1.
52. *Common Cause,* September 11, 1914, p.426.
53. *Common Cause,* June 18, 1915, p. 144.
54. Anon., "For the Glory of Ireland." *See illustrations.*
55. Headley Le Bas was appointed to direct the recruiting campaign in Ireland, where it was politically impossible to impose conscription even after 1916. Le Bas was also the head of Caxton's advertising agency, which was centrally involved in the government recruiting campaign. Because of his recruiting tactics, one critic argued that Le Bas's recruits were de facto conscripts. E. S. Turner, *Dear Old Blighty* (London: Michael Joseph Ltd., 1980), p. 67.
56. Hansard, *House of Commons Parliamentary Debates,* May 19, 1915, col. 2409. A marvelous discussion of the significance of "short-haired women" can be found in Mary Louise Roberts, *Civilization Without Sexes: Reconstructing Gender in Postwar France, 1917–1927* (Chicago: University of Chicago Press, 1994), pp. 63–87.
57. J. H. Morgan, *German Atrocities: An Official Investigation* 2nd ed. (London: T. Fisher Unwin, 1916), pp. 136 and 151. Committee on Alleged German Outrages, *Report of the Committee on Alleged German Outrages,* (London: H.M. Stationery Office, 1915), p. 40. It was also speculated that the Germans cut off women's breasts to warn their compatriots that the woman had been infected with syphilis in the process of being raped.
58. Committee on Alleged German Outrages, *Report,* pp. 39–40.
59. Jean Massart, *Belgians Under the German Eagle* (London: Fisher Unwin Ltd., 1916), pp. 340–341.
60. J. H. Morgan, *German Atrocities,* pp. 52–52.
61. Sandra Gilbert, "Soldier's Heart," pp. 197–198. For examples, see Will Dyson "The Wonders of Science" (1915) in Will Dyson, *Kulture Cartoons* (London: Stanley Paul & Co., 1915), p. 6. Foxe's *Book of Martyrs,* a standard work on Protestant hagiography and a ubiquitous text in Victorian households, illustrated tortures identical to many of those seized upon in atrocity propaganda. This fact is significant since, according to Christopher Hill, Foxe "depicted God's Englishmen as in the forefront of the battle for Christ versus Anti-Christ throughout the ages." Christopher Hill, "History and Patriotism," in Raphael Samuel, *Patriotism: The Making and Unmaking of British National Identity,* vol. I (London: Routledge, 1989), p. 6.
62. *South Wales Daily News,* September 30, 1914, p. 7.
63. "Women and the War," *PRC,* no. 23 (London: PRC, 1915), p. 1. This logic was also implicit in the government's defense of the necessity of calling up married men after the fiasco of Asquith's "pledge." "Statement on Compulsory Military Service," Bodleian, MM, MS Asquith, vol. 30, fol. 108.
64. C. Sheridan Jones, *The Unspeakable Prussian* (London: Cassell & Co. Ltd., 1914), p. 53.

65. With the reinstatement of the Contagious Diseases Acts, women could be jailed for infecting Tommies with venereal disease. Any official attempt to separate the men from women was undertaken on behalf of the soldiers. Turner, *Dear Old Blighty*, p. 210.

66. *Times*, August 19, 1914, p. 6.

67. *John Bull*, January 2, 1915, p. 7.

68. *Vote*, June 15, 1917, p. 252. See also Susan Kingsley Kent, "Love and Death: War and Gender in Britain, 1914–1918," in Frans Coetzee and Marilyn Shevin-Coetzee, eds., *Authority, Identity and the Social History of the Great War* (Oxford: Berghahn, 1995), p. 162.

69. *Weekly Dispatch*, September 6, 1914, quoted in the *Times*, September 12, 1914, p. 12.

70. Captain Martin Hardie, *Censor's Report*, October 19, 1917, p. 3, in IWM Documents, Collection of Captain Martin Hardie.

71. Home Office to Chief Constables, August 21, 1915, p. 2, in PRO, HO 45 10734/258929.

72. *The Times History of the World War*, vol. 4 no. 52, August 17, 1915, p. 509. For an excellent discussion of this theme, see Angela Woollacott, "'Khaki Fever' and its Control: Gender, Class, Age and Sexual Morality on the British Homefront in the First World War," *Journal of Contemporary History* (April 1994), pp. 325–347.

73. Jessie Pope, *More War Poems* (London: Grant Richards Ltd., 1915), pp. 42–43.

74. Siegfried Sassoon famously derided these sentiments in his poem "Glory of Women." Catherine Reilley, *Scars Upon My Heart* (London: Virago Press, 1981), p. xv.

75. For a discussion of several of these policies, see Arthur Marwick, *The Deluge: British Society and the First World War* (New York: Norton & Co., 1965), pp. 56–68.

76. F. E. Smith, "Preface," in Arthur Conan Doyle, *To Arms!* (London: Hodder and Stoughton, 1914), p. 10.

77. Smith, "Preface," p. 8.

78. For a typical British version of the toff slacker, see G. E. Studdy, "Beginning to Understand," *Tatler*, no. 691 (September 23, 1914), p. 341

79. Captain Tom Sherwood to Blanche, May 2, 1915, IWM Documents, Collection of Captain Tom Sherwood.

80. J. H. Balfour Browne, *War Problems*, pp. 87–92.

81. Anon., "Have You Womenfolk Worth Defending?" IWM Department of Art.

82. John Ferns, *Lytton Strachey* (Boston: Twayne Publishers, 1988), p. 15. Strachey's famous double-edged reply was, "I should attempt to come—between them."

83. Richard Williamson to T. J. Macnamara, October 27, 1915, in HLRO LG/D/17/13 #2.

84. Derby to Asquith, March 21, 1916, etc. MM, Bod., MS Asquith vol. 16 fols. 109, 127–30; Walter H. Long to M. Bonham Carter, April 16, 1916,

ibid., fol. 142; Derby to Asquith, April 8, 1916, etc., MS Asquith vol. 30; Lord Robert Cecil to Asquith, April 28, 1916, ibid., fol. 78. Wilson, *Myriad Faces*, p. 413. The original Military Service Act imposed conscription only on single men and childless widowers between the ages of eighteen and forty-one. Wilson, p. 396.

85. Mr. Henry Allen Ashton, "One Clear Call" (London: Voluntary Recruiting League, n.d.) reprinted in the *Recruiting Times*, March 1915, p. 4.

CHAPTER 3

1. "Heart to Heart Chats," *Woman's World*, September 19, 1914, p. 271.
2. "Heart to Heart Chats," *Woman's World*, September 19, 1914, p. 271.
3. Lord Derby, who was appointed the director general of recruiting in 1915, declared that under the new structure of recruiting, "the civilian [is] bringing the raw material to the soldier." Yet what the role of women was to be in the production of this "raw material" was never spelled out. In 1915, the Parliamentary Recruiting Committee rejected the idea of a women's PRC, although, according to Clive Hughes, it encouraged women, presumably soldier's mothers, to canvass house to house attempting to enlist or register potential recruits. According to the Beverly Parliamentary Recruiting Committee, local women were active in recruiting, whereas the women of Bristol were pointedly "not invited to take part in the canvass." Such local inconsistencies reveal an ambiguity and unsureness over what the role of women in recruiting should be. Women contributed large amounts of money to the recruiting effort and offered their organizational structures as well as their time and labor to the Parliamentary Recruiting Committee. They were indefatigable canvassers for Derby, and participated, along with men, in a number of semi-official recruiting schemes. See speech by Lord Derby to the Parliamentary Recruiting Committee, October 11, 1915, PRC Minutes, BL, ADD 54192b, p. 9; Clive Hughes, *Army Recruiting in Gwunedd, 1914–16* (M.A. Thesis, University of Wales, 1983), p. 299; Beverly Recruiting Committee, January 24 and 25, 1916, IWM, Documents, Recruiting and Conscription, Misc. Docs.; "Canvass for Recruits," *Bristol Times and Mirror*, October 27, 1915, p. 5; *Standard Recruiter*, August 31, 1914, p. 6.
4. Major Leonard Darwin, "On the Meaning of Honour" (London: The League of Honour, 1915), p. 5, in IWM, WW, BO6/2/8.
5. Anon., "The Kitchen is the Key to Victory"; Anon., "Don't Waste Bread!" IWM Department of Art. In the words of the *Win the War Cookery Book*, "The British fighting line shifts and extends and now *you* are in it. The struggle is not only on land and sea; it is in *your* larder, *your* kitchen and *your* dining room. Every meal *you* serve is now literally a battle." Martin Pugh, *Women and the Women's Movement in Britain 1914–1959* (New York: Paragon House, 1993), p. 13.

6. For a comprehensive study of the wartime ideology of motherhood in Britain and France see, Susan R. Grayzel, *Women's Identities at War: Gender, Motherhood, and Politics in Britain and France during the First World War* (Chapel Hill: University of North Carolina Press, 1999).

7. A. G. Hayes, "Have Ye Mothered a Man?," *John Bull*, March 6, 1915, p. 14.

8. "To the Mothers of Britain," *Mother and Home*, September 5, 1914, p. 425.

9. "Women and Patriotism," *Girl's Own Paper*, vol. 1914–15, p. 36.

10. "Women's Duty in Wartime," *The Primrose League Gazette*, June 1915, no. 68, p. 10 in IWM, WW, BO6/4/6.

11. The Mothers' Union, "To British Mothers, How They Can Help, By One of Them," (London: The Mothers Union and Mr. Wells Gardener, Darton & Co, n.d.), p. 1 in IWM, 325.1 K. # 6063.

12. The Mothers' Union, "To British Mothers," p. 1 in IWM, 325.1 K. # 6063.

13. "Where do boys go who tell lies?" asked *Punch* of an under-aged lad; "To the front, Sir," replied the boy in this timely cartoon. *Mr. Punch's History of the War* (London: Cassell & Co., 1919), p. 51.

14. While some mothers were eligible for separation allowances, many ineligible dependents, including parents and siblings, complained of the hardship that the loss of a son could entail. Even for eligible dependents, the absence of a high-wage-earning man would not be viewed with enthusiasm, since government allowances were notoriously small. For a comprehensive study of separation allowances, see Susan Pedersen, *Family, Dependence, and the Origins of the Welfare State: Britain and France, 1914–1918* (Cambridge: Cambridge University Press, 1993), pp. 107–119.

15. *The Spectator*, November 6, 1915, p. 612.

16. Coulson Kernahan, *The Experiences of a Recruiting Officer* (London: Hodder & Stoughton, 1915) p. 40.

17. Anna Davin, "Imperialism and Motherhood," *History Workshop Journal*, no. 5 (Spring 1978), pp. 9–65.

18. I am indebted to Susan R. Grayzel's excellent analysis of feminist pacifism, *Women's Identities at War*, pp. 157–165.

19. Olive Schreiner, *Women and Labour* (London: T. Fisher Unwin, 1911), p. 174.

20. Suffragists continually pointed out that rather than playing no part in war, as "Antis" asserted, women were crucial to national defense since they gave birth to and reared soldiers. See also Grayzel, *Women's Identities at War*, pp. 115–116.

21. Mrs. Alec Tweedie FRGS, *Women and Soldiers* (London: John Lane, 1918), p. 1.

22. For a discussion of Schreiner's logic and its impact on British feminist pacifism, see Grayzel, *Women's Identities at War*, pp. 159–161.

23. Tweedie, *Women and Soldiers*, p. 182.

24. "Mothers and their Boys," *Girl's Own Paper*, vol. 1914–1915, p. 48.

25. Lawrence Binyon, "To Women," *Times*, August 20, 1914, p. 7.

26. Margaret Peterson, "The Woman's Message," PRC, no. 26 (London: PRC, 1915).

27. For a thorough analysis of women's reproductive work during war, see Grayzel, *Women's Identities at War*, pp. 186–120.

28. Mrs. Hudson Pile to the editor of the *Chatham News*, "Appeal to the Mothers of England," *Chatham News*, September 5, 1914, p. 5.

29. The Munitions of War Act of 1915 and the Munitions of War (Amendment) Act of 1916 both facilitated the process of "dilution" whereby skilled male workers could be replaced by unskilled female workers in essential war industries. See Trevor Wilson, *The Myriad Faces of War* (Cambridge: Polity Press, 1986), pp. 226–227 and Angela Woollacott, *On Her Their Lives Depend* (Berkeley: University of California Press, 1994), pp. 90–91.

30. Mary Gabrielle Collins, "Women at Munitions Making," in Catherine Reilley, ed., *Scars Upon My Heart: Women's Poetry and Verse in the First World War* (London: Virago Press, 1981), p. 24.

31. Robert Graves, *Good-bye to All That* (New York: Doubleday & Co., 1957), p. 229.

32. "A Recruiting Enthusiast: What One Woman had Done for the Army and Navy," *The Tatler*, October 21, 1914, in IWM, Women's Work Collection [hereafter WW], Army/8.

33. Mrs. J. G. Paterson, "Recruiting for Ladies," *Daily Mail*, March 9, 1908, in IWM, WW, Army/20.

34. Paterson, "Recruiting for Ladies," *Daily Mail*, March 9, 1908.

35. Paterson, "Recruiting for Ladies," *Daily Mail*, March 9, 1908.

36. *Times*, August 25, 1914, p. 5; Anon., *Diary*, entry August 30, 1914, IWM, Documents, Misc. 522; Virginia Woolf, *Three Guineas* (New York: Harvest Books, 1966), p. 39.

37. Quoted in Sandra Gilbert, "Soldier's Heart: Literary Men, Literary Women, and the Great War," in Margaret Higonnnet, Jane Jenson, et al., eds., *Behind the Lines: Gender and the Two World Wars* (New Haven: Yale University Press, 1987), p. 214.

38. Tweedie, p. 182.

39. In 1914, Mrs. Hugh Ford of the Ladies Rifle Club suggested the use of armed women to put down riots, *Times*, August 11, 1914, p. 9; In a column on "How to be Useful in Wartime," the *Times* was flooded with suggestions from women who wished to use guns, to form women's home defense leagues, or to endorse the formation of female Territorial divisions. See *Times*, August 22, 1914, p. 8; August 28, 1914, p. 11; and September 4, 1914, p. 5.

40. R. C. Lyle, "Women and Rifles: Things to Remember," *The Ladies Field*, September 12, 1914, p. 94.

41. See, for example, Miss G. Holland, *Journal*, IWM, Documents, 88/26/1, p. 88.

42. "Girls Who Want to be in the Fighting Line," *Daily Sketch*, January 18, 1915, p. 2.

43. "Girls Who Want to be in the Fighting Line," p. 2.

44. "Girls Who Want to be in the Fighting Line," p. 2.

45. "Girls Who Want to be in the Fighting Line," p. 2.

46. "Girls Who Want to be in the Fighting Line," p. 2.

47. "I too am serving my country. I, too, have a right to my pay," *Votes for Women*, November 13, 1914, cover. For an excellent discussion of this issue, see Susan Pedersen, "Gender, Welfare, and Citizenship in Britain During the Great War," *The American Historical Review*, vol. 95, no. 4 (October 1990), pp. 983–1006.

48. *Common Cause*, June 30, 1916.

49. Anon., "Go! Its YOUR DUTY, Lad!," and E. V. Kealey "Women of Britain say *GO!. See illustrations.*

50. "Britain's Brave Women," *Women's World*, November 28, 1914, p. 559.

51. See Captain Martin Hardie, "Papers," IWM, Documents.

52. Mary Martindale, *One Englishwoman to Another* (Oxford: Oxford University Press, 1918), p.1 in National War Aims Committee Leaflets 1917–1918, BL, 1854.e.5.

53. *Times*, August 19, 1914, p. 7.

54. *Recruiting Times*, March 1915, p. 4; *Women's World*, October 10, 1914, p. 3.

55. Michael McDonagh, *In London During the Great War* (London: Eyre & Spottiswoode, 1935), p. 60.

56. *Times*, August 10, 1914, p. 3.

57. Kernahan, *Experiences*, p. 24.

58. Kernahan, *Experiences*, p. 24.

59. Kernahan, *Experiences*, p. 27.

60. As one bereaved mother supposedly put it: "pity is more needed by the mother whose sons won't go." Anon., "Women's Duty in War Time," *Primrose League Gazette*, no. 68 (June 1915), p. 10.

61. Kernahan, p. 40. The mother in Matilda Betham-Edwards's poem, "Two Mothers," told a stranger who saw her crying that she wept "not for the soldier son; / of shame, not grief my heart will break . . ." Quoted in Kernahan, p. 38.

62. *Spectator*, July 24, 1915, p. 101.

63. Will Crooks PC, MP, *The British Workman Defends his Home* (London: The Whitehall Press, 1917), p. 9.

64. Crooks, *British Workman*, p. 9.

65. Crooks, *British Workman*, p. 9.

66. Allan Monkhouse, *The Shamed Life*, in *War Plays* (London: Constable & Co, 1916), p. 17.

67. Monkhouse, p. 17.
68. Monkhouse, p. 8.
69. Monkhouse, p. 16.
70. Monkhouse, p. 20.
71. Monkhouse, p. 20. For a similar motif, see Lechmere Worall and J. E. Harold Terry, *The Man Who Stayed at Home* (London: Samuel French Ltd., 1916).
72. Thomas Macmillan, "Memoirs," 1935, p. 5, in IWM, Documents.
73. P. T. Bryant to Mrs. L. Hayman, [n.d.], IWM, Documents, Collection of Mrs. L. Hayman, 88/51/1.
74. Bryant to Hayman, IWM, Documents, 88/51/1.
75. Martin Hardie, "Censor's Log 1916," July 8 entry, IWM, Documents, Collection of Captain Martin Hardie.
76. Thomas Macmillan, "Memoirs," p. 1. The reference is to a famous war poster by Saville Lumley, "Daddy, what did *YOU* do in the Great War?" *See illustrations.*
77. Peter Simkins, *Kitchener's Army: the Raising of the New Armies, 1914–1916* (Manchester: Manchester University Press, 1988), p. 123.
78. Philip Dutton, "Moving Images? The PRC's Poster Campaign 1914–1916," *IWM Review*, no. 4, (1989), p. 54.
79. I am grateful to Mr. Keeble for discussing his collection with me; Macmillan, "Memoirs," p. 1.
80. For a masterful account of the depth of bereavement, see Jay Winter, *Sites of Memory, Sites of Mourning* (Cambridge: Cambridge University Press, 1995).

CHAPTER 4

1. "Women's War: White Feathers for 'Slackers'," *Daily Mail*, August 31, 1914, p. 3. The white feather of cowardice referred to the white feather in a game cock's tail, widely regarded as a mark of inferior breeding. In popular parlance, to "mount" or "show" the white feather was to display signs of cowardice. This chapter is an expanded and re-focused version of Nicoletta F. Gullace, "White Feathers and Wounded Men: Female Patriotism and the Memory of the Great War," *Journal of British Studies*, vol. 36, no. 2 (April 1997), pp. 178–206.
2. "Women's War: White Feathers for 'Slackers'," p. 3.
3. "'White Feathers' A Novel Method of Making Young Men Enlist," *Chatham News*, September 5, 1914, p. 8.
4. "'White Feathers' A Novel Method of Making Young Men Enlist," p. 8.
5. Although white feathers were given out in many parts of the country, the practice was most common in London and in port towns where the long history of impressment may have created a culture favorable to such coercive practices. For a sense of the geographical range of white feather incidents, see Imperial War Museum staff, "Great War Index to Letters of

Interest" [nd]. It is unclear exactly how the practice caught on, but it is probable that rumor, newspaper reports, and the depiction of the practice in popular theater and fiction helped spread the idea. Francis Almond to the BBC, May 25, 1964, IWM, BBC Great War Series, [hereafter BBC/GW] vol. ALL-ANT, fol. 339.

6. M. Yearsley, "Memoirs," IWM, Documents, DS/Misc./ 17, p.19.

7. For additional accounts, see Peter Simkins, *Kitchener's Army: The Raising of the New Armies, 1914–16* (Manchester: Manchester University Press, 1988), p. 119.

8. *Times,* September 1, 1914, p. 1.

9. Paper presented to the Cabinet by Mr. Gasilee, November 1, 1915, "The Northcliffe Press and Foreign Opinion," Cabinet Document #1184, p. 2, in PRO, INF 4/ 1B.

10. See for example Lord Northcliffe to Hedley Le Bas, April 26, 1916, BL, ADD 62170, vol. XVIII, fol. 188.

11. *Bystander,* December 9, 1914, p. 352. *See illustrations.*

12. Admiral Charles Cooper Penrose Fitzgerald, *From Sail to Steam: Naval Recollections, 1878–1905* (London: Edward Arnold, 1916), p. 288.

13. Penrose Fitzgerald, p. 291.

14. Penrose Fitzgerald., p. 291. The internal quote is a sarcastic reference to a speech by Lord Haldane.

15. Penrose Fitzgerald, p. 292.

16. Gasilee to the Cabinet, November 1, 1915, Cabinet Document #1184, PRO INF 4/1B, pp. 3–4. To many conservatives, and to increasing numbers of liberal and socialist observers, taunts to masculinity were a poor substitute for compulsion. *Labour Leader,* September 3, 1914, p 1; *Manchester Guardian,* August 6, 1915; George Riddell, *Diaries* BL, MS ADD 62976, August 1915, fol. 116.

17. Gasilee to the Cabinet, November 1, 1915, Cabinet Document #1184, PRO INF 4/1B, pp. 3–4.

18. Mrs. Kathleen Langmuir to BBC, June 9, 1964, IWM, BBC/GW, vol. LAB-LAZ, fol.140. Mrs. Langmuir did not see the advertisement herself and thus candidly admitted to having "sent several" and to having been one of the "Whitehall 'flappers.'" See also Mrs. Thyra Mitchell to BBC, IWM BBC/GW, vol. MIL-MIT, fols. 475–479.

19. For a fuller discussion of the available evidence testifying to the prevalence of white-feather–giving, see Gullace, "White Feathers and Wounded Men," pp. 180–182 and footnotes 12, 13, and 15.

20. See Gullace, "White Feathers and Wounded Men" for a discussion of the increasingly shameful memory of the white feather campaign.

21. See "BBC Seeking White Feather Women," *Daily Telegraph,* May 15, 1964, in IWM, BBC/GW, vol. APL-AYR, fol. 242; *Daily Mirror,* May 29, 1964, p. 7. The BBC advertisement was published in a variety of other newspapers, though not all of them even solicited letters from women.

22. Mrs. Thyra Mitchell to the BBC, April 16, 1964, IWM, BBC/GW, vol. MIL-MIT, fol. 479, and Nicholas Wall, "Notes on Telephone Interview with Mrs Thyra Mitchell," May 26, 1964, IWM, BBC/GW, vol. MIL-MIT, fol. 477–478. For a fuller account of this episode, see Mrs. Mitchell's interview with the *Daily Mirror,* May 29, 1964, p. 7.

23. T. A. Lowe to BBC, May 15, 1964, IWM, BBC/GW, vol. LID/LYO, fol. 268.

24. See Philippa Levine, "'Walking the Streets in a Way No Decent Woman Should': Women Police in World War I," *Journal of Modern History* (March 1994), pp. 34–78.

25. See, for example, John Osborne, *The Voluntary Recruiting Movement In Britain, 1914–1916* (Ann Arbor: University Microfilms International, 1983), p. 176; Claire Tylee, *The Great War and Women's Consciousness* (London: Macmillan, 1990), p. 58; and Virginia Woolf, *Three Guineas* (New York: Harvester Books, 1966), p. 182. For a fuller discussion of the relationship of white-feather-giving to feminist historiography, see Gullace, "White Feathers and Wounded Men," pp. 179–180.

26. T. O. Cunningham to BBC, May 22, 1964, IWM, BBC/GW, vol. CRA-CUT, fol. 245.

27. See also J. W. Besker to BBC, May 1964, IWM, BBC/GW, vol. BEL-BEX, fol. 269 and S. W. Buckingham to BBC, May 15, 1964, IWM, BBC/GW, vol. BUC-BUR, fol. 54.

28. C. G. Byrne to BBC, May 22, 1964, IWM, BBC/GW, vol. BUS-BYR, fol. 184.

29. Francis Almond to BBC, May 25, 1964, IWM, BBC/GW, vol. ALL-ANT, fol. 339.

30. Almond, fol. 340.

31. C. B. Abraham to BBC, May 16, 1964, IWM, BBC/GW, vol. AAR-ALL, fol. 46.

32. Mrs. J. UpJohn to BBC, May 15, 1964, IWM, BBC/GW, vol. UDA–VOS, fol. 32.

33. Harry Taylor to BBC, May 19, 1964, IWM, BBC/GW, vol. TAB-THO, fol. 98.

34. P. W. Bassatt to BBC, May 15, 1964, IWM, BBC/GW, vol. BAS-BAZ, fol. 11. See also J. W. Bacham to BBC, May 21, 1964, IWM, BBC/GW, vol. BAB-BAP, fol. [19].

35. Mr. J. Jones to the BBC, May 29, 1964, IWM, BBC/GW, fols. 285–286.

36. Jones, fol. 286.

37. Coulson Kernahan, *The Experiences of a Recruiting Officer* (London: Hodder & Stoughton, 1915), pp. 40, 69.

38. Alfred Allen to BBC, May 31, 1964, IWM, BBC/GW, vol. ALL-ANT, fol. 263. The elderly lady was by no means exceptional as a woman showing contempt for the white-feather-givers. A vivid articulation of some women's shame over the activities of the white feather women is found in Helen Hamilton's poem "Jingo Woman." In this poem, Hamilton im-

plored the "dealer in white feathers" to "hold your tongue! / You shame us women / Can't you see it isn't decent / To flout and goad men into doing / What is not asked of you?" Quoted in Catherine Reilley, ed., *Scars Upon My Heart: Women's Poetry and Verse of the First World War* (London: Virago, 1981) pp. 47–48.

39. E. Sylvia Pankhurst, *The Suffragette Movement: An Intimate Account of Persons and Ideals* (London: Longmans, 1931), p. 594.

40. Yearsley, "Memoirs," p. 20.

41. Yearsley, "Memoirs," p. 20.

42. Yearsley, "Memoirs," p. 20.

43. For a provocative discussion of gender, masculinity, and civic obligation see Robert Westbrook, "'I Want to Marry a Girl Just Like the Girl who Married Harry James': American Women and the Problem of Political Obligation in World War II," *American Quarterly*, vol. 42 (December 1990), pp. 587–614. An influential interpretation of the multivalent use of women in the promotion of war is found in Jean Bethke Elshtain, *Women and War* (New York: Basic Books, 1987), pp. x–xiv; 106–120.

44. The Germans apparently made much of a personal advertisement in which a woman named "Ethel M." informed her lover, "Jack F.G." that "if you are not in khaki by the 20th I shall cut you dead." The Germans, according to British sources, translated this as something closer to "hack you to death." *Times*, July 8, 1915, quoted in E. S. Turner, *Dear Old Blighty* (London: Michael Joseph, 1980), p. 70.

45. Contemporaries generally supposed such barbs were from women. In *The Experiences of a Recruiting Officer*, for example, Coulson Kernahan denounces "folk who inform me that this or that man 'ought to go.'" This practice he attributes primarily to malicious and jealous women. Quoting a letter that is both anonymous and addressless, Kernahan assumes that it is from a lady who wished to have other women's menfolk protect her. Kernahan, *Experiences*, pp. 54–55.

46. "Public Opinion and the Laggards, Unpatriotic or Afraid," *The Times*, August 28, 1914, p. 6.

47. Henry Arthur Jones to the *Times*, August 29, 1914, p. 9.

48. Duke of Bedford, "Recruiting Pamphlets and leaflets 1914–1915," IWM, 325.1 NP K.44699.

49. "To the Young Women of London," IWM, 4903, reproduced in Maurice Rickards, *Posters of the First World War* (New York: Walker & Co, 1968), no. 23.

50. Angelsey's Ellis John Griffith, MP protested in August 1915 that "the walls of our country and the pages of our newspapers are defaced by official jibes and taunts at our manhood, some of these actually being addressed to women." *Manchester Guardian*, August 6, 1915. He was not alone in opposing tactics that called upon women to do the dirty work of the state. *Vote* denounced "an insolent advertisement that has been published in the daily papers putting 'four questions to the women of England,' and accusing men

of having to be *sent* by them to 'join our glorious army.'" *Vote*, January 22, 1915, p. 472. *See illustrations.*

51. "A Fight to the Finish: Work of National Enlightenment," *Times*, August 31, 1914, p. 4.

52. See Susan Kingsley Kent, *Making Peace: The Reconstruction of Gender in Interwar Britain* (Princeton: Princeton University Press, 1993), pp. 12–30.

53. Major Leonard Darwin, "On the Meaning of Honour," a lecture delivered to The Women's League of Honour, 1915, IWM, WW, BO6/3/2/8, p. 6.

54. Kernahan, *Experiences*, p. 69.

55. Michael MacDonagh, *In London During the Great War* (London: Eyre & Spottiswoode, 1935), pp. 79–80.

56. J. P. Cope to BBC, May 1964, IWM, BBC/GW, vol. COC-COY, fol. 141.

57. Cope, fol. 141.

58. C. Berkeley to BBC, May 18, 1964, IWM, BBC/GW, vol. BEL-BEX, fols. 249–250.

59. Francis Almond to the BBC, May 25, 1964, IWM, BBC/GW, vol. ALL-ANT, fol. 339. Because of its origins as a breeding term in cock-fighting [see footnote 1], the symbol of the white feather bound together issues of sexual selection, bravery, and cowardice—a confluence highlighted in the novel, which had gone into four editions by 1918.

60. His mission is significantly to "avenge the death of General Gordon" by accompanying Kitchener's forces on the reconquest of Khartoum.

61. A. E. W. Mason, *The Four Feathers* (London: Smith Elder & Co, 1902), p. 35.

62. Mason, pp. 41–42.

63. Mason, p. 147.

64. Mason, p. 210.

65. *Times*, August 28, 1914, p. 11.

66. The dynamics and implications of "khaki fever" are well addressed in, Angela Woollacott, "'Khaki Fever' and its Control: Gender, Class, Age and Sexual Morality on the British Homefront in the First World War," *Journal of Contemporary History*, vol. 29, no. 2 (April 1994), pp. 325–347.

67. "Women and Patriotism," *Girl's Own Paper*, vol. 1914–1915, p. 36.

68. The Mother's Union, "To British Mothers: How They Can Help Enlistment, by One of Them," (London: Gardener, Dutton & Co,. n.d.), p. 1.

69. The Baroness Orczy, "To the Women of England, The Answer to 'What Can I Do?' . . . ," *Daily Mail*, September 4, 1914.

70. Orczy, *Daily Mail*, September 4, 1914.

71. Orczy, *Daily Mail*, September 4, 1914.

72. The Baroness Orczy to Miss Conway of the Imperial War Museum [1918], in IWM, WW, BO/6/6/2i. The Baroness's league was reputed to have raised 600,000 men for the army.

73. *John Bull*, March 6, 1915, p. 1.

74. According to Francis Almond, "Songs like: 'We Don't Want of Lose You, but We Think You Ought to Go . . . ' and 'On Monday I Walk out with a Soldier . . . ' were rendered by women vocalists throughout the land." Mr. Francis Almond to the BBC, May 1964, fol. 339. See also Woollacott, "Khaki Fever," pp. 325–327.

75. Tony Howarth, ed., *Joe Soap's Army Song Book,* IWM Great War Series (London: Longman's, 1976), p. 2.

76. Howarth, p. 2.

77. For a discussion of the patriotic and conservative nature of the music hall, see Gareth Stedman Jones, "Working-Class Culture and Working-Class Politics in London, 1870–1900: Notes on the Remaking of a Working Class," in Gareth Stedman Jones, *Languages of Class: Studies in English Working Class History 1832–1982* (Cambridge: Cambridge University Press, 1983), pp. 179–238.

78. Major D. K. Patterson to the BBC [May 1964], IWM, BBC/GW, vol. LIN-LYO, fol. 328.

79. Norah Kinnaird, "A Soldier's Wife," *Woman's World,* September 19, 1914, p. 262. Jules's mother was even commended by female readers in "Heart to Heart Chats." See "Auntie Jean" to the "Editoress," "Britain's Brave Women." *Women's World,* November 28, 1914, p. 559.

80. M. McD. Bodkin, "The White Feather," *Women at Home,* August 1917, pp. 153–160.

81. Bodkin, pp. 153–154.

82. Bodkin, p. 155.

83. Bodkin, p. 159.

84. Bodkin, p. 160.

85. Bill Lawrence to BBC, [May 1964], IWM, BBC/GW, vol. LAB-LAZ, fol. 275.

86. H. Symonds to BBC, May 18, 1964, IWM, BBC/GW, vol. SNE-SYM, fols. 427–428.

87. Symonds, fols. 427–428.

88. Caroline Rennles, IWM Department of Sound Records, 000566/07, p. 10, quoted in Angela Woollacott, *On Her Their Lives Depend,* (Berkeley: University of California Press, 1994), pp.197–98.

89. Vivid accounts of the treatment of these men can be found in memoirs and oral history interviews with conscientious objectors. See, for example, IWM Department of Sound Records, Oral History Recordings, "The Anti-War Movement, 1914–1918."

90. John W. Graham, M.A., *Conscription and Conscience* (London: George Allen & Unwin, 1922), p. 39.

91. Ronald W. Crawley to the BBC, May 16, 1964, IWM, BBC/GW, vol. CRA-CUT, fol. 67.

92. Harold Begbie, "Fall In!," in IWM Documents, Misc. 94, Item 1441, *side 1.*

93. Phyllis to Walter Ernest Bone [n.d.] IWM Documents, Misc. 94, Item 1441, *side 2.*

94. G. E. Studdy, "Beginning to Understand," *Tatler*, no. 691, September 23, 1914.

95. See R.W. Farrow, "Recollections of a Conscientious Objector," IWM, Documents, 75/111/1, fol. 289; Mr. B. Upton to BBC, May 15, 1964, IWM, BBC/GW, vol. UDA-VOS, fol. 38; For a fascinating discussion of women's relationship to military fashion, see Susan R. Grayzel, "'The Outward and Visible Sign of Her Patriotism': Women, Uniforms, and National Service During the First World War," *Twentieth Century British History* vol. 8, no. 2 (1997), pp. 145–164.

96. While the majority of those who received white feathers seem to have gotten them in 1915, the practice was still quite common in 1916 and 1917, and, though less frequent, was not unheard of in 1918. Imperial War Museum staff, "Great War Index to Letters of Interest," [n.d.].

97. MacDonagh, *In London*, p. 80.

98. P. C. S. Vince to BBC, May 18, 1964, IWM, BBC/GW, vol. UDA-VOS, fol. 199. See also, W. F. C. Ashworth to the BBC, May 18, 1964, BBC/GW, vol. ALP-AYR.

99. R. W. Farrow, "Recollections," p. 290.

100. See Mrs. Ruth L. Brown to BBC, May 16, 1964, IWM, BBC/GW, vol. BRO-BRY, fol. 261.

101. Mrs. G. Simns to BBC, April 27, 1964, IWM, BBC/GW, vol. SHA-SKI, fol. 361.

102. MacDonagh, *In London*, p. 79.

103. G. Backhaus to BBC, May 15, 1964, IWM, BBC/GW, vol. BAB-BAP, fol. 18.

104. Backhaus, fol. 19.

105. Ernest Barnby to BBC, May 19, 1964, IWM, BBC/GW, vol. BAR, fol. 393.

106. Granville Bradshaw to BBC, May 15, 1964, IWM, BBC/GW, vol. BRA-BRI, fol. 54.

107. Hansards, *House of Commons Parliamentary Debates*, March 1, 1915, col. 548.

108. John W. Graham, *Conscription and Conscience: A History, 1916–1919* (London: George Allen & Unwin, 1922), *passim*.

109. To illustrate this point, Woolf goes on to quote an often cited passage by George Bernard Shaw about the "pugnacity" of the white-feather women. Pointing out that "the number of 'civilized young women' who stuck feathers into coats must have been infintesimal compared with those who did nothing of the kind," Woolf speculates that "the male still preserves an abnormal susceptibility to such taunts; therefore that courage and pugnacity are still among the prime attributes of manliness; ... therefore that any derision of such qualities would have a proportionate effect." Virginia Woolf, *Three Guineas* (New York: Harvest Books [1938] 1966) p. 182.

110. As we know from the work of Judith Walkowitz and Erika Rappaport, urban women were frequently subjected to taunts and rudeness by men as they roamed city streets on shopping trips or traveling to and from work.

Judith R. Walkowitz, "Going Public: Shopping, Street Harassment, and Streetwalking in Late Victorian London," *Representations* 62 (Spring 1998) pp. 1–30; Erika Rappaport, "The Halls of Temptation: Gender, Politics, and the Construction of the Department Store in Late-Victorian London," *Journal of British Studies* 35 (January 1995), pp. 58–83.

111. Margaret Haig, *This Was My World* (1933), excerpted in Harold L. Smith, *The British Women's Suffrage Campaign* (London: Longmans, 1998), p. 91.

CHAPTER 5

1. This version of the execution was particularly popular in visual matter such as calendars and postcards. See Anon., "Miss Edith Cavell Cowardly Murdered," 1915 postcard, in Imperial War Museum [hereafter IWM], *Women in Wartime* (London: Imperial War Museum, [nd]), item # 3, side b and Anon., "German Crimes Calendar" (London: The London Electrotype Agency, 1918), October, IWM, GB 352.1 K49367. The Germans adamantly denied this far-fetched rumor, but their protests did little to stop it. For an extraordinary array of documents, news clippings, books, and ephemera, see IWM, Documents, Edith Cavell Collection, Box P 114 a and b; *Votes for Women*, October 22, 1915, p. 27.

2. Brand Whitlock, *Correspondence with the United States Ambassador Respecting the Execution of Miss Cavell at Brussels*, Cmd. 8013. October 1915, p. 17, quoted in Patricia Y. Lin, "From a Call to Arms to A Symbol for Peace: The Changing Image of Nurse Edith Cavell, 1915–1939" (Berkeley: Unpublished seminar paper, 1992), p. 5. Lin's paper is a splendid elucidation of the changing meaning of Edith Cavell, particularly as a pacifist symbol in the postwar period.

3. Quoted in William Thomas Hill, *The Martyrdom of Nurse Cavell: The Life and Story of the Victim of Germany's Most Barbarous Crime* (London: Hutchinson & Co, 1915), pp. 48–49.

4. Hill, pp. 47–49; Mrs. Jessie Burton to BBC, July 19, 1963, IWM, BBC/GW, vol. BUC-BUR, fol. 272. Mrs. Burton possessed a photo of the exhumation.

5. For an account of the funeral service, see Millicent Garrett Fawcett, "The Memorial Service in St. Paul's to Miss Edith Cavell," *Common Cause*, November 5, 1915, p. 380.

6. *Times*, October 19, 1915, p. 8.

7. Hansards, *House of Commons Parliamentary Debates*, November 2, 1915, col. 527.

8. Hill, *The Martyrdom of Nurse Cavell*, p. 47.

9. Hill, *The Martyrdom of Nurse Cavell*, p. 47.

10. *Times*, October 19, 1915, p. 8.

11. For an excellent discussion of the Military Service Acts and the various phases in which conscription was instated see R. J. Q. Adams and Philip

Poirier, *The Conscription Controversy in Great Britain, 1900–1918* (Columbus: Ohio State University Press, 1987), pp. 144–170 and Trevor Wilson, *The Myriad Faces of War* (Cambridge: Polity Press, 1988), pp. 166–169, 207–214, 396–400. For reservations about conscription, see Adams and Poirier, pp. 1–32 and 71–118 and J. G. Fuller, *Troop Morale and Popular Culture in the British and Dominion Armies 1914–1918* (Oxford: Clarendon Press, 1990), p. 32. For a detailed account of the organization of manpower, see J. M. Winter, *The Great War and the British People* (Cambridge: Harvard University Press, 1986), pp. 25–64.

12. See IWM, Documents, Conscription and Recruiting, "Recruitment— Misc. Documents." The folder includes numerous letters from local Parliamentary Recruiting Committees.

13. "Let the Government Act: An Appeal for Big and Drastic Measures," *Globe*, May 18, 1915 in BL, Northcliffe Papers, ADD, 62336, fol. 25.

14. Hansards, *House of Commons Parliamentary Debates*, July 28, 1915, col. 2435.

15. W. Bridgeman, *Diary*, entry for November 29, 1914, quoted in Wilson, *Myriad Faces*, p. 199.

16. A. B. Maitland to Lord Northcliffe, July 1, 1915, BL, ADD 62330/ fol. 1.

17. Arthur Conan Doyle, *To Arms!* (London: Hodder & Stoughton, 1914), p. 13. While strongly imperialistic, patriotic, and approving of military preparedness, Conan Doyle favored voluntarism in principal and had rebuffed an invitation by Lord Roberts, issued before the war, to speak in favor of compulsory National Service. See Ivor Brown, *Conan Doyle: A Biography of the Creator of Sherlock Holmes* (London: Hamish Hamilton, 1972), pp. 109–121 and Pierre Nordon, *Conan Doyle: A Biography* (New York: Holt, Rinehart and Winston, 1967), p. 86.

18. Ellis J. Griffith, "Military Compulsion," *Contemporary Review*, February 1916, p. 144. A typical example of the type of argument he is ridiculing can be found in the *Economist*, October 16, 1915, p. 569.

19. *Nation*, July 17, 1915, p. 507.

20. *Nation*, July 17, 1915, p. 508. See also *New Statesman*, September 25, 1915, pp. 584–586.

21. *Spectator*, November 6, 1915, p. 612.

22. "Can Compulsory be Combined with Voluntary Service," Cab Doc no. 1127, October 14, 1915, HLRO, LG/D/24/10/19.

23. "Can Compulsory be Combined with Voluntary Service," Cab Doc no. 1127, October 14, 1915, HLRO, LG/D/24/10/19.

24. Parliamentary Recruiting Committee, *Minute Book*, October 21, 1914, pp. 5–7 and April 16, 1915, pp. 23–24. For an account of Maitland's somewhat anomalous position see Roy Douglas, "Voluntary Enlistment in the First World War and the Work of the Parliamentary Recruiting Committee" *Journal of Modern History* (December 1970), pp. 571–572.

25. Douglas, "Voluntary Enlistment," p. 577.

26. J. Keating, "The Menace of the Slacker," *Month* (October 1915), p. 413.

27. Hansards, *House of Commons Parliamentary Debates*, November 2, 1915, col. 553.

28. *Standard Recruiter*, August 29, 1914, p. 6.

29. *Times Recruiting Supplement*, November 1915, p. 3. For an alternative perspective on the moralizing influence of conscription, see Joseph Thorpe, "Thoughts on National Service and National Unity," *Athenaeum*, October 1916, p. 463.

30. Headly Le Bas to Lord Northcliffe, November 16, 1915. ADD 62170 xviii, fol. 175; see also *Times Recruiting Supplement*, November 3, 1915, p. 3 col 4.

31. Headley Le Bas to Lord Northcliffe, November 16, 1915. ADD 62170 xviii, fol. 175; see also *Times Recruiting Supplement*, November 3, 1915, p. 3 col 4.

32. *The Times Recruiting Supplement*, November 3, 1915, p. 3, col 4.

33. Northcliffe to Le Bas November 30, 1915 ADD 62170 xviii, fol. 185.

34. Quoted in *The Times*, September 5, 1914, p. 9.

35. David French, "Spy Fever in Britain, 1900–1915," *Historical Journal*, vol. 21, no. 2 (1978), pp. 355–370.

36. *Nation*, July 17, 1915, p. 507. See also the *Times*, August 27, 1914, p. 3.

37. *Nation*, July 17, 1915, p. 506.

38. Conan Doyle, *To Arms!*, p. 14.

39. Anon., *Women and the War*, PRC no. 23, (London: PRC [1915]), p. 1.

40. Arthur Kitson, *The Great Pacifist Conspiracy!* (Stamford: Dolby Brothers Printers, 1918), pp. 22–24.

41. Quoted in Hill, *The Martyrdom of Nurse Cavell*, p. 47.

42. Anon., "October," *German Crimes Calendar* (London: The London Electrotype Agency, 1918) in IWM/GB/352.1/K49367.

43. Company Segt Major Healy to Mrs. Alice de Burgh Griffith, March 1915, quoted in Alice de Burgh Griffith to Arthur Gaitskell, November 30, 1915, National Army Museum, Aston letters, "Recruiting."

44. Alex Shaw to A.G. Gardiner, December 9, 1914, quoted in Wilson, p. 195.

45. W. Llewelyn Williams, "Military Compulsion: Another View," *Contemporary Review*, February 1916, p. 147.

46. An Independent Liberal, *Lloyd George and the War* (London: Hutchinson & Co., 1917), p. 45.

47. J. Keating, "The Menace of the Slacker," *Month*, October 1915, p. 412.

48. *The Spectator*, November 6, 1915, p. 612.

49. *The Nation*, July 29, 1916, excerpted in Marilyn Shevin-Coetzee and Frans Coetzee eds., *World War I & European Society: A Source book* (Lexington: D.C. Heath, 1995), pp. 198–199.

50. By the end of August 1915, forty-five Liberal MPs already supported National Service. George Riddell, *Diary* of August 1915, MM, BL, MS ADD 62976 fol. 113. For a discussion of the collapse of practical opposition to conscription among Liberal and Labour members see Wilson, *Myriad*

Faces, pp. 396–398 and Adams and Poirier, *Conscription Controversy,* pp. 166–170. With the exception of some radical labor unions, pro-conscription feeling in the country at large seems to have been even broader than it was in Parliament. Arthur Marwick, *The Deluge: British Society and the First World War* (London: W. W. Norton, 1965), p. 82. The third reading division in the Commons was 252 to 37, the minority being twenty-seven Liberals and ten Labor. Douglas, "Voluntary Recruiting," p. 585, fn. 80.

51. For a defense of voluntarism and a contemporary discussion of its demise, see Richard C. Lambert, *The Parliamentary History of Conscription in Great Britain* (London: George Allen & Unwin, 1917), pp. i-iv.

52. For a good personal account, see John W. Graham, *Conscription and Conscience: A History, 1916–1919* (London: George Allan & Unwin, 1922).

53. David Lloyd George, "The Training of Boys" [n.d.], HLRO, LG/F/79/23; Graham, *Conscription and Conscience,* p. 30.

54. J. A. Seddon, *Why British Labor Supports the War* (London: L. Upcott, Grill & Sons Ltd., 1917), p. 11.

55. Lord Derby, "Recruiting Interviews," [n.d.], PRO, WO/106/370.

56. See H. H. Asquith, *A Call To Arms a Speech by the Prime Minister at the Guildhall, September 4, 1914* (London: Methuen & Co., 1914), p. 5 and Robert Roberts, *The Classic Slum: Salford Life in the First Quarter of the Century* (Manchester: Manchester University Press, 1971), pp. 152.

57. Caldwell Harper to the *Egoist,* July 1, 1915, p. 115.

58. No-Conscription Fellowship, "The C.O. in Prison" and "International Brotherhood" (London: No-Conscription Fellowship, [n.d.]). *See illustrations.*

59. Wilson, *Myriad Faces,* pp. 167–168; Jay Winter, *Great War and the British People* (Cambridge: Harvard University Press, 1986), p. 38.

60. Trevor Wilson, pp. 167–169; Jay Winter, *Great War and British People,* pp. 38–39.

61. *Spectator,* November 6, 1915, p. 612.

62. F. E. Smith, "Preface," to Conan Doyle, *To Arms!,* p. 4.

63. For a sense of the isolation and moral purpose felt by hold-outs against conscription, see Lambert, *The Parliamentary History of Conscription,* pp. iii-iv.

64. Quoted in Trevor Wilson, *Myriad Faces,* p. 396–397.

65. For an account of the passage of the first Military Service Act see Adams and Poirier, pp. 139–143. This Act was known colloquially as the "Bachelor's Bill" because it applied only to unmarried men, yet it paved the way for the far more sweeping Military Service Act of May 1916. Those who voted against conscription included such famous pacifists as Philip Morell, Arthur Ponsonby, Ramsay MacDonald, and Philip Snowdon, all of whom had their patriotism and loyalty impugned during the war for their stance on conscription. Sir John Simon was the one member of the Cabinet to resign over conscription. Simon was exceptional in objecting to conscription on purely libertarian grounds. Marwick, *Deluge,* p. 79. For a voting breakdown, see Hansards, *House of Commons Parliamentary Debates,* January 12, 1916, cols. 1736–1739 and January 24, 1916, cols.

1040–1042. A more extensive Bill was passed in May 1916, opposed by only 37 MPs. Douglas, "Voluntary Enlistment," p. 585, fn. 80. An excellent account of the fate of the Military Service Bill in Parliament can be found in John Rae, *Conscience and Politics: The British Government and the Conscientious Objector to Military Service 1916–1919* (London: Oxford University Press, 1970), pp. 32–51.

66. Unions saw the Derby plan as being in good faith and were much more amendable to conscription after it had been tried. The Labour Party went through motions of dissent but accepted the move in actuality. Wilson, pp. 396–398.

67. Coulson Kernahan, *The Experiences of a Recruiting Officer* (London: Hodder & Stoughton, 1915), p. 52.

68. James Maxton, "War Resistance by Working-Class Struggle," excerpted in Shevin-Coetzee and Coetzee, pp. 259–260.

69. Graham, *Conscription and Conscience*, pp. 248–249.

70. "Women and the War," *Spectator*, July 24, 1915, p. 101.

71. Quoted in J. Keating, "The Menace of the Slacker," *Month*, October 1915, p. 413.

72. Quoted in Roberts, *The Classic Slum*, pp. 154–155.

73. Caldwell Harper to the *Egoist*, July 1, 1915, p. 115.

74. The pacifist Philip Snowden frequently complained of such disruptions. See, for example, *House of Commons Parliamentary Debates*, December 8, 1915, col. 1390 and January 26, 1916, col. 1262. Excellent contemporary accounts chronicling the treatment of conscientious objectors and pacifists can be found in Sylvia Pankhurst's journal the *Women's Dreadnought*, May-July 1916.

75. Roberts, *The Classic Slum*, p. 155.

CHAPTER 6

1. For a lucid discussion of the application of the term terrorism to suffragette militants see Cheryl R. Jorgensen-Earp, ed., *Speeches and Trials of the Militant Suffragettes: The Women's Social and Political Union, 1903–1918* (London: Associated University Presses, 1999), pp. 135–137.

2. Jessie Kenney, *The Price of Liberty*, typescript diary of her trip to Russia with Mrs. Pankhurst, June-September, 1917, p. 15, Fawcett Library, 7/yyy5 Box 639; *Britannia*, July 13, 1917, p. 44.

3. Benjamin Sacks, *J. Ramsay MacDonald in Thought and Action: An Architect for a Better World* (Albuquerque: University of New Mexico Press, 1952), p. 499, fn 111.

4. *Manchester Guardian*, June 8, 1917 quoted in *Britannia*, June 13, 1917.

5. Sacks, pp. 499–500.

6. Jessie Kenney, a working woman, had to make a trip to Paris to ransack Christabel's closet for suitably elegant hand-me-downs for the trip. For

WSPU attitudes to Mr. MacDonald, see "Ramsay MacDonald receiving Iron Cross from the Kaiser," *Britannia*, June 22, 1917, cover. Christabel later declared that she wished he'd been thrown overboard rather than simply escorted down the gangplank. E. Sylvia Pankhurst, *The Life of Emmeline Pankhurst: The Suffragettes Struggle for Women's Citizenship* (London: T. Werner Laurie Ltd., 1935), p. 161.

7. Lisa Tickner, *The Spectacle of Women: Imagery of the Suffrage Campaign, 1907–1914* (Chicago: University of Chicago Press, 1988), p. 230.

8. The classic example of this interpretation is Ray Strachey, *The Cause: A Short History of the Women's Movement in Great Britain* (Bath: Cedric Chivers Portway, 1928). This interpretation has been most influentially endorsed by Arthur Marwick, *Women at War, 1914–1918* (London: Croom Helm, 1977).

9. Susan Kinglsey Kent suggests that fear of renewed suffrage militancy persuaded Parliament to retain the controversial women's suffrage clause in the Representation of the People Bill, while Sandra Stanley Holton goes so far as to argue that the war actually delayed the passage of women's suffrage. Kent is highly convincing in her analysis of the underlying psychological need for domestic reconciliation that made MPs in both houses susceptible to a solution that would ward off a renewed "sex war," but she does not look extensively at the rationale of war service that was crucial to justifying this change of heart. For the two most influential contemporary feminist accounts of the relationship of war to suffrage, see Susan Kingsley Kent, *Making Peace: The Reconstruction of Gender in Interwar Britain* (Princeton: Princeton University Press, 1993) and Sandra Stanley Holton, *Feminism and Democracy: Women's Suffrage and Reform Politics in Britain, 1900–1918* (Cambridge, Cambridge University Press, 1986).

10. For Mrs. Pankhurst's explanation of the decision to drop militant suffrage agitation, see Emmeline Pankhurst, "Speech Delivered to Militant Suffragists," excerpted in Midge MacKenzie, ed., *Shoulder to Shoulder: A Documentary* (London: Alfred A. Knopf, 1975), p. 280, and Mrs. Emmeline Pankhusrt to WSPU, August 13, 1914, quoted in MacKenzie, *Shoulder to Shoulder*, p. 282. See also Jacqueline de Vries, "Gendering Patriotism: Emmeline and Christabel Pankhurst in World War I," in Sybil Oldfield, ed., *This Working-Day World: Women's Lives and Cultures(s) in Britain 1914–1945* (London: Taylor & Francis, 1994), pp. 75–76. For Christabel's decision to return to England, see Dame Christabel Pankhurst, *Unshackled: The Story of How We Won the Vote* (London: Hutchinson, 1959), pp. 287–288.

11. For those feminists who remained adamant in their opposition to the war, loss of life took precedence over every other claim. Pacifists from both the constitutionalist and the militant wings of the suffrage movement were furious that female citizenship might be advanced through participation in such carnage, and many dissenters remained skeptical about the violent

images used to fuel support of the war. See Jo Vellacott, "Feminist Consciousness and the First World War," *History Workshop Journal* 23 (Spring 1987), pp. 81–101.

12. *Suffragette*, August 7, 1914, p. 301. A number of influential feminist pacifists including Emmeline Pethick Lawrence, Charlotte Despard, and Olive Schreiner were at this meeting, held at the Kingsway Hall, London. Unlike Mrs. Fawcett, they retained their pacifist commitment. For an account of the rally, see *Votes for Women*, August 7, 1914, p. 680.

13. Despite the inordinate amount of attention feminist pacifism has received from scholars, the pacifist Women's International League of Peace and Freedom had only 2,458 members in 1916 and 3,687 by 1918. Martin Pugh, *Women and the Women's Movement in Britain, 1914–1959* (New York: Paragon House, 1993), p. 10. Indeed, the extent of the feminist antiwar movement has probably been exaggerated. Sylvia Pankhurst never doubted that her mother and sister had followers, despite deploring their pro-war attitude. Indeed, announcements in *Britannia* make clear that the WSPU retained numerous local branch offices and continued to sell papers, raise money, and fill meetings, despite its newfound jingoism. See de Vries, "Gendering Patriotism: Emmeline and Christabel Pankhusrst and World War One," pp. 76–77 and Kent, *Making Peace*, pp. 77–78. For an important recent discussion of feminism's imperial tendencies during this period, see Antoinette Burton, *Burdens of History: British Feminists, Indian Women and Imperial Culture, 1865–1915* (Chapel Hill: University of North Carolina Press, 1994).

14. Mrs. Pankhurst was also concerned that militants be allowed to recuperate physically and financially from their strenuous guerilla campaign and debilitating prison sentences. See Emmeline Pankhurst to the WSPU, August 13, 1914, in MacKenzie, *Shoulder to Shoulder*, p. 282. For a thoughtful account of the suspension of militancy and the adoption of pro-war positions, see deVries, pp., 76–77.

15. Kent, *Making Peace*, p. 76.

16. E. Sylvia Pankhurst, *The Life of Emmeline Pankhurst: The Suffragette Struggle for Women's Citizenship* (New York: Kraus Reprint Co., 1969), pp. 150–151.

17. Kent, *Making Peace*, pp. 26, 33–34, 75–76. For a seminal discussion of the centrality of sexual exploitation to prewar suffrage argumentation, see also Susan Kingsley Kent, *Sex and Suffrage in Britain, 1860–1914* (Princeton: Princeton University Press, 1987).

18. Quoted in Kent, *Making Peace*, pp. 77–78.

19. David Mitchell, *Women on the Warpath: The Story of the Women of the First World War* (London: Jonathan Cape, 1966), p. 187.

20. *Common Cause*, August 14, 1914, p. 385.

21. *Daily Sketch*, January 27, 1915 quoted in David Mitchell, *Queen Christabel* (London: Macdonald and Jane's, 1977), p. 252. Mrs. Pankhurst's characterization of her own activities was slightly exaggerated. While she did

adopt four "war babies" in 1915 in the unrealized hope of establishing a national refuge for dislocated children, the majority of WSPU war projects were stridently nationalistic. Pankhusrt, *Life of Emmeline Pankhurst*, pp. 154–155; For an illuminating discussion of the problem of "war babies," see Susan R. Grayzel, *Women's Identities at War: Gender, Motherhood, and Politics in Britain and France During the First World War* (Chapel Hill: University of North Carolina Press, 2000), pp. 89–103.

22. Annie Kenney, *A Militant* (London: Routledge [1924], 1994), p. 255. In some cases, this defection had little to do with pacifism and much to do with a desire to continue the militant campaign. The "Independent WSPU," the "Suffragettes of the WSPU," and the "East London Federation of Suffragettes" broke with the Pankhursts in 1914 in order to continue overt, militant agitation for the vote. Of the splinter groups, Sylvia Pankhurst's East London Federation was alone committedly pacifist, and according to Sylvia Pankhurst herself, it suffered greatly for this position. See *The Independent Suffragette* [1914]; *The Suffragette New Sheet*, December 1915, p. 2; and *The Women's Dreadnought*, August 8, 1914. For an excellent account of wartime splits, see deVries, pp. 79–80.

23. Mitchell, *Warpath*, p. 51.

24. Mrs. Edith Ellis to Havelock Ellis, quoted in Havelock Ellis, *My Life: Autobiography of Havelock Ellis* (Boston: Houghton Mifflin, 1939), p. 515.

25. Mitchell, *Warpath*, p. 51.

26. Mitchell, *Warpath*, p. 51.

27. Christabel Pankhurst, *America and the War: A Speech Delivered at Carnegie Hall New York, October 24, 1914* (London: WSPU, 1914), p. 6.

28. Christabel Pankhurst, *America and the War*, p. 3. For an insightful discussion of "just war" rhetoric in WSPU discourse and its relationship to the war, see Cheryl R. Jorgensen-Earp, *"The Transfiguring Sword:" The Just War of the Women's Social and Political Union* (Tuscaloosa: University of Alabama Press, 1997), pp. 147–151.

29. Christabel Pankhurst, *America and the War*, pp. 10–15. For a fascinating analysis of such imagery in suffrage discourse, see Kent, *Making Peace*, pp. 75–78.

30. Christabel Pankhurst, *The War: A Speech Delivered at the London Opera House on September 8, 1914* (London: WSPU, 1914), p. 6. This point was made by a variety of feminist organizations, regardless of their stance on the war. See, for example, the *Women's Dreadnought*, December 26, 1914, p. 162; *Votes for Women*, August 14, 1914, p. 690 and June 4, 1915, p. 292; *Common Cause*, November 24, 1916, cover.

31. Pankhurst, *The War*, p. 16.

32. The *Star*, quoted in David Mitchell, *Queen Christabel: A Biography of Christabel Pankhurst* (London: Macdonald and Jane's, p. 1977), p. 248.

33. "War and Duty. Mrs. Pankhurst's Exhortation to Patriotism," *Times*, December 1, 1914.

34. E. Sylvia Pankhurst, *The Suffragette Movement: An Intimate Account of Persons and Ideals* (London, Longmans, 1931), p. 594.
35. These were the cities visited on recruiting missions as of April 1915. *The Suffragette*, April 16, 1915 p. 12.
36. Mrs. Emmeline Pankhurst, "What is Our Duty," a speech delivered at the Sun Hall, Liverpool, reprinted in the *Suffragette*, April 23, 1914, p. 25.
37. Flora Drummond, "Our Present Duty," a speech delivered in the Town Hall, Blackburn, reprinted in the *Suffragette*, May 21, 1915, p. 85.
38. Sylvia Pankhurst, *The Suffragette Movement*, p. 594–595.
39. *Daily Sketch*, January 27, 1915, quoted in Mitchell, *Queen Christabel*, p. 252.
40. Sylvia Pankhurst, *The Suffragette Movement*, p. 594.
41. Adela Pankhurst, who lived in Australia, shared Sylvia's pacifist sympathies. For accounts, see Mitchell, *Warpath*, pp. 289–291; *Britannia*, April 28, 1916, in Sylvia Pankhurst, *The Suffrage Movement*, p. 595; *Votes for Women*, May 1916, p. 162. Sylvia complained bitterly that following her pacifist or anti-conscription demonstrations, contributions to her clinics for working-class mothers dropped precipitously.
42. See also Christabel Pankhurst, *The War*, p. 13.
43. Pankhurst, *The War*, p. 15.
44. Feminists debated the merits of recruiting, some being strongly opposed, others finding it better than compulsion, and still others regarding it as a patriotic duty. For a thoughtful discussion of some positions, see "On Recruiting," *Common Cause*, June 18, 1915, pp. 146–147. Margaret Ashton was taken to task in *Common Cause* for making a recruiting speech. For the tenor of this controversy, see *Common Cause*, June 25, 1915.
45. *Common Cause*, June 18, 1915, p. 146.
46. *Vote*, September 11, 1914, p. 310.
47. *John Bull* March 6, 1915, p. 1; J.C. Carlie, *In Folkstone During the Great War* (Folkstone: F. J. Parsons, Ltd., 1922), p. 60.
48. *Manchester Guardian*, September 9, 1914, reprinted in MacKenzie, pp. 286–287.
49. For some accounts, see *Votes for Women*, March 19, 1915, p. 203; *Suffragette*, July 9, 1915, p. 200 in House of Lords Record Office [hereafter HLRO] LG/D/24/10/ # 39; *Times*, July 12, 1915. While all suffrage organization experienced an overall decline in revenue during the war, as wealthy contributors tightened their belts and made charitable contributions to the war effort, the patriotic fundraising of both the Pankhursts and the NU, which sponsored all female hospital units in the war zones, was quite remarkable.
50. *Suffragette*, May 21, 1915, p. 85.
51. Sylvia Pankhurst, *The Suffrage Movement*, pp. 593–595.
52. The *Suffragette* reemerged in 1915 just in time to castigate the pacifist wing of the NU which was embroiled in internecine strife over whether or not some of its ranking members could attend an international peace conference of women to be held at the Hague. Taking advantage of this

moment of division and apparent disloyalty within the NU, the WSPU captured the limelight of the women's movement and used the opportunity to subvert a variety of arguments against female citizenship. Helena Swanwick and others were furious about the WSPU's claim to speak for the women's movement. See Mitchell, *Warpath*, p. 321, and Pankhurst, *Unshackled*, pp. 290- 291.

53. The government funding of WSPU activities was several times protested in Parliament by Philip Snowdon, Richard Lambert, and other opponents of the war. See *Britannia*, March 31, 1916. Sylvia Pankhurst believed that her mother had received as much as £3,000 to put on the parade.

54. The tendency to dismiss the influence of the Pankhursts began with irate contemporaries who loathed their militaristic stance and their claim to speak for women. Typical is Ray Strachey, who declared that "Militancy faded away, and no more was ever heard of the Women's Social and Political Union." Strachey, p 337. Splits in the movement also gave the impression that the Pankhursts had lost their following, a position comforting to feminist who disapproved of their nationalism. For an account of the difficulty in gauging the actual level of support enjoyed by the WSPU leadership, see de Vries, pp. 79–80.

55. *Observer*, July 18, 1915, reprinted in *Britannia*, March 22, 1918, p. 394. The March 22, 1918, issue of *Britannia* commemorated the great parade by reprinting the original 1915 press coverage.

56. Michael MacDonagh, *In London During the Great War* (London: Eyre & Spottiswoode, 1935), p. 71. *See illustrations.*

57. *Daily Mail*, July 19, 1915 reprinted in *Britannia*, March 22, 1918, p. 393.

58. *Daily Chronicle*, July 19, 1915, reprinted in *Britannia*, March 22, 1918, p. 393–394.

59. The WSPU offices in Kingsway were flooded with mail from women looking for patriotic work. Mitchell, *Warpath*, pp. 59–60.

60. The Women's Labour League worried about this, as did Sylvia Pankhurst. See *Votes for Women*, January 28, 1916, p. 139 and *The Woman's Dreadnought*, March 11, 1916, p. 439.

61. Emmeline Pankhurst, "A Speech Delivered at the London Pavilion, October 5, 1915," reprinted in Midge MacKenzie ed., *Shoulder to Shoulder: A Documentary* (London: Alfred A. Knopf, 1975), p. 294.

62. Speeches delivered July 17, 1915, in *Suffragette*, July 23, 1915, and fuller accounts reprinted in *Britannia*, March 27, 1918.

63. *Sunday Times*, July 18, 1915 and *Daily Express*, July 19, 1915, reprinted in *Britannia*, March 22, 1918, p. 394. For an account of the strike, see Trevor Wilson, *The Myriad Faces of War* (Cambridge: Polity Press, 1988), pp. 223–224.

64. From interviews in the *Egoist*, quoted in Mitchell, *Queen Christabel*, p. 360.

65. Leo Maxse, speaking at a "Votes for Servicemen" rally with Mrs. Pankhurst, described Asquith's "conversion" as a plan to "enfranchise the conscientious objector and disenfranchise the Victoria Cross." *Britannia*, October 6, 1916.

66. On August 14, 1916 Asquith made the speech that Mrs. Pankhurst reacted to, stating that any franchise awarded on the basis of state service would "open the floodgates" to women's claims. For documents and commentary see Mackenzie, pp. 320–324.

67. *Britannia*, August 18, 1916.

68. Bellairs speech was delivered in the House of Commons on August 16, 1916, just two days after Asquith's speech saying that he could not oppose women suffrage if a new franchise were introduced on the basis of state service. *Britannia*, August 18, 1916, p. 236. The Pankhursts insisted that women's voteless condition was "made even more intolerable by the war" but wanted soldiers to vote regardless of what happened to the female franchise. *Britannia*, August 25, 1916.

69. The WSPU was unanimously barred from being an official sponsor of the march because of the Bellairs affair, but significantly Mrs. Pankhurst herself was invited to attend and spoke formally at the request of Lloyd George. In her speech she presented herself as in full agreement with Mrs. Fawcett on the need for a compromise Bill that would grant a measure of female suffrage but survive legislative debate. *Britannia*, April 9, 1917, p. 358; For an account of the meeting, see Sylvia Pankhurst, *The Suffragette Movement*, p. 606, and *Britannia*, April 2, 1917, p. 354.

70. Jorgensen-Earp, p. 128.

71. In the end, Mary Leigh was acquitted of the hatchet-throwing incident for "lack of evidence." Van Wingerden, pp. 140–141. For the Lloyd George conspiracy trial, see *Britannia*, February 19, 1917, p. 332. Interestingly, Lord Russell, in advocating the Women's Clause in the House of Lords in 1917, gave fear of "riot, revolution, and the rifle" as one reason to resolve the issue, while the Marquess of Crewe reminded his colleagues that "it would have been no surprise to us . . . if any one of our colleagues . . . had been assassinated in the street." Hansards, *House of Lords Debates*, December 17, 1917, col. 216 and January 9, 1918, col. 448. For an incisive discussion of the way prewar militancy haunted wartime debates see Kent, pp. 84–85.

72. *Britannia*, February 18, 1916, p. 133.

73. *Times*, December 1, 1914.

74. See, for example, the *Times*, May 18, 1915 and May 21, 1915.

75. *Britannia*, February 12, 1917, p. 328.

76. See *Britannia*, October 5, 1917, p. 143, and *Britannia*, June 23, 1916.

77. Mitchell, *Queen Christabel*, p. 271. Christabel herself longed to see a woman in the cabinet. Christabel Pankhurst to Lloyd George, July 6, 1918, in HLRO/ LG/F/94/3/#60.

78. Mitchell, *Queen Christabel*, p. 252.

79. *Britannia*, April 9, 1917, p. 356.

80. "When is an Alien not an Alien?," *Votes for Women*, September 4, 1914, cover. For the treatment of Germans in Britain during World War I, see Panikos Panayi, *The Enemy in our Midst: Germans in Britain during the First World War* (Oxford: Berg, 1991).

81. Restrictions on aliens' franchise privileges were clarified in the Municipal Corporation Act of 1882 and the County Electors Act of 1888. See J. Renwick Seager, J. P., *The Reform Act of 1918* (London: Liberal Publication Department, 1918), p. 48. For feminist irritation over the Alien's Act, which conferred alien status upon British born women married to aliens, while granting foreign-born women married to Britons British nationality, see *Votes for Women*, September 4, 1914, cover and *Common Cause*, September 4, 1914, p. 417.

82. Mitchell, *Queen Christabel*, p. 256.

83. See *Britannia*, March 17, 1916. For harassment of Haldane, see *Britannia*, October 20, 1916, p. 278, and *Britannia*, October 27, 1916, p. 288.

84. *Britannia*, April 28, 1916, pp. 173–174. The final sentence concludes the article.

85. *Britannia*, July 28, 1916.

86. *Globe*, July 25, 1916 reprinted in *Britannia*, July 28, 1916; *Morning Post*, reprinted in *Britannia*, July 28, 1916.

87. *Morning Post*, reprinted in *Britannia*, July 28, 1916.

88. "A Strong Protest," *Vote*, July 28, 1916. Boyle was also irritated by the Lloyd George's collaboration with the Pankhursts. As she wrote in the *Vote*, it was "indeed a remarkable spectacle to see [Lloyd George's] open patronage of those who have left no stone unturned to wreck his colleagues."

89. *Lady's Pictorial*, reprinted in *Britannia*, July 28, 1916.

90. *Britannia*, May 28, 1915, p. 102. The difficulties of aliens were exacerbated by the kaiser's nationality proclamation of July 27, 1914, which granted dual citizenship to all Germans naturalized by another power. To Christabel and many others, this was "Bigamy in the national sense."

91. *Britannia*, March 3, 1916, p. 140.

92. *Britannia*, January 28, 1916, p. 127. While initially the WSPU claimed to be combating the "German Canker on the Clyde," it soon came to regard its campaign as part of a larger international struggle against bolshevism and revolution. Like many contemporaries, these perceived evils were compatible since they regarded Germany and German agents as responsible for both domestic pacifism and international bolshevism.

93. Mitchell, *Queen Christabel*, p. 265 and *Britannia*, September 7, 1917, p. 112. Impressive lists of "Victory Fund" contributors and money raised were printed in *Britannia* during 1917, but it is not always clear what projects the funds were to be used for. See, for example, *Britannia*, June 6, 1917 and June 13, 1917.

94. From March 1916 to August 1918, the *Times* printed frequent accounts of strikes, causing much unease and consternation, particularly about the Clyde. For an account of this activity see Wilson, pp. 228–230.

95. Mrs. Drummond was proud of the fact that she spoke at both "factory gates and in Great Halls," *Britannia*, September 28, 1917, p. 135. For examples of her diatribes, see the *Northern Western Mail*, April 3, 1917 and *Britannia*, April 9, 1917, p. 356; *Britannia*, June 29, 1917, p. 30.

96. *Britannia*, February 18, 1916, p. 134.

97. Interview with the *Sunday Herald* reprinted in *Britannia*, August 25, 1918, p. 109.

98. Interview with the *Sunday Herald*, August 25, 1918, reprinted in *Britannia*, August 30, 1918, p. 109.

99. Accounts in the *Empire News*, the *Glasgow Evening Times*, the *Glasgow Evening News*, and the *Glasgow Record and Mail* reported in *Britannia*, February 22, 1918.

100. "General Drummond and Lloyd George with Munitionettes at Manchester," Museum of London. *See illustrations*. See also "Flora Drummond Speaking to Munitionettes from a Tank," *Britannia*, February 15, 1918; *Britannia*, March 22, 1918, pp. 386–387.

101. Annie Kenney, who "spoke at practically all the large munitions centers," attributed her own popularity to the fact that she was a former factory worker. Annie Kenney, *A Militant* (London: Routledge [1924], 1994), pp. 271–273.

102. *Britannia* and other conservative papers gave extensive coverage to a resolution by 4000 female munitions workers on the Clyde who voted to denounce striking male workers and to take on their work themselves. *Britannia*, February 15, 1918. Flora Drummond frequently paraded loyal munitions girls for Lloyd George and Christabel claimed their support during her 1918 political campaign. See, for example, *Britannia*, December 6, 1918, pp. 222–223.

103. *Britannia*, August 2, 1918, p. 79.

104. *Woolwich Herald*, March 8, 1918, reprinted in *Britannia*, March 15, 1918, p. 372.

105. *Western Mail* reprinted in *Britannia*, October 19, 1917, p. 157.

106. Mitchell, *Warpath*, p. 370–371.

107. Christabel Pankhusrt, "Warning to all Women Workers," *Empire News*, August 25, 1918, reprinted in *Britannia*, August 30, 1918, p. 110.

108. Christabel Pankhurst, "To Abolish the Proletariat," *Britannia*, September 6, 1918, p. 116.

109. The fullest and most riveting account of this trip is to be found in Jessie Kenney's *Price of Liberty*, a diary of her trip with Mrs. Pankhurst. For excellent additional information see MacKenzie, pp. 312–315 and Margaret R. Higonnet, ed., *Lines of Fire: Women Writers of World War I* (New York: Penguin, 1999), pp. 157–166.

110. Kenney, *Price of Liberty*, p. 67. This was the implication of an account of a conversation between Mrs. Pankhurst and Countess Orloff Davidoff.

111. "Madame Botchkareva," *Britannia*, August 3, 1917, cover; Kenney, *Price of Liberty*, p. 32.

112. Russian Women's "Manifesto," reprinted in *Britannia*, August 10, 1917, p. 78; "Russian Women's Challenge," *Britannia*, June 29, 1917, p. 25. See also Kenney, *Price of Liberty*, pp. 34–35 and 54–55. For a short history of the Russian Women's Battalion of Death see, Laurie Stoff, "They Fought

for Russia: Female Soldiers of the First World War," in Gerard DeGroot and Corinna Peniston-Bird, eds., *A Soldier and a Woman: Sexual Integration in the Military* (Harlow: Pearson Education Ltd., 2000), pp. 66–82.

113. MacKenzie, p. 314. *Britannia* continued to report on Botchkareva's exploits even after Botchkareva herself was forced to flee the Bolshevik revolution. *Britannia*, May 17, 1918, p. 462.

114. See photograph of Mrs. Pankhusrt reviewing the Russian women's Battalion of Death, *Britannia*, August 10, 1917, p. 77.

115. Quoted in Jorgensen-Earp, *Speeches and Trials*, p. 367.

116. *Britannia*, February 18, 1916, p. 132. That which *Britannia* considered to be "untrue" was also the idea that Haldane's pernicious influence had been removed from the War Office.

117. *Britannia*, November 2, 1917.

118. *Britannia*, March 22, 1918, p. 386.

119. *Britannia*, November 2, 1917, p. 171.

120. *Britannia*, November 2, 1917, p. 172.

121. Christabel Pankhusrt, "Industrial Salvation," *Britannia*, August 30, 1918, p. 107.

122. *Britannia*, September 6, 1918, p. 117; Mitchell, *Warpath*, pp. 370–372.

123. For an excellent discussion of feminists relationship to contemporary cultural attitudes see Burton, *Burdens of History*, pp. 204–205.

124. Pankhurst, *Life of Emmeline Pankhurst*, p.162.

CHAPTER 7

1. David Mitchell, *Women on the Warpath: The Story of the Women of the First World War* (London: Jonathan Cape, 1966), pp. 247–248.

2. *New York Tribune*, October 31, 1914, reprinted in Midge Mackenzie ed., *Shoulder to Shoulder A Documentary* (London: Alfred Knopf, 1975), p. 290.

3. Mitchell, *Warpath*, p. 183

4. *Votes for Women*, September 11, 1914, p. 726.

5. For an excellent account of the terrifying first weeks of war, see Trevor Wilson, *The Myriad Faces of War* (Cambridge: Polity Press, 1986), pp. 41–49.

6. Mrs. Dawson Scott (Women's Defense Relief Corps) and the Hon. Mrs. Evelina Haverfield (Women's Volunteer Rifle Corps) both proposed establishing female combatant corps for home defense. See the *Times*, September 6, 1914. These ideas received quite a bit of play in the feminist press. See, for example, *Votes for Women*, August 28, 1914, p. 713, followed by a regular column entitled "Should Women Shoot," which aired letters from readers on the subject for the next several months. *Votes for Women*, September 25, 1914, p. 746 and *Common Cause*, December 24, 1914, p. 618. For a discussion of the laws governing the treatment of irregulars see

Nicoletta F. Gullace, "Sexual Violence and Family Honor: British Propaganda and International Law during the First World War," *The American Historical Review*, June 1997, pp. 730–735.

7. "Women's Service Under Fire," *Common Cause*, December 24, 1914, p. 618, and February 19, 1915, p. 719. For an excellent discussion of paramilitary women's organizations see Jenny Gould, "Women's Military Service in First World War Britain," in Margaret Higonnet, Jane Jenson et al., eds., *Behind the Lines: Gender and the Two World Wars* (New Haven: Yale University Press, 1987), pp. 114–125.

8. *Votes for Women*, September 4, 1914, p. 718.

9. Numerous women were afraid that armed women would be shot as irregulars since it was unlikely that the government would ever recognize them as a militia. For a lucid discussion of this issue, see Mrs. Cavendish Bentinck, *Votes for Women*, September 4, 1914, p. 718, and Gullace, "Sexual Violence and Family Honor," pp. 730–735.

10. *Votes for Women*, September 4, 1914, p. 718.

11. Violet Markham, *Anti-Suffrage Review*, August 1915, p. 59; Gladys Medwin, *The Anti-Suffrage Review*, March 1915, p. 22.

12. *Common Cause*, January 21, 1916, p. 548.

13. Susan R. Grayzel, "'The Outward and Visible Sign of her Patriotism': Women, Uniforms, and National Service During the First World War," *Twentieth Century British History*, vol. 8, no. 2 (1977), pp. 145–164. See also Gould, "Women's Military Services," pp. 114–125.

14. Margaret R. Higonnet, ed., *Lines of Fire: Women Writers of World War I* (New York: Penguin, 1999), pp. 152–154.

15. Mrs. Alec Tweedie, FRGS, *Women and Soldiers* (London: John Lane, 1918), p. 26.

16. *Britannia*, May 24, 1918. Drummond was simply building on an idea long held by the WSPU leadership. As early as September 1914, Christabel Pankhurst had declared in a speech at the London Opera House that women were "as willing to serve as men" and that "if we are needed in the fighting line we shall be there." Christabel Pankhurst, *The War: A Speech Delivered at the London Opera House on September 8, 1914* (London: WSPU, 1914), p. 12.

17. Miss Edith Milner, *The Anti-Suffrage Review*, February 1915, p. 12; J. Masssie, *The Anti-Suffrage Review*, March 1915, p. 21.

18. For a lucid discussion of militant "reformist terrorism," see Cheryl R. Jorgensen-Earp, ed., *Speeches and Trials of the Militant Suffragettes: The Women's Social and Political Union, 1903-1918* (London: Associated University Presses, 1999), pp.135–137.

19. *Common Cause*, January 1, 1915, p. 631.

20. "War is a Man's Show, Old Dear," *Votes for Women*, December 18, 1914; *Votes for Women*, May 14, 1915, p. 267.

21. Ray Strachey, *The Cause: A Short History of the Women's Movement in Great Britain* (Bath: Cedrick Chivers Portway, 1928), p. 347.

22. Arthur Marwick, *The Deluge: British Society and the First World War* (New York: Norton, 1965), p. 89.

23. Strachey, *The Cause*, p. 348

24. Kathleen Hodges North, *Diary*, excerpted in Margaret Higonnet, ed., *Lines of Fire*, pp. 188- 190.

25. Arthur Marwick, *Women at War, 1914–1918* (London: Croom Helm, 1977), p. 107.

26. *Common Cause*, April 22, 1916, p. 29; Strachey, *The Cause*, p. 348.

27. *Lancet*, quoted in *Common Cause*, December 14, 1917.

28. *Votes for Women*, January 28, 1916, pp. 146.

29. *Common Cause*, March 19, 1915.

30. *Common Cause*, August 14, 1914, p. 385.

31. *Common Cause*, August 14, 1914, p. 385.

32. E. Sylvia Pankhurst, *The Suffrage Movement* (London: Longmans, 1931), p. 608.

33. *Common Cause*, April 30, 1915, p. 42.

34. *Common Cause*, June 25, 1915, p. 158.

35. *Common Cause*, May 7, 1915; *Anti-Suffrage Review*, May 1915; *Anti-Suffrage Review*, March 1915, p. 19.

36. Agatha M. Richardson to *Common Cause*, October 2, 1914; Ellen Capman to *Common Cause*, October 2, 1914.

37. Dr. Ethyl Smyth to the *Morning Post*, reprinted in the *Anti-Suffrage Review*, July 1915.

38. Harrison believed herself to have been misquoted in C. K. Ogden's *Militarism and Feminism* and wanted to clarify her support for the present war. *Common Cause*, March 5, 1915.

39. Marion Chadwick, *Common Cause*, April 16, 1915, p. 16; Harriet Powell, *Common Cause*, April 16, 1915, p. 16.

40. *Common Cause*, April 23, 1915, p. 32.

41. *Common Cause*, April 23, 1915, and *Anti-Suffrage Review*, May 1915. Mrs. Fawcett also wrote a scathing article against the pacifists published in the *Englishwoman*. Fawcett carried the day when the Executive Committee voted 2–1 against sending delegates to the Women's Peace Meeting at the Hague. See the *Englishwoman*, June 1915, pp. 193–200.

42. *Common Cause*, May 21, 1915.

43. *The Anti-Suffrage Review*, March, 1915.

44. "Eminent Woman Surgeon," *Punch*, no. 149 (1915). Mitchell, *Warpath*, pp. 187–196.

45. See Vera Brittain, *Testament of Youth* (London: Penguin [1933], 1989), p. 372. Anne Summers, *Angels and Citizens: British Women as Military Nurses 1854–1914* (London: Routledge, 1988). Summers points out that many nurses did not actually favor women's suffrage. Interestingly, such conservatism in no way prevented British suffragists from making use of their heroism for the suffrage cause.

46. For a comment on photographic images, see *Common Cause*, January 19, 1917.

47. For an extraordinary array of documents, news clippings, books, and ephemera, see Imperial War Museum, London [hereafter IWM], Documents, Edith Cavell Collection, Box P 114 a and b; Anon., "German Crimes Calendar" (London: The London Electrotype Agency, 1918), October IWM, GB 352.1 K49367; *Votes for Women*, October 22, 1915, p. 27.

48. *The Women's Dreadnought*, November 6, 1915, pp. 387 and 392; Patricia Y. Lin, "From a Call to Arms to a Symbol for Peace: The Changing Image of Nurse Edith Cavell, 1915–1939" (Berkeley: Unpublished seminar paper, 1992).

49. *Votes for Women*, November 5, 1915, p. 44.

50. *Votes for Women* November 12, 1915, p. 52.

51. See, for example, Christabel Pankhurst, *International Militancy: A Speech Delivered at Carnegie Hall, New York, January 31, 1915* (London: WSPU, 1915); *Common Cause*, December 24, 1914, *Votes For Women*, August 7, 1914, and *Votes for Women*, August 14, 1914.

52. Notice of the *Times History* in *Common Cause*, July 9, 1915, p. 190; *The Daily Telegraph* quoted in *Common Cause*, June 30, 1916.

53. *Anti-Suffrage Review*, September 1915, p. 71.

54. Asquith's speech quoted in *Votes for Women*, November 12, 1915, p. 52; Lord Haldane, *House of Lords Debates*, January 9, 1918, col. 425.

55. Nina Boyle, *Vote*, February 19, 1915.

56. As Bonnie Smith has pointed out, the female war worker replaced the suffragette as the dominant image of the woman in the public sphere and established a highly flattering profile "of a patriotic working woman, contributing to the war effort . . . in solidarity with men." Bonnie Smith, *Changing Lives* (Lexington: D.C. Heath, 1989), p. 372. The *Tatler* published a cartoon entitled "The Key of the Situation," which depicted a female munitions worker unlocking the houses of Parliament (and the vote) with a key labeled "National Work." She had laid down her militant's axe, inspiring John Bull to remark, "It was no good axeing for it, but now you've worked for it . . . it's a different matter." *Tatler*, April 11, 1917, p. 40.

57. Mitchell, *Warpath*, pp. 83–84.

58. *Britannia*, July 28, 1916, p. 225. While this was not explicitly staged as a suffrage parade, the press nevertheless read it as one, highlighting once again the indivisablity of the name "Pankhurst" with the suffrage cause. Nina Boyle, "A Strong Protest," *Vote*, July 28, 1916.

59. Strachey, *The Cause*, p. 358.

60. *Common Cause*, April 7, 1917, p. 685.

61. Strachey, *The Cause*, p. 344–345.

62. *Suffragette News Sheet*, April 1916, p. 1.

63. Angela Woollacott, *On Her Their Lives Depend: Munitions Workers in the Great War*, (Berkeley: University of California Press, 1994), pp. 2 and 7.

64. "Fuze 106: The Adventures of a Detonator Plug" by a Detonator Plug Girl, in Perivale, *The War-Worker* 2, no. 4 (September 1918), p. 66 quoted in Woollacott, p. 200; Mary Macleod Moore, "Women as Munitions Workers," *Sunday Times*, July 23, 1916, quoted in Woollacott, p. 195.

65. Alec Holmes, "The Munition Worker: A Play in Once Scene," *Englishwoman* (March 1917), pp. 255–270, quoted in Woollacott, pp. 8–9.

66. Holmes, quoted in Woollacott, pp. 8–9.

67. Woollacott, p. 9.

68. *Votes for Women*, January 1917, p. 225.

69. Woollacott, pp. 84–87.

70. Woollacott, p. 8.

71. Mrs. Dean, IWM, DSR, 9381/01 and Lilian Miles, IWM, DSR, 000854/04, quoted in Woollacott, p. 81–82.

72. Woolacott, p. 82

73. *Common Cause*, October 6, 1916.

74. "Rudheath Girl Dies for Her Country: 'If I Die, I've Done My Bit,'" *Chronicle*, May 19, 1917, quoted in Woollacott, p. 82.

75. For information on pay rates, see Marwick, *Women at War*, pp. 60–82, and Gail Braybon, *Women Workers in the First World War* (London: Croom Helm, 1981), pp. 96–111.

76. Mrs. H. A. Felstead to IWM, January 17, 1976, excerpted in Marwick, pp. 67–68.

77. For a fascinating discussion of these issues, see Woollacott, pp. 134–152.

78. Mary Macarthur, 'The Flaunting Flapper," *Women's Life*, no. 302 (November 17, 1917), p. 202, quoted in Woollacott, p. 144.

79. H. G. Wells, in *Ladies Home Journal*, June 1916, quoted in Woollacott, p. 188.

80. *Daily Telegraph*, June 21, 1915, quoted in *Common Cause*, July 2, 1915.

81. *Glasgow Herald*, quoted in *Common Cause*, February 25, 1916; *Globe*, quoted in *Common Cause*, June 2, 1916.

82. *Common Cause*, April 9, 1915, p. 6; *Common Cause*, January 26, 1917.

83. Mackenzie, *Shoulder to Shoulder*, p. 323.

84. Selected correspondence between Mrs. Fawcett and Mr. Asquith, May-August, 1916, reprinted in Mackenzie, *Shoulder to Shoulder*, p. 321.

85. *Common Cause*, May 19, 1916, p. 82.

86. Strachey, *The Cause*, p. 349.

87. Quoted in Susan Kingsley Kent, *Making Peace: The Reconstruction of Gender in Interwar Britain* (Princeton: Princeton University Press, 1993), p. 83.

Chapter 8

1. See Janet Penrose Trevelyan, *The Life of Mrs. Humphry Ward* (New York: Dodd, Mead & Co, 1923), pp. 269–287 and John Sutherland, *Mrs.*

Humphry Ward: Eminent Victorian, Pre-eminent Edwardian (Oxford: Clarendon, 1990), pp. 350–367.

2. Sutherland, p. 342.
3. Sutherland, p. 299.
4. Martin Pugh, *The March of Women: A Revisionist Analysis of the Campaign for Women's Suffrage 1866–1914* (Oxford: Clarendon, 2000), pp. 36–49.
5. Sutherland, p. 345 and pp. 326–356; Pugh, *March of Women*, p. 152.
6. Brian Harrison, *Separate Spheres: The Opposition to Women's Suffrage in Britain* (London: Croom Helm, 1978), pp. 212–213.
7. Harold L. Smith, *The British Women's Suffrage Campaign 1866–1928* (London: Longman, 1988), p. 67.
8. Hansards, *House of Lords Debates*, January 10, 1918, cols. 521–523. This appeal was all the more treacherous since Curzon at the time was the President of the National League for Opposing Women's Suffrage. Harrison, p. 221.
9. Ray Strachey, *The Cause: A Short History of the Women's Movement in Great Britain* (Bath: Cedric Chivers Portway, 1928), p. 365, and Harrison, p. 221.
10. David Close, "The Collapse of Resistance to Democracy: Conservatives, Adult Suffrage, and Second Chamber Reform, 1911–1928," *The Historical Journal*, 20, 4 (1977), p. 913. See also Smith, p. 69. Historians differ widely on the actual numbers in part because of contemporary miscalculations of the electorate. The Speaker's Conference estimated that an age bar of thirty, combined with property qualifications, would enfranchise only six million women. In fact eight and a half million women were actually placed on the register, making up nearly 40 percent of the total electorate.
11. Although the terms of female enfranchisement in 1918 were partial and far from equal to those of men, they were considerably more generous than the provisions found in most of the forty-five other suffrage proposals that had gone down in defeat between 1867 and 1914. For an excellent summary of the fate of some of those proposals, see Constance Rover, *Women's Suffrage and Party Politics In Britain, 1866–1914* (London: Routledge, 1967), pp. 211–223, and Marian Ramelson, *Petticoat Rebellion* (London: Lawrence & Winhart, 1967) p. 162.
12. The idea that women's suffrage was granted for loyal wartime service was long regarded as axiomatic by contemporaries and historians alike. While some historians still maintain this position, it has come under increasing challenge by feminist historians. See, for example, Cheryl Law, "The Old Faith Living and the Old Power There: The Movement to Extend Women's Suffrage," in Maroula Joannou and June Purvis, eds., *The Women's Suffrage Movement: New Feminist Perspectives* (Manchester: Manchester University Press, 1998), p. 204; Angela Woollacott, *On Her Their Lives Depend: Munitions Workers in the Great War* (Berkeley: University of California Press, 1994), p. 89; Susan Kingsley Kent, *Making Peace: The Reconstruction of Gender in Interwar Britian* (Princeton:

Princeton University Press, 1993), p. 82; Susan R. Grayzel, "'The Out-ward and Visible Sign of her Patriotism': Women, Uniforms, and National Service During the First World War," *Twentieth Century British History*, vol. 8, no. 2 (1997), p. 148.

13. Sandra Holton's influential claim that women's suffrage was "near resolution" in 1914 and that the war may actually have "delayed" the vote has been used to support the idea that women's wartime efforts made no difference to the arrival of the franchise. Although this is not Holton's contention, it has proved to be one of her most influential statements. See Sandra Holton, *Feminism and Democracy*, p. 130; Martin Pugh, *Women and the Women's Movement in Britain, 1914–1959*, pp. 36–39; Martin Pugh, "Politicians and the Women's Vote, 1914–1918," *History* 59 (October 1974), p. 358; and Martin Pugh, *The March of Women*, p. 286.

14. For an excellent account of the fundamentally gendered basis of the franchise in Britain, see Anna Clark, "Gender, Class and the Nation: Franchise Reform in England, 1822–1928," in James Vernon, ed., *Re-reading the Constitution* (Cambridge: Cambridge University Press, 1996), pp. 230–253.

15. While householders could move to a different house in the same constituency without losing their votes, lodgers were automatically disenfranchised upon changing their residence. Because the residency period had to be established by the July preceding the holding of the election (to allow time to compile and contest the register) most men had to have inhabited their homes for well over a year before being able to vote. Lodgers were also the only category of voter who was required to reapply every year to be included on the electoral register, and lodgers' electoral qualification was that most likely to be challenged by electoral agents, effectively making the lodger franchise a sham. Neal Blewett has noted the disproportionately low percentage of lodger voters, attributing this to a combination of registration hurdles and difficulty meeting the £10 rental qualification. Neal Blewett, "The Franchise in the United Kingdom, 1885–1918," *Past and Present*, December 1965, pp. 36–43. In addition to the residency hurdles faced by poor men wishing to vote was the provision that automatically disenfranchised anyone who had accepted poor relief or whose dependents had received poor relief. Even those who had received as little as a single loaf of bread from the parish were disqualified along with criminals, aliens, lunatics, and women. See Blewett, pp. 33.

16. Because only the head of household was qualified to vote as a "householder," all those other adult men living under his roof, including adult sons, male servants, and laborers living with their masters, were left without a vote. Duncan Tanner estimates that of the 4 million men who obtained the parliamentary vote in 1918, the majority were young men living in furnished rooms. Duncan Tanner, *Political Change and the Labour Party, 1900–1918* (Cambridge: Cambridge University Press, 1990), pp.

387–388. See also H. J. Hanham, *The Nineteenth Century Constitution, Documents and Commentary* (Cambridge, Cambridge University Press, 1969), pp. 273–274 and 280–281, and Blewett, pp. 36–43.

17. Blewett, p. 27.

18. A "householder" was a man who owned or rented a single-family dwelling and paid the "rates"—taxes used to support poor relief—on that home. Many older, married urban workers, particularly those in skilled jobs, were able to meet this qualification, making the 1867 Reform Bill the first to enfranchise significant numbers of working-class men. The household franchise, however, operated only in the boroughs, and it was not until 1884 that rural workers enjoyed the same franchise qualification as urban workers. Hanham, pp. 273–274.

19. Tanner, pp. 387–388.

20. Neal R. McCrillis, *The British Conservative Party in the Age of Universal Suffrage: Popular Conservatism, 1918–1929* (Columbus: Ohio State University Press, 1998), pp. 12–13.

21. McCrillis, p. 4.

22. Malcolm Pearce and Geoffrey Stewart, *British Political History, 1867–1990* (Routledge, 1992), p. 25. R. K. Webb, *Modern England*, 2nd ed. (New York: Harper & Row, 1980), p. 330.

23. For an excellent summary of the "physical force" argument, see Pugh, *March of Women*, p. 55.

24. Clark, p. 253. For the definitive work on the use of the sexual exploitation of women in suffragist argumentation see Susan Kingsley Kent, *Sex and Suffrage in Britain, 1860–1918* (Princeton: Princeton University Press, 1990).

25. The residential disenfranchisement of soldiers was upheld in two court cases, "Spittal v. Brook, 1886" and "Ford v. Elmsley, 1885." J. Renwick Seager, J.P. ed., *The Reform Act of 1918: Full Text, Annotated with Explanatory Notes* (London: The Liberal Publication Department, 1918), p. 31. See also Blewett, p. 33 and Pugh, *March of Women*, p. 56.

26. "Votes for Valour," *Common Cause*, June 1, 1917, p. 90.

27. See Tanner, pp. 385–386.

28. Martin Pugh, *Electoral Reform in War and Peace, 1906–1919* (Routledge & Kegan Paul, 1978), pp. 50–55.

29. See Sir Edward Carson's speeches on this theme. Hansards, *House of Commons Debates*, July 19, 1916; August 14, 1916.

30. "Into the Melting Pot," *The Common Cause*, August 25, 1916, p. 250.

31. James Bryce to A.V. Dicey, November 21, 1917, cited in Pugh, *Electoral Reform*, p. 87; McCrillis, p. 14.

32. Close, p. 908.

33. George F. Shee, *The Briton's First Duty* (London: Grant Richards, 1901), p. 252; Coulson Kernahan, "Why I Support Lord Roberts," *Wesleyan Methodist Magazine*, March 1914.

34. Martin Pugh makes a similar observation in *Electoral Reform*, p. 51.

35. Lord Selborne to Lord Salisbury, September 12, 1916, cited in Pugh, *Electoral Reform*, pp. 80–81 and 113.
36. Pugh argues that their error was in assuming that temporary volunteers and conscripts would share the outlook of regular professional soldiers. Pugh, *Electoral Reform*, p. 81.
37. Hansards, *Commons*, July 19, 1916, col. 1049.
38. Hansards, *Commons*, August 14, 1916, col. 1461.
39. Hansards, *Commons*, August 14, 1916, p. 1461. The heckler was Mr. W. Thorne.
40. Pugh, *Electoral Reform*, p. 51.
41. Close, pp. 900–901; McCrillis, pp. 14–15; Close, p. 895.
42. Pugh, *Electoral Reform*, p. 92.
43. McCrillis, p. 15. The latter half of the quote is Neal McCrillis's paraphrase. See also Close, pp. 899–902.
44. Close, p. 895.
45. Hansards, *Commons*, August 14, 1916, col. 1461.
46. Mrs. H. Ward to the *Times*, May 23, 1917 quoted in *Common Cause*, June 1, 1917, p. 90.
47. Quoted in David Mitchell, *Women on the Warpath: The Story of the Women of the First World War* (London: Jonathan Cape, 1966), p. 63.
48. *Common Cause*, May 19, 1916, p. 84.
49. Pugh, *Electoral Reform*, pp. 61–63.
50. Hansards, *Commons*, August 14, 1916, cols. 1451–1452.
51. Ninety-eight local Conservative associations now supported women's suffrage, while only forty-four opposed it. Smith, p. 61.
52. A. Patriot, "Votes for Heroines as Well as Heroes," *Votes for Women*, November 26, 1915.
53. The main provision of the military service franchise, in its final form, was to reduce the residential qualifying period for naval and military voters from six months to one month. It further required that the prospective military voter prove he would have met the male parliamentary qualification (six months residency in a single constituency and a roof over his head) but for war service. The word of a soldier was supposed to be good enough proof, but it could be subject to challenge from someone who had evidence that he would not have otherwise qualified under the male franchise. Thus, despite Carson's inclusive rhetoric, even the military service franchise, in the end, excluded vagrants, transients and itinerants. Both the military service franchise and the male franchise did, however, vastly expand the number of males who could vote by reducing the qualifying period and allowing lodgers of rooms of any value to vote. See Seager, *Reform Act of 1918*, pp. 29–40 and pp. 41–43.
54. Seager, *The Reform Act of 1918*, pp. 42–43. See also *Times*, February 7, 1918.
55. This was of course a tiny fraction of the male military service register which had almost 4 million men on it. But given women's age bar and the

fact that they could not join the armed forces until the last months of the war, their inclusion within this particular franchise is significant. Pugh, *Electoral Reform,* pp. 196 and 173.

56. For statistics on conscientious objection see John W. Graham, *Conscription and Conscience: A History 1916–1919* (London: George Allen & Unwin, 1922), pp. 348–350.

57. Hansards, *Commons,* June 26, 1917, cols. 339–340.

58. *Britannia,* October 6, 1916, p. 265.

59. *Times,* October 25, 1917, quoted in John Rae, *Conscience and Politics: The British Government and the Conscientious Objector to Military Service, 1916–1919* (London: Oxford University Press, 1970), p. 219.

60. Hansards, *Commons,* June 26, 1917, cols. 313–314.

61. Disenfranchisement was advocated in the *Times* on July 6, 1916. While at that point the position still had few parliamentary advocates, the idea would gain force gradually. Rae, p. 170.

62. *Common Cause,* November 23, 1917; Hansards, *Commons,* November 20, 1917, col. 1138.

63. *Common Cause,* November 30, 1917, p. 406.

64. Rae, p. 223 and Pugh, *Electoral Reform,* p. 126.

65. Hansards, *Commons,* June 26, 1917, col. 316. See also November 21, 1917, col. 1215.

66. Hansards, *Commons,* November 21, 1917, col. 1215.

67. Hansards, *Lords,* December 17, 1917, col. 219.

68. Hansards, *Commons,* November 21, 1917, col. 1232.

69. Hansards, *Commons,* November 21, 1917, col. 1242 (Rowntree was quoting Gilbert Murray to this effect); Mr. Caradoc Rees, November 21, 1917, col. 1260.

70. Hansards, *Commons,* June 26, 1917, cols. 318–319 and November 21, 1917, cols. 1222–1223.

71. Hansards, *Commons,* November 21, 1917, col. 1270.

72. Hansards, *Lords,* December 18, 1917, col. 242.

73. Hansards, *Commons,* November 21, 1917, col. 1237.

74. Hansards, *Commons,* November 20, 1917, col. 1139.

75. *Britannia,* August 25, 1916, cover.

76. Graham, p. 341.

77. Rae, p. 220; Graham, p. 326.

78. Harrison, p. 202.

79. Such observations were not exclusive to the Pankhursts. See, for example, Irene E. Toye Warner to *Votes for Women,* September 25, 1914, p. 746.

80. Hansards, *Commons,* November 20, 1917, col. 1140.

81. Hansards, *Commons,* June 26, 1917, col. 312.

82. Hansards, *Commons,* November 20, 1917, col. 1142.

83. According to Martin Pugh, "In Britain the anti-war movement remained very small and unpopular." Pugh, *Women and the Women's Movement,* p. 10.

84. Pugh, *Electoral Reform*, p. 126.
85. Rae, pp. 234–245.
86. Pugh, *Electoral Reform*, p. 125.
87. Seager, *Reform Act of 1918*, pp. 40–43.
88. Seager, *Reform Act of 1918*, p. 41; Smith, pp. 68–71.
89. Law, p. 203. The distinctions between the male and the female franchise were most marked around the issues of age, property, and marriage. Under each franchise, women were held to an age bar of thirty; under each franchise a woman was barred from exercising a second vote (which was an option for male electors who owned a business premises worth ten pounds or held a university degree), and in the final case, women were held to an implicit property qualification, embedded in the household and lodger franchise, which required the payment of rates or the ownership of furniture—provisions that most eligible women qualified for through their husbands. These differences were often galling. Whereas boys of nineteen could vote as long as they had seen combat (and had resided for at least one month in the same constituency before the outbreak of war), no woman, regardless of how rich, how well-educated, how stable her habitation, or how heroic she had been, could vote before her thirtieth birthday. Finally, a British-born women married to an alien was not qualified to vote, due to nationality laws that automatically conferred upon married women the nationality of their husbands. British-born husbands, of course, experienced no such restrictions. For a discussion of women married to aliens, see *Common Cause*, December 8, 1916, p. 461. In certain exceptional circumstances, women actually held the advantage in the 1918 Bill. The wives of peers (who did not have the parliamentary vote) and the wives of conscientious objectors were both entitled to vote. Also, under the local government franchise, men needed to occupy unfurnished rooms valued at £10 in order to vote in municipal elections, whereas women needed only to occupy unfurnished rooms valued at £5. Married women could also qualify to vote through their husbands' eligibility. Thus while women were disadvantaged under the parliamentary franchise, they actually had the advantage over men in the municipal franchise. See Seager, *Reform Act of 1918*, pp. 36–41.
90. Seager, *Reform Act of 1918*, pp. 29–36, 43–46, 46–49.
91. *Nation*, May 27, 1916.
92. *Daily Chronicle*, June 22, 1916, quoted in *Common Cause*, June 30, 1916, p. 153; *Common Cause*, July 7, 1916. During this period *Common Cause* was replete with such press cuttings, revealing a news media wildly enthusiastic about the prospect of enfranchising women on the basis of their service to the state. See *Common Cause*, July and August 1916.
93. Quoted in Andrew Rosen, *Rise Up Women!: The Militant Campaign of the Women's Social and Political Union, 1903–1914* (London: Routledge & Kegan Paul, 1974), p. 263.
94. Hansards, *Lords*, January 9, 1918, col. 426. Haldane makes this point, which is also acknowledged by Selborne and Curzon.

95. Holton, p. 146; *Common Cause,* April 7, 1917, p. 683.
96. Pugh, "Politicians and the Women's Vote, 1914–1918," *History,* vol. 59, #197 (October 1974), p. 365; Blewett, p. 365.
97. Harrison, p. 224.
98. McCrillis, p. 16.
99. On insincerity, see, for example, Blewett, p. 366. The prevalence of a rationale based on service is more than evident in the speeches given on this subject in the House of Commons. The issue of women's suffrage was debated on March 28, 1917; April 7, 1917; May 15, 1917; May 22 and 23, 1917; and June 19, 1917, when the final vote was taken. See Hansards, *House of Commons Debates,* March-June 1917.
100. Harrison, p. 204.
101. Pugh, *Electoral Reform,* p. 152; Sophia A. van Wingerden, *The Women's Suffrage Movement in Britain, 1866–1928* (London: Macmillan, 1999), p. 154.
102. *Common Cause,* May 26, 1916, p. 93.
103. *Common Cause,* January 26, 1917, p. 547.
104. As *Common Cause* exclaimed with joy, Anti arguments were "melting down in the fire of war." *Common Cause,* August 25, 1916.
105. *Common Cause,* April 7, 1917, p. 683.
106. Hansards, *Commons,* June 19, 1917. The speaker was Ramsay MacDonald and the dramatic landslide in favor of women's suffrage on June 19— no less than 385 to 55—suggests that he may have been right. For suffragist lobbying tactics, see Smith, p. 67.
107. Hansards, *Lords,* January 9, 1918, col. 412.
108. Hansards, *Lords,* January 9, 1918, cols. 415–416. The idea of an age limit of thirty for women was first suggested by W. H. Dickinson, a confidant of Mrs. Fawcett and one of the most committed suffragists on the Speaker's Conference, to offset the objection that an equal franchise would result in a predominantly female electorate—a prospect that even some Labourites did not relish. Pugh, *Electoral Reform,* p. 85.
109. Pugh, "Women and the Women's Movement," p. 39
110. *The Englishwoman,* March 1917, p. 197, quoted in Wingerden, p. 170. "Adultist" suffragists vehemently opposed a female franchise that was not fully equal, but the main women's suffrage organizations accepted the age bar as a compromise necessary to allay fears of a female majority, break down the sex barrier, and commit women's groups to the fight for an equal franchise later on. Particularly hostile to the age bar were those like Sylvia Pankhurst and Mary Macarthur who worked with young female industrial workers. See E. Sylvia Pankhurst, *The Suffragette Movement* (London: Longmans, 1931), pp. 602–608.
111. Hansards, *Lords,* January 10, 1918, col. 471.
112. For the most accurate figures regarding the 1918 electoral register see Pugh, *Electoral Reform,* Appendix 10, "The 1918 Electorate," p. 196. According to Pugh, 12,913,166 men and 8,479,156 women registered to vote.

113. Hansards, *Lords,* January 10, 1918, col. 520; *Times,* reported in *Votes for Women,* January 1917, p. 225.
114. Hansards, *Lords,* January 9, 1918, col 456. Lord Burnham is the speaker.
115. Harrison, p. 203; *Anti-Suffrage Review,* July 1915, p. 55.
116. Smith, pp. 58–59; *Times,* May 21, 1915; *The Times,* November 6, 1918; Harrison, p. 215.
117. Hansards, *Lords,* January 10, 1918, col. 507.
118. Hansards, *Lords,* January 9, 1918, cols. 460–462.
119. Woollacott, pp. 124–133.
120. Hansards, *Lords,* December 17, 1917, cols. 182–184. A "tweenie" was an inferior domestic, usually young, who assisted both the cook and the housemaid.
121. Lord Balfour, Hansards, *Lords,* January 9, 1918, col. 435; Law, p. 201; Close, p. 915; Bryce, Hansards, *Lords,* December 17, 1917, col. 185.
122. See, for example, James Bryce to A.V. Dicey, January 22, 1919, Bodleian, Modern Manuscripts, MS Bryce 4, fol. 212.
123. See, for example, Viscount Chaplin, Hansards, *Lords,* January 10, 1918, col. 502, and Close, p. 895. No doubt owing to the tremendous embarrassment that would have come from disenfranchising soldiers whose families had accepted poor relief, the pauper disqualification was eliminated by the Speakers Conference, meaning that even the poorest male civilians—as long as they had roofs over their heads—would be eligible to vote. This unpalatable prospect could at least be offset by ensuring that the poorest women would not share this privilege—a consideration strikingly revealed in the 1920s when Tories tried to restore the pauper disqualification for both sexes. See Close, p. 914 and Seager, *Reform Act of 1918,* p. 46.
124. Hansards, *Lords,* January 10, 1918, col. 480.
125. Close, p. 914.
126. Hansards, *Lords,* January 10, 1918, col. 515.
127. Susan R. Grayzel, *Women's Identities at War: Gender, Motherhood and Politics in Britain and France during the First World War* (Chapel Hill: University of North Carolina Press, 1999).
128. Pugh, *Electoral Reform,* p. 144.
129. Executive Committee of the Consultive Committee of Women's Suffrage Societies to Prime Minister Asquith, August 4, 1916, p. 2, reprinted in Midge Mackenzie, ed., *Shoulder to Shoulder: A Documentary* (London: Alfred A. Knopf, 1975), p. 323; *Contemporary Review,* July 1916, pp. 40–46.
130. R. M. Wilson, *Wife: Mother: Voter: Her Vote. What Will She Do With It?* (London: Hodder & Stoughton, 1918), p. ix–x.
131. Hansards, *Lords,* January 9, 1918, p. 436.
132. It is also possible that without "votes for valour," the girl of twenty-one who quit her factory in 1918 might have waited even longer than she did to cast a ballot. The ten-year struggle for an equal franchise reveals a decidedly more hostile environment in which to press for women's rights than existed during the war. Indeed, the case of France, where women did

not receive the vote until after World War II, demonstrates British women's indebtedness to a shrewdly opportunistic feminist movement, able to seize the day in a cultural environment where the voluntary nature of service evoked encomiums for those simply doing what the State would have compelled them to do anywhere else.

133. Hansards, *Lords*, December 19, 1917, cols. 302–303.
134. Hansards, *Lords*, January 10, 1918, col. 523.
135. The Parliament Act of 1911 restricted the veto power of the House of Lords. It was passed following a series of partisan vetoes that culminated in the rejection of Lloyd George's popular "People's Budget" in 1909. Webb, pp. 464–466.

EPILOGUE

1. The definitive account of the invasion of Belgium is John Horne and Alan Kramer, *German Atrocities, 1914: A History of Denial* (New Haven: Yale University Press, 2000). Classic exposés of World War I propaganda are Harold Laswell, *Propaganda Technique in World War I* (Cambridge, MA: M.I.T. Press, 1927); Arthur Ponsonby, *Falsehood in War-Time* (London: George Allen & Unwin, 1928); George Silvester Viereck, *Spreading Germs of Hate* (London: Duckworth Press, 1931); James Morgan Read, *Atrocity Propaganda 1914–1918* (New Haven: Yale University Press, 1941).

2. Gail Braybon, *Women Workers in the First World War: The British Experience* (London: Croom Helm, 1981), pp. 173–210.

3. Quoted in Ruth Roach Pierson, "'Did Your Mother Wear Army Boots?': Feminist Theory and Women's Relation to War, Peace, and Revolution" in Sharon MacDonald, et al., *Images of Women in Peace and War* (London: Macmillan, 1987), p. 217. See also Trevor Wilson, *The Myriad Faces of War: Britain and the Great War, 1914–1918* (Cambridge: Polity Press, 1988), p. 725. For a fascinating discussion of literary women and conservatism, see Alison Light, *Forever England: Femininity, Literature and Conservatism between the Wars* (London: Routledge, 1991).

4. Martin Pugh, *Electoral Reform in War and Peace, 1906–1919* (Routledge & Kegan Paul, 1978), p. 174.

5. See David Close, "The Collapse of Resistance to Democracy: Conservatives, Adult Suffrage and Second Chamber Reform, 1911–1928," *The Historical Journal* 20, 4 (1977), p. 917, and Neil R. McCrillis, *The British Conservative Party in the Age of Universal Suffrage: Popular Conservatism, 1918–1929* (Columbus: Ohio State University Press, 1998), pp. 46–82.

6. Christabel Pankhurst lost the Smethwick election by a hair's breadth and received a total of 8,000 votes—the most cast for any woman candidate in the 1919 election. Marion Ramelson, *The Petticoat Rebellion* (London: Lawrence and Wishart), p. 169. Given Christabel's popularity among

right-wing female munitions workers, it is likely that the enfranchisement of younger women might have changed the outcome of the election.

7. David Mitchell, *Queen Christabel* (London: Macdonald and Jane's, 1977), ch. 16; E. Sylvia Pankhurst, *The Life of Emmeline Pankhurst* (London: T. Werner Laurie Ltd., 1969), ch. 11; R. M. Douglas, *Feminist Freikorps: The British Voluntary Women Police, 1914–1940* (London: Praeger, 1999). Significantly, it was Emmeline Pankhurst's statue that was erected in Westminster to commemorate the passage of women's suffrage.

8. Harold Smith, *The British Women's Suffrage Campaign, 1866–1928* (London: Longmans, 1998), p. 69.

9. Brian Harrison, *Separate Spheres: The Opposition to Women's Suffrage in Britain* (London: Croom Helm, 1978), pp. 223–224.

10. Bryce seems to allude to his own reservations in an address delivered at the British Academy. See Viscount James Bryce, *Some Historical Reflections on War, Past and Present: Being Portions of Two Annual Presidential Addresses delivered to the British Academy June 1915 and July 1916* (London: Oxford University Press, 1916), pp. 5–11. His official biographies also gloss over the Bryce Report as quickly as possible, raising questions about the degree Bryce wished to be remembered for the atrocity report. Given his distrust of the relationship between democracy and the media, such reservations might be understandable. See James Bryce to A. V. Dicey, December 28, 1915, Bodleian, Modern Manuscripts, MS Bryce 4, fol. 96.; 29 October, 1916, fol. 123; September 15, 1917, fols. 145–146; September 19, 1917, fols. 147–149; February 15, 1918, fols. 171–172.

11. The bill reduced the residency period to one month for military service voters, but women still needed to meet the age and property or educational requirements to qualify, even under this franchise.

12. J. Renwick Seager, J.P. ed., *The Reform Act of 1918: Full Text, Annotated with Explanatory Notes* (London: The Liberal Publication Department, 1918), pp. 40–41.

13. This criticism was made at the time of the Speakers Conference and would be reiterated by "adultists" feminists who continued to object to the unequal and inconsistent nature of the franchise. E. Sylvia Pankhurst, *The Suffragette Movement: An Intimate Account of Persons and Ideals* (London: Longmans, 1931), pp. 602–603.

Selected Bibliography

I. Primary Sources

Archival Sources

Bodleian Library, Oxford*
Asquith MSS
Bryce MSS
John Johnson Collection
Simon MSS
*In all cases, those materials concerning the years 1914–19 were examined

British Library, London

Austin-Lee MSS	Add. MSS 46772
Cecil MSS	Add. MSS 51092
Davies MSS	Add. MSS 54192–54192b
Northcliffe MSS	Add. MSS 62153–62339
Riddell MSS	Add. MSS 62974–62978
Parliamentary Recruiting Committee Add 54192 a and b	

Fawcett Library, London
Consultative Committee of Women's Suffrage Societies Collection
Emily Davison Collection
Jessie Kenney Collection
National Union of Women's Suffrage Societies Collection

Hoover Institute on War Revolution and Peace, Stanford University, CA
Great Britain—Director of Propaganda in Enemy Countries
Great Britain—Foreign Office (Wellington House)
Great Britain—Ministry of Information

House of Lords Records Office, London

Beaverbrook MSS	BBK C/39-BBK C/1276
Lloyd George MSS	LG C/1-LG F/229

Imperial War Museum, London
  Department of Art
    WWI British Art, (transparency room and open display)
    WWI British Posters
    WWI Postcards
  Department of Documents
    Atrocities, WWI
    BBC TV Great War Series Correspondence
    Censorship and Propaganda, WWI
    Conscription and Recruiting, WWI
    Edith Cavell Collection
    Ephemera Collection, WWI
    Women at Work Collection

Museum of London, London
  Department of Later London History
    David Mitchell Collection
    Suffragette Collection

National Army Museum, London
  Recruiting correspondence

The Public Records Office, Kew
  Advertising   HO 174
  Defense of the Realm Act   WO 32/4893
  Kitchener Papers   WO 159/1–23
  National War Aims Committee   T 102/1–26
  Misc.   FO 395/147
  Parliamentary Recruiting Committee   WO 106/367
  Police and Aliens   HO 45/139441–37196
  Press Bureau   HO 139/1–44
  Press and Propaganda   INF 4/1–10

Parliamentary Sources

Hansards, *Parliamentary Debates,* House of Commons, 5th series (1914–1919)
Hansards, *Parliamentary Debates,* House of Lords, 5th series (1914–1919)

Newspapers and Periodicals

Anti-Suffrage Review
Athenaeum
Birmingham Daily Post

Brighton Herald
Bristol Times and Mirror
Britannia (formerly the *Suffragette*)
Bystander
Chatham News
Clarion
Common Cause
Contemporary Review
Daily Express
Daily Chronicle
Daily Graphic
Daily Mail
Daily Mirror
Daily Sketch
Daily Telegraph
Dumfries Standard
Economist
Egoist
Empire News
Empire Review
Englishwoman
Eugenics Review
Fortnightly Review
Gentlewoman
Girl's Own Paper
Girl's Realm
Glasgow Evening News
Glasgow Evening Times
Glasgow Record and Mail
Globe
Illustrated London News
Independent Suffragette
John Bull
Labour Leader
Ladies Field
Ladies Pictorial
Lady's Realm
Lady's World
Literary Digest
London Illustrated Weekly
Manchester Guardian
Methodist Times
Month
Morning Post
Mother and Home

Nation
New Statesman
New York Times
New York Tribune
Nineteenth Century and After
Northern & Western Mail
Observer
Primrose League Gazette
Punch
Quarterly Review
Quest: A Quarterly Review
Recruiting Times
Round Table
Southend Standard
South Wales Daily News
Spectator
Statist
Standard Recruiter
Suffragette News Sheet
Sunday Herald
Sunday Pictorial
Sunday Times
Standard Recruiter
Suffragette (later *Britannia*)
Tatler
Times of London
Times Literary Supplement
Times Recruiting Supplement
Vote
Votes for Women
War Illustrated
Weekly Dispatch
Western Daily Press
Western Mail
Woman at Home
Woman's Dreadnought
Woman's World
Woman's Home Magazine
Young Ladies Weekly Journal
Young Woman

PRINTED SOURCES AND PUBLISHED MEMOIRS

Anon. *A "Corpse Conversion Factory" A Peep Behind the German Lines*. London: Darling & Sons, [n.d.].

Anon. *The Deportation of Women and Girls from Lille: Translated Textually from the Notes Addressed by the French Government to the Government of Neutral Powers on the Conduct of the German Authorities Towards the Population of the French Departments in the Occupation of the Enemy*. London: Hodder and Stoughton, 1916.

Anon. *German Crimes Calendar, 1918*. IWM GB 352.1 K 49367.

Asquith, H. H. *A Call to Arms: A Speech by the Prime Minister at the Guildhall September 14, 1914*. London: Methuen & Co., 1914.

————. *What We Are Fighting For. A Speech by Mr. Asquith Delivered at Leeds September 26, 1917*. London: NWAC no. 16, 1917.

Aston, Major-General Sir George, K.C.B. *The Triangle of Terror in Belgium*. London: John Murray, 1918.

"A Suffragette." *The Representation of the People Bill*. London: W. Godbold, 1917.

Balfour Browne, J. H. *War Problems*. London: Longmans, Green & Co., 1915.

Beck, James M. *The Case of the Lusitania*. Boston: Citizen's League for America and the Allies, 1916.

Bedford, Duke of. "Recruiting Pamphlets and leaflets, 1914–1915." IWM, 325.1 NP K 44699.

Bédier, Joseph. *German Atrocities: Studies and Documents on the War from German Evidence*. Translated by Bernard Harrison. Paris: Librairie Armand Colin, 1915.

The Belgian Official Commission of Inquiry. *The Martyrdom of Belgium: Official Report of Massacres of Peaceable Citizens, Women and Children by the German Army, Testimony of Eye-Witnesses*. Report XI. Baltimore: W. Steward Brown, [nd].

————. *Violation of the Rights of Nations and the Laws and Customs of War*. Vol. I. London: H.M. Stationery Office, [1914].

Berden, Louis. *Pictures of Ruined Belgium*. London: John Lane, 1917.

Boas, Mrs. F. S. *Our Village and the War*. London: PRC no. 33, [1915].

Brex, Twells. *"Scare Mongering" From the Daily Mail 1896–1914, the Paper that Fortold the War*. London: The Daily Mail [1914].

The British Empire Union. "The Perils of Pacifism." The British Empire Union no. 20, 1917. In *Pamphlets and Leaflets*. London: The British Empire Union, 1919.

Brittain, Vera. *Testament of Youth: An Autobiographical Study of the Years 1900–1925*. [1933] London: Penguin, 1989.

Bryce, James. *The Last Phase in Belgium*. London: Spaight & Sons, 1916.

————. *Some Historical Reflections on War Past and Present: Being Portions of Two Annual Presidential Addresses Delivered to the British Academy June 1915 and July 1914*. London: Oxford, 1916.

The Bystander. *Fragments from France*. London: H.R. Baines, [n.d.].

Cabberton, Dr. J. H. *Belgium and Germany: a Dutch View*. Translated by W.E. Leonard. London: Open Court, 1916.

Carlie, J. C. *In Folkstone During the Great War*. Folkstone: F. J. Parsons, Ltd., 1922.

Chamberlain, W. J. *Fighting for Peace: The Story of the War Resistance Movement*. London: No More War Movement, 1928.

Central Committee for National Patriotic Organizations. *Tracts Relating to the European War 1914-*. London: John Murray, 1914.

Committee on Alleged German Outrages. *Appendix to the Report of the Committee on Alleged German Outrages, Evidence and Documents*. London: H.M Stationery Office, 1915.

———. *Report of the Committee on Alleged German Outrages*. London: H.M. Stationery Office, 1915.

Conan Doyle. Arthur. *"To Arms!."* London: Hodder & Stoughton, 1914.

Cook, Sir Edward. *The Press In War Time*. London: Macmillan & Co., 1920.

Cook, Theodore A. *The Crimes of Germany: Being an Illustrated Synopsis of the Violations of International Law and of Humanity by the Armed Forces of the German Empire*. London: The Field & Queen, [1917].

Crooks, Will, MP. *The British Workman Defends his Home*. London: The Whitwell Press, 1917.

Daily Chronicle. In the Trail of the German Army. London: The Daily Chronicle, 1915.

———. *Where the German Army has Passed*. London: The Daily Chronicle, 1915.

Darwin, Major Leonard. *"On the Meaning of Honour."* London: The League of Honour, 1915.

Davignon, Henri. *Belgium and Germany: Texts and Documents*. London: Thomas Nelson, 1915.

"Dikaios Logos." *"An Ordinary Briton's View of the War": An Open Letter to a Senator of the USA*. London: Darling & Sons, 1915.

The Duty and Discipline Movement. *All Can Help: A Handbook for War-Time*. London: The Duty and Discipline Movement, 1915.

Dyson, Will. *Kultur Cartoons*. London: Stanley Paul, 1915.

Ellis, Havelock. *My Life: Autobiography of Havelock Ellis*. Boston: Houghton Mifflin, 1939.

Fawcett, Millicent Garrett. "The National Union of Women's Suffrage Societies and the Hague Congress." *The Englishwoman* (June 1915), pp. 193–200.

———. *The Women's Victory—and After*. London: Sidgwick & Jackson Ltd., 1920.

———. *What I Remember*. London: T. Fisher Unwin Ltd., 1925.

Fichte Association. *Confutation of the Lies About German Atrocities during the War*. Hamburg: Fichte Association, [1925].

Fight for Right Movement. *Fight for Right*. London: Fight For Right Movement, [1917].

Fitzgerald, Admiral Charles Cooper Penrose. *From Sail to Steam: Naval Recollections, 1878- 1905*. London: Edward Arnold, 1916.

Foxe, John. *The Lives of the English Martyrs*. Ed. Edwin H. Burton, D.D. London: Longmans, 1914.

Fraser, Helen. *Women and War Work*. New York: G.A. Shaw, 1918.

Gardner, Alice. *Our Outlook as Changed by War. A Paper Read in Newnham College on Sunday, 25 October 1914.* London: Simpkin Marshall, 1914.

Graham, John W., M.A. *Conscription and Conscience: A History 1916–1919.* London: George Allen and Unwin, 1922.

Graves, Robert. *Good-Bye to All That.* New York: Doubleday [1929], 1957.

The Grotius Society. *Problems of the War: Papers Read before the Society in the Year 1915.* London: Sweet & Maxwell, 1916.

Hamund, St. John. *The Rubaiyat of William the War Lord.* London: Grant Richards, 1915.

Hanham, J. H. *The Nineteenth Century Constitution Documents and Commentary* Cambridge: Cambridge University Press, 1969.

Headlam, J. W., M.A. *The Truth about England Exposed in a Letter to a Neutral.* London: Thomas Nelson, 1915.

Higgins, Pearce A. *The Hague Peace Conference and Other International Conferences Concerning the Laws and Usages of War: Texts of the Conventions with Commentaries.* Cambridge: Cambridge University Press, 1915.

———. "The Law of Nations and the War." *Oxford Pamphlets* no 24. London: Oxford University Press, 1914.

Hill, William Thomas. *The Martyrdom of Nurse Cavell: The Life and Story of the Victim of Germany's Most Barbarous Crime.* London: Hutchinson, 1915.

Holls, Frederick. *The Peace Conference at the Hague; and its Bearings on International Law and Policy.* New York: Macmillan, 1900.

Howarth, Tony, ed. *Joe Soap's Army Song Book.* Imperial War Museum Great War Series. London: Longmans, 1976.

Kipling, Rudyard. "Tommy," in Irving Howe, ed. *The Portable Kipling.* New York: Penguin, 1982.

Hurd, Archibald. *An Incident of War by Order of the Kaiser.* London: Sir Joseph Causton & Sons, 1916.

An Independent Liberal. *Lloyd George and the War.* London: Hutchinson & Co., 1917.

Irvine, Dr. Alexander. *God and Tommy Atkins.* London: Hutchinson, 1918.

Jones, Kennedy. *Fleet Street and Downing Street.* London: Hutchinson & Co., 1920.

Jones, Sheridan C. *The Unspeakable Prussian.* London: Cassel & Co., 1914.

Kelynack, M. D., ed. *Pro Patria: A Guide to Public and Personal Service in Wartime.* London: John Bale & Sons, 1916.

Kennedy, William Antony, LLB. *As Britons See It.* London: Henry Good & Son, 1914.

Kenney, Annie. *A Militant.* [1924] London: Routledge, 1994

Kernahan, Coulson. *The Experiences of a Recruiting Officer.* London: Hodder & Stoughton, 1915.

Kitson, Arthur. *The Great Pacifist Conspiracy! An Appeal to the British Public.* Stamford: Dolby Bros., 1918.

Lambert, Richard. *The Parliamentary History of Conscription in Great Britain.* London: George Allen & Unwin, 1917.

Lauterpacht, H. *Private Law Sources and Analogies of International Law*. London: Longmans, Green & Co., 1927.

Lechmere, Worall, and J. E. Harold Terry. *The Man Who Stayed at Home*. London: Samuel French Ltd., 1916.

Le Queux, William. *German Atrocities: A Record of Shameless Deeds*. London: George Newnes, [1914].

Lloyd George, David. *British War Aims*. New York: George H. Doran, 1918.

———. "Mr. Lloyd George's Speech at Glasgow, 29 June 1917." In Anon. *When the War Will End*. London: Hayman, Christy, and Lilly, [1917].

———. *Through Terror to Triumph: An Appeal to the Nation, A Speech Delivered at the Queen's Hall, London September 19, 1914*. London: Parliamentary Recruiting Committee, 1914.

Lind-Af-Hageby, L. *Women's Function in Social Development*. London: League of Peace and Freedom, 1915.

MacDonagh, Michael. *In London During the Great War*. London: Eyre & Spottiswoode, 1935.

Marshall, Catherine E. "Women in War." In Margaret Kamester and Jo Vellacott, eds., *Militarism versus Feminism: Writings on Women and War*. London: Virago, 1987.

Martindale, Mary. *One Englishwoman to Another*. NWAC Pamphlets. London, Oxford, 1918.

Mason, A. E. W. *The Four Feathers*. London: Smith Elder & Co., 1902.

Massart, Jean. *Belgians under the German Eagle*. Translated by Bernard Miall. London: T. Fisher Unwin, 1916.

Monkhouse, Allan. *War Plays*. London: Constable & Co., 1916.

Morgan, J. H. *German Atrocities: An Official Investigation*. London: T. Fisher Unwin, 1916.

———. *Leaves from a Field Notebook*. London: Macmillan, 1916.

The Mothers Union. *To British Mothers, How they Can Help, By One of Them*. London: Wells, Gardner, Darton & Co.,[n.d.].

Müller-Meiningen, Ernst. *Who are the Huns? The Law of Nations and its Breakers*. Berlin: Georg Reimer, 1915.

National War Aims Committee. *A Kalender of "Kultur."* NWAC no. 15 [1917].

———. *Leaflets 1917–1918*. BL 1854.e.5.

———. *Searchlights*. Nos. 2–19, 21–26. London: NWAC, 1917–18.

Nettleingham, F. T. *Tommy's Tunes*. London: Erskine MacDonald, 1917.

No-Conscription Fellowship. *Pamphlets*. London: No-Conscription Fellowship, 1915–1919.

Noyes, Alfred. *Rada: A Belgian Christmas Eve*. London: Methuen & Co., 1915.

Oakes, Sir Augustus and R. B. Mowat, eds. *The Great Treaties of the Nineteenth Century*. Oxford: Clarendon Press [1918], 1970.

Ogden, C. K. *Militarism versus Feminism*. London: Allen Unwin, 1915.

Osborne, Margaret. *The War and Myself, A Woman's Point of View*. NWAC Pamphlets. London: R. Clay & Sons, [1917].

Oxenham, John. "The League of Honour War Memorial." London: The League of Honour, [1914].

Oxford Faculty of Modern History. *Why We are at War.* 3d ed. Oxford: Clarendon, 1914.

Pankhurst, Christabel. *America and the War: A Speech Delivered at Carnegie Hall, New York October 24, 1914.* London: WSPU. 1914.

———. *International Militancy: A Speech Delivered at Carnegie Hall, January 13, 1915.* London: WSPU, 1915.

———. *Industrial Salvation.* London: Women's Party, 1918.

———. *The Lord Cometh: The World Crisis Explained.* London: Marshall Morgan Scott, Ltd., 1934.

———. *Speech delivered by Christabel Pankhurst at Washington, U.S.A., January 24, 1915.* London: Jones & Co, 1915.

———. *Unshackled: The Story of How We Won the Vote.* London: Hutchinson, 1957.

———. *The War: A Speech Delivered at the London Opera House on September 8, 1914.* London: WSPU, 1914.

Pankhurst, Emmeline. *My Own Story.* London: Eveleigh Nash, 1914.

Pankhurst, E. Sylvia. *The Home Front: A Mirror to Life in England During the First World War* [1932]. London: Cresset Library, 1987.

———. *The Suffragette Movement: An Intimate Account of Person and Ideals.* London: Longmans, 1931.

———. *The Life of Emmeline Pankhurst: The Suffragette Struggle for Women's Citizenship.* London: T. Werner Laurie Ltd., 1935.

Parliamentary Recruiting Committee. *4 Questions to Women.* London: PRC no. 31 [1914–5].

———. *"To the Men of Great Britain: A CALL TO ARMS."* London: PRC no. 6, 1914.

———. *A Reason—or An Excuse?.* London: PRC no. 34 [1915].

———. *Scientific Savagery.* London: PRC no. 32 [1915].

———. *The Truth about German Atrocities.* London: PRC no. 43, 1915.

———. *Women and the War.* London: PRC no. 23 [1915].

Peterson, Margaret. "The Woman's Message." London: PRC no. 26, 1915.

Phillipson, Coleman. *International Law and the Great War.* London: Fisher Unwin, 1915.

Pope, Jessie. *More War Poems.* London: Grant Richards, 1915.

———. *Simple Rhymes for Stirring Times.* London: C. Arthur Penrose, 1916.

Prothero, G. W. "Our Duty and Our Interest in the War." In Central Committee for National Patriotic Organizations. *Tracts Relating to the European War 1914-.* London: John Murray, 1914.

Punch. *Mr. Punch's History of the Great War.* London: Cassell & Co., 1919.

Raemaekers, Louis. *Raemaekers Cartoons.* London: Hodder & Stoughton, [nd].

Richards, H. E. "Does International Law Still Exist?" In *Oxford Pamphlets.* Vol. XV. London: Fisher Unwin, 1915.

Roberts, Robert. *The Classic Slum: Salford Life in the First Quarter of the Century.* Manchester: Manchester University Press, 1971.

Russell, Bertrand. *Why Men Fight.* New York: Century, 1917.

Sanders, Stephen. *If the Kaiser Governed Britain: The Lesson of Germany.* London: Hayman, Christy, & Lilly, 1918.

Sarolea, Charles. *The Curse of the Hohenzolern.* London: George Allen & Unwin, 1915.

Schreiner, Olive. *Women and Labour.* London: Fisher Unwin, 1911.

Seager, J. Renwick, J.P. *The Reform Act of 1918: Full Text, Annotated with Explanatory Notes.* London: The Liberal Publication Department, 1918.

Seddon, J. A. *Why British Labour Supports the War.* London: Avenue Press, 1917.

Shee, George F. *The Briton's First Duty.* London: Grant Richards, 1901.

Smith Dorien, General Sir Horace. *A Message from the Front to the Womenfolk at Home.* PRC no. 19 [1915].

Spurgeon, Caroline F. E. *The Privilege of Living in Wartime: An Inaugural Address to King's College for Women, Delivered at the University of London on October 16, 1914.* London: University of London, 1914.

Stallings, Lawrence, ed. *The First World War: A Photographic History.* New York: Simon & Schuster, 1933.

Strachey, Ray. *The Cause: A Short History of the Women's Movement in Great Britain.* Bath: Cedric Chivers, 1928.

———. *Women's Suffrage and Women's Service: The History of the London and National Society for Women's Service.* London: London and National Society for Women's Service, 1927.

Sullivan, Edmund J. *The Kaiser's Garland.* London: Heineman, 1915.

Swanwick, Helena. *I Have Been Young.* London: Victor Gollancz, 1935.

———. *The War and Its Effect Upon Women.* [1915] New York: Garland, 1971.

———. *Women and War.* [1916] NY: Garland, 1971.

Tillet, Ben, MP. *My Message to Labour.* NWAC *Searchlights* no.7, [1917].

The Times of London. *The Times History of the World War, 1914–1918.* 18 vols. London: Times, 1914–1918.

Toynbee, Arnold. *Armenian Atrocities: The Murder of a Nation.* London: Hodder & Stoughton, 1915.

———. *The Belgian Deportations.* London: Fisher Unwin, [1917].

Tweedie, Mrs. Alec, FRGS. *Women and Soldiers* London: John Lane, 1918.

Ward, Mrs. Humphry. *England's Effort: Letters to an American Friend.* New York: Scribner, 1916.

Webster, Nesta H. *Britain's Call to Arms: An Appeal to our Women.* London: Hugh Rees, 1914.

Whitlock, Brand. *Correspondence with the United States Ambassador Respecting the Execution of Miss Edith Cavell at Brussels,* Cmd. 8013. October, 1915.

Willis, W. N. *The Kaiser and His Barbarians.* London: Anglo Eastern [n.d.].

Wilson, R. M. *Wife, Mother Voter: Her Vote What Will She Do with It?.* London: Hodder & Stoughton, 1918.

Woolf, Virginia. *Three Guineas.* [1933] New York: Harvest Books,1966.

Worall, Lechmere, and J. E. Harold Terry. *The Man Who Stayed at Home.* London: Samuel French, 1916.

II. SECONDARY SOURCES

Adams, R. J. Q., and P. Poirier. *The Conscription Controversy in Great Britain 1900–1918*. Columbus: Ohio State University Press, 1987.

Alberti, Johanna. *Beyond Suffrage: Feminists in War and Peace, 1914–1928*. New York: St. Martin's Press, 1989.

Bailey, Peter, ed. *Music Hall: The Business of Pleasure*. Milton Keynes: Open University Press, 1986.

Baker, Steve. "Describing Images of the National Self: Popular Accounts of the Construction of Pictorial Identity in the First World War Poster." *Oxford Art Journal* 13, 2 (1990), pp. 24–30.

Blewett, Neal. "The Franchise in the United Kingdom, 1885–1918." *Past and Present* (December 1965), pp. 27–56.

Bourke, Joanna. *Dismembering the Male: Men's Bodies, Britain and the Great War*. Chicago: University of Chicago Press, 1996.

Bristow, Nancy. *Making Men Moral: Social Engineering During the Great War*. New York: New York University Press, 1996.

Braybon, Gail. *Women Workers in the First World War*. London: Croom Helm, 1981.

Brown, Ivor. *Conan Doyle: A Biography of the Creator of Sherlock Holmes*. London: Hamish Hamilton, 1972.

Buitenhuis, Peter. *The Great War of Words: British, American, and Canadian Propaganda and Fiction 1914–1933*. Vancouver: University of British Columbia Press, 1987.

Burton, Antoinette. *Burdens of History: British Feminists, Indian Women and Imperial Culture, 1865–1915*. Chapel Hill: University of North Carolina Press, 1994.

Bussey, Gertrude, and Margaret Tims. *Pioneers for Peace*. London: Allen & Unwin, 1965.

Byles, Joan Montgomery. "Women's Experience of World War One: Suffragists, Pacifists and Poets." *Women's Studies International Forum* 8, no. 5 (1985), pp. 473–487.

Caedel, Martin. *Pacifism in Britain 1914–1945: The Defining of a Faith*. Oxford: Oxford University Press, 1980.

Chenault, Libby, ed. *Battlelines: World War I Posters from the Bowman Gray Collection, The Rare Book Collection, Wilson Library, the University of North Carolina at Chapel Hill*. Chapel Hill: University of North Carolina Press, 1988.

Clark, Anna. "Gender, Class and the Nation: Franchise Reform in England, 1822–1928." In James Vernoen, ed., *Re-reading the Constitution*. Cambridge: Cambridge University Press, 1996.

Close, David. "The Collapse of Resistance to Democracy: Conservatives, Adult Suffrage, and Second Chamber Reform, 1911–1928." *The Historical Journal* 20, 4 (1977), pp. 893–918.

Coetzee, Frans and Marilyn Shevin-Coetzee, eds. *Authority, Identity and the Social History of the Great War*. Oxford: Berghahn Books, 1995.

Colley, Linda. *Britons: Forging the Nation 1707–1837*. New Haven: Yale University Press, 1992.

Collini, Stefan. *Public Moralists: Political Thought and Intellectual Life in Britain 1850–1930.* Oxford: Clarendon, 1991.

Colls, Robert and Philip Dodd, eds. *Englishness: Politics and Culture 1880–1920.* London: Croom Helm, 1986.

Condell, Diana and Jean Liddiard. *Working for Victory? Images of Women in the First World War, 1914–1918.* London: Routledge & Kegan Paul, 1987.

Cooke, Miriam, and Angela Woollacott, eds. *Gendering War Talk.* Princeton: Princeton University press, 1993.

Cooper, Helen M., Adrienne Munich, and Susan Merrill Squier, eds. *Arms and the Woman: War, Gender, and Literary Representation.* Chapel Hill: University of North Carolina Press, 1989.

Dangerfield, George. *The Strange Death of Liberal England, 1910–1914.* [1935] New York: Perigee, 1980.

Daracott, Joseph, and Belinda Loftus. *First World War Posters.* London: Imperial War Museum, 1972.

Davin Anna. "Imperialism and Motherhood." *History Workshop* 5 (Spring 1978), pp. 9–65.

de Vries, Jacqueline. "Gendering Patriotism: Emmeline and Christabel Pankhurst and World War One," in Sybil Oldfield, ed. *This Working-Day World: Women's Lives and Culture(s) in Britain, 1914–1945.* London: Taylor & Francis, 1994.

Douglas, R. M. *Feminist Freikorps: The British Voluntary Women Police, 1914–1940* London: Praeger, 1999.

Douglas, Roy. "Voluntary Enlistment in the First World War and the Work of the Parliamentary Recruiting Committee." *Journal of Modern History* (December 1970), pp. 564–585.

Dutton, Philip. "Moving Images? The PRC's Poster Campaign, 1914–1916." *IWM Review* 4 (1989), pp. 43–58.

Elshtain, Jean Bethke. *Woman and War.* New York: Basic Books, 1987.

Elshtain, Jean Bethke, and Sheila Tobias, eds. *Women, Militarism, and War: Essays in History, Politics, and Social Theory.* Savage: Rowman & Littlefield, 1990.

Enloe, Cynthia. *Does Khaki Become You?: The Militarization of Women's Lives.* London: South End Press, 1983.

Evans, Richard J. *Comrades and Sisters: Feminism, Socialism, and Pacifism in Europe, 1870- 1945.* New York: St. Martin's Press, 1987.

Farrar, L. L. "Nationalism in Wartime: Critiquing Conventional Wisdom," in Franz Coetzee and Marilyn Shevin-Coetzee, eds. *Authority, Identity and the Social History of the Great War.* Oxford: Berghahn Books, 1995.

Fehl, Philip. *World War I Posters of the University of North Carolina.* Durham: University of North Carolina Press, 1969.

Ferguson, Niall. *The Pity of War: Explaining World War I.* New York: Basic Books, 1999.

Ferns, John. *Lytton Strachey.* Boston: Twayne, 1988.

Fisher, H. A. L. *James Bryce.* New York: Macmillan, 1927.

Foster, Catherine. *Women for All Seasons: The Story of the Women's International League for Peace and Freedom.* Athens: University of Georgia Press, 1989.

French, David. "Spy Fever in Britain, 1900–1915." *Historical Journal* 21 (1978), pp. 355–370.

Fuller, J. G. *Troop Morale and Popular Culture in the British and Dominion Armies 1914–1918.* Oxford: Clarendon, 1990.

Fussell, Paul. *The Great War and Modern Memory.* Oxford: Oxford University Press, 1977.

Gallo, Max. *The Poster in History.* New York: American Heritage, 1974.

Garner, Les. *Stepping Stones to Women's Liberty: Feminist Ideas in the Women's Suffrage Movement 1900–1918.* London: Heinemann, 1984.

Gilbert, Sandra M. "Soldier's Heart: Literary Men, Literary Women, and the Great War." In Margaret Higonnet et al., eds. *Behind the Lines: Gender and the Two World Wars.* New Haven: Yale University Press, 1987.

Glover, Jon and Jon Silken, eds. *First World War Prose.* London: Penguin, 1990.

Gould, Jenny. "Women's Military Service in First World War Britain." In Margaret Higonnet et al., eds. *Behind the Lines: Gender and the Two World Wars.* New Haven: Yale University Press, 1987.

Grayzel, Susan R. "'The Mothers of Our Soldiers' Children': Motherhood, Immorality, and the War Baby Scandal, 1914–1918." In Claudia Nelson and Ann Sumner Holmes, eds. *Maternal Instincts: Motherhood and Sexuality in Britain, 1875–1925.* Houndsmills: Macmillan, 1997.

———. "'The Outward and Visible Sign of Her Patriotism': Women, Uniforms, and National Service During the First World War." *Twentieth Century British History* 8, no. 2 (1997), pp. 145–164.

———. *Women's Identities at War: Gender, Motherhood, and Politics in Britain and France During the First World War.* Chapel Hill: University of North Carolina Press, 1999.

Gubar, Susan. "'This is My Rifle, This is My Gun': World War II and the Blitz on Women." In Margaret Higonnet et al. eds. *Behind the Lines: Gender and the Two World Wars.* New Haven: Yale University Press, 1987.

Gullace, Nicoletta F. "Sexual Violence and Family Honor: British Propaganda and International Law during the First World War." *American Historical Review* (June 1997), pp. 714–747.

———. "White Feathers and Wounded Men: Female Patriotism and the Memory of the Great War." *Journal of British Studies* (April 1997), pp. 178–206.

Harris, Ruth. "'The Child of the Barbarian': Rape, Race and Nationalism in France During the First World War. *Past and Present* (November 1993), pp. 170–141.

Harrison, Brian. *Peaceable Kingdom: Stability and Change in Modern Britain.* Oxford: Clarendon, 1982.

———. *Separate Spheres: The Opposition to Women's Suffrage in Britain.* London: Croom Helm, 1978.

———. "Women's Suffrage at Westminster 1866–1928." In Michael Bentley and John Stevenson, eds. *High and Low Politics in Modern Britain.* Oxford: Clarendon, 1983.

Haste, Cate. *Keep the Home Fires Burning: Propaganda in the First World War.* London: Allen Lane, 1978.

Higonnet, Margaret R., and Patrice Higonnet. "The Double Helix." In Margaret Randolph Higonnet, Jane Jenson, Sonya Michel, and Margaret Collins Weitz, eds. *Behind the Lines: Gender and the Two World Wars.* New Haven: Yale University Press, 1987.

Higonnet, Margaret R., Jane Jenson, Sonya Michel, and Margaret Collins Weitz eds. *Behind the Lines: Gender and the Two World Wars.* New Haven: Yale University Press, 1987.

Higonnet, Margaret R., ed., *Lines of Fire: Women Writers of World War I.* New York: Penguin, 1999.

Hill, Christopher. "History and Patriotism." In Raphael Samuel, ed. *Patriotism: The Making and Unmaking of British National Identity.* Vol. I. London: Routledge, 1989.

Hiller, Bevis. *Posters.* New York: Stern & Day, 1969.

Holton, Sandra Stanley. *Feminism and Democracy: Women's Suffrage and Reform Politics in Britain 1900–1918.* Cambridge: Cambridge University Press, 1986.

———. "The Making of Suffrage History." In June Purvis and Sandra Stanley Holton eds. *Votes for Women.* London: Routledge, 2000.

Horne, John, and Alan Kramer. *German Atrocities, 1914: A History of Denial.* New Haven: Yale University Press, 2001.

———. "German 'Atrocities' and Franco-German Opinion, 1914: The Evidence of German Soldiers' Diaries." *Journal of Modern History* (March 1994), pp. 1–33.

Howarth, Tony, ed. *Joe Soap's Army Song Book.* Imperial War Museum Great War Series. London: Longmans, 1976.

Hughes, Clive. *Army Recruiting in Gwenedd, 1914–16.* M.A. thesis. University of Wales, 1983.

Hunt, Lynn, ed., *The New Cultural History.* Berkeley: University of California Press, 1989.

Hutchinson, H. F. *The Poster: An Illustrated History from 1860.* New York: Viking, 1968.

Hynes, Samuel. *The Edwardian Turn of Mind.* Princeton: Princeton University Press, 1975.

———. *A War Imagined: The First World War and English Culture.* London: Pimlico, 1992.

Joannou, Maroula, and June Purvis. *The Women's Suffrage Movement: New Feminist Perspectives.* Manchester: Manchester University Press, 1998.

Jones, Nora, and Liz Ward, eds. *The Forgotten Army: Women's Poetry of the First World War.* Beverly: Highgate, 1991.

Jorgensen-Earp, Cheryl R., ed. *Speeches and Trials of the Militant Suffragettes: The Women's Social and Political Union 1903–1918.* London: Associated University Press, 1999.

———. *"The Transfiguring Sword": The Just War of the Women's Social and Political Union.* Tuscaloosa: University of Alabama Press, 1987.

Kahn, Nosheen. *Women's Poetry of the First World War.* London: Harvester, 1988.

Kamester, Margaret, and Jo Vellacott. *Militarism versus Feminism: Writing on Women and War—Catherine Marshall, C. K. Ogden, and Mary Sargent Florence.* London: Virago Press, 1987.

Kent, Susan Kingsley. "Love and Death: War and Gender in Britain, 1914–1918." In Frans Coetzee and Marilyn Shevin-Coetzee, eds. *Authority, Identity and the Social History of the Great War.* Oxford: Berghahn Books, 1995.

———. *Making Peace: Gender Reconstruction in Interwar Britain.* Princeton: Princeton University Press, 1993.

———. "The Politics of Sexual Difference: World War I and the Demise of British Feminism." *Journal of British Studies* 27 (July 1988), pp. 232–253.

———. *Sex and Suffrage in Britain, 1860–1914.* Princeton: Princeton University Press, 1987.

Laswell, Harold. *Propaganda Technique in World War I.* Cambridge: MIT Press, 1927.

Law, Cheryl. "The Old Faith Living and the Old Power There: The Movement to Extend Women's Suffrage." In Maroula Joannou and June Purvis, eds. *The Women's Suffrage Movement: New Feminist Perspectives.* Manchester: Manchester University Press, 1998.

Layton, Lynn. "Vera Brittain's Testament(s). In Margaret Higonnet et al., eds. *Behind the Lines: Gender and the Two World Wars.* New Haven: Yale University Press, 1987.

Laffin, John. *Tommy Atkins: The Story of an English Soldier.* London: Cassell, 1966.

Leed, Eric. *No Man's Land: Combat and Identity in World War I.* Cambridge: Cambridge University Press, 1979.

Levine, Philippa. "'Walking the Streets in a Way No Decent Woman Should': Women Police in World War I. *Journal of Modern History* (March 1994), pp. 34–78.

Lewis, Jane. *The Politics of Motherhood: Child and Maternal Welfare in England, 1900–1939.* London: Croom Helm, 1982.

Liddington, Jill. *The Road to Greenham Common: Feminism and Anti-Militarism since 1820.* Syracuse: Syracuse University Press, 1989.

Light, Alison. *Forever England: Femininity, Literature and Conservatism between the Wars.* London: Routledge, 1991.

Lin, Patricia Y. "From a Call to Arms to A Symbol fro Peace: The Changing Image of Nurse Edith Cavell, 1915–1939." Berkeley: Unpublished Seminar Paper, 1992.

MacDonald, Sharon, et al., eds. *Images of Women in War and Peace.* London: Macmillan, 1987.

MacKenzie, John M. *Propaganda and Empire: The Manipulation of British Public Opinion 1880- 1960.* Manchester: Manchester University Press, 1984.

MacKenzie, Midge. *Shoulder to Shoulder: A Documentary.* London: Alfred A. Knopf, 1975.

Martin, Christopher. *English Life in the First World War.* London: Wayland, 1974.

Marwick, Arthur. *The Deluge: British Society and the First World War.* New York: Norton, 1965.

———. *Women at War 1914–1918.* London: Croom Helm, 1977.

Mayhall, Laura E. Nym. "Creating the 'Suffragette Spirit': British Feminists and Historical Imagination." *Women's History Review* 4, no. 3 (1995).

———. "Defining Militancy: Radical Protest, the Constitutional Idiom, and Women's Suffrage in Britian, 1908–1909." *Journal of British Studies* (July 2000).

McCrillis, Neal. *The British Conservative Party in the Age of Universal Suffrage.* Columbus: Ohio State University Press, 1998.

McEwen, John M. "The National Press during the First World War: Ownership and Circulation." *Journal of Contemporary History.* 17 (1982), pp. 459–486.

Messinger, Gary. *British Propaganda and the State in the First World War.* Manchester: Manchester University Press, 1992.

Mitchell, David. *Queen Christabel: A Biography of Christabel Pankhurst.* London: Macdonald and Jane's, 1977.

———. *Women on the Warpath: The Story of Women of the First World War.* London: Jonathan Cape, 1968.

Morgan, David. *Suffragists and Liberals: The Politics of Woman's Suffrage in England.* Totowa, N.J.: Rowman & Littlefield, 1975.

Mosse, George L. *Fallen Soldiers: Reshaping the Memory of the World Wars.* Oxford: Oxford University Press, 1990.

Nordon, Pierre. *Conan Doyle: A Biography.* New York: Holt, Rinehart and Winston, 1967.

Osborne, John. *The Voluntary Recruiting Movement in Britain.* Ann Arbor: University Microfilms International, 1983.

Ouditt, Sharon. *Fighting Forces, Writing Women: Identity and Ideology in the First World War.* London: Routledge, 1994.

Panayi, Panikos. *The Enemy in Our Midst: Germans in Britain during the First World War.* Oxford: Berg Press, 1991.

Paret, Peter, Beth Irwin Lewis, and Paul Paret, eds. *Persuasive Images: Posters of War and Revolution from the Hoover Institution Archives.* Princeton: Princeton University Press, 1992.

Parker, Peter. *The Old Lie: The Great War and the Public School Ethos.* London: Constable, 1987.

Pearce, Malcolm, and Geoffrey Stewart. *British Political History, 1867–1990.* London: Routledge, 1992.

Pedersen, Susan. *Family, Dependence, and the Origins of the Welfare State: Britain and France, 1914–1945.* Cambridge: Cambridge University Press, 1993.

———. "The Future of Feminist History." *Perspectives* (October 2000).

———. "Gender, Welfare, and Citizenship in Britain During the Great War." *American Historical Review* (October 1990).

Peterson, H. C. *Propaganda for War: The Campaign Against American Neutrality, 1914–1917.* Norman: University of Oklahoma Press, 1939.

Pierson, Ruth Roach. "'Did Your Mother Wear Army Boots?' Feminist Theory and Women's Relation to War, Peace, and Revolution." In Sharon MacDonald, et al., eds. *Images of Women in War and Peace.* London: Macmillan, 1987.

Ponsonby, Arthur. *Falsehood in War-Time.* London: George Allen & Unwin, 1928.

Pugh, Martin. *Electoral Reform in War and Peace, 1906–18.* London: Routledge & Kegan Paul, 1978.

———. *The March of Women: A Revisionist Analysis of the Campaign for Women's Suffrage, 1866–1914.* Oxford. Oxford University Press, 2000.

———. "Politicians and the Women's Vote, 1914–1918." *History* 59, 197 (October 1974).

———. *Women and the Women's Movement in Britain, 1914–1959.* New York: Paragon, 1993.

Purvis, June, and Sandra Stanley Holton, eds. *Votes for Women.* London: Routledge, 2000.

Rappaport, Erika. "The Halls of Temptation: Gender, Politics, and the Construction of the Department Store in Late-Victorian London." *Journal of British Studies* 35 (January 1995).

———. *Shopping for Pleasure: Women in the Making of London's West End.* Princeton: Princeton University Press, 2000.

Rae, John. *Conscience and Politics: The British Government and the Conscientous Objector to Military Service 1916–1919.* London: Oxford, 1970.

Raeburn, Antonia. *The Suffragette View.* New York: St. Martin's Press, 1976.

Ramelson, Marian. *Petticoat Rebellion.* London: Lawrence & Winhart, 1967.

Read, James Morgan. *Atrocity Propaganda 1914–1918.* New Haven: Yale University Press, 1941.

Reilley, Catherine. *Scars Upon My Heart: Women's Poetry and Verse of the First World War.* London: Virago, 1981.

Rhodes, Anthony. *Propaganda: The Art of Persuasion in World War II.* New York: Chelsea House, 1976.

Rickards, Maurice. *Posters of the First World War.* New York.: Walker & Co., 1968.

Roberts, Kristina. "Gender, Class, and Patriotism: Women's Paramilitary Units in First World War Britain." *International History Review* (February 1997).

Roberts, Mary Louise. *Civilization Without Sexes: Reconstructing Gender in Postwar France, 1917–1927.* Chicago: University of Chicago Press, 1994.

Rose, Sonya. "Sex, Citizenship, and the Nation in World War II Britian." *American Historical Review* (October, 1998).

Rosen, Andrew. *Rise Up Women! the Militant Campaign of the Women's Social and Political Union 1903–1914.* London: Routledge and Kegan Paul, 1974.

Rover, Constance. *Women's Suffrage and Party Politics in Britain 1866–1914.* London: Routledge, 1967.

Sacks, Benjamin. *J. Ramsay MacDonald in Thought and Action: An Architect for a Better World.* Albuquerque: University of New Mexico Press, 1952.

Samuel, Raphael, ed. *Patriotism: The Making and Unmaking of British National Identity.* London: Routledge, 1989.

Sanders, Michael, and Philip Taylor. *British Propaganda During the First World War.* London: Macmillan, 1982.

Shevin-Coetzee, Marilyn, and Frans Coetzee, eds. *World War I and European Society: A Sourcebook.* Lexington, MA: D.C. Heath, 1995.

Scott, Joan Wallach. *Gender and the Politics of History.* New York: Columbia, 1988.

Stanley, Peter. *What Did YOU Do in the Great War, Daddy?: A Visual History of Propaganda Posters.* Melbourne: Oxford University Press, 1983.

Stoff, Laurie. "They Fought for Russia: Female Soldiers of the First World War." In Gerard DeGroot and Corinna Peniston-Bird, eds. *A Soldier and a Woman: Sexual Integration in the Military.* Harlow: Pearson Education Ltd., 2000.

Stuart, Sir Campbell. *The Secrets of Crewe House.* London: Hodder and Stoughton, 1920.

Summers, Anne. *Angels and Citizens: British Women as Military Nurses 1854–1914.* London: Routledge, 1988.

Summerfield, Penny. *Reconstructing Women's Wartime Lives.* Manchester: Manchester University Press, 1998.

Silkin, Jon, ed. *First World War Poetry.* London: Penguin, 1979.

Simkins, Peter. *Kitchener's Army: The Raising of the New Armies, 1914–16.* Armed Forces and Society Series. Manchester: Manchester University Press, 1988.

Smith, Bonnie. *Changing Lives.* Lexington: D. C. Heath, 1989.

Smith, Harold L. *The British Women's Suffrage Campaign.* London: Longmans, 1998.

Stedman Jones, Gareth. *Languages of Class: Studies in English Working Class History 1832- 1982.* Cambridge: Cambridge University Press, 1983.

Sutherland, John. *Mrs. Humphry Ward: Eminent Victorian, Pre-eminent Edwardian.* Oxford: Clarendon, 1990.

Tanner, Duncan. *Political Change and the Labour Party, 1900–1918.* Cambridge: Cambridge University Press, 1990.

Thom, Deborah. "Tommy's Sister: Women at Woolwich in World War I." In Raphael Samuel ed. *Patriotism: The Making and Unmaking of British National Identity.* Vol 2. London: Routledge, 1989.

Tickner, Lisa. *The Spectacle of Women: Imagery of the Suffrage Campaign 1907–1914.* Chicago: University of Chicago Press, 1988.

Trevelyan, Janet Penrose. *The Life of Mrs. Humphry Ward.* New York: Dodd, Mead & Co., 1923.

Turner, E. S. *Dear Old Blighty.* London: Michael Joseph, 1980.

Tylee, Claire M. "'Maleness Run Riot'—The Great War and Women's Resistance to Militarism." *Women's Studies International Forum* 11, 3 (1988), pp. 199–210.

———. *The Great War and Women's Consciousness: Images of Militarism and Womanhood in Women's Writings, 1914–64.* Iowa City: University of Iowa Press, 1990.

Vellacott, Jo. "Feminist Consciousness and the First World War." *History Workshop* 23 (Spring 1987).

Viereck, George Silvester. *Spreading Germs of Hate.* London: Duckworth, 1931.

Walkowitz, Judith R. *City of Dreadful Delight: Narratives of Sexual Danger in Late Victorian London.* Chicago: University of Chicago Press, 1992.

———. "Going Public: Shopping, Street Harassment, and Streetwalking in Late Victorian London." *Representations* 62 (Spring 1998).

Wall, Richard, and Jay Winter, eds. *The Upheaval of War: Family, Work, and Welfare in Europe 1914–1918.* Cambridge: Cambridge University Press, 1988.

Walzer, Michael. *Just and Unjust Wars: A Moral Argument with Historical Illustrations.* New York: Basic Books, 1977.

Ward, Paul. *Red Flag and Union Jack: Englishness, Patriotism and the British Left, 1881–1924.* Rochester: Royal Historical Society, 1998.

Watson, Janet S. K. ""Khaki Girls, VADs and Tommy's Sister: Gender and Class in First World War Britain." *International History Review* 19, 1 (February 1997).

Westbrook, Robert. "'I Want to Marry a Girl Just Like the Girl who Married Harry James': American Women and the Problem of Political Obligation in World War II." *American Quarterly* 42 (December 1990).

Whol, Robert. *The Generation of 1914.* Cambridge: Harvard University Press, 1979.

Wilson, Trevor. "Lord Bryce's Investigation into Alleged German Atrocities in Belgium, 1914- 1915." *Journal of Contemporary History* (July 1979).

———. *The Myriad Faces of War: Britain and the Great War, 1914–1918.* Cambridge: Polity Press, 1988.

Wiltshire, Anne. *Most Dangerous Women: Feminist Peace Campaigners of the First World War.* London: Pandora, 1985.

Wingerden, Sophia A. van. *The Women's Suffrage Movement in Britain, 1866–1928.* London: Macmillan, 1999.

Winter, Jay. "British National Identity and the First World War." Address delivered to the NACBS Santa Clara, CA (March 1991).

———. "The Era of Total War: Gender Sexuality, and the State 1914–1918." AHA annual meeting Washington, D.C. (December 1991).

———. *The Experience of World War I.* New York: Oxford University Press, 1989.

———. *The Great War and the British People.* Cambridge: Harvard University Press, 1986.

———. *Sites of Memory, Sites of Mourning: The Great War in European Cultural History.* Cambridge: Cambridge University Press, 1996.

Winter Jay and Jean-Louis Robert. *Capital Cities at War: London, Paris, Berlin, 1914–1919.* Cambridge: Cambridge University Press, 1997.

Woollacott, Angela. "'Khaki Fever' and its Control: Gender, Class, Age and Sexual morality on the British homefront in the First World War." *Journal of Contemporary History.* (April 1994), pp. 325–347.

———. *On Her Their Lives Depend: Munitions Workers in the Great War.* Berkeley: University of California Press, 1994.

———. "Sisters and Brothers in Arms: Family, Class, and Gendering in World War I Britain." in Miriam Cooke and Angela Woollacott eds. *Gendering War Talk.* Princeton: Princeton University Press, 1993.

INDEX

Printed in the United States
69385LVS00003B/97-249

9 781403 967107